Governance for Structural Transformation in Africa

Adam B. Elhiraika · Gamal Ibrahim
William Davis
Editors

Governance
for Structural
Transformation
in Africa

Editors
Adam B. Elhiraika
Economic Commission for Africa (ECA)
Addis Ababa, Ethiopia

William Davis
Economic Commission for Africa (ECA)
Addis Ababa, Ethiopia

Gamal Ibrahim
Economic Commission for Africa (ECA)
Addis Ababa, Ethiopia

The views expressed herein are those of the authors and do not necessarily reflect the views of the United Nations.

ISBN 978-3-030-03963-9   ISBN 978-3-030-03964-6   (eBook)
https://doi.org/10.1007/978-3-030-03964-6

Library of Congress Control Number: 2018960883

This Palgrave Macmillan imprint is published by the registered company Springer Nature Switzerland AG
The registered company address is: Gewerbestrasse 11, 6330 Cham, Switzerland

Contents

Notes on Contributors

Abidemi C. Adegboye is currently a Ph.D. student in Development Economics at the Department of Economics, University of Benin, Benin City Nigeria. He is also a lecturer in Economics at Adeyemi College of Education. His areas of interest include labour markets in SSA and fiscal policy.

Jean Balié is Senior Economist in the FAO Agricultural Development Economics Division, where he manages the Monitoring and Analyzing Food and Agricultural Policies (MAFAP) Programme. He has over 20 years of experience in policy analysis in developing and developed countries. He also worked for the French Ministry of Agriculture on bilateral cooperation and international trade negotiations. He wrote several papers, articles and reports on topics such as policy processes, policy monitoring, commodity chain analysis and price volatility.

Abiodun Surajudeen Bankole is Professor of Economics in the Department of Economics at the University of Ibadan, Nigeria.

William Davis is Economic Affairs Officer working with the Macroeconomic and Governance Division of the Economic Commission for Africa.

Davide Del Prete is Economist at the FAO Agricultural Development Economics Division, where he is currently working at the Monitoring and Analyzing Food and Agricultural Policies (MAFAP) Programme and as an Assistant Professor at University of Naples Parthenope. He holds a Ph.D. in Economics from Sapienza University of Roma, Italy. His research interests cover: international trade, value chains, applied economics and micro-econometrics. He has experience consulting with the International Trade Center (UN), UNCTAD and the Italian Ministry of Foreign Affairs.

Joel Edafe is a Ph.D. student in Economics at the Benson Idahosa University, Benin City Nigeria. He is also a lecturer in Economics at Adeyemi College of Education. His area of interest is development finance and household welfare.

Tafah Edokat is Professor of Economics and former Vice-Chancellor of The University of Bamenda.

Rapuluchukwu Efobi Uchenna holds a Ph.D. from the College of Business and Social Sciences Covenant University with a special interest in Development Economics. He is a Hewlett Fellow and is interested in issues on household and firm outcomes, while considering sustainability.

Monday I. Egharevba is a Ph.D. student in Economics at the Benson Idahosa University, Benin City, Nigeria. He focuses on demographic implications of government policies. He is also a lecturer in Economics at Adeyemi College of Education.

Dr. Adam B. Elhiraika is the Director of the Macroeconomic and Governance Division of the United Nations Economic Commission for Africa (ECA). He directly supervises ECA work on macroeconomics, development planning and economic governance and public finance, including key flagship publications: The Economic Report on Africa, the African Governance Report and the Sustainable Development Report. Before joining the United Nations, Elhiraika served as Economist at the Islamic Development Bank (Saudi Arabia), Associate Professor of Economics at the United Arab Emirates University (UAE),

Senior Lecturer at the University of Fort Hare (South Africa) and the University of Swaziland (Swaziland) and Assistant Professor at the University of Gezira (Sudan). In addition to the contribution to official reports and publications, he has published extensively in internationally refereed journals, books and monographs.

Gamal Ibrahim leads the technical work on public finance and illicit financial flows in ECA and has been a member of the secretariat of the High Level Panel on Illicit Financial Flows from Africa since its inception in 2011. Dr. Ibrahim has an M.A. in Development Economics from the University of Leeds, UK and a Ph.D. from Nottingham Trent University, UK. He taught Economics at Nottingham Business School, Nottingham Trent University before joining the Arab Monetary Fund in Abu Dhabi as a Senior Economist. In 2010, he joined the United Nations Economic Commission for Africa. Dr. Ibrahim has published widely in books and leading economics Journals. His main field of specialisation is institutional economics with a particular emphasis on economic governance, finance for development, illicit financial flows and private sector development. He served as a resource person for the African Economic Research Consortium (AERC) research and training programmes. Gamal is a research fellow for the Economic Research Forum (ERF).

Beecroft Ibukun is Economics Researcher and Faculty at Covenant University (CU), Nigeria. Her research is centred on Fiscal Studies and Economic Development in Africa, and she has collaborated with a number of scholars in her field on various grants and award-winning research projects.

Emiliano Magrini is Economist at the FAO Agricultural Development Economics Division, where he is currently working in the Monitoring and Analyzing Food and Agricultural Policies (MAFAP) Programme. His research focuses on agricultural and food value chain analysis in Sub-Saharan Africa, with particular interest in the impact of domestic and trade policies on price fluctuations, production choices and farmers' poverty and food security. He obtained a Ph.D. in Development Economics from the University of Rome "Sapienza" and a Masters in International Economics from the University of Sussex.

Ita M. Mannathoko is an independent researcher formerly of the Bank of Botswana, World Bank and International Monetary Fund.

Isaac Marcelin has taught finance for the past 8 years at University of Maryland Eastern Shore, served as the Senior Advisor in Finance to two Prime Ministers; has published in top-tier journals and conducted M&E of public or social programs along with authoring policy briefs.

Pedro M. G. Martins is Senior Economist for Timor-Leste at the World Bank. Prior to joining the World Bank, Pedro had been an Economic Affairs Officer at the Economic Commission for Africa, a Research Specialist at UNDP's Human Development Report Office and a Research Fellow at the Overseas Development Institute (UK). He holds an M.A. in Development Economics and a Ph.D. in Economics, both from the University of Sussex (UK).

Pierluigi Montalbano is Associate Professor of International Economic Policy, Chair Holder of the Jean Monnet Chair on "EU Trade Policy for Development" and Associate Faculty at the University of Sussex (UK). He holds a Ph.D. in Quantitative Methods from Sapienza University and in Economics from Sussex University. He is author and co-author of several articles and scientific publications in peer-reviewed international journals and an invited speaker at several national and international conferences and seminars. His research interests lie at the crossover between International Economics and Development.

Malokele Nanivazo is a visiting scholar at the University of Kansas. She worked as a research fellow at the United Nations University— World Institute for Development Economics Research (UNU-WIDER). She contributed to several projects on the roots causes of conflicts for the Economic Commission for Africa of the United Nations.

Silvia Nenci is Associate Professor of Economic Policy at the Roma Tre University, Italy. She holds a Ph.D. in Economics from Sapienza University of Rome. Her research interests focus on international trade and development, trade policy, global value chains and network analysis. She is author and co-authors of several publications, included articles in internationally-refereed journals. She has experience consulting with the Inter-American Development Bank, the Italian Ministry of Foreign Affairs, the Global Development Network and the Food and Agriculture Organization of the United Nations.

Aloysius Njong is Associate Professor of Economics and Dean of the Faculty of Economics and Management Sciences at The University of Bamenda.

Musibau Adekunle Oladapo works as a Research Executive at the Centre for Trade and Development Initiatives (CTDi), Bodija, Ibadan, Nigeria. He is also a Doctoral Student in the Department of Economics at the University of Ibadan, Nigeria.

Belmondo Tanankem Voufo holds a Statistician Economist Engineer diploma from the Sub regional Institute of Statistics and Applied Economics of Cameroon. He also holds an M.Sc. in development economics from the University of Antwerp, Belgium. He is currently employed as a Research Officer in the Department of Analysis and Economic Policies of the Ministry of Economy, Planning and Regional Development of Cameroon where he is involved in the realisation of studies for policy and decision-making. He has experience in research and consultancy, specialising in policy analysis, quantitative modelling and econometric applications. His areas of interest include labour and education economics, international trade and development, inequalities and gender, as well as industrial policies and structural transformation. He has authored a number of articles in journals and books on these issues and has presented research papers at various local and international conferences.

List of Figures

List of Tables

1

Overview

Adam B. Elhiraika, Gamal Ibrahim and William Davis

Introduction

The present book is entitled "governance for structural transformation in Africa." The concepts of "governance" and "structural transformation" and the links between them is unpacked at the book's outset and these will help to illuminate the book's objectives and its contribution to the understanding of effective economic governance in Africa.

First, "governance" can be understood, broadly, as the set of factors that influence how power is exercised. It comprises the complex range of mechanisms, processes, relationships and institutions through which citizens and societal groups articulate their interests, exercise their rights

A. B. Elhiraika (✉) · G. Ibrahim · W. Davis
Economic Commission for Africa (ECA), Addis Ababa, Ethiopia
e-mail: elhiraika@un.org

G. Ibrahim
e-mail: ibrahim-eca@un.org

W. Davis
e-mail: d.davis@un.org

© The Author(s) 2019
A. B. Elhiraika et al. (eds.), *Governance for Structural Transformation in Africa*,
https://doi.org/10.1007/978-3-030-03964-6_1

and meet their obligations and mediate differences. As such, governance determines which public policies get adopted and how they are implemented. There is a growing consensus that African countries require a more effective governance architecture for them to be able to pursue better public policies and ultimately to achieve better outcomes, including structural transformation and inclusive development.

Structural transformation is understood to be the reallocation of factors of production (capital, land and labour) within all different segments of the economy to better support inclusive development, increased value addition, increased diversification and increased productivity and industrialisation. Historically, structural transformation has been key to the achievement of sustained, inclusive, job-rich development (see, e.g. Economic Commission for Africa and African Union Commission 2014).

Effective governance and institutions are prerequisites for the attainment of structural transformation and sustainable development (Jakšić and Jakšić 2018). These allow governments to formulate and execute the industrial policies that are required for their economies to structurally transform; they discourage unproductive rent-seeking and harmful business practices[1]. In addition, structural transformation, once unleashed, can also help to improve governance (particularly political governance)—giving rise, for example, to interest groups that push for accountable leadership and effective institutions. As countries get more transformed, more effective institutions also become more affordable. Over time, economic transformation can advance core governance objectives of accountability, participation and transparency. This means that there is a positive feedback loop from more effective governance to structural transformation and vice versa.

It is in this context that we have prepared the present book on "Governance for structural transformation in Africa." The book aims to analyse different governance questions facing African countries

---

[1]Though rent-seeking can be harmful, in some cases the use of contingent rents can be an effective tool for encouraging investment and performance in key sectors of the economy.

and provide recommendations regarding how African countries can most effectively respond to them. This chapter offers an overview of the arguments and conclusions of the various chapters on how African countries can pursue "governance for structural transformation."

This book comprises nine chapters divided into three thematic sections: (i) background on governance and structural transformation—theoretical and empirical overview; (ii) institutions and structural transformation and (iii) industrial and trade policies for structural transformation. Each of these thematic sections is summarised in turn.

Background on Governance and Structural Transformation—Theoretical and Empirical Overview

This section comprises two chapters: (i) Institutional and Governance Weaknesses and African Transformation by Tafah Edokat and Aloysius Njong and (ii) Sub-Regional Perspectives on Structural Change by Pedro M. G. Martins.

Insights from Economic Theory on the Causal Links Between Governance and Structural Transformation and the State of Governance in Africa

Economic theory offers an interpretation of the empirical evidence on the links between governance and structural transformation. This helps to understand the key challenges facing African countries in this area and how they can be addressed. It also helps to interpret the empirical findings presented later in the book and whether they confirm or contradict various different theories of the links between governance and structural transformation. In Chapter 2, Tafah Edokat and Aloysius Njong present an overview of economic theories explaining the relationship between governance and structural transformation. They outline the importance of effective governance for structural transformation and what such governance looks like. The chapter also includes an overview of the existing empirical literature and stylised facts on the state of governance in Africa, which help to underline the importance of the various policy questions that are addressed in detail later in the book.

Overview of Trends and Patterns in Structural Change Worldwide

Understanding which regions, and which countries, in particular, have had success in achieving structural transformation can help us to understand where to find approaches to governance and policies that can support its achievement. In this context, in Chapter 3 Pedro M. G. Martins provides a comprehensive assessment of structural change patterns in the world economy (structural change is the movement of labour across sectors, and is closely related to structural transformation). It uses a new dataset on sectoral employment produced by the International Labour Organization, which is complemented by national accounts and population data from the United Nations Department of Economic and Social Affairs. The sample includes 169 countries, representing about 99% of the world's output and population in 2013.

One of the main contributions of this paper is its focus on the sub-regional level, which has been hitherto absent from the literature. The chapter provides an assessment of 13 sub-regions in Africa, Asia and Latin America in order to offer deeper and richer insights into the recent dynamics of structural change. Overall, the results suggest that within-sector productivity improvements were the key driver of output per capita growth in most sub-regions. Nonetheless, structural change has also played a critical role in enhancing economic performance since 2002—mainly through services. Changes in the demographic structure and employment rates have also contributed to the recent performance, albeit to a much lesser extent. The paper concludes that accelerating the pace of structural change—by exploiting existing productivity gaps—will be crucial to sustain current economic growth rates in developing regions.

Institutions and Structural Transformation

This section comprises three chapters: (i) Economic Regulation and Employment Elasticities of Growth In Sub-Saharan Africa by Abidemi C. Adegboye, Monday I. Egharevba and Joel Edafe, (ii) Governance in the Mineral Dependent Economy—The Case of Botswana by Ita M. Mannathoko and (iii) Can Export Promotion Agencies Stem the Deindustrialisation in Sub-Saharan Africa? by Isaac Marcelin and Nanivazo Malokele. The following sections provide a synopsis of the findings, rationale and methodology used by each of the authors.

The Impact of Regulations, Legal Systems and Government Participation in the Economy on Structural Transformation

In Chapter 4, Abidemi C. Adegboye, Monday I. Egharevba and Joel Edafe investigate how economic regulation and the effectiveness of Government can impact the job-richness of growth (a variable that is closely related to structural transformation). In particular, the paper uses the employment elasticity of growth for a group of 37 African countries. The paper finds that structural changes and demographic transitions are not enough to ensure that growth is strongly employment-enhancing. Rather, the level of regulation also affects the employment elasticity of growth, though the effect differs according to the type of employment. As a result, for Africa (excluding North Africa), deep duality in both product and labour markets provides that additional policy stance would be required to guarantee adequate changes and integration in the sectors over time as output grows.

In particular, the chapter also shows that there is a strong distinction between active regulation and institutional quality in terms of their effects on employment elasticities. Less economic regulation essentially enhances formal sector activities and employment, while the effects on informal and pro-poor employment is not straight-forward. Although overall regulation tends to improve both formal and informal sector employment, labour market flexibility tends to worsen informal sector employment.

In the same vein, legal institutions appear to be pro-poor in terms of employment effects, though legal system quality can depress other types of employment. Government participation in economic activities strongly decreases employment elasticity of output growth in Africa (excluding North Africa). The chapter also finds that intersectoral integration and adjustments play little role in ensuring employment benefits from output growth when regulations are minimal. There is, therefore, a need for careful balancing of regulations to address structural bottlenecks, improve informal sector activities and employment and ensure pro-poor growth in the region.

Impacts of Resource Dependence on Government Effectiveness

In Chapter 5, Ita M. Mannathoko investigates the impacts of Botswana's changing degree of mineral dependence on the effectiveness of the country's Government. As background, the chapter notes that in general, governments that are dependent on mining receipts for a significant share of their revenue face different performance incentives from those that source their revenues from a broad and diversified tax base. These different incentives can influence how government prioritises its engagement with economic actors and the citizenry; rewarding government performance that gives precedence to what is best for the mining sector rather than what is best for the economy as a whole. This bias then undermines efforts to achieve the type of structural transformation needed for diversification of production and of the fiscal revenue base, both of which are essential to avoid Dutch disease and generate long-term sustainable growth and employment. While the governance challenges associated with mineral dependency are well established in the literature, most recent studies are cross-country analyses and not much country-specific empirical analysis has been done on the relationship between mineral dominance and governance, especially in Africa. The chapter, therefore, uses a country-specific study of Botswana, a mineral-dependent economy.

The author employs a time-series cointegration methodology and a dynamic error-correction model. The results establish that mining dominance in Botswana has indeed had a long-term influence on government effectiveness, such that the effectiveness of governance systems has been predicated on strong mining sector receipts. The dynamic error correction model shows that the influence from mineral dependency feeds back into current changes in government effectiveness on an annual basis as the system adjusts towards the long-run level of government effectiveness. In addition, improvements in the control of corruption in the preceding year and in citizen participation (represented by voice and accountability data) in the current year both have a significant and positive impact, generating improvements in government effectiveness.

The Role of Export Promotion Agencies in Supporting Industrialisation

In Chapter 6, Isaac Marcelin and Malokele Nanivazo investigate how export promotion agencies affect the growth of the manufacturing sector outcomes in Africa using the propensity score matching technique. The results indicate that creating an export promotion agency drives up boosts the manufacturing sector significantly. Countries in Africa (excluding North Africa) without an export promotion agency (EPA) might, therefore, have missed out on an opportunity to boost their manufacturing sector. Export promotion agencies have strong effects on manufacturing in as early as three years following their implementation. The results found in the chapter are robust to various matching strategies. Results also suggest that the joint effect of export promotion agencies and export processing zones is beneficial to manufacturing activities. The authors conclude that, since many conditions required for well-functioning financial markets for manufacturing firms to finance their expansion are missing, government intervention through export promotion agencies directed at counteracting some distortions may be growth enhancing.

Industrial and Trade Policies for Structural Transformation

This section comprises three chapters: (i) Incentives and Firms' Productivity: Exploring Multidimensional Fiscal Incentives in a Developing Country by Rapuluchukwu Efobi Uchenna, Belmondo Tanankem Voufo and Ibukun Beecroft, (ii) Does trade policy impact food and agriculture global value chain participation of Sub-Saharan African countries? by Jean Balié, Davide Del Prete, Emiliano Magrini, Pierluigi Montalbano and Silvia Nenci and (iii) The role of Regional Trade Integration and Governance in Structural Transformation: Empirical Evidence from ECOWAS Trade Bloc by Abiodun Surajudeen Bankole and Musibau Adekunle Oladapo. The following sections provide a synopsis of the findings, rationale and methodology used by each of the authors.

The Role of Fiscal Incentives in Boosting Productivity

In Chapter 7, Rapuluchukwu Efobi Uchenna, Belmondo Tanankem Voufo and Ibukun Beecroft investigate the impact of fiscal incentives on firms' productivity using Cameroonian firms as a case. The authors use data from the World Bank Enterprise Survey for over 300 firms to calculate firm productivity and measure the extent to which firms benefit from different categories of fiscal incentives, including import duty exemptions, profit tax exemptions and export financing. The authors use propensity score matching to assess the impact of firms benefiting from such incentives on their productivity. The results show a significant and positive impact of the productivity of firms that benefit from profit tax exemptions and export financing. However, when considering import duty exemptions, the significance of this variable was not consistent. The chapter thus provides support for the argument that the government's involvement in the firm should be targeted at rewarding outputs and not supporting processes, and thus provides an essential element of a strategy for industrialisation.

Trade Policy and Global Value Chain Participation in the Food and Agriculture Sectors

In Chapter 8, Jean Balié, Davide Del Prete, Emiliano Magrini, Pierluigi Montalbano and Silvia Nenci investigate how a country's trade policy affects its participation in food and agriculture global value chains. The authors first note that the most recent literature on international trade highlights the key role of global value chains in structural transformation, development and growth. The common perception is that Africa (excluding North Africa), unlike most Latin American and Asian countries, has not been able to successfully engage into global production networks. By applying the bilateral gross exports decomposition method developed by Wang et al. (2013) to panel data from EORA Input-Output Tables, the chapter provides two main contributions to the literature: (i) an extensive investigation of sectoral and bilateral participation of Africa (excluding North Africa) in global food and agriculture value chains and (ii) a sound empirical test to estimate the impact of bilateral trade protection on their backward and forward linkages. The chapter shows that: (i) despite their low world trade shares, participation of African (excluding North African) countries in agriculture and food global value chains is higher than that of many other regions in the world and is increasing over time (ii) bilateral protection significantly affects backward and forward global value chain participation; that is, import tariffs may have a depressing impact on the domestic value added content embodied in partner countries' exports as well as provide rents to foreign suppliers of inputs. These results call for a refinement of trade policy priorities in Africa (excluding North Africa).

Trade Policy, Governance and Structural Transformation

In Chapter 9, Abiodun Surajudeen Bankole and Musibau Adekunle Oladapo examine the effect of regional trade integration and governance on the structural transformation in the ECOWAS trade bloc covering the period 2000–2015. In estimating a regional trade index, the authors use the methodology developed for the Africa Regional

Integration Index developed by African Union Commission, the African Development Bank and the Economic Commission for Africa. The authors use a panel regression. The results of the panel regression show that poor governance negatively affects structural transformation while openness of member states' economies to both intra-regional trade and the rest of the world promote positive transformation towards the industrial sector. Trade integration alone as measured by its index, TINT, records neither a positive nor a negative statistically significant effect on any of the measures of structural transformation. The authors find that ECOWAS countries require both intra-regional and international trade with the rest of the world to structurally transform from dependence on the primary sector towards sustained industrialisation.

References

Economic Commission for Africa and African Union. (2014). Economic Report on Africa 2014 Dynamic Industrial Policy in Africa: Innovative Institutions, Effective Processes and Flexible Mechanisms. Economic Commission for Africa, Addis Ababa.

Jakšić, M., Jakšić, M. (2018). Inclusive Institutions for Sustainable Economic Development. *Journal of Central Banking Theory and Practice, 1,* 5–16

Wang, Z., Wei, S.-J, Zhu, K. (2013). *Quantifying International Production Sharing at the Bilateral and Sector Levels.* National Bureau of Economic Research. Available via http://www.nber.org/papers/w19677.pdf. Accessed 7 Feb 2017.

2

Institutional and Governance Weaknesses and African Transformation

Tafah Edokat and Aloysius Njong

Africa is world's greatest sources of raw materials used in different parts of the world. That alone puts Africa at the forefront in terms of growth prospects in the future. This however, depends on various variants like technological advancement, bureaucracy, corruption, skill shortages and personal safety and regulatory environment. (Kajuju Murori, World Fact Book, WB, July 13, 2015)

Tafah Edokat is a Professor of Economics and former Vice-Chancellor of The University of Bamenda.

Aloysius Njong is Associate Professor of Economics and Dean of the Faculty of Economics and Management Sciences at The University of Bamenda. His contribution to the Principal–Agent Problem Model has enhanced the article.

The authors greatly acknowledge the contribution of our research student Badjo Martial in sourcing some of the literature, relevant to the topic and some of the 2017 Ph.D students in the African Economic Research Consortium (AERC) collaborative Ph.D economic programme (JFE 2017), Nairobi.

T. Edokat (✉) · A. Njong
The University of Bamenda, Bamenda, Cameroon

© The Author(s) 2019
A. B. Elhiraika et al. (eds.), *Governance for Structural Transformation in Africa*,
https://doi.org/10.1007/978-3-030-03964-6_2

The opportunity to find a job or develop one's business idea is crucial in most people's personal satisfaction. It creates a sense of belonging and purpose and can provide an income that delivers financial stability. It can raise people out of poverty or prevent them from falling into it. (World Bank Doing Business Report: Equal Opportunity for All, 2017)

Introduction

Significant progress has been made in the economic transformation of many economies, especially in the developing countries in the past few decades with considerable growth gains resulting in poverty reductions, income distributions, productivity growth and shifts in labour market structures. While some regions have demonstrated similar patterns and signs of convergence others lag behind in most of the indicators of development. The literature has indicated that economic growth and transformation in South East Asia, China and most recently India was precipitated by the industrial sector, with manufacturing playing a key role (Enache et al. 2016).

However, the recent gains in economic growth in Sub-Saharan Africa (SSA) in the past decade still come from the export of natural resources and according to Enache et al. (ibid.) "the region's economies are developing in unexpected ways". The region is bypassing industrialisation as a major driver of growth and creator of jobs.

Africa possesses great potential. According to Murori (2015), "Africa is world's greatest sources of raw materials used in different parts of the world. That alone puts Africa at the forefront in terms of growth prospects in the future. This however, depends on various variants like technological advancement, bureaucracy, corruption, skill shortages and personal safety and regulatory environment". In addition, the rising population of Africa is a huge potential human resource base, which if properly harnessed could be another source of growth. However, growth and transformation in Africa has been slowed down by a number of obstacles including weak institutions, poor infrastructure, inadequate policies and volatility in natural resources and commodity markets. These obstacles need to be overcome in order to accelerate African economic growth and transformation. The questions that beg for answers are: why have other regions that were at the same level of development with Africa at independence advanced and transformed their economies to or near the levels of developed economies? In other words, why has Africa unable to rapidly overcome the constraints mentioned above in order to take advantage of its huge potentials? Why is Africa so rich but too poor and underdeveloped? Why is Africa unable to maintain sustained economic growth in order to transform their economies? What is wrong with Africa?

Research on the determinants of long-term and sustainable economic development have emphasised a series of factors evolving from traditional determinants (factors of production and technology) to a range of additional factors, such as government size, trade, human capital, financial system, etc. as outlined by new theories of economic growth (Romer 1986; Lucas 1988; Barro 1991, etc.). However, recent theories also explain that differences and fluctuations in economic performance of countries can be attributed to the quality of institutions and the governance structure (Easterly et al. 2004; Glaeser et al. 2004; Ansell and Gash 2008).

The relationship between institutional quality and economic performance has been widely analysed in theoretical and empirical literature. Since the pioneering work of North (1991), there has been increasing convergence of scholars on the importance of sound institutions to promote economic growth and development. Strong institutions guarantee a good climate for investment through macroeconomic and political stability. On the contrary, poor institutions can increase uncertainty, unpredictability, instability, corruption and transaction costs (Zouhaier 2012). Such a macroeconomic and political environment can deter private investment and lead to poor economic performance. The rationale behind the relationship between institutional quality and economic development is that institutions define the "rule of games" and conditions under which economic agents operate in an economy. The functioning of institutions in any economy depends on the governance system. The woes of SSA have been attributed to either weak and bad institutions or bad governance. The question then is: What is Governance, how does it relate to institution and how do these concepts affect the transformation of countries, especially SSA?

In this paper, we attempt to define these concepts and relate them to economic transformation. The paper is therefore purely conceptual and theoretical, void of empirical analysis. It draws on the existing literature, especially those linking institutions and governance to economic growth with implications for economic transformation. *The main proposition is that institutions and governance matter in economic growth and transformation, but poor crafting of institutions and bad governance have truncated the economic transformation and retarded the growth of African economies.*

The rest of the paper is structured as follows. "Concepts of Institutions, Governance and Transformation" takes a cursory look at the three concepts of institutions, governance and transformation. "The Principal–Agent Problem Model" elaborates the principal–agent model which best captures the relationship between these concepts. "Empirical Literature Linking Growth with Institutions" attempts a brief literature review on the link between institutional quality and economic growth. It attempts to examine some global institutional quality indictors and show the position of Africa in the global context with the objective of highlighting the weaknesses of these institutions in promoting rapid growth and thus transformation. "Economic Transformation in Africa" examines the raison d'etre of transformation and "Conclusion" concludes the paper with some reflections on the perspective of African transformation.

Concepts of Institutions, Governance and Transformation

Institutions

Institutions have been widely used in different domains in the social sciences, such as political science, economics, sociology and anthropology. In all the domains institutions are either formal or informal mechanisms or structures that govern the pattern of behaviour in a given society (North 1991). Institutions can be created by individuals or groups of individuals and or the state or other institutions. Institutions are therefore identified with a social purpose, transcending individuals and intentions by mediating the rules that govern living behaviour. As mechanisms of social interactions, institutions manifest themselves in *formal* organisations, such as the church, market or the legislature of a country. In addition, instruments of governance, such as the constitution, investment code and written rules and regulations are aspects of formal institutions. On the other hand, *informal* institutions manifest themselves in human psychology, culture (sanctions, taboos, customs, traditions and codes of conduct), etc. Denhart and Jeffress (1971) corroborate this by noting that: "Formal institutions are explicitly set forth by a relevant authority and informal institutions are generally unwritten societal rules, norms, and traditions."

Whether institutions shape policies and politics, or whether it is politics and policies that shape institutions, there is no doubt that political, economic and social institutions are the conveyor belts for collective action. There is abundant literature that has explored the importance of varying institutions in the field. They include political institutions (March and Olsen 1983), budget institutions (Padgett 1981), legislatures (Shepsle and Weingast 1987), local and state government institutions (Kjellberg 2005), administrative capacity (Skowronek 1982) and so on.

Acemoglu et al. (2005) defined institutions as a combination of three interrelated concepts:

Economic institutions They include factors governing the structure of incentives in society (i.e. incentives of economic actors to invest, accumulate factors, make transactions, etc.) and the distribution of resources. For example, the structure of property rights, entry barriers, set of contract, types of business offered in contract law; redistributive tax-transfer schemes are affecting economic performance and growth.

Political power—Economic institutions are themselves the outcome of collective choices of the society. A society is made of different groups with conflicting interests. The relative political power of these groups governs their capacity to decide the administration of resources and implement policies. The distribution of political power determines the design and the quality of economic institutions, that is, whether power is acquired de facto (political power emerging from economic outcomes) or de jure (power emerging from legal outcomes).

Political institutions—They include institutions allocating legal political power across groups. They are linked to the characteristics of the government and the design of the constitution. This raises numerous questions which include among others: Who elects the empowered? How is power distribution structured? Where is decision-making power held?

While formal institutions have received the bulk of attention in economic and political analysis, informal institutions, which have been given little attention, tend to govern the economic and political landscape of most LDCs, especially Sub-Saharan African (SSA) countries. An informal institution tends to have socially shared rules, which are unwritten and yet are often known by all inhabitants of a certain country, as such they are often referred to as being an inherent part of the culture of a given country. Informal practices are often referred to as "cultural", for example clientelism or corruption is sometimes stated as a part of the political culture in a certain place, but an informal institution itself is not cultural, it may be shaped by culture or behaviour of a given political landscape, but they should be looked at in the same way as formal institutions to understand their role in a given country. Informal institutions might be particularly used to pursue a political agenda, or a course of action that might not be publicly popular, or even legal, and can be seen as an effective way of making up for lack of efficiency in a formal institution. It is at this level that *the interplay between institutions and governance either enhance or constrain economic transformation*. But before we show the interplay of these concepts it would be proper to explore the concepts of governance and transformation in the next two sections.

Governance

Governance is a multidimensional and pervasive concept in constant evolution. According to Bevir (2013), "Governance is all of the processes of governing, whether undertaken by a government, market or network, whether over a family, tribe, formal or informal organization or territory and whether through the laws, norms, power or language of an organized society." As the act of governing, it refers to the way rules, norms and actions are structured, sustained, regulated and held accountable. Governance is thus multijurisdictional and often transnational combining people and institutions across different policy sectors and different levels of government (Bevir 2013). For example, Dolan and Humphrey (2000) show how international governance works in the horticulture market between Africa and Europe through some specifications that must be respected. These specifications determine the inclusion or exclusion of actors in the trade.

Governance, whether in the formal or informal form, is driven by different motivations and with different results. However, the outcomes of governance can be influenced by external actors not belonging to the governing institution, especially in collaborative governance.

Considering governance as the act of governing, therefore, collapses it into assessing how institutions are managed. A proper management of institutions to achieve the desired goals results in good governance, while bad governance is the reverse. As such institutions and governance are used synonymously and they matter in economic growth and transformation.

Economic Transformation

Traditional macroeconomics of development in Less Developed Countries (LDCs) tends to concentrate on the growth–poverty nexus. It is asserted that the adoption of certain macroeconomic fundamentals with good governance would induce growth which in turn would lead to poverty reduction (Wuyts and Kilama 2014). This assertion does not show the mechanism through which poverty is reduced, except under the assumption that per capita GDP growth translates itself into improved standards of living. The issue of economic transformation was ignored and has only recently come to focus as a challenge in LDCs, especially in SSA (Osman et al. 2011; te Velde 2013; Wuyts and Kilama 2014).

Transformation is an outcome of economic growth and development. Economic development is simply a sustained increase in national output accompanied by a structural transformation of the different sectors of the economy and the quality of life of the citizens. Transformation encompasses "*moving labour from low to higher productive activities. This includes between sectors to higher value activities* (for example, from agriculture to manufacturing) and within sectors (for example, from subsistence farming to high-value crops). It is widely accepted that poverty reduction and economic growth cannot be sustained without economic transformation and productivity change but, despite this obvious point, the development community has traditionally paid relatively little attention to these long-term determinants of development" (te Velde 2013). Transformation, according to Wikipedia, "is unidirectional and irreversible change in dominant human economic activity (economic sector). Such change is driven by slower or faster continuous improvement in sector productivity growth rate. Productivity growth itself is fueled by advances in technology, inflow of useful innovations, accumulated practical knowledge and experience, levels of education, viability of institutions, quality of decision-making and organised human effort, which are features of institutional quality and governance. Individual sector transformations are the outcomes of human socioeconomic evolution". Strictly speaking, economic and social transformation is thus a shift in the composition of output and employment away from agriculture towards industry and services, that is, a shift from an agricultural-based to an industry-based economy (Wuyts and Kilama 2014) conditioned by the quality of institutions and governance.

The three concepts are interrelated and affect the economic development and transformation of countries. Their interrelationship and effect on development is best captured in the Principal-Agency model which is discussed in "The Principal–Agent Problem Model".

The Principal–Agent Problem Model

Understanding the Principal–Agent Model

The relationship between the concepts of institutions, governance and transformation could be anchored on the principal–agent model. Essentially, the principal–agent approach looks at the interaction of two actors: the principal (ownership) on the one hand and the agent (management) on the other hand (Ricketts 2002). In modern-day management of business activities/production, there is a divorce between ownership and management. This divorce is achieved in most organisations through delegation of powers.

Delegation is the starting point of the principal–agent problem. It occurs when the principal decides that an activity has to be accomplished but cannot easily perform the task themselves, and so hires an agent to act on their behalf. Unfortunately, just as principals cannot do the task themselves, they often have difficulty knowing if they have hired the right person for the task and whether the task is being accomplished appropriately. The two problems—hiring the right agent and knowing that they will do the job appropriately—are known respectively as adverse selection and moral hazard (Ricketts 2002). The principal–agent problem (otherwise simply referred to agency problem) arises because there is always the possibility that the agent will not act in the best interests of the principals but may serve their own interests first. If the agent shares the same interests and concerns as the principal there will be no agency problem: the agent will always do his best to fulfil the objectives of the principal. However, such congruent interests are unlikely: usually, agents will have their own distinct interests. School teachers may prefer not to turn up to school each day and doctors may prefer to remain on the public payroll but spend their time practicing privately.

A second step in the principal–agent framework is that the principal is not able to fully observe what the agent does. Such monitoring activities may be costly to the principal. Since the agent obviously knows what he does, and the principal does not, there exists asymmetric information in the model. Although the principal is dependent upon an agent whose interests often diverge from his own, he the principal is not powerless. The principal pays the agent for his work and has some scope to make his payments conditional through an incentive scheme. This way, the principal may be able to inflict penalties where agent interest diverges as well as pay rewards to agents to implement the interests of the principal.

Applying the Principal-Agency Theory to the Institutions-Transformation Nexus

In the private sector, there are two actors and it is relatively easy to identify which actor is the principal and which the agent. For instance, in a private firm, the principal is the employer who is dependent upon the worker (the agent) for the attainment of some objective. The principal may as well be a parent who wants his child to be well-taught, and the agent the school teacher whose effort determines the quality of teaching. In the public sector, an additional actor—the government or individual politicians come into the picture. They can influence the activities of the public enterprise through influence over the management. This difference has a direct bearing on the overall performance of public enterprises as compared to private firms. African transformation requires more effective use of resources to improve service delivery, such as water, sanitation, energy, healthcare and education that contribute to human development. We limit our analysis to production in the public sector which is more to provide such goods or services. According to the World Bank (2004), the principal–agent relationships established between citizens, politicians and goods/service providers may be referred to as accountability relations. Citizens (clients) delegate responsibilities to elected officials (state) to provide public services and pay taxes to fund them. Politicians in turn delegate service delivery to provider organisations by creating incentives and appropriating budgets. The model stipulates two layers of agency problems: between the citizens and politicians (elected officials) and between elected officials and goods/service providers. The role of intermediary agent played by the state in the principal–agent relationship creates a situation where it is difficult for the principal (citizens) to evaluate and control the actions of the decentralised agent (goods/service providers). According to Besley and Ghatak (2003), we may identify four aspects in which public goods/services differ from private provision.

a. *Multiplicity of tasks*

Goods/service providers (agents) perform a multiplicity of tasks which renders evaluation of results difficult. For instance, health workers perform vaccination or other preventive activities as well as curative activities, which generally compete with each other in terms of limited time and other resources. This makes provision of incentives difficult when workers have to perform such multiple tasks.

b. *Measurability problems of the output*

Measurability problems are associated with the complexity of service provision. Agents' activities in public organisations are generally unobservable by the principal (citizens). Typically, citizens only get to observe the aggregate output of the production process. Citizens cannot easily determine who is responsible for the situation they observe: the front-line service providers, politicians or bureaucrats. They cannot observe the specific contribution that a politician makes to a program and it is also difficult to link this potential contribution to the program outcome and their own welfare.

c. *Multiple principals*

Service delivery is also characterised by the presence of multiple principals. There are several actors who are directly affected by the actions of an agent in the provision of public services. For instance, in the education sector, the parents, school boards, Ministry of Education officials and politicians could be seen as the principals, while the agents are the teachers. These different principals might have different preferences concerning the outcome of the various tasks carried out by the agents. In other words, each principal would like to induce the agent to put more effort into activities that he cares more about.

d. *Multilevel structure of agents*

The provision of a public good/service is characterised by the presence of multiple agents engaged in the production process. In this set up, the responsibilities are shared between several decision-making levels, often following a central-regional/provincial-local authority pattern. These multilevel structures are characterised by situations of functional interdependence between levels: rather than being independent, one unit's (or level's) action has repercussions upon the effectiveness of a second unit's action. Functional interdependence between agents potentially gives rise to specific problems, in particular, related to the difficulty of dissociating the individual contribution of the different levels of agents.

The World Bank (2004) describes two accountability 'routes' or relationships in this multilevel principal–agent relationship of public goods and service provision. First, we have the short route of accountability between citizens and providers. This relationship involves direct accountability of providers to clients, a situation typically encountered in the private sector. Second, we have the long route of accountability between citizens and government and then between government and providers. Inadequate goods/service delivery is usually associated with failures in one or both of the links along the long route of accountability. The dismal performance of African economies may be attributed to the shortcomings in the long route accountability relationships. To redress this situation, there must be a mechanism that enables clients to monitor and directly discipline service providers through sanctions or rewards (an incentive scheme).

Empirical Literature Linking Growth with Institutions

Empirical Literature

Economic development is the ultimate goal of any policy or system of governance in the economic domain. If there seems to be an increased consensus of what economic development is all about, there has been a plurality of the measurements of economic development. Most commonly used measurements of economic development include gross domestic product per capita (GDPPC) and Human Development Index (HDI). There is increased attention of researchers on the channels through which institutions and governance as a whole affect economic growth and development. Failure to address the question of why some countries succeed and others fail despite capital accumulation, technology and human capital, a new stream of economists have emerged to look into deep determinants of long-term economic performance of economies. This is the New Institutional Economics (NEI) which extends the neoclassical economics by incorporating the role played by institutions in promoting economic growth and development. Several studies have emerged in that direction. Some studies relating institutions and/or governance with development are examined below.

Salahodjaev and Chepel (2014) empirically investigated the effects of institutional quality on inflation. Using panel data from 1991 to 2007, they found that increase in institutional development measured by the ratio of domestic credit to private sector over GDP has significant and sizeable effect on inflation. Their paper showed that in countries with high inflation rates, financial sectors cannot resist current levels of inflation and banking system does not decrease inflation in the environment where private banks and financial companies have adapted to existing monetary environment.

Iqbal and Daly (2014) argued that weak institutions increase rent-seeking activities and by so doing divert resources from productive sector to unproductive sector. On the other hand, strong institutions reduce the chances of rent-seeking activities and accelerate economic growth process and productivity. The consequences of rent-seeking activities for growth can be negative: resources may not be efficiently allocated, externalities may be ignored and transaction costs may be increased. North (1991) argues that institutional weaknesses lead to rent-seeking activities hence low development. The incomplete rule of law, no enforcement of property rights, inadequate policies and the lack of reliable infrastructure constitute a weak institutional framework that may promote rent-seeking activities (Iqbal and Daly 2014).

Nawaz et al. (2014) examined the impact of institutional quality on economic growth in selected Asian countries over the period 1996–2012. The authors used the static and dynamic panel Generalized Methods of Moments to analyse the data. Results from the analyses revealed that institutions exert a significant effect on the long run economic growth of Asian countries. However, the study also indicates that the impact of institutions on economic growth differs from one country to another depending on the level of economic development. The impact of institutions was more pronounced in developed countries as compared to developing countries of the region.

Zouhaier (2012) analysed the effect of institutional factors on investment and economic growth in 11 countries of the Middle East and North Africa (MENA) region during the period 2000–2009, using a model of dynamic panel data. The major findings generated by his empirical tests revealed a significant relationship between institutional variables and investment on the one hand and economic growth on the other hand. Further results also showed that there was a positive interaction between political institutions and investment and a negative interaction between political instability and investment.

A study by Osman et al. (2011) explored the role of institutions in economic development in 27 Sub-Saharan countries over the period running from 1984–2003. Using a panel data analysis alongside four institutional quality indicators namely government stability, corruption, ethnic tensions and socioeconomic conditions, along with other control and policy variables, these authors found that institutional factors were key determinants of economic development whereas the control variables had limited effect. Thus, the traditional variables of economic theory can only explain long-term economic performance in SSA partially.

Ifere et al. (2015) examined the relationship between institutional quality, macroeconomic policy and economic development in Nigeria. The authors employed data from four development indicators: the prevalence of undernourishment, life expectancy at birth, the Human Development Index (HDI) and Gross Domestic Product (GDP) per-capita from 1995 to 2013 to achieve the above objective. Results revealed an insignificant impact of domestic institution on Nigerian development indices. Interest rate was also found to have an insignificant impact on economic development in Nigeria, even when growth related indices were considered. On the other hand, government expenditure was found to exert a significant, though small, impact on the country's development indices. Based on these, a holistic approach of attitudinal change, systematic strengthening and development of institutions was recommended for the attainment of the country's developmental objectives.

These studies and many others in the literature indicate the importance of institutional quality on economic growth and development and by implication economic transformation.

Indicators of Institutions and Governance

Institutional quality has been looked at in different ways by different authors, emphasising different indicators or group of indicators that act together to shape interactions in the economies of countries. Different indices have been contrived as dependent or independent variables of institutions by the World Bank, Experts and international organisations that affect development and/or growth. Although some controversies exist in contriving these indices, they are useful in their own right as measurement of institutions is a difficult process. These indices can, therefore, be used to assess and compare countries, regions and even societies in their development and transformation processes. Although not perfect, they are useful in producing guides for policy formulation. We use some of these indicators as produced by the various organisations to compare SSA with other regions of the world. The indices selected include *Corruption Perception Index, Doing Business, Voice and Accountability, Regulatory Quality and Government Effectiveness*. The choice of these variables is arbitrary. However, African countries were selected on the basis of their classification as the fastest growing economies in Africa in recent years (Murori 2015) to juxtapose them with some high performing economies of South East Asia. The data were taken from the World Bank Governance Indicators (WBGI) 2016. The corruption perception index comes from Transparency International Corruption Perception Index, 2017 (Table 2.1).

These indicators show that there is a correlation between economic growth and the quality of institutions and governance. While higher indexes indicate good governance lower ones show the reverse. An examination of the table indicates that the selected African countries, except Botswana (which consistently scores above 50%) had very low scores as compared to the high performing economies of South East Asia. This is an indication of the weaknesses of institutions and

Table 2.1 Some indicators of governance in selected countries 2016

Country	Corrupt. PI	Doing Bus.	Voice & Acc	Regul Qlity	Govt Effec
New Zealand	90	87.01	97.54	97.04	98.2
Singapore	84	85.05	NA	36.94	100
Hong kong	77	98.08	65	NA	98.08
Korea	53	84.07	68.97	NA	NA
Rwanda	54	69.81	17.24	NA	NA
Tanzania	32	54.48	41.87	40.39	34.13
Mozambique	NA	53.78	40.89	33.99	18.75
Ivory Coast	34	52.31	32	36.45	26.92
Congo, DRC	21	37.57	18.23	10.84	5.77
Ethiopia	34	28.05	12.81	NA	28.37
Botswana	60	65.55	61.58	59.11	70.67

Note All the indexes are graded up to 100% with 100% being the highest score indicating highest level of performance on that index, while a 0% score indicates the lowest level of perception of performance of that index. Scores above 50% indicate average and above performance. NA are statistics that were not available
Source The World Governance Indicators (2017) and Transparency International Corruption Perception Index (2017)

governance in Africa, which have, to some reasonable extent, been responsible for the low growth performance of these countries and by implications slowing down transformation.

Economic Transformation in Africa

Transformation in Africa has been a topic of concern for some time. The topic has generated debates, brainstorming and resolutions have been taken by African Heads of state within the context of the African Union (AU). The topic is emerging as a consensus in Africa, but the implementation of the various resolutions on this issue is still a topic of debate. Why is there a need for transformation in Africa?

Why Transformation and What Kind of Transformation?

African economic performance has been very impressive in the past decade but the structural change that has emerged does not follow the classical pattern that produced high economic growth and transformation during and after the industrial revolution in Europe, North America and especially in the Asian high performing economies such as "the Asian Tigers", China and India. From the quotation at the beginning of this paper Africa has a lot of potentials in both natural and human resources which if properly harnessed would ensure faster growth and a better life for the vast majority of its people. Recent growth experience in Africa has shown some distinctive characteristics:

i. Growth has been led by growing exports of agricultural raw materials and mineral resources, with very little changes in the industrial (manufacturing) sector.

ii. Labour is moving out of the agricultural and rural areas, but formal manufacturing industries are not the main beneficiaries of this rural exodus as perceived in classical economic thought.

iii. The growing urban population from rural–urban migration is absorbed largely into services of the urban informal sector, with very low productivity.

iv. Growth has not been accompanied by widespread changes in the social wellbeing of a large majority of the people. Rural production is still on small scale, while the few small scaled industries that exist operate on artisanal basis. Poverty, especially rural poverty is still a distinct feature and many countries in the region are classified as the poorest and least developed in the world.

v. Growth is not accompanied by application of science, technology and innovation and foreign aid and foreign investments are on the decline.

vi. Growth has taken place under very weak institutions, bad governance and poor infrastructure.

Based on these characteristics it becomes necessary to have a comprehensive structural transformation in Africa that guarantees growth with equity and other dimensions of social development. The need for such transformation has been muted in various reflections and seminars/conferences, some of which are outlined below:

a. Africa's historical position as an exporter of raw materials and natural resources for the industries of the Developed Countries (DCs) and other emerging countries. This situation needs to be reversed. Such exports are low valued, having diminishing returns and subject to the volatility of the international commodity markets.

b. Africa as a continent has the huge potential not only to attain high food security but also to generate surplus that can be internationally traded; however, it is still performing below capacity with very low productivity.

c. Africa's recent experience with Structural Adjustment Programs (SAPs) and the Millennium Development Goals (MDGs) executed under the auspices of International Finance Institutions, did not reduce the dependence of Africa on raw material and mineral resource exports. Globalisation has not helped Africa either. It has rendered Africa vulnerable, poor and dependent.

d. Africa will need to develop an array or network of highly productive sectors to complement the huge traditional and small modern sectors. There should be different industries that can add value to raw farm produce at different stages of production. This will increase the returns to farmers and encourage further investments and serve as an incentive to the farmers as well.

e. Africa needs "to move from a 'production system' dominated by primary extraction and low value-added agriculture and services to a high value-added industrial production system," that adopts science, technology and innovation for better linkages between sectors. This is to enable Africa to get a fair share of its natural resources rents.

f. Africa needs to develop a vibrant private sector with small, medium and large enterprises with employment opportunities in order to empower more people by putting money and wealth in their hands. This will enhance savings and investments which are necessary conditions for economic growth. More investments funds generated by Africans will reduce its dependence on foreign investments and aid.

g. Transformation is needed to generate rapid, sustained and inclusive growth with vertical and horizontal equity and to ensure universal "access to essential services, providing additional protection for the poorest and weakest in the society and ensuring an equitable, peaceful and harmonious society."

h. Transformation needs to be accompanied by transformed social, economic and political institutions and good governance, that is, "a transformed relationship between state and citizens."

i. The need to be resilient in the face of global challenges, such as food, financial, energy and environmental crisis and the spread of terrorism.

j. The need to build international cooperation between Africa and international community on the "principles of equality of nations and peoples" and mutual respect.

These and other issues are the main focus of reflections on African transformation which has dominated policy agenda in many high levels discussions.

What Should Be Done to Ensure Effective Transformation in Africa? (Perspectives)

The need for African transformation is more urgent now than ever before. Africa needs to take advantage of its enormous human and natural resources and the growth potentials to change the socio-economic and political landscape of the continent. African scholars and researchers need to scale up their examination of the drivers and implications of economic transformation and productivity change in the continent, e.g. what are the direct and indirect links with development and poverty; what is holding back or promoting transformation; what is the role of institutions and governance and how can the global community support this? These questions and many others necessitate some reflections on the way forward. While not pretending to have exhaustive answers or reflection on the gambit of necessary conditions for successful African transformation, our contribution is on four key issues, which in our opinion are the bedrock on which transformation depends. The issues are: self-transformation, harnessing of African human capital, designing and implementing a comprehensive compensation scheme, and return to planning.

a. *Self-Transformation*

Transformation implies change, which can be systemic or organic and social network is critical in the institution-governance-development nexus. Social network begins with the INDIVIDUAL whose first instinct is self-preservation—the "***self-syndrome***". Self-syndrome manifests itself in self-interest where the principle is "***Me, myself and I***". This principle has played a dominant role in the African governance system, especially in SSA. In this, principle actions taken or envisaged are egocentric in nature and the ***tribe/family*** sometimes comes into play. The agency problem is highly in play here. The politicians who are supposed to perform tasks on behalf of the citizens act to serve their interest first. The self-syndrome limits thinking within the box and decisions are therefore taken within the box. This syndrome has given rise to entrenched corruption (with its consequences of poor infrastructure, poor medical care), long stay in power by leaders, lack of transparency in elections and management of public affairs, poverty, capital flight, conflicts, etc. This has been one of the major causes of institutional weakness, failures and bad governance in many counties, thereby slowing growth.

The African needs to transform the mindset to start thinking of the collective good (the state and/or community) before self or tribe/family. In this way public property will no longer be perceived as someone else's property and therefore to be looted; appointments into government and public corporations will be based on merit rather than the tribe/family and self-gains; rules and regulations will be crafted collectively and transparently for the common good. Self-transformation when collectively done will engender institutional transformation and thus good governance, which is one of the prerequisites for socio-economic and political transformation of the African society.

b. *Harnessing African Human capital*

It has been asserted that the continued investment in people's skills, knowledge, education, health and nutrition is one of the most important investments in any society. Human capital is the "software" and "brainware" of any nation and constitutes the most important form of capital. The population of the African continent is large and growing. The literature indicates that the rising population, especially the urban population has contributed to the growth of African economies through jobs in the service sector. This is at odd with orthodox economic theory in which industrialisation is the engine of growth through the absorption of excess labour from the rural sector. On the growing population of Africa, Enache et al. (2016) assert that "The demographic dividend will make the region's labor force much larger and better than that of any nation, including China or India if young children in Africa could be better educated than in the past." The implication of this assertion is that the educational system is poor, not adapted to the needs of the local economy and therefore needs to be restructured and transformed and adapted to local needs to play its important role in the transformation of Africa. The reform envisaged should be in the following domains:

i. Curriculum reforms: Most educational institutions in SSA still operate on curricula inherited from the colonial masters, which aimed at training students for white collar jobs (Tafah 2003). This has resulted in the training of jobless and unsuitable unemployed graduates. There is an urgent need for curricula revision tailored to the needs of the different economies. Curriculum review should involve all stakeholders in the labour market so as to tailor these curricular to the needs of industries.[1]

ii. Reversal of the funding structure of education where tertiary education is prioritised and highly subsidised as against the lower levels. Experience in Asia and China indicates that more attention was paid to the lower levels making them universal. This reversal will increase the social and private returns to education.

---

[1] *Our experience at The University of Bamenda in this direction has borne a lot of fruits. In opening the School of Transport and Logistic we associate all stakeholders in the transport sector in curriculum design and teaching. The students alternate between the classroom (theory) and the world of work (internship). Some of the lecturers from the private and public sectors handle the students on internship.*

iii. The need for vocational and technological teaching with emphasis on skills, knowledge and application at the tertiary level. This is a deviation from the present emphasis on general knowledge which produces a large army of unemployed graduates.[2]

iv. Linkages between state, enterprise and university academics in serving local economy needs. In this case, the state should involve professors and researchers in major consultancy jobs rather than awarding such consultancies to external experts at exorbitant costs. These foreign experts turn round to recruit locals to do the job. The relation between enterprise and university academics should be symbiotic in which there is cross fertilisation in teaching and curriculum design.

c. *Designing and implementing a comprehensive compensation scheme*

The solution to the principal–agent problem is to design a compensation scheme that will motivate the agent with incentives to implement the interests of the principal. In the language of principal–agent theory, the optimal contract satisfies both an *incentive compatibility constraint*, meaning that the workers (agents) are encouraged to choose high effort, and a *participation constraint*, meaning that the workers accept the contract. The general issue in designing incentives for the agent to exert the appropriate level of effort is to link the agent's compensation to their performance.

d. *Return to Economic Planning*

As indicated above, there are many other constraints that have to be overcome for African transformation. We may sound bizarre here, but we believe and evidence in the literature show that SSA countries performed better during the post-independent periodic planning era than it is the case today. The classical notion of respecting the fundamentals

---

[2] *This point is supported by experience during the construction of the Chad-Cameroon Pipeline Project where professional welders were imported from Asia. The Cameroonian tertiary education system failed to produce this quality of human resources.*

through SAPs plunged many countries into negative growth and increased poverty. The growth process was reversed. Public wealth was transferred to wealthier domestic and foreign owners through privatisation. The market has served the rich better and makes them richer. It has transferred wealth from the poor to the rich. Failure of state enterprises was due to poor governance and the <u>self and tribe syndrome</u> in the management of these enterprises. A careful planning system, with functioning institutions, good governance and proper allocation of resources will ensure balanced and harmonious growth. Botswana which is cited as a success story in economic performance in Africa operates a number of state-owned enterprises that function on profit basis and practices planning.

There are a number of other factors that will promote African transformation which could be economic, social or political but the transformation of the 'individual' and the educational system will provide the necessary conditions for reforming institutions and practicing good governance. These variables have been proven to be weak and have been a hindrance to economic growth in Africa.

Conclusion

The question of African transformation has become imperative in the face of a global world full of challenges. It has been demonstrated that institutional and governance weaknesses have to a large extent slowed growth and transformation in Africa. In addition, growth in Africa does not conform to orthodox economic prescriptions. Most of the growth is still generated from natural resources and agricultural exports. Agriculture still is, and will remain, a dominant activity for some time to come. Its productivity is still low and both natural resources and agricultural exports are subject to the volatility of international commodity markets. In most cases, growth has not been accompanied by changes in the welfare of the people. In other words, it has not been inclusive. Goods and service providers, even when resources are available, are often mired in a system where the incentives for effective delivery are weak, corruption is rife, and political patronage is common. These weaknesses constitute the main reasons why transformation becomes more relevant. Transformation has been discussed in different fora and resolutions adopted. This should not end at the level of rhetoric and brainstorming, reflections and resolutions at conferences and summits. Concrete action is needed. To achieve this Africa needs visionary and dynamic leaders to overcome the hurdles posed by institutions and governance in order to drive the African agenda forward.

Bibliography

Acemoglu, D., Johnson, S., & Robinson, J. (2005). Institutions as the Fundamental Cause of Long-Run Growth. In P. Aghion & S. Durlauf (Eds.), *Handbook of Economic Growth* (Vol. 1A, pp. 385–472). Amsterdam: North Holland.

Aisen, A., & Veiga, F. (2008). Political Instability and Inflation Volatility. *Public Choice, 135,* 207–223.

Ansell, C., & Gash, A. (2008). Collaborative Governance in Theory and Practice. *Journal of Public Administration Research and Theory, 18*(4), 543–571.

Barro, R. J. (1991). Economic Growth in a Cross-Section of Countries. *Quarterly Journal of Economics, 106,* 407–443.

Besley, T., & Ghatak, M. (2003). Incentives, Choice and Accountability in the Provision of Public Services. *Oxford Review of Economic Policy, 19*(2), 235–249.

Bevir, M. (2013). *Governance: A Very Short Introduction.* Oxford: Oxford University Press.

Denhart, R. B., & Jeffress, P. W. (1971). Social Learning and Economic Behavior: The Process of Economic Socialization. *American Journal of Economics and Sociology, 30*(2), 113–125.

Dreher, A., Gaston, N., & Pim, M. (2008). *Measuring Globalisation—Gauging Its Consequences.* New York: Springer.

Dolan, C. S., & Humphrey, J. (2000). Governance and Trade in Fresh Vegetables: The Impact of UK Supermarkets on the African Horticulture Industry. *The Journal of Development Studies, 37,* 147–176.

Easterly, W., Levine, R., & Roodma, D. (2004). Aid, Policies, and Growth: Comment. *American Economic Review, 94*(3), 774–780.

Enache, M., Ghani, E., & O'Connell, S. (2016). *Structural Transformation in Africa: A Historical View.* World Bank. Available via https://openknowledge.worldbank.org/handle/10986/24824. Accessed 10 Oct 2017.

Glaeser, E. L., La Porta, R., Lopez-de-Silanes, F., & Shleifer, A. (2004). Do Institutions Cause Growth? *Journal of Economic Growth, 9*(2), 271–303.

Hattam, V. C. (1993). *Labor Visions and State Power: The Origins of Business Unionism in the United States*. Princeton Studies in American Politics: Historical, International, and Comparative Perspectives. Princeton: Princeton University Press.

Hodgson, G. M., & Knudsen, T. (2006). Why We Need a Generalized Darwinism, and Why a Generalized Darwinism Is Not Enough. *Journal of Economic Behavior & Organization, 61,* 1–19.

Ifere, E. O., Okoi, O. B., & Bassey, C. E. (2015). Institutional Quality, Macroeconomic Policy and Economic Development in Nigeria. *Journal of Economics and Development Studies, 3*(2), 140–145.

Iqbal, N., & Daly, V. (2014). Rent Seeking Opportunities and Economic Growth in Transitional Economies. *Economic Modelling, 37,* 16–22.

Kaufmann, D., Kraay, A., & Mastruzzi, M. (2010). *Governance Matters viii: Aggregate and Individual Governance Indicators 1996–2009*. World Bank. Available via https://openknowledge.worldbank.org/handle/10986/4170. Accessed 15 Oct 2017.

Kjellberg, A. (2005). Mergers in a Class-Segmented Trade Union System. In J. Waddington (Ed.), *Restructuring Representation: The Merger Process and Trade Union Structural Development in Ten Countries*. Brussels: P.I.E Peter.

Lang Knight, J. (1994). *Institutions and Social Conflict*. Southern Political Science Association. Chicago: University of Chicago Press.

Lucas, R. E. (1988). On the Mechanics of Economic Development. *Journal of Monetary Economics, 22*(1), 3–42.

March, J. G., & Olsen, P. (1983). Organising Political Life: What Administrative Reorganization Tells Us About Government. *American Political Science Review, 77,* 281–296.

Murori, K. (2015). The 6 Fastest Growing Economies in Africa. In *CIA World Factbook 2015*. Washington, DC: Central Intelligence Agency.

Nawaz, S., Iqbal, N., & Khan, M. A. (2014). The Impact of Institutional Quality on Economic Growth: Panel Evidence. *Pakistan Development Review, 53*(1), 15–31.

North, D. C. (1991). *Institutions, Institutional Change and Economic Performance*. Cambridge: Cambridge University Press.

Osman, R. H., Alexiou, C., & Tsaliki, P. (2011). The Role of Institutions in Economic Development: Evidence from 27 Sub-Saharan African Countries. *International Journal of Social Economics, 39*(1), 142–160.

Padgett, J. F. (1981). Hierarchy and Ecological Control in Federal Budgetary Decision Making. *American Journal of Sociology, 87*(1), 75.

Ricketts, M. (2002). *The Economics of Business Enterprise: An Introduction to Economic Organization and the Theory of the Firm.* Ashgate: Edward Elgar.

Romer, P. M. (1986). Increasing Returns and Long-Run Growth. *Journal of Political Economy, 94*(5), 1002–1037.

Salahodjaev, R., & Chepel, S. (2014). Institutional Quality and Inflation. *Modern Economy, 5,* 219–223.

Shepsle, K. A., & Weingast, B. R. (1987). Structure-Induced Equilibrium and Legislative Choice. *Public Choice, 37,* 503–519.

Siba, E. G. (2008). *Determinants of Institutional Quality in Sub-Saharan African Countries.* School of Business, Economics and Law, University of Gothenburg. Available via https://scholarworks.wmich.edu/cgi/viewcontent.cgi?article=1116&context=africancenter_icad_archive. Accessed 25 Oct 2017.

Skowronek, S. (1982). *Building a New American State: The Expansion of National Administrative Capacities.* Cambridge and London: Cambridge University Press.

Tafah, E. (2003). Cameroon's Education: Retrospection and Perspective. In T. M. Bekolo-Ebe & S. M. Fouda (Eds.), *Dynamiques de Development: Debats Theoriques et Enjeux Politiques à l'aube du 21ᵉ Siècle.* Paris: Edition Montchrestien.

te Velde, D. W. (2013). Economic Transformation: Where Are We Heading Post-2015? Comment. Mimeograph, 17 December 2013.

The Worldwide Governance Indicators. (2017). Accessed from http://info.worldbank.org/governance/wgi/mc_countries.asp.

Transparency International. (2017). *Corruption Perception Index 2017.* Available via https://www.transparency.org/cpi/2017/.

World Bank. (1992). *Governance and Development.* Washington, DC: The World Bank.

World Bank. (2004). *World Development Report 2004: Making Services Work for Poor People.* Washington, DC: The World Bank and Oxford University Press.

World Bank. (2017). *World Bank Doing Business Report: Equal Opportunities for All, 2017.* Washington, DC: World Bank.

Wuyts, M., & Kilama, B. (2014). *Economic Transformation in Tanzania: Vicious or Virtuous Circle?* The Economic and Social Research Foundation. Available via http://esrf.or.tz/docs/THDR-BP-2.pdf. Accessed 27 Oct 2017.

Zouhaier, H. (2012). Institutions, Investment and Economic Growth. *International Journal of Economics and Finance, 4*(2), 152–162.

3

Sub-Regional Perspectives on Structural Change

Pedro M. G. Martins

Introduction

There is a renewed interest in the role that structural change can play in stimulating economic growth (McMillan and Heady 2014). Developing countries have significantly improved their economic performance since the early 2000s, but there are mounting concerns about the inclusiveness and sustainability of current growth patterns. In particular, the recent growth accelerations have not always been translated into concomitant improvements in socio-economic indicators—such as the poverty headcount—and broad-based economic development. This chapter investigates the pace and pattern of structural change in developing regions with a view to better understand the key drivers of economic growth and provide insights on how to enhance it.[1]

---

[1] This chapter is based on the gross domestic product (GDP) production approach, rather than the (perhaps more common) expenditure approach. Therefore, instead of assessing whether it is

---

P. M. G. Martins (✉)
World Bank, Washington, DC, USA
e-mail: pmartins@worldbank.org

© The Author(s) 2019
A. B. Elhiraika et al. (eds.), *Governance for Structural Transformation in Africa*,
https://doi.org/10.1007/978-3-030-03964-6_3

The early literature on structural change dates back to the 1950s and 1960s. For instance, Kuznets (1957), Chenery (1960) and Chenery and Taylor (1968) uncover important stylised facts on the relationship between a country's economic structure and its income level. This literature posits that structural change is a key characteristic and driver of economic and social development. Structural change can be narrowly defined as a process whereby labour moves from low-productivity to higher-productivity sectors. This relocation of labour raises workers' productivity, which contributes to accelerating economic growth. In developing countries, labour productivity in agriculture is considerably lower than in the non-agricultural sector (Gollin et al. 2014). This suggests that a reallocation of labour from agriculture to industry and services would considerably boost aggregate productivity and economic growth. Broader definitions of structural change go beyond changes in economic structure—such as production and employment—as they also encompass changes in other aspects of society (Kuznets 1966). For instance, structural change may entail a spatial reorganisation of the population, through rural-urban migration, and demographic change, arising from lower fertility rates. This chapter adopts a broader view of structural change.

The recent emphasis on structural change has led to a rapidly expanding body of theoretical and empirical work. Herrendorf et al. (2014) review recent advances in the literature. Datasets have been compiled to document regional patterns—with varying degrees of sectoral disaggregation and country coverage. This chapter, however, uses a much more comprehensive dataset and focuses on the sub-regional level in order to offer deeper and richer insights into the recent dynamics of structural change. Moreover, the empirical literature decomposes aggregate labour productivity growth into within-sector and between-sector (structural) effects. In this chapter, we adopt an empirical methodology based on the decomposition of output per capita—rather than output per worker. This strategy enables an empirical assessment that is compatible with a broader concept of structural change. In addition to evaluating within-sector and between-sector productivity effects, we estimate the

---

consumption, investment or exports that is stimulating economic growth, we investigate which economic sectors are driving economic performance.

contribution of demographic and employment changes to economic growth. Lower dependency ratios can generate a sizeable demographic dividend, while social preferences can impact on employment rates—through economic inactivity—which in turn affect economic growth.

This chapter is structured as follows. "Methodology and Data" presents the empirical methodology and the data used in this study. "Trends in Economic Structure" discusses trends in output, employment and labour productivity by economic sector—for regions and sub-regions. "Empirical Results" provides estimates on the relative contribution of within-sector and between-sector productivity improvements to output per capita growth, as well as the contribution of demographic change and employment rates. "Other Empirical Studies" compares these results with the evidence emerging from the existing literature. "Conclusion" concludes by summarising the main findings.

Methodology and Data

Shapley Decompositions

Most empirical studies on structural change focus on the decomposition of labour productivity growth. In this chapter, we adopt a broader framework that provides additional insights, namely, on the contribution of the employment rate and demographic change to output growth. Hence, our starting point is output per capita, which can be expressed as:

$$\frac{Y}{N} = \frac{Y}{E} \cdot \frac{E}{A} \cdot \frac{A}{N}$$

where Y is total output (value added), N is total population, E is total employment and A is the working-age population. Output per capita is represented by y, while the remaining components consist of output per worker (w), the employment rate (e) and the relative size of the working-age population (a).

$$y = w \cdot e \cdot a$$

To calculate the contribution of each of these components to changes in output per capita, we employ Shapley decompositions—see below.[2] This decomposition has the advantage of being additive and that each component has the interpretation of a counterfactual scenario.

$$\Delta y = \Delta w \left[\frac{1}{3}(e_{t=1}a_{t=1} + e_{t=0}a_{t=0}) + \frac{1}{6}(e_{t=1}a_{t=0} + e_{t=0}a_{t=1}) \right]$$

$$+ \Delta e \left[\frac{1}{3}(w_{t=1}a_{t=1} + w_{t=0}a_{t=0}) + \frac{1}{6}(w_{t=1}a_{t=0} + w_{t=0}a_{t=1}) \right]$$

$$+ \Delta a \left[\frac{1}{3}(w_{t=1}e_{t=1} + w_{t=0}e_{t=0}) + \frac{1}{6}(w_{t=1}e_{t=0} + w_{t=0}e_{t=1}) \right]$$

We can express these contributions as a share of output per capita growth by dividing each of the three terms above by Δy. Denoting $\bar{w}$, $\bar{e}$ and $\bar{a}$ as the share of growth that can be attributed to each component, output per capita growth can then be expressed as:

$$\frac{\Delta y}{y} = \bar{w} \frac{\Delta y}{y} + \bar{e} \frac{\Delta y}{y} + \bar{a} \frac{\Delta y}{y}$$

At this point, we can decompose output per worker—a measure of labour productivity. We start with the following equation:

$$w = \sum_{i=1}^{n} w_i s_i$$

where w_i represents output per worker in sector i (Y_i/E_i), s_i is the sectoral employment share (E_i/E) and n is the total number of economic sectors. This can then be decomposed into within-sector and between-sector effects, respectively:

---

[2]The Shapley decomposition considers the marginal effect on a variable (in our case, output per capita growth) of sequentially eliminating each of the contributory factors, and then assigns to each factor the average of its marginal contributions in all possible elimination sequences (Sorrocks 2013). See also World Bank (2015).

$$\Delta w = \sum_{i=1}^{n} \Delta w_i \left(\frac{s_{i,t=0} + s_{i,t=1}}{2} \right) + \sum_{i=1}^{n} \Delta s_i \left(\frac{w_{i,t=0} + w_{i,t=1}}{2} \right)$$

It is important to note that this decomposition differs from other studies in the literature, which will be taken into consideration when comparing results.[3] Finally, the sectoral pattern of employment rate changes can be calculated as:

$$\Delta e = \sum_{i=1}^{n} \Delta e_i$$

Figure 3.1 provides a schematic representation of the stepwise decomposition strategy used in this chapter.

Data Sources and Aggregation

This chapter uses three main sources of data. Data on sectoral employment comes from the World Employment and Social Outlook (WESO) database of the International Labour Organization (ILO). The latest release constitutes the most comprehensive source of sectoral employment data in existence. It includes annual employment data for 174 countries, which is disaggregated by 14 economic sectors and covers the period from 1991 to 2013. It should be noted that the dataset relies on modelled estimates for years and countries for which country-reported data is unavailable.

Data on sectoral output comes from the National Accounts Main Aggregates database of the United Nations Statistics Division (UNSD)—which serves under the United Nations Department of Economic and Social Affairs (UNDESA). The database provides a consistent annual dataset of national accounts aggregates for 212 countries and territories. It is based on official data reported to UNSD—through an annual questionnaire—and supplemented with data estimates for

---

[3]For instance, McMillan et al. (2014) use $\Delta w = \sum_{i=1}^{n} \Delta w_i(s_{i,t=0}) + \sum_{i=1}^{n} \Delta s_i(w_{i,t=1})$, while Timmer et al. (2015) use an empirically equivalent decomposition that further disaggregates the between-sector component into static and dynamic reallocation effects.

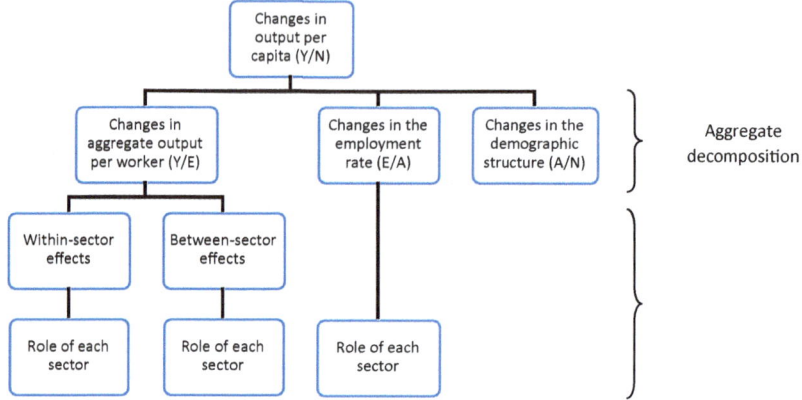

Fig. 3.1 Stepwise decomposition approach

years and countries with incomplete or inconsistent information. For the purpose of this chapter, we use gross value added (GVA) by kind of economic activity in US dollars at constant market prices.

Finally, data on total population and working-age population (i.e. 15–64 years old) comes from the World Population Prospects (2012 Revision) database of the United Nations Population Division (UNPD)—which is also under UNDESA. The database provides demographic estimates and projections for 233 countries and territories.

The consolidation of these three data sources led to a large annual dataset comprised of 169 countries. The employment data was the key binding constraint for the country sample, although Guadeloupe, Macau (China), Martinique, Réunion and Taiwan (China) had to be excluded due to the lack of (or incomplete) data on sectoral output. In 2013, these 169 countries had a combined total population of 7072 million inhabitants (compared to 7162 million for the whole world) and a total GVA of $53,139 billion (compared to $53,191 billion for the whole world). This suggests that this sample represents 98.7% of the world's population and 99.9% of global GVA.

The countries were then grouped into four main world regions—Africa, Asia, Latin America and Other (Developed). Since the aim of this chapter is to investigate patterns of structural change at the sub-regional level—with a special focus on developing countries—these countries were also classified according to 13 sub-regions in Africa, Asia and Latin America (Table 3.1). See Table 3.A1 in the Appendix for the countries included these regions and sub-regions.

Table 3.1 Sample

UN classification		Structure of study sample	
Geographical (continental) regions and sub-regions	UN member countries	Regions and sub-regions[a]	Countries
Africa	**54**	**Africa**	**49**
Eastern Africa	18	Eastern Africa	14
Middle Africa	9	Middle Africa	8
Northern Africa	6	Northern Africa	6
Southern Africa	5	Southern Africa	5
Western Africa	16	Western Africa	16
Americas	**35**	**Asia**	**48**
Caribbean	13	Central Asia	5
Central America	8	Eastern Asia	4
Northern America	2	South-Eastern Asia	14
South America	12	Southern Asia	9
		Western Asia	16
Asia	**47**		
Central Asia	5	**Latin America**	**28**
Eastern Asia	5	Caribbean	8
South-Eastern Asia	11	Central America	8
Southern Asia	9	South America	12
Western Asia	17		
		Other (Developed)	**44**
Europe	**43**		
Eastern Europe	10		
Northern Europe	10		
Southern Europe	14		
Western Europe	9		
Oceania	**14**		
Australia and New Zealand	2		
Melanesia	4		
Micronesia	5		
Polynesia	3		
Total	**193**	**Total**	**169**

[a]Due to the lack of disaggregated data, Sudan refers to 'former Sudan' and is included in Northern Africa. Eastern Asia includes Hong Kong, China (not a UN member country); South-Eastern Asia includes Fiji, Papua New Guinea and Solomon Islands (all from Melanesia); Western Asia includes West Bank & Gaza Strip (not a UN member country). The Caribbean includes Puerto Rico (not a UN member country). Following common practice, 'developed' includes Europe, as well as Canada and United States (both from Northern America), Australia and New Zealand (both from Oceania) and Japan (from Eastern Asia)—see http://unstats.un.org/unsd/methods/m49/m49regin.htm

The output data determined the level of sectoral disaggregation. The UNSD data is disaggregated into seven sectors of economic activity, which meant that the ILO 14-sector data had to be aggregated in order to ensure data consistency (Table 3.2). Both sources report data according to the third revision of the International Standard Industrial Classification of All Economic Activities (ISIC Rev.3.1). In our dataset, agriculture includes fishing (section B), while mining & quarrying (section C) and electricity, gas & water supply (section E) are lumped together. Commerce includes wholesale & retail trade (section G) and hotels & restaurants (section H). Finally, other services includes a wide range of service activities: financial intermediation (section J), real estate & business activities (section K), public administration & defence (section L), education (section M) and health & social work (section N), other service activities (section P) and activities of private households

Table 3.2   Data aggregation by ISIC section

ISIC Rev.3.1		Aggregation for this chapter	
Sector	Section	Short name	Section(s)
Agriculture, hunting & forestry	A	Agriculture	A, B
Fishing	B	Mining & utilities	C, E
Mining and quarrying	C	Manufacturing	D
Manufacturing	D	Construction	F
Electricity, gas and water supply	E	Commerce	G, H
Construction	F	Transport	I
Wholesale and retail trade; repair of motor vehicles (…)	G	Other services	J–P
Hotels and restaurants	H		
Transport, storage and communications	I		
Financial intermediation	J		
Real estate, renting and business activities	K		
Public administration and defence; compulsory social security	L		
Education	M		
Health and social work	N		
Other community, social and personal service activities	O		
Activities of private households as employers (…)	P		
Extraterritorial organizations and bodies	Q		

Note See http://unstats.un.org/unsd/cr/registry/regcst.asp?Cl=17&Lg=1&Top=1

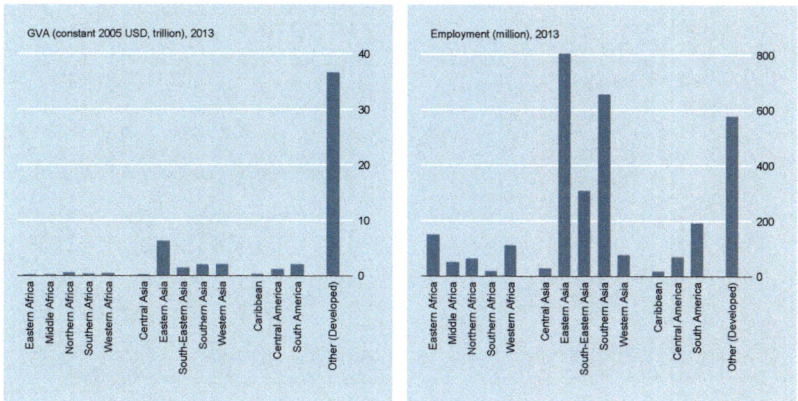

Fig. 3.2 Output and employment by sub-region

(section P). Section Q is not quantified in national accounts (output) data and is usually negligible in terms of employment.

Figure 3.2 shows aggregate output and employment levels for the 13 sub-regions.

Trends in Economic Structure

Regions

The structure of output and employment varies considerably across regions (Fig. 3.3). In 2013, the share of agriculture in total GVA ranged from 15% in Africa to under 2% in developed countries. Other services accounted for 52% of total GVA in developed countries, but represented less than 30% in Africa and Asia. Finally, manufacturing contributed to 26% of GVA in Asia, but only 11% in Africa. In terms of employment, the differences are even starker. Agriculture employed over 55% of Africa's workers while accounting for less than 5% of total employment in developed countries. Other services represented 44% of total employment in developed countries, but only 15% in Asia.

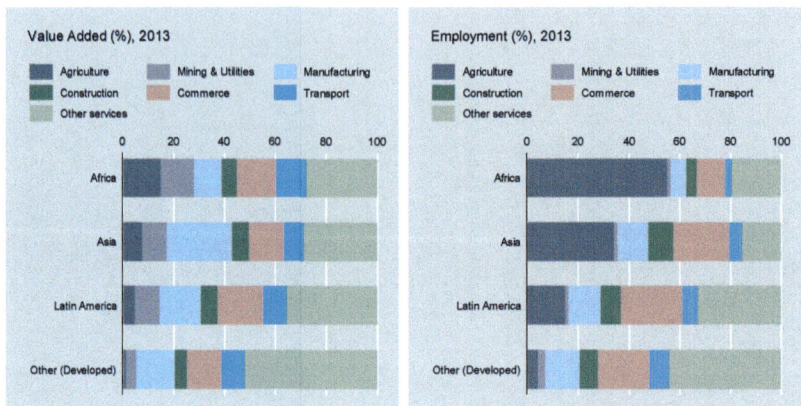

Fig. 3.3 Structure of output and employment—regions

As noted in the early literature on structural change, these differences in economic structure are partly responsible for the large income gaps observed across regions.

Africa's real GVA more than doubled between 1991 and 2013, mainly due to the strong economic performance registered since the early 2000s—see Table 3.A2 in the Appendix. The structure of production remains relatively diversified, with other services accounting for 27% of total GVA in 2013 and most other sectors also in the double-digits—construction is the only exception. Mining & utilities has seen its GVA share decline from 22% in 1991 to 13% in 2013, suggesting that the economic acceleration was not predominantly driven by natural resources, as it is often portrayed. On the other hand, transport has substantially increased its share in total GVA—from 7% in 1991 to 12% in 2013—while the share of agriculture stagnated at about 15%. Asia nearly quadrupled its real GVA in these 22 years, which led to a remarkable increase in its share of global GVA—from 10% in 1991 to 22% in 2013. The share of manufacturing in total GVA rose from 17% in 1991 to 26% in 2013, while the share of agriculture nearly halved—to 8%. Latin America achieved lower GVA growth rates than Africa and Asia, but also experienced a stronger performance during 2002–2013. Other services represented about 35% of total GVA throughout the period, while commerce and manufacturing were also important sectors. Developed countries have lagged significantly behind in terms of economic performance. In fact, aggregate GVA growth decelerated in 2002–2013—from 2.2 to 1.4%—and the construction sector even contracted. This slower growth was partly due to the global financial crisis of the late 2000s, and contributed to a declining weight in global GVA—from 82% in 1991 to 69% in 2013. Other services accounted for the majority of GVA in 2013—52%—while manufacturing and commerce accounted for a combined 29%.

The structure of employment has not changed significantly in Africa over the past 22 years, although there are encouraging signs since 2002. Employment in agriculture fell from 60% of total employment in 2002 to 55% in 2013, while other services absorbed most of this change. In Asia, the share of employment in agriculture dropped from 56% in 1991 to 34% in 2013. In fact, the absolute number of workers in agriculture fell between 2002 and 2013. Commerce, construction and other services observed large relative gains—more than 6 percentage points since 1991—while the share of manufacturing remained around 12%. There was a similar shift away from agriculture in Latin America—albeit less pronounced. The share of employment in agriculture fell from 25% in 1991 to 15% in 2013, while manufacturing also recorded a decline. Other services accrued the largest relative gains—6 percentage points. In developed countries, the share of manufacturing dropped from 22% in 1991 to 14% in 2013, while other services made important gains over this period—9 percentage points.

Sectoral output and employment data provide valuable insights on economic structure—see Fig. 3.A1 in the Appendix for annual trends. However, the concept of structural change is intrinsically linked to labour productivity. In this chapter, we use GVA per worker as a measure of labour productivity. At the global level, we note that agriculture has the lowest labour productivity by a wide margin. On average, each agricultural worker produced 2019 of output in 2013, while mining & utilities workers produced 30 times more. Exploiting these large productivity gaps can significantly boost incomes and accelerate economic development. However, the employment-generation potential of some high-productivity sectors is rather limited—such as mining & utilities—owing to their high capital intensity.

In Africa, aggregate labour productivity stagnated in the 1990s. Stronger output growth since 2002 was crucial to achieve a 2% average annual growth in productivity. Mining & utilities had the highest labour productivity in 2013—37 times higher than agriculture—despite declining since 1991.[4] The transport sector has consistently experienced strong labour productivity growth—2.5% per year since 1991. Asia has experienced very strong productivity growth over the past two decades. Despite having a lower starting point than Africa in 1991, aggregate labour productivity nearly tripled by 2013. Productivity growth in manufacturing was particularly high—7% per year—as well as in agriculture since 2002—6% per year. In Latin America, aggregate productivity growth was negligible in the 1990s. Since 2002, agriculture became an important source of aggregate productivity growth, with some support from commerce, transport and even manufacturing. However, labour productivity in mining & utilities declined significantly. Productivity growth in developed countries decelerated considerably in 2002–2013, with only agriculture and manufacturing showing positive signs.

Countries can considerably enhance their economic performance by taking advantage of existing labour productivity gaps, especially in Africa and Asia—see Fig. 3.A2 in the Appendix. As noted earlier, the employment share of agriculture—the least productive sector—declined in all regions. The key question, however, is whether agricultural labour is moving to dynamic sectors that have above-average (and growing) levels of labour productivity (Fig. 3.4). Africa observed an employment shift towards other services, a sector that lags behind mining & utilities, transport and manufacturing in terms of labour productivity. In Asia, employment shifted towards construction, commerce and other services. However, both construction and commerce had labour productivity levels below the economy-wide average, which has somewhat limited the impact of labour relocation. In Latin America, labour mainly relocated to other services, but the labour productivity of the sector is only

---

[4] The observed decline in labour productivity is partly due to stronger employment growth in public utilities (section E)—which is observed across all regions.

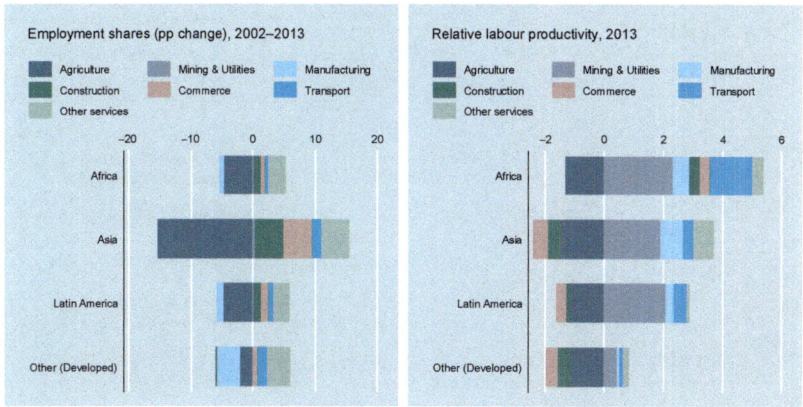

Fig. 3.4   Changes in employment and labour productivity gaps—regions (*Note* Relative labour productivity is calculated as the natural logarithm of the ratio of sectoral productivity to aggregate productivity. If a sector has the same productivity level as the whole economy, then it will not be shown in the graph—since log(1) equals zero. Large productivity gaps are represented by wider bar areas—positive or negative. If the width of a bar measures 1 unit, then the sector's productivity is 10 times higher than the average—or a tenth of the average if negative)

marginally above that of the aggregate level. Developed countries shed a considerable amount of manufacturing jobs, but since productivity gaps are small, the potential impact of structural change is more limited than in developing countries.

Africa

In this chapter, we are especially interested in sub-regional dynamics. The African region comprises five sub-regions: Eastern, Middle, Northern, Southern and Western Africa.[5] The structure of output varies

---

[5]It should be noted that South Africa accounted for 91% of Southern Africa's GVA in 2013 and 85% of employment, while Nigeria represented 76% of Western Africa's GVA in 2013 and 45% of employment.

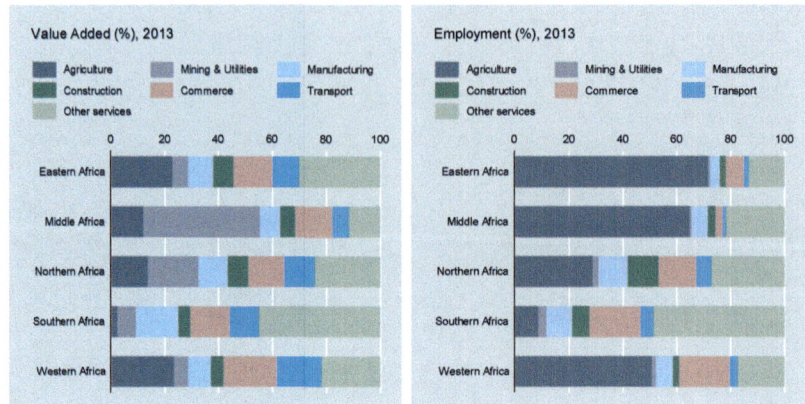

Fig. 3.5 Structure of output and employment—Africa

significantly across these sub-regions (Fig. 3.5). In 2013, mining & utilities accounted for more than 43% of total GVA in Middle Africa, but less than 7% in Eastern, Southern and Western Africa. The agriculture share of GVA was about 23% in Eastern and Western Africa, but less than 3% in Southern Africa. Finally, other service s accounted for 45% of GVA in Southern Africa, but only 12% in Middle Africa. The structure of employment is even more diverse across the region. Employment in agriculture ranged from 72% of total employment in Eastern Africa to 9% in Southern Africa, while employment in other services ranged from 48% in Southern Africa to 13% in Eastern Africa. In addition, commerce accounted for 19% of employment in Southern and Western Africa, but less than 3% in Middle Africa.

All African sub-regions improved their economic record in 2002–2013. GVA growth was particularly strong in Western Africa (7.1%), Middle Africa (6.3%) and Eastern Africa (6.2%)—see Table 3.A3 in the Appendix. In Eastern Africa, the share of agriculture in GVA remained constant in 1991–2002, but then declined from 29% in 2002 to 23% in 2013. This was compensated by relative increases in construction and transport. In Middle Africa, the weight of mining & utilities in total GVA increased from 34% in 1991 to 43% in 2002, though it has flattened since then. Manufacturing, on the other hand, saw its share decline from 14% in 1991 to 8% in 2013. Northern Africa has gradually reduced its reliance on mining & utilities—from 33% of total GVA in 1991 to 19% in 2013—with concomitant increases in the remaining sectors. Southern Africa also registered a decline in the share of mining & utilities—from 14% in 1991 to 7% in 2013—while agriculture and manufacturing also had relative declines. Transport and other services increased their weight in total GVA. Finally, the relative importance of mining & utilities in Western Africa dropped from 15% of total GVA in 1991 to less than 6% in 2013, while transport increase by almost 10 percentage points—to 17% in 2013.

Employment growth rates were relatively stable in Eastern, Middle and Western Africa—around 3% per year—while Southern Africa registered a sharp fall—from 2.9 to 1.3%. In Southern Africa, the share of employment in agriculture halved—from 18% in 1991 to 9% in 2013—while other services recorded an increase of nearly 10 percentage points. Changes in the structure of employment were less pronounced in Eastern Africa. The share of agriculture declined by nearly 5 percentage points since 2002—to 72% in 2013—most of which was absorbed by other services. In Middle Africa, agricultural employment fell from 72 to 65% between 1991 and 2013, which was met by relative increases in all remaining sectors. Northern Africa saw its share of employment in agriculture decline by more than 6 percentage points—to 29% in 2013—while manufacturing fell to a lesser extent. The relative weight of the remaining sectors increased, especially the construction sector. Agriculture and manufacturing declined in Western Africa to a similar extent, while other services significantly increased their weight in total employment.

Eastern Africa had the lowest aggregate labour productivity—just above $1000 per worker in 2013—while Southern Africa's was 17 times larger. Nonetheless, all sub-regions registered an acceleration in labour productivity growth. In Eastern Africa, labour productivity was stagnant in 1991–2002, but grew by an average of about 3% per year in the subsequent period. Construction, commerce and transport were the best-performing sectors since 2002. Labour productivity declined in Middle Africa between 1991 and 2002—by 1.5% a year—although it bounced back strongly since then. Construction recorded a strong growth in productivity in 2002–2013, while the increase in

Fig. 3.6 Changes in employment and labour productivity gaps—Africa

manufacturing and other services was almost negligible. The mining & utilities sector is associated with very high productivity levels—nearly $144,000 per worker in 2013—leaving commerce (the second highest) at a considerable distance—about $15,000. Northern Africa only had a small improvement in productivity growth. Mining & utilities registered strong declines in both periods, thus dampening the improvements of the remaining sectors. Manufacturing and construction also had disappointing performances in 2002–2013. In Southern Africa, transport was the only sector that had a positive performance in 1991–2002, while construction suffered the largest relative decline in productivity—2.4% a year. Since 2002, transport broadly maintained its pace of improvement, while the remaining sectors improved considerably—especially agriculture. Western Africa had the strongest rate of productivity growth in 2002–2013—4% per year—despite a strong decline in mining & utilities. Manufacturing, commerce and transport all posted productivity growth rates above 6% in the 2002–2013 period.

Between 2002 and 2013, the share of employment in agriculture declined by about 5 percentage points in three African sub-regions—the reduction was smaller in Northern Africa and larger in Western Africa (Fig. 3.6). With the exception of Northern Africa, other services gained the most ground in terms of employment shares. However, we note

Fig. 3.7 Structure of output and employment—Asia

that the productivity of the sector is not often higher than the aggregate level. This may suggest that the benefits of structural change could have been significantly higher, had labour relocated to other sectors—such as manufacturing.

Asia

The Asian region comprises five sub-regions: Eastern, Central, South-Eastern, Southern and Western Asia.[6] The economic structure is less heterogeneous across Asian sub-regions than in Africa, although there are still significant variations (Fig. 3.7). For instance, mining & utilities accounted for about 24% of Western Asia's GVA in 2013, but less than 6% in Eastern Asia. Conversely, manufacturing comprised 34% of total GVA in Eastern Asia, but only 13% in Western Asia. In terms of employment, the share of agriculture ranged from 47% in Southern Asia to 17% in Western Asia, while commerce and other services also varied considerably across sub-regions.

---

[6]In 2013, China accounted for 78% of Eastern Asia's GVA and 96% of employment; while India was responsible for 70% of Southern Asia's GVA and 71% of employment.

Central Asia presents a fairly diversified economic structure—see Table 3.A4 in the Appendix. While there have not been major changes in the structure of output since 1991, real GVA growth rates do capture the economic decline experienced by many ex-USSR countries in the early 1990s. Manufacturing was the fastest growing sector in Eastern Asia, which led to a considerable increase in its share of GVA—rising from 22% in 1991 to 34% in 2013. Agriculture, on the other hand, saw its relative importance fall by nearly 10 percentage points. Southern Asia also observed a relative decline in agriculture—11 percentage points—which was mainly captured by transport and other services. In South-Eastern Asia, agriculture experienced a relative decline of about 5 percentage points between 1991 and 2013, while transport recorded the largest relative increase—probably supported by India's information technology (IT) sector. In Western Asia, the weight of mining & utilities and agriculture in total GVA declined, while transport increased by nearly 4 percentage points. It is worth noting that the share of manufacturing in total GVA increased in all Asian sub-regions between 1991 and 2013, while it declined in most of Africa.

Central Asia observed a considerable decline in the share of workers employed in agriculture—from 37% in 1991 to 27% in 2013—while other services recorded the largest relative increase in that period (4 percentage points). Eastern Asia is the sub-region with the largest number of workers—more than 800 million—but employment growth has been weak. Agriculture shed a substantial number of workers—about 150 million between 1991 and 2013—which has played a critical role in the overall trends. The share of employment in agriculture shrunk by 29 percentage points, which was met by increases in commerce (13 percentage points), construction (8 percentage points) and other services (nearly 8 percentage points). This points to a dramatic change in the structure of employment in a fairly short period of time, even though agriculture remains the second largest employer in the sub-region. In South-Eastern Asia, the share of workers in agriculture dropped by almost 20 percentage points. Commerce and other services made significant gains—about 5 and 7 percentage points, respectively.

Southern Asia and Western Asia also registered a sizeable reduction in the share of agricultural employment—about 15 percentage points. These shares were mainly captured by construction in Southern Asia (6 percentage points) and other services in Western Asia (8 percentage points).

Aggregate labour productivity fell sharply in Central Asia during 1991–2002, mainly due to the economic decline mentioned earlier. Nonetheless, most sectors bounced back strongly. Perhaps surprisingly, transport is the sector with the highest productivity level—rather than mining & utilities. Eastern Asia achieved the highest aggregate labour productivity growth rate in the region—above 7 percentage points—by a considerable margin. Manufacturing had a very strong performance in both periods, while productivity growth in agriculture accelerated remarkably in the second period. Southern-Eastern Asia improved its productivity growth rate by 1.1 percentage points per year, despite the decline in mining & utilities. The transport sector, in particular, registered a strong performance since 2002. Southern Asia had a stronger acceleration in aggregate productivity growth—to nearly 5% a year in 2002–2013—but the construction sector was subdued in both periods. Productivity in transport, commerce and manufacturing grew by about 5% since 2002. In Western Asia, aggregate productivity growth remained at a low 1.7% a year. Productivity in mining & utilities is extremely high—more than $320,000 per worker in 2013—despite a recent decline. However, this large productivity gap is difficult to seize upon, since the employment-generation potential of the sector is quite limited.

In sum, Eastern Asia dramatically reduced its employment share in agriculture, while the remaining sub-regions also achieved considerable reductions (Fig. 3.8). Labour relocated mainly to construction, commerce and other services. Nonetheless, labour productivity in both construction and commerce were below the aggregate level in most regions. Once again, the impact of structural change could have been larger if a greater proportion of labour had relocated to higher-productivity sectors—such as manufacturing, transport or other services.

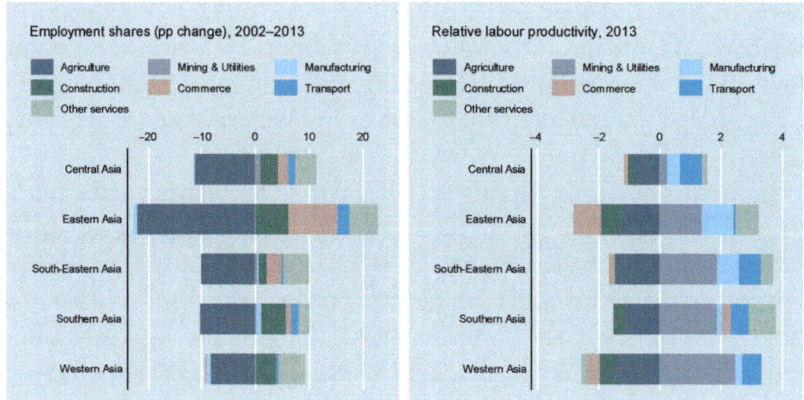

Fig. 3.8 Changes in employment and labour productivity gaps—Asia

Latin America

The Latin America region comprises three sub-regions: the Caribbean, Central America and South America.[7] In our sample, the Caribbean sub-region encompasses eight small island developing states (SIDS), which nonetheless have a combined GVA larger than Central Asia, Eastern Africa and Middle Africa—$219 billion in 2013. Latin America seems considerably less heterogeneous than Africa and Asia in terms of the structure of output and employment (Fig. 3.9).

In the Caribbean, the share of manufacturing and agriculture in total GVA declined, while the weight of transport and other services increased by almost 3 percentage points each—see Table 3.A5 in the Appendix. However, it should be noted that the Caribbean was the only sub-region—out of the 13 sub-regions under analysis—that suffered a deceleration in its real GVA growth rate between the two periods. In Central America, the transport sector made significant relative gains—more than 4 percentage points—while mining & utilities declined from

---

[7]In 2013, Mexico accounted for 88% of Central America's GVA and 74% of employment; while Brazil represented 49% of South America's GVA and 52% of employment.

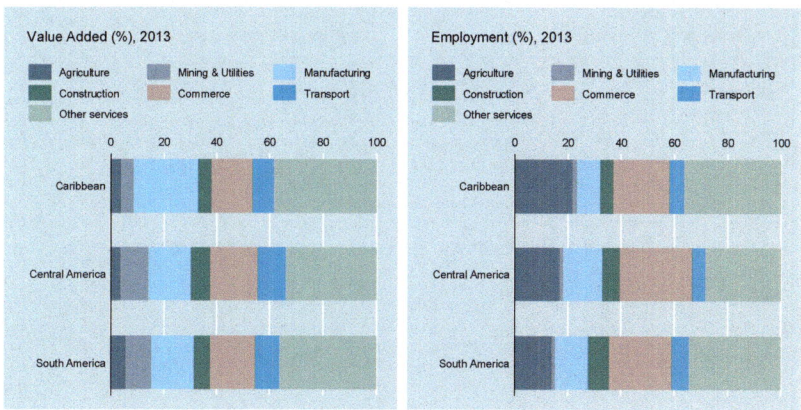

Fig. 3.9 Structure of output and employment—Latin America

13% in 1991 to 10% in 2013. South America accounted for 60% of the region's GVA in 2013. The share of manufacturing decline from 19% in 1991 to 16% in 2013, while transport increased by 2 percentage points. Overall, the structure of output in Latin America has not shifted significantly over time, at least when compared to Asia or even Africa.

In the Caribbean, employment in agriculture declined from about 26% of total employment in 1991 to under 22% in 2013. Manufacturing also lost some ground—more than 3 percentage points. Commerce and other services, on the other hand, registered the largest improvements. Central America experienced a large relative decline in agricultural employment—from 28% in 1991 to 17% in 2013—which was mostly compensated by other services (nearly 8 percentage points). South America also had a considerable fall in the share of agricultural employment—10 percentage points—which was partly offset by a rise in other services (6 percentage points). Latin America's employment structure has changed to a lesser extent than in Asia.

Compared to other regions, aggregate labour productivity levels are relatively homogeneous across Latin America. Nonetheless, the performance has varied within the region. The Caribbean experienced a significant deceleration in aggregate labour productivity growth,

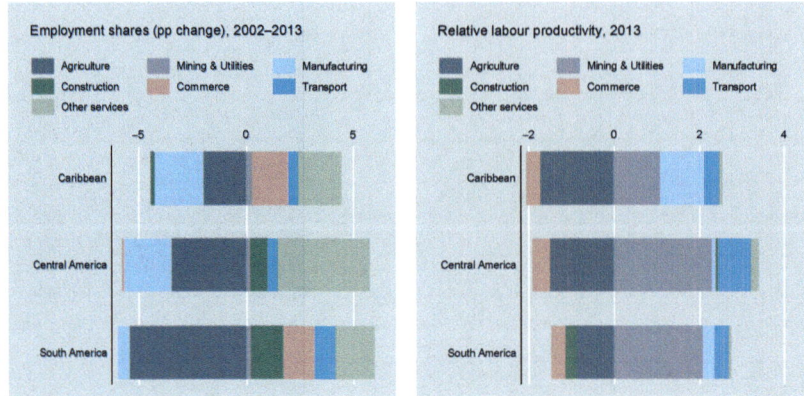

Fig. 3.10 Changes in employment and labour productivity gaps—Latin America

notwithstanding an improvement in agriculture. Labour productivity in manufacturing is relatively high—at par with mining & utilities—and the highest in the region. Labour productivity growth in Central America has been disappointing. The strong decline in mining & utilities—almost 3% a year since 1991—has certainly contributed to this performance, although productivity growth in construction and other services has also been negative since 1991. South America has the lowest level of productivity in the region. Although aggregate productivity declined by 0.2% a year in 1991–2002, it has shown many positive signs since 2002. Agriculture was the best performing sector over the entire period, while productivity in mining & utilities fell considerably—the only sector to register a productivity decline in 2002–2013.

Overall, both agriculture and manufacturing registered significant reductions in the employment share—much of which was absorbed by other services (Fig. 3.10). Apart from mining & utilities, the sectors with the highest labour productivity levels were manufacturing and transport—which either saw their employment share decline or increase by a small amount. This is likely to have hampered the potential of structural change in the region, and thus economic growth.

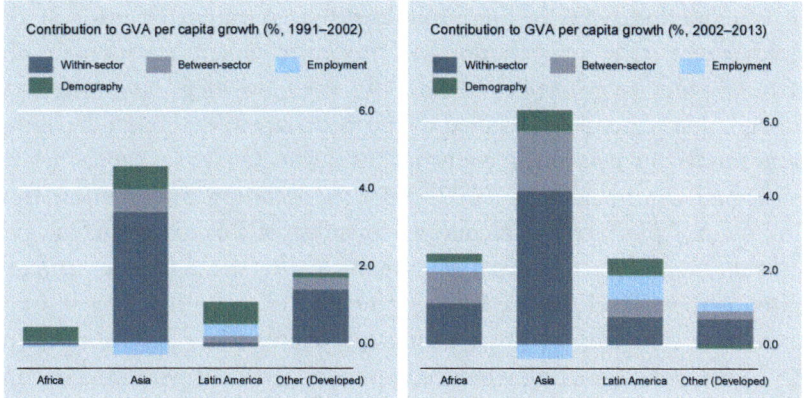

Fig. 3.11 Decomposition of GVA per capita growth—regions

Empirical Results

Regions

Africa's economic performance has improved remarkably since 2002 (Fig. 3.11)—see also Table 3.A7 in the Appendix. Annual GVA per capita growth accelerated from 0.3% in 1991–2002 to 2.4% in 2002–2013—which mainly reflected improvements in labour productivity. In fact, both within-sector and between-sector components provided strong contributions since 2002. Employment also emerged as a positive influence in the latter period, mainly due to an increase in the employment rate—see Table 3.A6 in the Appendix. The contribution of the demographic structure declined, owing to a slower increase in the share of the working-age population. GVA per capita growth was outstandingly high in Asia—accelerating from 4.3% in 1991–2002 to 5.9% in 2002–2013. Within-sector productivity improvements have been the main driver of this strong performance, but the contribution of structural change has also been substantial and growing. Employment has dampened growth—as the employment rate declined in both periods—but demographic changes supplemented output per capita growth with over 0.5 percentage points. In Latin America, GVA per capita growth also accelerated in the latter period, with labour productivity accounting for most of this improvement. The contribution of the employment component also increased—due to a stronger increase in the employment rate—while the demographic structure continued to provide a sizeable (though declining) contribution. In developed countries, however, GVA per capita growth decelerated considerably in 2002–2013. A declining contribution from within-sector productivity accounted for most of this disappointing performance, although the negative impact of the demographic structure component was also noticeable—partly due to population ageing and the relative shrinking of the working-age population. The only positive sign came from the employment component. Overall, within-sector and between-sector productivity trends seem promising in developing countries, while employment and demography played a relatively minor role in boosting output per capita growth—with the exception of Latin America.

The aggregate results provide a useful overview of the key contributors to output per capita growth. Nevertheless, we are also interested in identifying the economic sectors that have been driving these trends. Table 3.3 decomposes the results discussed above by sector for the period 2002–2013 and reports them as percentages of GVA per capita growth.

In Africa, within-sector productivity improvements accounted for 46% of output per capita growth, especially due to commerce, agriculture and transport. Mining & utilities had a negative impact, partly a consequence of the labour productivity declines experienced by Northern Africa and Western Africa. Agriculture provided the largest contribution to the structural change component, while manufacturing had a negative impact.[8] If labour had not reallocated between economic sectors—predominantly from agriculture to other services—output per capita growth would have been over one-third lower (35%). Finally, changes in the agricultural employment rate dampened growth, but were more than compensated by the services sectors.[9] Overall, the three service sectors—commerce, transport and other services—contributed

---

[8]A sector provides a positive contribution to the between-sector component if: (i) its labour productivity is above the aggregate average and its employment share increases or (ii) its labour productivity is below the aggregate average and its employment share declines (this is often the case of agriculture).

[9]The structural change component is intrinsically linked to the employment share (Ei/E), while the employment component relates to the (sectoral) employment rate (Ei/A).

to most of the output growth in 2002–2013. Contrary to common perception, mining & utilities did not drive economic performance in Africa—rather, it seems that the sector has undermined it.

Within-sector productivity was the key driver of Asia's economic performance—accounting for 70% of output per capita growth. Manufacturing was the most important sector within this component, representing 29% of total output per capita growth. Structural change—which itself contributed with 27%—was mainly driven by agriculture and other services. Changes in the employment rate had a negative impact, mainly due to agriculture. Overall, manufacturing and other services were the sectors that provided the strongest contributions to output per capita growth in Asia.

The results for Latin America point to a fairly even contribution across the four key components. On the whole, other services was the key driver of economic performance, followed by commerce. Manufacturing had a negative impact on both the structural change and employment components. Mining & utilities undermined the contribution of within-sector productivity, but provided a significant contribution to between-sector effects—the sector marginally increased its share in total employment.

In developed countries, manufacturing provided a strong boost to within-sector productivity, but had a large negative impact on the employment component—the sector recorded a strong increase in productivity levels coupled with a relative decline in employment shares. As a result, its overall contribution to output per capita growth was significantly reduced. Other services provided very strong contributions throughout and were by far the largest contributors to overall economic performance.

Agriculture was the largest contributor to the structural change component across all regions. However, this is because the sector—which has below-average productivity levels—experienced considerable declines in employment shares.[10] In practice, it is the reallocation of labour from agriculture to higher-productivity sectors that is driving structural change. In fact, there is a clear negative relationship between agricultural employment and average incomes—both within and across regions (Fig. 3.12). It also seems that the faster labour moves out of agriculture,

---

[10]In fact, agriculture is the least productive sector in all regions (and sub-regions).

Table 3.3 Decomposition of GVA per capita growth, 2002–2013—regions

Region/sector	Contribution from (%)				Total contribution (%)
	Within-sector productivity	Between-sector productivity	Changes in employment	Changes in demography	
Africa	**45.9**	**34.9**	**11.4**	**7.8**	**100.0**
Agriculture	15.5	13.0	−11.1		17.3
Mining & utilities	−17.1	8.2	0.8		−8.1
Manufacturing	8.8	−1.9	−1.7		5.1
Construction	3.6	1.9	4.7		10.2
Commerce	18.2	0.8	3.8		22.7
Transport	12.5	7.5	2.7		22.7
Other services	4.5	5.6	12.2		22.3
Asia	**69.6**	**27.4**	**−6.1**	**9.1**	**100.0**
Agriculture	9.6	19.3	−27.6		1.3
Mining & utilities	4.3	2.5	0.3		7.0
Manufacturing	28.7	0.2	−0.6		28.3
Construction	1.3	−1.8	7.1		6.7
Commerce	9.5	−2.5	6.3		13.3
Transport	4.1	1.5	2.2		7.9
Other services	12.1	8.3	6.1		26.5
Latin America	**32.1**	**20.6**	**28.4**	**18.9**	**100.0**
Agriculture	6.5	13.4	−14.1		5.8
Mining & utilities	−9.2	7.5	1.2		−0.5
Manufacturing	7.6	−1.4	−0.5		5.7
Construction	0.0	−0.4	6.9		6.5
Commerce	11.4	−1.3	11.3		21.4
Transport	5.5	1.9	4.9		12.2

(continued)

Table 3.3 (contiuned)

Region/sector	Contribution from (%)				Total contribution (%)
	Within-sector productivity	Between-sector productivity	Changes in employment	Changes in demography	
Other services	10.2	1.1	18.7		30.0
Other (Developed)	**67.6**	**23.3**	**20.4**	**−11.3**	**100.0**
Agriculture	6.2	14.2	−18.5		2.0
Mining & utilities	−1.2	0.9	2.0		1.7
Manufacturing	47.7	−0.1	−30.2		17.4
Construction	−6.1	0.3	0.3		−5.5
Commerce	6.0	−1.9	10.3		14.4
Transport	−0.9	2.7	15.6		17.5
Other services	15.8	7.1	40.9		63.8

Note Changes in employment refer to changes in the ratio of sectoral employment to the working-age population (Ei/A). It is not possible to disaggregate the working-age population by sector. Moreover, changes in the demographic structure cannot be related to sectors

the larger is the increase in output per capita. Moreover, the contribution of manufacturing has been partly hampered by negative impacts on the between-sector and employment components—its share in total employment declined in all regions, except Asia (where it stagnated). Other services has been a consistently strong sector across regions.

Africa

GVA per capita growth accelerated in all African sub-regions after 2002 (Fig. 3.13)—see also Table 3.A8 in the Appendix. In Eastern Africa, growth registered in 2002–2013 was mostly due to improvements in labour productivity—both within and between sectors. Changes in the demographic structure are also playing an increasing (albeit much smaller) role. Middle Africa experienced a significant decline in output per capita in 1991–2002, mainly due to a broad-based fall in sectoral labour productivity. The recent performance is mainly explained by a sharp reversal of these sectoral productivity trends. Like in Eastern Africa, changes in the demographic structure have also provided a small

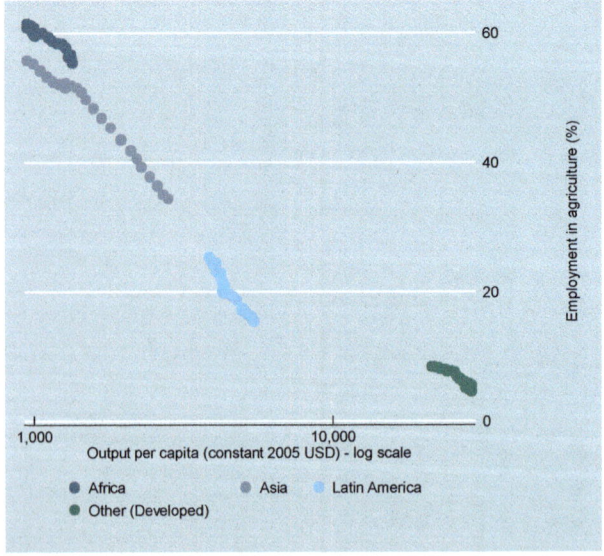

Fig. 3.12 Trends in agricultural employment and output per capita, 1991–2013

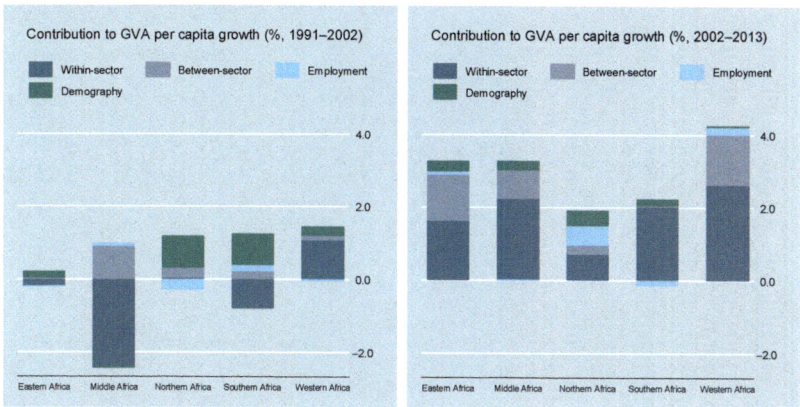

Fig. 3.13 Decomposition of GVA per capita growth—Africa

contribution to economic growth. In Northern Africa, the improved economic performance was due to both within-sector productivity and employment improvements. Nevertheless, a lower increase in the working-age population share drove down the contribution of demography. Structural change has played a limited role in Southern Africa, especially in recent years. Employment undermined output growth in 2002–2013, while the contribution of demography shrunk significantly. Hence, the positive economic performance was mainly due to within-sector productivity growth. Western Africa accelerated output per capita growth from 1.4% in 1991–2002 to 4.2% in 2002–2013—owing to both within-sector and between-sector productivity. Overall, the improved economic performance of African sub-regions was mainly due to enhanced labour productivity. Within-sector productivity played a major role in accelerating output per capita growth, while the contribution of structural change rose significantly in Eastern Africa and Western Africa. The contribution of the employment component grew in Eastern, Northern and Western Africa, and that of the demographic structure in Eastern and Middle Africa. Nonetheless, the relative importance of these two components was rather limited—with the exception of Northern Africa.

In Eastern Africa, other services provided the largest sectoral contribution to output per capita growth, mostly through structural change (15%) but also due to changes in employment (10%) (Table 3.4). Transport, construction and commerce also provided sizeable contributions. In Middle Africa,

Table 3.4 Decomposition of GVA per capita growth, 2002–2013—Africa

Region/sector	Contribution from (%)				Total contribution (%)
	Within-sector productivity	Between-sector productivity	Changes in employment	Changes in demography	
Eastern Africa	**50.1**	**38.0**	**3.0**	**8.9**	**100.0**
Agriculture	11.0	8.4	−10.7		8.7
Mining & utilities	0.3	4.7	0.7		5.7
Manufacturing	6.3	−0.3	−0.1		5.9
Construction	5.8	5.1	2.1		12.9
Commerce	14.6	−0.2	0.0		14.4
Transport	8.3	5.4	1.2		14.8
Other services	3.9	15.1	9.8		28.8
Middle Africa	**68.7**	**23.9**	**−0.1**	**7.4**	**100.0**
Agriculture	9.5	11.2	−13.9		6.8
Mining & utilities	31.7	8.5	0.2		40.4
Manufacturing	1.4	0.6	1.2		3.1
Construction	6.4	1.6	2.4		10.4
Commerce	13.1	3.1	0.7		16.9
Transport	5.3	2.5	0.7		8.5
Other services	1.3	−3.5	8.8		6.6
Northern Africa	**37.3**	**13.0**	**27.8**	**21.9**	**100.0**
Agriculture	18.8	8.6	−6.9		20.5
Mining & utilities	−34.8	5.7	1.1		−28.0
Manufacturing	3.5	0.0	1.4		4.9
Construction	0.8	−5.7	19.5		14.5
Commerce	13.3	0.1	2.8		16.2

(continued)

Table 3.4 (continued)

Region/sector	Contribution from (%)				Total contribution (%)
	Within-sector productivity	Between-sector productivity	Changes in employment	Changes in demography	
Transport	12.0	3.8	5.8		21.6
Other services	23.5	0.6	4.2		28.3
Southern Africa	**96.6**	**0.7**	**-6.1**	**8.8**	**100.0**
Agriculture	7.0	18.0	-25.2		-0.1
Mining & utilities	8.6	-9.7	-7.3		-8.4
Manufacturing	23.9	-6.3	-10.9		6.7
Construction	5.1	-2.6	6.0		8.6
Commerce	14.3	-1.1	3.9		17.1
Transport	6.7	3.7	2.5		12.9
Other services	31.0	-1.3	24.8		54.4
Western Africa	**62.2**	**32.5**	**5.1**	**0.2**	**100.0**
Agriculture	22.1	8.9	-14.1		16.9
Mining & utilities	-16.4	8.6	1.4		-6.4
Manufacturing	13.3	-0.7	-2.9		9.7
Construction	3.0	1.3	1.5		5.9
Commerce	23.6	-0.2	6.9		30.3
Transport	17.8	9.7	2.6		30.1
Other services	-1.1	4.9	9.7		13.5

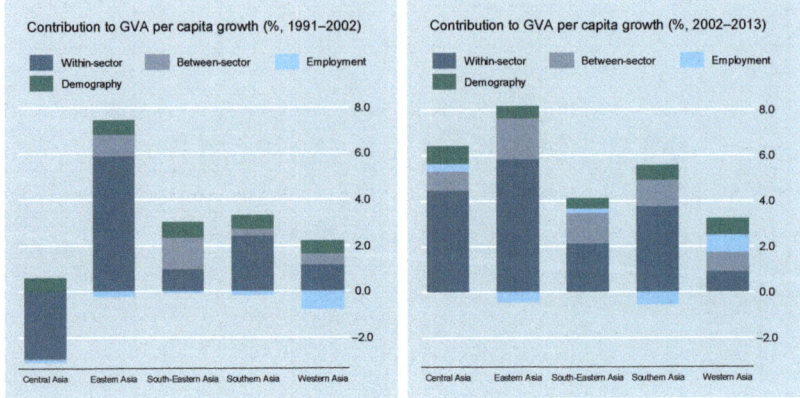

Fig. 3.14 Decomposition of GVA per capita growth—Asia

mining & utilities played the vital role in boosting output per capita—especially through enhanced sectoral productivity (32%). In Northern Africa, however, the performance of the mining & utilities sector severely undermined aggregate output growth. Other services and transport were the most dynamic sectors. In Southern Africa, other services accounted for most of the positive economic performance. Mining & utilities and agriculture had a net negative impact. In West Africa, commerce and transport were the most important sectors. In sum, the three service sectors accounted for most of the stronger economic record since 2002—except in Middle Africa—while manufacturing has provided a limited boost to output growth.

Asia

GVA per capita growth accelerated in all Asian sub-regions in 2002–2013 (Fig. 3.14)—see also Table 3.A9 in the Appendix. Central Asia, in particular, underwent notable changes. Growth improved considerably in 2002–2013—following a negative performance in the previous period—mainly owing to sectoral productivity growth. The remaining components also boosted economic growth, although to a much lesser extent. Eastern Asia experienced remarkably strong and consistent growth. Although the contribution of structural change nearly doubled in percentage points, within-sector productivity remained the key driver of economic performance. The negative impact of employment was more than compensated by demographic changes. In South-Eastern Asia, structural change provided the largest contribution to output growth in 1991–2002, which remained strong in the subsequent period. However, the improved economic record was mainly due to within-sector productivity changes. Southern Asia registered substantial increases in both components of aggregate labour productivity, which accounted for much of the overall progress—despite a negative effect from employment. The employment component seems to have played a key role in Western Asia—rising from 0.76 percentage points in the earlier period to 0.74 percentage points in the later period. The contribution of within-sector productivity declined in 2002–2013, while the weight of the between-sector component increased. Overall, these decompositions suggest that Asia's story is also predominantly one of enhanced labour productivity—especially within sectors, but also structural change. There is some variation within the region, but with the exception of Western Asia, changes in employment and demographic structure have been relatively less important.

Other services were the leading contributor to GVA per capita growth, except for Eastern Asia. Manufacturing, commerce and transport also provided strong contributions, often in the double-digits (Table 3.5). In Eastern Asia, manufacturing provided the largest sectoral contribution, although exclusively through increases in within-sector productivity. Manufacturing also played an important role in South-Eastern Asia, but other services provided even higher net contributions to output per capita growth. Overall, most of the between-sector improvements were attributable to agriculture, which is not surprising—since declining employment shares in the least-productive sector (i.e. agriculture) implicitly boost aggregate productivity levels. With the exception of Eastern Asia, other services was the main contributor to output per capita growth in Asian sub-regions. However, the three service sectors were often (meaningfully) supported by the manufacturing and construction sectors.

Latin America

GVA per capita growth declined in the Caribbean during 2002–2013, mainly owing to a much lower contribution from within-sector productivity (Fig. 3.15)—see also Table 3.A10 in the Appendix. The between-sector

Table 3.5 Decomposition of GVA per capita growth, 2002–2013—Asia

Region/sector	Contribution from (%)			Total contribution (%)
	Within-sector productivity	Between-sector productivity	Changes in employment	Changes in demography	
Central Asia	**69.5**	**13.2**	**5.2**	**12.2**	**100.0**
Agriculture	12.1	10.0	−15.2		6.9
Mining & utilities	3.2	0.8	1.9		5.9
Manufacturing	14.4	−0.1	0.3		14.6
Construction	4.0	−0.5	5.3		8.8
Commerce	10.0	−0.3	3.6		13.3
Transport	9.1	2.1	2.2		13.4
Other services	16.7	1.3	7.0		25.0
Eastern Asia	**75.5**	**23.0**	**−5.4**	**7.0**	**100.0**
Agriculture	11.1	21.2	−30.6		1.7
Mining & utilities	5.0	0.6	0.1		5.8
Manufacturing	39.2	−1.2	−1.4		36.6
Construction	1.6	−2.7	7.4		6.3
Commerce	8.3	−6.4	10.4		12.3
Transport	1.2	1.1	2.6		4.9
Other services	9.1	10.3	6.1		25.5
South-Eastern Asia	**51.7**	**32.5**	**5.8**	**10.1**	**100.0**
Agriculture	9.3	17.0	−20.1		6.3
Mining & utilities	−7.5	7.6	1.0		1.1
Manufacturing	18.3	0.9	1.5		20.7
Construction	2.5	0.0	3.6		6.1
Commerce	12.5	−0.9	7.3		18.9
Transport	10.7	0.7	1.0		12.4
Other services	5.8	7.2	11.5		24.5

(continued)

Table 3.5 (continued)

Region/sector	Contribution from (%)				Total contribution (%)
	Within-sector productivity	Between-sector productivity	Changes in employment	Changes in demography	
Southern Asia	**75.3**	**23.0**	**−10.5**	**12.2**	**100.0**
Agriculture	13.8	13.0	−24.6		2.1
Mining & utilities	1.9	2.2	0.2		4.3
Manufacturing	13.4	0.4	0.6		14.4
Construction	−0.2	−1.0	8.0		6.9
Commerce	14.4	0.6	0.7		15.7
Transport	9.2	2.0	2.0		13.2
Other services	22.9	5.8	2.6		31.3
Western Asia	**28.6**	**25.8**	**23.1**	**22.5**	**100.0**
Agriculture	2.8	18.1	−18.8		2.2
Mining & utilities	−7.1	12.2	1.4		6.5
Manufacturing	11.3	−0.4	0.0		10.8
Construction	0.5	−3.6	12.4		9.3
Commerce	8.1	0.1	3.9		12.1
Transport	7.8	0.9	2.5		11.2
Other services	5.1	−1.5	21.8		25.4

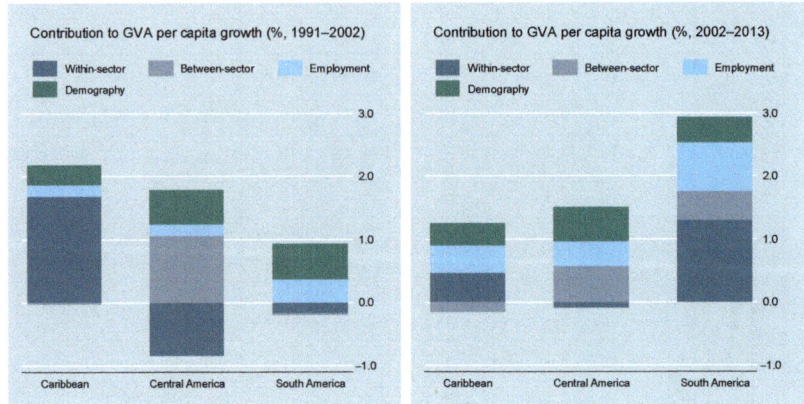

Fig. 3.15 Decomposition of GVA per capita growth—Latin America

component was negative—the only occurrence in all 13 sub-regions—which suggests that, on average, workers moved towards lower-productivity sectors. The positive impact of employment and demography were not sufficient to counter these productivity trends. In Central America, output per capita growth accelerated in 2002–2013. Nonetheless, the contribution of within-sector productivity growth remained negative, while the positive impact of structural change weakened. The employment component improved somewhat. South America enjoyed considerably faster output growth in 2002–2013, predominately due to stronger within-sector productivity. However, structural change and employment also played an important role. Overall, changes in employment and demographic structure were relatively important in the Caribbean and Central America, but mostly because the productivity performance was very disappointing. This is likely to explain much of the performance differential between Latin America and the other two regions.

As indicated above, the Caribbean was the only sub-region (out of 13) that showed a pattern of growth-reducing structural change in 2002–2013. This was largely due to the manufacturing sector, which experienced a significant relative decline in sectoral employment (Table 3.6). Its negative impact on overall economic performance was offset by other services, but also by commerce and transport. In Central America, other services were also the most dynamic sector, while mining

Table 3.6 Decomposition of GVA per capita growth, 2002–2013—Latin America

Region/sector	Contribution from (%)				Total contribution (%)
	Within-sector productivity	Between-sector productivity	Changes in employment	Changes in demography	
Caribbean	**42.0**	**−14.1**	**40.2**	**31.8**	**100.0**
Agriculture	4.5	13.6	−7.2		10.8
Mining & utilities	−10.0	5.6	3.0		−1.5
Manufacturing	29.0	−32.3	−15.3		−18.6
Construction	3.3	0.1	1.0		4.3
Commerce	−0.1	−3.5	22.1		18.5
Transport	11.0	1.4	6.0		18.4
Other services	4.4	1.2	30.6		36.2
Central America	**−5.9**	**40.8**	**26.7**	**38.4**	**100.0**
Agriculture	3.9	17.7	−17.4		4.1
Mining & utilities	−24.9	13.0	1.4		−10.5
Manufacturing	9.8	−1.1	−10.2		−1.5
Construction	−6.1	0.9	7.1		2.0
Commerce	11.9	0.1	7.0		18.9
Transport	13.1	2.8	4.1		20.1
Other services	−13.6	7.4	34.6		28.5
South America	**44.3**	**15.7**	**26.3**	**13.7**	**100.0**
Agriculture	7.6	10.7	−12.7		5.7
Mining & utilities	−4.7	6.0	1.0		2.2
Manufacturing	8.0	−0.6	1.5		9.0
Construction	2.2	−0.9	6.6		7.9
Commerce	12.5	−1.3	10.7		21.8
Transport	3.6	1.4	4.7		9.7
Other services	15.1	0.5	14.4		30.0

& utilities and manufacturing undermined output per capita growth. In South America, the key sectors were other services and commerce, while transport and manufacturing also had sizeable positive impacts. Overall, mining & utilities had a consistently negative impact on Latin America's within-sector productivity, while agriculture was the key contributor to the structural change component. Other services was the strongest economic sector by a considerable margin.

Other Empirical Studies

This section compares our results with those of the recent literature. In particular, we focus our attention on five key empirical studies: McMillan et al. (2014), McMillan and Harttgen (2015), Timmer et al. (2015), UNCTAD (2014) and Kucera and Roncolato (2012). It is worth noting that our country sample is significantly larger than that of previous studies, which enhances the representativeness of the findings (Table 3.7). Our dataset includes 169 countries, compared to the 81 of Kucera and Roncolato (2012) and the 38 of McMillan et al. (2014). We have data since the early 1990s, which we decide to split in half in order to look at two subperiods—knowing that economic growth accelerated in most developing countries since the early 2000s. Our sector coverage is determined by the national accounts data and thus restricted to seven sectors. It would have been useful to separate the mining and utilities sectors, as well as further disaggregate other services.

Since most studies decompose output per worker growth—rather than output per capita growth—we adjust our results as necessary to facilitate comparisons. In addition, we report within-sector and between-sector effects both as compound annual growth rates and shares. In the first case, the contributions add up to the annual compound growth rate of output per worker, while in the second they add up to 100%. Finally, we are only able to compare results for the 'macro' regions.

There are significant discrepancies in terms of the contribution of structural change to output per worker growth (Table 3.8). For instance, our results point to positive within-sector and between-sector productivity changes for all regions, which is not always the case in the literature.

Table 3.7 Coverage, sector aggregation and data sources of selected studies

	This study	Kucera and Roncolato (2012)	UNCTAD (2014)	McMillan et al. (2014)	McMillan and Harttgen (2015)	Timmer et al. (2015)
Countries	169	81	...	38	37	31
Aggregation	Africa (49) Asia (48) Developed (44) LAC (28)	Developed (25) Europe & CIS (18) LAC (19) Asia (14) MENA (3) SSA (2)	Developed (..) ODC (..) LDC (38)	Asia (10) Africa (9) LAC (9) Developed (9) Turkey	Asia (10) Africa (9) LAC (9) Developed (9)	Africa (11) Asia (11) LAC (9)
Years	22	24	2-	15	5	20
Period(s)	1991–2002 2002–2013	1984–1998 1999–2008	1991–2012	1990–2005	2000–2005	1960–1975 1975–1990 1990–2010
Sectors	7	7	3	9	9	8
ISIC Rev. 3.1 (sections)	(1) A, B (2) C, E (3) D (4) F (5) G, H (6) I (7) J–P	(1) A, B (2) C, E (3) D (4) F (5) G, H (6) I (7) J–P	(1) A, B (2) C–F (3) G–Q	(1) A, B (2) C (3) D (4) E (5) F (6) G, H (7) I (8) J, K (9) L–P	(1) A, B (2) C (3) D (4) E (5) F (6) G, H (7) I (8) J, K (9) L–P	(1) A, B (2) C (3) D (4) E, F (5) G–I (6) J (7) L–N (8) O–P K excluded
Data sources						
Population	UNDESA	n/a	UNDESA	n/a	n/a	n/a
Employment	ILO	ILO, GGDC	ILC	GGDC, national	GGDC, national	GGDC
Value added	UNDESA	UNDESA, GGDC	UNDESA	GGDC, national	GGDC, national	GGDC

Note It is unlikely that studies include section Q (extraterritorial organizations and bodies), since this section is not usually reported in national accounts data. Latin America & the Caribbean (LAC), Least Developed Countries (LDC), Middle East and North Africa (MENA), Other Developing Countries (ODC), Sub-Saharan Africa (SSA)

Table 3.8 Comparison with other empirical studies

Study	Period	Region	Output per worker growth	Compound annual growth rate (%) Contribution from		Share of contribution from (%)[a]	
				Within sectors	Between sectors	Within sectors	Between sectors
This study	1991–2013	Africa	1.0	0.5	0.4	54	46
		Asia	4.8	3.7	1.1	77	23
		Latin America	0.7	0.3	0.4	46	54
		Other (Developed)	1.3	1.1	0.3	80	20
This study	2002–2013	Africa	1.9	1.1	0.8	57	43
		Asia	5.8	4.1	1.6	72	28
		Latin America	1.2	0.7	0.5	61	39
		Other (Developed)	0.9	0.7	0.2	75	25
McMillan et al. (2014)	1990–2005	Africa	0.9	2.1	−1.3	248	−148
		Asia	3.9	3.3	0.6	86	15
		Latin America	1.4	2.2	−0.9	166	−65
		High income	1.5	1.5	−0.1	105	−6
McMillan and Harttgen (2015)	2000–2005	Africa	2.1	1.2	0.9	57	43
		Asia	3.9	3.5	0.4	89	11
		Latin America	1.0	1.9	−0.9	186	−86
		High Income	1.2	1.4	−0.2	116	−16
Timmer et al. (2015)[b]	1990–2010	Africa	1.9	1.7	0.1	94	6
		Asia	3.6	3.1	0.6	85	15

(continued)

Table 3.8 (continued)

Study	Period	Region	Compound annual growth rate (%)			Share of contribution from (%)[a]	
			Output per worker growth	Contribution from		Within sectors	Between sectors
				Within sectors	Between sectors		
UNCTAD (2014)[c]	1991–2012	Latin America	0.9	1.1	−0.1	113	−13
		LDCs	2.3	1.5	0.7	65	33
		ODCs	3.7	2.4	1.2	66	33
		Developed	1.4	1.2	0.1	90	9
Kucera and Roncolato (2012)	1999–2008	Sub-Saharan Africa	3.0	2.4	0.5	80	17
		Asia	3.8	2.9	1.0	76	26
		Middle East & North Africa	2.2	2.5	−0.2	114	−9
		Latin America	1.2	1.1	0.0	92	0
		Developed	1.1	1.2	0.0	109	0

[a]These shares do not always add up to 100—especially for Kucera and Roncolato (2012)—due to rounding of reported results

[b]Between-sector effects are further disaggregated into static and dynamic reallocation effects. This table reports the combined effect

[c]UNCTAD also estimates the contribution of changes in relative prices across sectors—though these are small

McMillan et al. (2014) point to a considerable growth-reducing structural change in Africa and Latin America during the 1990–2005 period, McMillan and Harttgen (2015) suggest the same for Latin America in 2000–2005 and ditto for Timmer et al. (2015) regarding Latin America in 1990–2010. Not even our results for 1991–2002 (not shown here) corroborate these finding. Despite this, our results for Africa are very similar to those reported by McMillan and Harttgen (2015).[11] Our results for Asia suggest a stronger contribution from structural change than that reported in other studies. The findings from UNCTAD (2014) and Kucera and Roncolato (2012) are not directly comparable to ours, due to different regional aggregates. Nevertheless, UNCTAD (2014) suggest that structural change accounted for about 33% of GVA per worker growth in developing countries, which is similar to what we obtain when aggregating Africa, Asia and Latin America into a single region.[12] Kucera and Roncolato (2012), however, suggest a negligible role of structural change in Latin America and the Middle East & North Africa (MENA), and a relatively small role in sub-Saharan Africa (SSA).

A range of factors might explain these discrepancies, including different country samples, time frames, level of sectoral aggregation, data sources and empirical methodologies. Therefore, we undertake additional calculations and checks to ensure that our results are robust to different choices, namely, the method of aggregation and the decomposition methodology.

Most studies compute results at the country level and then report unweighted regional averages. This strategy can be misleading, since it treats all countries equally—regardless of their relative importance in terms of output and employment.[13] In practice, the prospects of a worker in a larger country are deemed less important than those of workers in

---

[11]McMillan and Harttgen (2015) also report results for an expanded African sample (19 countries), but disaggregated into four sectors only. The findings are broadly similar to the main results.

[12]Such a decomposition yields an output per worker growth rate of 3.4% per year for 1991–2013, of which 72% is due to within-sector improvements and the remaining 28% is due to structural change.

[13]For instance, China accounts for most of GVA and employment in Eastern Asia. As a comparison, GVA per worker growth declines from 7.6% (our result) to 5.3% (when unweighted) in 2002–2013, while the between-sector effect drops from 1.8 percentage points to 0.9 percentage points. Similar discrepancies emerge when McMillan and Harttgen (2015) apply employment weights and Kucera and Roncolato (2012) apply GDP weights to their respective results.

smaller countries. Moreover, weighing countries ex-post entails several arbitrary decisions, such as choosing the weighting variable and the type of weight.[14] In this chapter, we consider each region (and sub-region) as a unit of analysis. This means that output, employment and population data is aggregated in absolute terms before the analysis is carried out. As a robustness check, we also calculate unweighted, employment-weighted and GDP-weighted averages from individual country results. Interestingly, the unweighted averages significantly underestimate output per worker growth in Asia and Africa, probably because some large economies are performing better than the average—such as China, India, Ethiopia and Nigeria. See Table 3.A11 in the Appendix. Nonetheless, the weighted results are broadly in line with our findings on the pattern and pace of structural change. In addition, we apply the decomposition method used by McMillan et al. (2014) and Timmer et al. (2015) to our data. In 2002–2013, the contribution of between-sector effects increases from 43% to 44% for Africa and from 28 to 31% in Asia. On the other hand, this share declines from 39 to 37% in Latin America and from 25 to 19% in developed countries. Overall, it seems that different empirical methodologies and strategies to estimate regional trends do not account for the different results across studies. Hence, it might be that a more representative country sample and the availability of recent data explain some of these discrepancies.

Conclusion

This chapter uncovered evidence of growth-enhancing structural change in 12 out of the 13 sub-regions analysed—the exception being the Caribbean. All sub-regions recorded a reduction in the share of employment in agriculture between 2002 and 2013, often by a large amount. Moreover, the manufacturing's employment share also declined in all

---

[14]A single weight needs to be used across all components to ensure consistency, but while output would probably be more suitable for weighing within-sector effects, employment is likely to be more appropriate for between-sector effects. This can be problematic, since a country's weight may vary considerably according to which variable is chosen. For example, D.R. Congo accounts for 50% of Middle Africa's employment, but only 14% of GVA.

but four sub-regions: South-Eastern Asia, Southern Asia, Middle Africa
and Eastern Africa—it actually remained constant in the latter. On average, other services achieved the largest relative increases in employment,
although construction and commerce also made important gains in some
sub-regions. Since agriculture has the lowest level of labour productivity across all sub-regions, the relocation of workers from agriculture to
other sectors led to positive structural change, which helped boost aggregate productivity and thus economic growth. Improvements in within-
sector productivity were the key driver of economic performance in
2002–2013—as noted in earlier studies—but the contribution of structural change has also been considerable and often growing in importance.
Changes in the demographic structure had a positive impact on output
per capita growth in developing regions, while the impact of changes in
the employment rate has varied considerably across sub-regions. In sum,
labour productivity growth—especially within sectors—has been the
main force behind the recent acceleration of output per capita growth
in developing countries, although a demographic dividend and rising
employment rates have also added to this performance (Fig. 3.16).

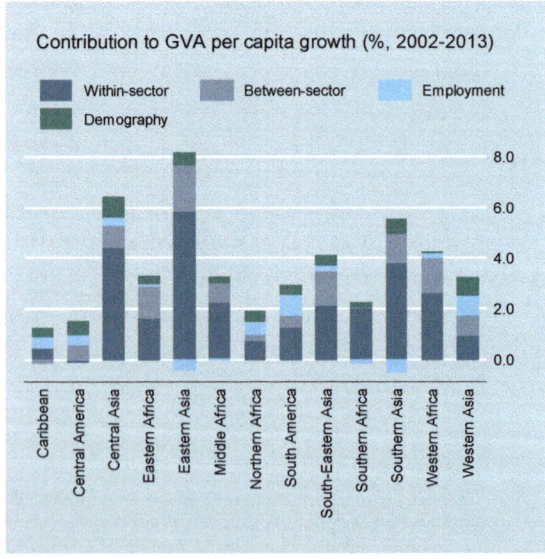

Fig. 3.16 Decomposition of GVA per capita growth—sub-regions

Despite these positive findings, there is still much scope for accelerating structural change. For instance, the (relative) reductions in agricultural employment are not uniform across regions—for instance, they have happened much faster in Asia than in Africa. Moreover, the sectors with the largest increases in the labour share do not always have above-average productivity. Large labour productivity gaps remain in many developing regions, which suggests that there remains significant scope to improve the current growth performance. The period since 2002 has been unquestionably positive for developing regions, but it is important to accelerate the pace of structural change in order to fully seize its benefits—especially for the poorest countries. Even if the structure of employment does not change considerably in a short period of time, economic gains can still be substantial due to very large productivity gaps—especially between agriculture and non-agricultural sectors.

Appendix

Table 3.A1 Country composition of regions and sub-regions

Sub-region	Country	Code	Sub-region	Country	Code	Sub-region	Country	Code	Sub-region	Country	Code
AFRICA			Western Africa	Mauritania	MRT	Western Asia	Israel	ISR	Other (Developed)	Belarus	BLR
Eastern Africa	Burundi	BDI	Western Africa	Niger	NER	Western Asia	Jordan	JOR	Other (Developed)	Belgium	BEL
Eastern Africa	Comoros	COM	Western Africa	Nigeria	NGA	Western Asia	Kuwait	KWT	Other (Developed)	Bosnia and Herzegovina	BIH
Eastern Africa	Eritrea	ERI	Western Africa	Senegal	SEN	Western Asia	Lebanon	LBN	Other (Developed)	Bulgaria	BGR
Eastern Africa	Ethiopia	ETH	Western Africa	Sierra Leone	SLE	Western Asia	Oman	OMN	Other (Developed)	Canada	CAN
Eastern Africa	Kenya	KEN	Western Africa	Togo	TGO	Western Asia	Qatar	QAT	Other (Developed)	Croatia	HRV
Eastern Africa	Madagascar	MDG	**ASIA**			Western Asia	Saudi Arabia	SAU	Other (Developed)	Czech Republic	CZE
Eastern Africa	Malawi	MWI	Central Asia	Kazakhstan	KAZ	Western Asia	Turkey	TUR	Other (Developed)	Denmark	DNK
Eastern Africa	Mauritius	MUS	Central Asia	Kyrgyzstan	KGZ	Western Asia	United Arab Emirates	ARE	Other (Developed)	Estonia	EST
Eastern Africa	Mozambique	MOZ	Central Asia	Tajikistan	TJK	Western Asia	West Bank and Gaza Strip	PSE	Other (Developed)	Finland	FIN
Eastern Africa	Rwanda	RWA	Central Asia	Turkmenistan	TKM	Western Asia	Yemen	YEM	Other (Developed)	France	FRA
Eastern Africa	Tanzania, United Rep.	TZA	Central Asia	Uzbekistan	UZB	**LATIN AMERICA & THE CARIBBEAN**			Other (Developed)	Germany	DEU
Eastern Africa	Uganda	UGA	Eastern Asia	China	CHN	Caribbean	Bahamas	BHS	Other (Developed)	Greece	GRC

(continued)

Table 3.A1 (continued)

Sub-region	Country	Code	Sub-region	Country	Code	Sub-region	Country	Code	Sub-region	Country	Code
Eastern Africa	Zambia	ZMB	Eastern Asia	Hong Kong China	HKG	Caribbean	Barbados	BRB	Other (Developed)	Hungary	HUN
Eastern Africa	Zimbabwe	ZWE	Eastern Asia	Korea, Republic of	KOR	Caribbean	Cuba	CUB	Other (Developed)	Iceland	ISL
Middle Africa	Angola	AGO	Eastern Asia	Mongolia	MNG	Caribbean	Dominican Republic	DOM	Other (Developed)	Ireland	IRL
Middle Africa	Cameroon	CMR	South-Eastern Asia	Brunei Darussalam	BRN	Caribbean	Haiti	HTI	Other (Developed)	Italy	ITA
Middle Africa	Central African Republic	CAF	South-Eastern Asia	Cambodia	KHM	Caribbean	Jamaica	JAM	Other (Developed)	Japan	JPN
Middle Africa	Chad	TCD	South-Eastern Asia	East Timor	TLS	Caribbean	Puerto Rico	PRI	Other (Developed)	Latvia	LVA
Middle Africa	Congo	COG	South-Eastern Asia	Indonesia	IDN	Caribbean	Trinidad and Tobago	TTO	Other (Developed)	Lithuania	LTU
Middle Africa	Congo, D. R.	COD	South-Eastern Asia	Lao P.D.R.	LAO	Central America	Belize	BLZ	Other (Developed)	Luxembourg	LUX
Middle Africa	Equatorial Guinea	GNQ	South-Eastern Asia	Malaysia	MYS	Central America	Costa Rica	CRI	Other (Developed)	Malta	MLT
Middle Africa	Gabon	GAB	South-Eastern Asia	Myanmar	MMR	Central America	El Salvador	SLV	Other (Developed)	Montenegro	MNE
Northern Africa	Algeria	DZA	South-Eastern Asia	Philippines	PHL	Central America	Guatemala	GTM	Other (Developed)	Netherlands	NLD
Northern Africa	Egypt	EGY	South-Eastern Asia	Singapore	SGP	Central America	Honduras	HND	Other (Developed)	New Zealand	NZL
Northern Africa	Libya	LBY	South-Eastern Asia	Thailand	THA	Central America	Mexico	MEX	Other (Developed)	Norway	NOR
Northern Africa	Morocco	MAR	South-Eastern Asia	Viet Nam	VNM	Central America	Nicaragua	NIC	Other (Developed)	Poland	POL
Northern Africa	Sudan (former)	SDN	South-Eastern Asia	Fiji	FJI	Central America	Panama	PAN	Other (Developed)	Portugal	PRT
Northern Africa	Tunisia	TUN	South-Eastern Asia	Papua New Guinea	PNG	South America	Argentina	ARG	Other (Developed)	Republic of Moldova	MDA

(continued)

Table 3.A1 (continued)

Sub-region	Country	Code	Sub-region	Country	Code	Sub-region	Country	Code	Sub-region	Country	Code
Southern Africa	Botswana	BWA	South-Eastern Asia	Solomon Islands	SLB	South America	Bolivia	BOL	Other (Developed)	Romania	ROU
Southern Africa	Lesotho	LSO	Southern Asia	Afghanistan	AFG	South America	Brazil	BRA	Other (Developed)	Russian Federation	RUS
Southern Africa	Namibia	NAM	Southern Asia	Bangladesh	BGD	South America	Chile	CHL	Other (Developed)	Serbia	SRB
Southern Africa	South Africa	ZAF	Southern Asia	Bhutan	BTN	South America	Colombia	COL	Other (Developed)	Slovakia	SVK
Southern Africa	Swaziland	SWZ	Southern Asia	India	IND	South America	Ecuador	ECU	Other (Developed)	Slovenia	SVN
Western Africa	Benin	BEN	Southern Asia	Iran, Islamic Rep.	IRN	South America	Guyana	GUY	Other (Developed)	Spain	ESP
Western Africa	Burkina Faso	BFA	Southern Asia	Maldives	MDV	South America	Paraguay	PRY	Other (Developed)	Sweden	SWE
Western Africa	Cape Verde	CPV	Southern Asia	Nepal	NPL	South America	Peru	PER	Other (Developed)	Switzerland	CHE
Western Africa	Côte d'Ivoire	CIV	Southern Asia	Pakistan	PAK	South America	Suriname	SUR	Other (Developed)	FYR of Macedonia	MKD
Western Africa	Gambia	GMB	Southern Asia	Sri Lanka	LKA	South America	Uruguay	URY	Other (Developed)	Ukraine	UKR
Western Africa	Ghana	GHA	Western Asia	Armenia	ARM	South America	Venezuela	VEN	Other (Developed)	United Kingdom	GBR
Western Africa	Guinea	GIN	Western Asia	Azerbaijan	AZE	OTHER (DEVELOPED)	Albania	ALB	Other (Developed)	United States	USA
Western Africa	Guinea-Bissau	GNB	Western Asia	Cyprus	CYP	Other (Developed)	Australia	AUS			
Western Africa	Liberia	LBR	Western Asia	Georgia	GEO	Other (Developed)	Austria	AUT			
Western Africa	Mali	MLI	Western Asia	Iraq	IRQ						

Table 3.A2 Output, employment and labour productivity by sector—regions

Region/sector	GVA (constant 2005 USD, billion)			GVA (% total GVA)			GVA (annual growth, %)			Employment (million)			Employment (% total employment)			Employment (annual growth, %)			GVA per worker (constant 2005 USD)			GVA per worker (annual growth, %)		
	1991	2002	2013	1991	2002	2013	1991–2002	2002–2013	1991–2013	1991	2002	2013	1991	2002	2013	1991–2002	2002–2013	1991–2013	1991	2002	2013	1991–2002	2002–2013	1991–2013
World	**30,160**	**40,091**	**53,151**	**100.0**	**100.0**	**100.0**	**2.6**	**2.6**	**2.6**	**2232**	**2664**	**3111**	**100.0**	**100.0**	**100.0**	**1.6**	**1.4**	**1.5**	**13,515**	**15,047**	**17,086**	**1.0**	**1.2**	**1.1**
Agriculture	1091	1367	1865	3.6	3.4	3.5	2.1	2.9	2.5	958	1052	924	42.9	39.5	29.7	0.9	-1.2	-0.2	1140	1299	2018	1.2	4.1	2.6
Mining & utilities	1957	2418	3124	6.5	6.0	5.9	1.9	2.4	2.1	40	38	50	1.8	1.4	1.6	-0.4	2.5	1.0	49,174	63,527	62,590	2.4	-0.1	1.1
Manufacturing	4810	6526	9318	15.9	16.3	17.5	2.8	3.3	3.1	320	338	364	14.3	12.7	11.7	0.5	0.7	0.6	15,038	19,321	25,627	2.3	2.6	2.5
Construction	2090	2307	2701	6.9	5.8	5.1	0.9	1.4	1.2	103	147	263	4.6	5.5	8.5	3.3	5.4	4.4	20,345	15,718	10,266	-2.3	-3.8	-3.1
Commerce	3827	5558	7435	12.7	13.9	14.0	3.4	2.7	3.1	350	466	636	15.7	17.5	20.5	2.6	2.9	2.7	10,922	11,914	11,685	0.8	-0.2	0.3
Transport	2137	3236	4747	7.1	8.1	8.9	3.5	3.5	3.7	85	116	176	3.8	4.4	5.7	2.9	3.8	3.4	25,077	27,846	26,967	1.0	-0.3	0.3
Other services	14,246	18,679	23,962	47.2	46.6	45.1	2.5	2.3	2.4	376	507	698	16.9	19.0	22.4	2.7	3.0	2.9	37,885	36,872	34,336	-0.2	-0.6	-0.4
Africa	**644**	**876**	**1490**	**100.0**	**100.0**	**100.0**	**2.8**	**5.0**	**3.9**	**207**	**282**	**389**	**100.0**	**100.0**	**100.0**	**2.8**	**3.0**	**2.9**	**3108**	**3103**	**3834**	**0.0**	**1.9**	**1.0**
Agriculture	93	137	226	14.4	15.6	15.2	3.6	4.7	4.1	126	169	215	60.7	60.0	55.4	2.7	2.2	2.5	739	809	1,052	0.8	2.4	1.6
Mining & utilities	141	165	198	21.9	18.8	13.3	1.4	1.7	1.6	2	3	5	1.2	1.1	1.3	2.6	4.3	3.5	58,687	51,510	38,832	-1.2	-2.5	-1.9
Manufacturing	84	107	163	13.1	12.2	10.9	2.2	3.9	3.0	15	19	24	7.4	6.8	6.2	2.1	2.0	2.1	5530	5573	6796	0.1	1.8	0.9
Construction	23	34	82	3.6	3.9	5.5	3.5	8.2	5.9	5	8	15	2.5	2.7	3.9	3.8	6.3	5.0	4581	4473	5463	-0.2	1.8	0.8
Commerce	85	114	233	13.2	13.0	15.6	2.7	6.7	4.7	21	30	44	10.3	10.7	11.4	3.2	3.5	3.3	3959	3780	5273	-0.4	3.1	1.3
Transport	44	75	182	6.8	8.5	12.2	4.9	8.4	5.7	5	6	11	2.2	2.2	2.9	2.9	5.3	4.1	9625	11,921	16,399	2.3	2.9	2.5
Other services	173	243	406	26.9	27.8	27.3	3.1	4.8	4.0	33	46	74	15.7	16.4	19.1	3.2	4.4	3.8	5309	5247	5474	-0.1	0.4	0.1
Asia	**2956**	**5475**	**11,687**	**100.0**	**100.0**	**100.0**	**5.8**	**7.1**	**6.4**	**1339**	**1617**	**1867**	**100.0**	**100.0**	**100.0**	**1.7**	**1.3**	**1.5**	**2208**	**3385**	**6259**	**4.0**	**5.7**	**4.9**
Agriculture	451	616	926	15.2	11.2	7.9	2.9	3.8	3.3	746	802	639	55.7	49.6	34.2	0.7	-2.0	-0.7	604	768	1448	2.2	5.9	4.1
Mining & utilities	388	619	1107	13.1	11.3	9.5	4.3	5.4	4.9	20	19	26	1.5	1.2	1.4	-0.3	2.9	1.3	19,670	32,496	42,285	4.7	2.4	3.5
Manufacturing	515	1241	3039	17.4	22.7	26.0	8.3	8.5	8.4	168	194	226	12.5	12.0	12.1	1.3	1.4	1.4	3071	6390	13,449	6.9	7.0	6.9
Construction	190	297	736	6.4	5.4	6.3	4.2	8.6	6.4	51	86	187	3.8	5.3	10.0	4.9	7.2	6.1	3721	3440	3941	-0.7	1.2	0.3
Commerce	378	698	1606	12.8	12.7	13.7	5.7	7.9	6.8	195	279	408	14.6	17.3	21.9	3.3	3.5	3.4	1937	2498	3936	2.3	4.2	3.3
Transport	189	409	925	6.4	7.5	7.9	7.3	7.7	7.5	41	63	102	3.0	3.9	5.5	4.1	4.4	4.3	4634	6458	9073	3.1	3.1	3.1
Other services	846	1595	3347	28.6	29.1	28.6	5.9	7.0	6.5	118	173	279	8.8	10.7	14.9	3.5	4.4	4.0	7150	9224	12,010	2.3	2.4	2.4
Latin America	**1745**	**2309**	**3375**	**100.0**	**100.0**	**100.0**	**2.6**	**3.5**	**3.0**	**166**	**217**	**279**	**100.0**	**100.0**	**100.0**	**2.5**	**2.3**	**2.4**	**10,518**	**10,626**	**12,116**	**0.1**	**1.2**	**0.6**
Agriculture	95	127	169	5.4	5.5	5.0	2.7	2.6	2.7	42	44	43	25.2	20.1	15.4	0.4	-0.2	0.1	2264	2895	3933	2.3	2.8	2.5
Mining & utilities	188	258	324	10.8	11.2	9.6	2.9	2.1	2.5	2	2	2	1.2	1.0	1.2	0.3	4.1	2.2	91,902	121,970	97,981	2.6	-2.0	0.3
Manufacturing	325	424	559	18.6	18.4	16.6	2.5	2.5	2.5	24	30	35	14.6	13.7	12.6	1.9	1.5	1.7	13,375	14,248	15,884	0.6	1.0	0.8
Construction	120	143	219	6.9	6.2	6.5	1.6	4.0	2.8	9	14	21	5.6	6.3	7.5	3.6	4.0	3.8	12,966	10,440	10,433	-2.0	0.0	-1.0
Commerce	294	372	591	16.8	16.1	17.5	2.2	4.3	3.2	37	51	68	22.0	23.4	24.5	3.0	2.7	2.9	8032	7324	8669	-0.8	1.5	0.3

(continued)

Table 3.A2 (continued)

Region/sector	GVA (constant 2005 USD, billion)			GVA (% total GVA)			GVA (annual growth, %)			Employment (million)			Employment (% total employment)			Employment (annual growth, %)			GVA per worker (constant 2005 USD)			GVA per worker (annual growth, %)		
	1991	2002	2013	1991	2002	2013	1991–2002	2002–2013	1991–2013	1991	2002	2013	1991	2002	2013	1991–2002	2002–2013	1991–2013	1991	2002	2013	1991–2002	2002–2013	1991–2013
Transport	116	185	320	6.6	8.0	9.5	4.3	5.1	4.7	7	11	17	4.3	5.2	6.0	4.2	3.7	3.9	16,089	16,372	19,164	0.2	1.4	0.8
Other services	608	802	1193	34.8	34.7	35.4	2.6	3.7	3.1	45	66	91	27.0	30.4	32.8	3.6	3.0	3.3	13,592	12,149	13,063	–1.0	0.7	–0.2
Other	24,815	31,431	36,599	100.0	100.0	100.0	2.2	1.4	1.8	520	547	576	100.0	100.0	100.0	0.5	0.5	0.5	47,749	57,431	63,495	1.7	0.9	1.3
(Developed)																								
Agriculture	453	488	544	1.8	1.6	1.5	0.7	1.0	0.8	44	37	27	8.4	6.8	4.6	–1.4	–3.0	–2.2	10,392	13,115	20,392	2.1	4.1	3.1
Mining & utilities	1240	1376	1495	5.0	4.4	4.1	0.9	0.8	0.9	16	14	15	3.0	2.5	2.7	–1.2	1.0	–0.1	79,329	100,536	97,528	2.2	–0.3	0.9
Manufacturing	3886	4754	5556	15.7	15.1	15.2	1.9	1.4	1.6	113	95	78	21.7	17.3	13.6	–1.6	–1.7	–1.6	34,530	50,251	70,872	3.5	3.2	3.3
Construction	1756	1833	1664	7.1	5.8	4.5	0.4	–0.9	–0.2	37	39	40	7.2	7.1	7.0	0.4	0.3	0.3	47,006	47,038	41,251	0.0	–1.2	–0.6
Commerce	3071	4374	5005	12.4	13.9	13.7	3.3	1.2	2.2	97	106	116	18.7	19.4	20.1	0.8	0.8	0.8	31,523	41,199	43,214	2.5	0.4	1.4
Transport	1789	2568	3320	7.2	8.2	9.1	3.3	2.4	2.8	33	35	46	6.3	6.5	8.0	0.7	2.5	1.6	54,648	72,565	71,761	2.6	–0.1	1.2
Other services	12,619	16,038	19,015	50.9	51.0	52.0	2.2	1.6	1.9	180	221	254	34.7	40.4	44.0	1.9	1.2	1.6	69,952	72,483	74,985	0.3	0.3	0.3

Source Calculated from UNSD and ILO

Table 3.A3 Output, employment and labour productivity by sector—Africa

Region/sector	GVA (constant 2005 USD, billion)			GVA (% total GVA)			GVA (annual growth, %)			Employment (million)			Employment (% total employment)			Employment (annual growth, %)			GVA per worker (constant 2005 USD)			GVA per worker (annual growth, %)		
	1991	2002	2013	1991	2002	2013	1991–2002	2002–2013	1991–2013	1991	2002	2013	1991	2002	2013	1991–2002	2002–2013	1991–2013	1991	2002	2013	1991–2002	2002–2013	1991–2013
Eastern Africa	**62.2**	**84.7**	**163.6**	**100.0**	**100.0**	**100.0**	**2.8**	**6.2**	**4.5**	**76.8**	**106.2**	**149.9**	**100.0**	**100.0**	**100.0**	**3.0**	**3.2**	**3.1**	**810**	**797**	**1091**	**-0.1**	**2.9**	**1.4**
Agriculture	18.0	24.6	37.9	29.0	29.0	23.2	2.8	4.0	3.4	58.8	80.9	107.4	76.6	76.2	71.6	2.9	2.6	2.8	307	304	353	-0.1	1.4	0.6
Mining & utilities	4.8	4.7	9.5	7.7	5.6	5.8	-0.1	6.6	3.2	0.6	0.7	1.3	0.7	0.6	0.9	1.6	6.4	3.9	8372	6988	7123	-1.6	0.2	-0.7
Manufacturing	6.7	9.0	15.6	10.7	10.7	9.6	2.8	5.1	3.9	3.3	4.1	5.6	4.3	3.8	3.8	1.9	3.0	2.5	2028	2226	2781	0.8	2.0	1.4
Construction	2.3	3.8	11.8	3.7	4.5	7.2	4.8	10.8	7.7	0.8	1.4	3.0	1.1	1.3	2.0	4.7	7.3	6.0	2745	2752	3903	0.0	3.2	1.6
Commerce	8.0	11.6	23.4	12.9	13.7	14.3	3.4	6.6	5.0	5.1	7.5	10.5	6.6	7.1	7.0	3.7	3.7	3.4	1583	1534	2223	-0.3	3.4	1.6
Transport	3.8	6.4	16.3	6.0	7.5	10.0	4.9	9.0	6.9	0.9	1.4	2.5	1.1	1.3	1.7	3.7	5.7	4.7	4084	4620	6470	1.1	3.1	2.1
Other services	18.6	24.6	48.9	29.9	29.0	29.9	2.6	6.5	4.5	7.3	10.3	19.5	9.5	9.7	13.0	3.2	6.0	4.6	2559	2394	2509	-0.6	0.4	-0.1
Middle Africa	**58.5**	**68.4**	**133.4**	**100.0**	**100.0**	**100.0**	**1.4**	**6.3**	**3.8**	**25.5**	**35.2**	**49.5**	**100.0**	**100.0**	**100.0**	**3.0**	**3.1**	**3.1**	**2292**	**1943**	**2698**	**-1.5**	**3.0**	**0.7**
Agriculture	8.4	9.7	16.4	14.4	14.2	12.3	1.3	4.9	3.1	18.3	24.6	32.1	71.7	69.8	64.9	2.7	2.5	2.6	461	395	510	-1.4	2.4	0.5
Mining & utilities	20.1	29.5	57.6	34.3	43.1	43.2	3.5	6.3	4.9	0.2	0.3	0.4	0.7	0.8	0.8	4.0	3.8	3.9	116,833	110,784	143,764	-0.5	2.4	0.9
Manufacturing	8.4	6.5	10.4	14.3	9.5	7.8	-2.3	4.3	1.0	0.9	1.9	2.9	3.6	5.5	5.9	7.1	3.8	5.4	9197	3367	3564	-8.7	0.5	-4.2
Construction	1.3	1.9	6.9	2.3	2.8	5.2	3.4	12.2	7.9	0.5	0.7	1.4	2.0	2.0	2.9	3.0	6.5	4.7	2626	2741	4900	0.4	5.4	2.9
Commerce	8.3	8.3	18.5	14.2	12.2	13.9	0.0	7.5	3.7	0.6	0.8	1.3	2.3	2.3	2.6	3.1	4.1	3.6	14,383	10,295	14,691	-3.0	3.3	0.1
Transport	3.5	3.4	8.2	6.0	5.0	6.2	-0.3	8.3	3.9	0.3	0.4	0.7	1.1	1.1	1.3	3.2	5.0	4.1	13,112	8,967	12,557	-3.4	3.1	-0.2
Other services	8.4	9.0	15.3	14.4	13.2	11.5	0.6	4.9	2.8	4.8	6.5	10.7	18.7	18.6	21.7	2.9	4.6	3.7	1762	1375	1427	-2.2	0.3	-1.0
Northern Africa	**224.9**	**303.3**	**454.7**	**100.0**	**100.0**	**100.0**	**2.8**	**3.7**	**3.3**	**35.3**	**45.8**	**61.8**	**100.0**	**100.0**	**100.0**	**2.4**	**2.8**	**2.6**	**6379**	**6617**	**7353**	**0.3**	**1.0**	**0.6**
Agriculture	28.8	39.1	63.6	12.8	12.9	14.0	2.8	4.5	3.7	12.6	14.9	18.0	35.7	32.4	29.2	1.5	1.8	1.7	2291	2633	3527	1.3	2.7	2.0
Mining & utilities	74.0	83.1	86.2	32.9	27.4	19.0	1.1	0.3	0.7	0.6	0.9	1.2	1.8	1.9	2.0	3.1	3.3	3.2	118,630	95,281	69,236	-2.0	-2.9	-2.4
Manufacturing	23.4	35.7	49.7	10.4	11.8	10.9	3.9	3.1	3.5	4.7	5.2	6.8	13.2	11.3	10.9	1.0	2.5	1.7	5038	6894	7360	2.9	0.6	1.7
Construction	10.7	16.1	32.5	4.8	5.3	7.1	3.8	6.6	5.2	2.4	3.5	6.9	6.8	7.7	11.2	3.6	6.3	4.9	4447	4546	4671	0.2	0.2	0.2
Commerce	25.9	37.2	61.3	11.5	12.2	13.5	3.3	4.7	4.0	4.4	6.4	8.5	12.5	14.0	13.7	3.5	2.6	3.0	5893	5808	7220	-0.1	2.0	0.9
Transport	16.3	25.6	52.7	7.2	8.4	11.6	4.2	6.8	5.5	1.9	2.2	3.6	5.4	4.9	5.8	1.8	4.4	3.1	8786	11,378	14,674	2.4	2.3	2.4
Other services	45.8	66.7	108.7	20.3	22.0	23.9	3.5	4.5	4.0	8.7	12.8	16.8	24.8	27.8	27.1	3.5	2.5	3.0	5232	5228	6484	-0.6	2.0	1.0
Southern Africa	**171.1**	**221.0**	**317.5**	**100.0**	**100.0**	**100.0**	**2.4**	**3.3**	**2.8**	**10.9**	**15.0**	**17.2**	**100.0**	**100.0**	**100.0**	**2.9**	**1.3**	**2.1**	**15,684**	**14,736**	**18,424**	**-0.6**	**2.1**	**0.7**
Agriculture	6.5	7.0	8.5	3.8	3.2	2.7	0.7	1.7	1.2	2.0	2.2	1.5	18.2	14.5	9.0	0.9	-3.1	-1.1	3296	3215	5473	-0.2	5.0	2.3
Mining & utilities	23.2	23.6	21.8	13.6	10.7	6.9	0.1	-0.7	-0.3	0.6	0.7	0.5	5.1	4.5	2.9	1.8	-2.7	-0.5	41,950	34,997	43,853	-1.6	2.1	0.2

(continued)

Table 3.A3 (continued)

Region/sector	GVA (constant 2005 USD, billion)			GVA (% total GVA)			GVA (annual growth, %)			Employment (million)			Employment (% total employment)			Employment (annual growth, %)			GVA per worker (constant 2005 USD)			GVA per worker (annual growth, %)		
	1991	2002	2013	1991	2002	2013	1991–2002	2002–2013	1991–2013	1991	2002	2013	1991	2002	2013	1991–2002	2002–2013	1991–2013	1991	2002	2013	1991–2002	2002–2013	1991–2013
Manufacturing	31.7	40.5	51.3	18.5	18.3	16.1	2.3	2.2	2.2	1.3	1.8	1.7	12.0	12.0	9.6	2.9	-0.7	1.1	24,205	22,503	30,869	-0.7	2.9	1.1
Construction	5.4	5.9	12.7	3.1	2.7	4.0	0.9	7.1	4.0	0.5	0.7	1.1	4.6	4.9	6.3	3.4	3.7	3.6	10,671	8146	11,624	-2.4	3.3	0.4
Commerce	21.6	30.3	46.8	12.6	13.7	14.7	3.1	4.0	3.6	1.9	2.7	3.3	17.5	17.8	19.0	3.1	1.9	2.5	11,343	11,355	14,307	0.0	2.1	1.1
Transport	11.6	22.1	34.0	6.8	10.0	10.7	6.1	4.0	5.0	0.4	0.6	0.8	3.7	4.2	4.8	4.1	2.6	3.4	28,794	35,320	41,010	1.9	1.4	1.6
Other services	71.1	91.6	142.5	41.6	41.4	44.9	2.3	4.1	3.2	4.3	6.3	8.3	39.0	42.1	48.4	3.7	2.6	3.1	16,709	14,491	17,084	-1.3	1.5	0.1
Western Africa	**127.3**	**198.3**	**421.2**	**100.0**	**100.0**	**100.0**	**4.1**	**7.1**	**5.6**	**58.7**	**80.0**	**110.3**	**100.0**	**100.0**	**100.0**	**2.9**	**3.0**	**2.9**	**2167**	**2478**	**3819**	**1.2**	**4.0**	**2.6**
Agriculture	31.1	56.5	99.9	24.4	28.5	23.7	5.6	5.3	5.4	34.1	46.8	56.1	58.1	58.5	50.9	2.9	1.7	2.3	912	1208	1780	2.6	3.6	3.1
Mining & utilities	19.1	24.1	23.1	15.0	12.2	5.5	2.1	-0.4	0.9	0.5	0.7	1.6	0.8	0.9	1.5	3.6	7.8	5.7	39,396	33,832	14,203	-1.4	-7.6	-4.5
Manufacturing	14.2	15.6	36.0	11.2	7.9	8.5	0.9	7.9	4.3	5.1	6.3	7.0	8.7	7.8	6.4	1.9	1.0	1.5	2791	2482	5121	-1.1	6.8	2.8
Construction	3.8	6.6	18.1	2.9	3.3	4.3	5.3	9.6	7.4	0.9	1.3	2.5	1.5	1.7	2.3	4.0	6.0	5.0	4345	4991	7176	1.3	3.4	2.3
Commerce	21.0	26.7	82.8	16.5	13.5	19.6	2.2	10.8	6.4	9.5	12.8	20.6	16.1	16.0	18.7	2.7	4.4	3.6	2213	2093	4020	-0.5	6.1	2.7
Transport	8.9	17.2	70.4	7.0	8.7	16.7	6.2	13.7	9.9	1.1	1.6	3.5	1.9	2.0	3.2	3.4	7.1	5.2	7863	10,536	20,231	2.7	6.1	4.4
Other services	29.3	51.6	90.9	23.0	26.0	21.6	5.3	5.3	5.3	7.6	10.5	18.9	12.9	13.1	17.2	3.0	5.5	4.2	3866	4911	4806	2.2	-0.2	1.0

Source Calculated from UNSD and ILO

Table 3.A4 Output, employment and labour productivity by sector—Asia

Region/sector	GVA (constant 2005 USD, billion)			GVA (% total GVA)			GVA (annual growth, %)			Employment (million)			Employment (% total employment)			Employment (annual growth, %)			GVA per worker (constant 2005 USD)			GVA per worker (annual growth, %)		
	1991	2002	2013	1991	2002	2013	1991–2002	2002–2013	1991–2013	1991	2002	2013	1991	2002	2013	1991–2002	2002–2013	1991–2013	1991	2002	2013	1991–2002	2002–2013	1991–2013
Central Asia	**79.8**	**66.6**	**151.6**	**100.0**	**100.0**	**100.0**	**-1.6**	**7.8**	**3.0**	**18.2**	**21.2**	**27.4**	**100.0**	**100.0**	**100.0**	**1.4**	**2.3**	**1.9**	**4374**	**3140**	**5535**	**-3.0**	**5.3**	**1.1**
Agriculture	12.3	9.8	16.9	15.4	14.8	11.1	-2.0	5.0	1.5	6.7	8.1	7.3	37.0	38.0	26.8	1.6	-0.9	0.4	1822	1221	2303	-3.6	5.9	1.1
Mining & utilities	8.0	8.9	15.9	10.0	13.4	10.5	1.0	5.4	3.2	1.2	1.5	2.2	6.4	7.1	8.2	2.3	3.6	3.0	6792	5905	7124	-1.3	1.7	0.2
Manufacturing	13.2	11.8	26.4	16.5	17.8	17.4	-1.0	7.6	3.2	2.3	2.5	3.2	12.5	11.9	11.7	0.9	2.2	1.5	5768	4703	8255	-1.8	5.2	1.6
Construction	7.4	4.2	12.0	9.2	6.3	7.9	-5.0	10.1	2.3	1.4	1.3	2.6	7.6	6.2	9.5	-0.4	6.3	2.9	5319	3152	4624	-4.6	3.5	-0.6
Commerce	8.5	7.4	19.6	10.6	11.2	12.9	-1.2	9.2	3.9	2.3	2.6	3.9	12.3	12.3	14.2	1.3	3.7	2.5	3761	2859	5039	-2.5	5.3	1.3
Transport	11.4	7.1	19.6	14.3	10.7	12.9	-4.2	9.6	2.5	0.9	1.1	1.7	4.9	5.0	6.2	1.5	4.5	3.0	12,663	6753	11,449	-5.6	4.9	-0.5
Other services	19.2	17.2	41.2	24.0	25.9	27.2	-1.0	8.2	3.5	3.5	4.1	6.4	19.2	19.5	23.5	1.5	4.1	2.8	5462	4167	6412	-2.4	4.0	0.7
Eastern Asia	**1083.4**	**2549.6**	**6190.9**	**100.0**	**100.0**	**100.0**	**8.1**	**8.4**	**8.2**	**651.2**	**741.0**	**802.3**	**100.0**	**100.0**	**100.0**	**1.2**	**0.7**	**1.0**	**1664**	**3441**	**7717**	**6.8**	**7.6**	**7.2**
Agriculture	175.7	264.1	416.5	16.2	10.4	6.7	3.8	4.2	4.0	348.9	347.6	197.9	53.6	46.9	24.7	0.0	-5.0	-2.5	504	760	2105	3.8	9.7	6.7
Mining & utilities	47.0	136.7	351.0	4.3	5.4	5.7	10.2	8.9	9.6	11.1	9.6	11.6	1.7	1.3	1.4	-1.4	1.8	0.2	4223	14,313	30,335	11.7	7.1	9.4
Manufacturing	235.3	753.7	2115.4	21.7	29.6	34.2	11.2	9.8	10.5	93.0	93.0	96.3	14.3	12.5	12.0	0.0	0.3	0.2	2529	8106	21,974	11.2	9.5	10.3
Construction	79.8	143.9	390.4	7.4	5.6	6.3	5.5	9.5	7.5	26.2	43.5	96.1	4.0	5.9	12.0	4.7	7.5	6.1	3049	3306	4061	0.7	1.9	1.3
Commerce	140.8	300.2	802.2	13.0	11.8	13.0	7.1	9.3	8.2	115.6	160.7	247.3	17.8	21.7	30.8	3.0	4.0	3.5	1218	1869	3244	4.0	5.1	4.6
Transport	62.4	168.3	359.4	5.8	6.6	5.8	9.4	7.1	8.3	17.3	23.7	43.4	2.7	3.2	5.4	2.9	5.7	4.3	3598	7103	8272	6.4	1.4	3.9
Other services	342.6	782.7	1756.1	31.6	30.7	28.4	7.8	7.6	7.7	39.1	63.0	109.8	6.0	8.5	13.7	4.4	5.2	4.8	8770	12,423	16,000	3.2	2.3	2.8
South-Eastern Asia	**477.2**	**783.8**	**1400.6**	**100.0**	**100.0**	**100.0**	**4.6**	**5.4**	**5.0**	**195.9**	**249.7**	**307.3**	**100.0**	**100.0**	**100.0**	**2.2**	**1.9**	**2.1**	**2436**	**3139**	**4558**	**2.3**	**3.4**	**2.9**
Agriculture	67.4	90.5	131.3	14.1	11.5	9.4	2.7	3.4	3.1	112.6	119.7	117.0	57.5	48.0	38.1	0.6	-0.2	0.2	599	756	1122	2.1	3.7	2.9
Mining & utilities	51.7	83.7	108.5	10.8	10.7	7.7	4.5	2.4	3.4	1.4	1.9	3.6	0.7	0.8	1.2	2.9	5.8	4.3	36,279	43,031	30,110	1.6	-3.2	-0.8
Manufacturing	108.4	202.1	352.3	22.7	25.8	25.2	5.8	5.2	5.5	19.2	30.0	38.0	9.8	12.0	12.4	4.1	2.2	3.2	5647	6737	9273	1.6	2.9	2.3
Construction	28.3	38.1	76.7	5.9	4.9	5.5	2.7	6.6	4.6	5.8	11.2	18.2	2.9	4.5	5.9	6.2	4.5	5.4	4914	3407	4215	-3.3	2.0	-0.7
Commerce	78.1	124.3	245.0	16.4	15.9	17.5	4.3	6.4	5.3	31.1	45.1	63.9	15.9	18.1	20.8	3.4	3.2	3.3	2509	2754	3838	0.9	3.1	2.0
Transport	28.1	57.3	133.3	5.9	7.3	9.5	6.7	8.0	7.3	6.0	11.0	14.6	3.1	4.4	4.7	5.7	2.6	4.1	4692	5196	9133	0.9	5.3	3.1
Other services	115.3	187.8	353.5	24.2	24.0	25.2	4.5	5.9	5.2	19.8	30.6	52.0	10.1	12.3	16.9	4.0	4.9	4.5	5819	6126	6797	0.5	0.9	0.7
Southern Asia	**556.4**	**959.8**	**1919.9**	**100.0**	**100.0**	**100.0**	**5.1**	**6.5**	**5.8**	**432.3**	**555.0**	**654.3**	**100.0**	**100.0**	**100.0**	**2.3**	**1.5**	**1.9**	**1287**	**1729**	**2934**	**2.7**	**4.9**	**3.8**
Agriculture	141.2	185.1	278.9	25.4	19.3	14.5	2.5	3.8	3.1	264.5	313.9	304.0	61.2	56.6	46.5	1.6	-0.3	0.6	534	590	918	0.9	4.1	2.5
Mining & utilities	60.6	87.4	138.3	10.9	9.1	7.2	3.4	4.3	3.8	5.3	5.2	7.2	1.2	0.9	1.1	-0.2	3.1	1.4	11,432	16,833	19,129	3.6	1.2	2.4

(continued)

Table 3.A4 (continued)

Region/sector	GVA (constant 2005 USD, billion)			GVA (% total GVA)			GVA (annual growth, %)			Employment (million)			Employment (% total employment)			Employment (annual growth, %)			GVA per worker (constant 2005 USD)			GVA per worker (annual growth, %)		
	1991	2002	2013	1991	2002	2013	1991–2002	2002–2013	1991–2013	1991	2002	2013	1991	2002	2013	1991–2002	2002–2013	1991–2013	1991	2002	2013	1991–2002	2002–2013	1991–2013
Manufacturing	69.3	134.4	283.9	12.5	14.0	14.8	6.2	7.0	6.6	48.9	62.9	80.6	11.3	11.3	12.3	2.3	2.3	2.3	1418	2136	3522	3.8	4.7	4.2
Construction	32.6	56.5	127.6	5.9	5.9	6.6	5.1	7.7	6.4	15.2	27.0	61.9	3.5	4.9	9.5	5.4	7.8	6.6	2146	2094	2063	-0.2	-0.1	-0.2
Commerce	72.6	145.6	307.5	13.1	15.2	16.0	6.5	7.0	6.8	39.4	61.9	79.6	9.1	11.1	12.2	4.2	2.3	3.2	1844	2353	3864	2.2	4.6	3.4
Transport	33.6	75.7	199.0	6.0	7.9	10.4	7.7	9.2	8.4	14.5	24.8	37.8	3.4	4.5	5.8	5.0	3.9	4.5	2317	3055	5263	2.5	5.1	3.8
Other services	146.5	275.0	584.7	26.3	28.7	30.5	5.9	7.1	6.5	44.5	59.4	83.2	10.3	10.7	12.7	2.7	3.1	2.9	3289	4631	7027	3.2	3.9	3.5
Western Asia	**759.0**	**1115.5**	**2023.6**	**100.0**	**100.0**	**100.0**	**3.6**	**5.6**	**4.6**	**41.2**	**50.6**	**75.9**	**100.0**	**100.0**	**100.0**	**1.9**	**3.8**	**2.8**	**18,419**	**22,061**	**26,673**	**1.7**	**1.7**	**1.7**
Agriculture	54.0	66.4	82.2	7.1	6.0	4.1	1.9	2.0	1.9	13.5	12.9	13.1	32.9	25.5	17.3	-0.4	0.1	-0.1	3989	5142	6267	2.3	1.8	2.1
Mining & utilities	220.6	302.6	492.9	29.1	27.1	24.4	2.9	4.5	3.7	0.7	0.9	1.5	1.7	1.7	2.0	2.1	5.5	3.8	323,396	353,884	321,499	0.8	-0.9	0.0
Manufacturing	89.3	138.6	261.5	11.8	12.4	12.9	4.1	5.9	5.0	4.4	5.7	7.9	10.7	11.4	10.5	2.4	3.0	2.7	20,234	24,135	32,930	1.6	2.9	2.2
Construction	41.6	54.9	129.2	5.5	4.9	6.4	2.6	8.1	5.3	2.5	3.5	8.0	6.0	6.9	10.5	3.2	7.8	5.5	16,822	15,730	16,230	-0.6	0.3	-0.2
Commerce	77.7	120.4	232.0	10.2	10.8	11.5	4.1	6.1	5.1	6.7	9.1	13.6	16.2	18.0	17.9	2.8	3.7	3.3	11,648	13,252	17,100	1.2	2.3	1.8
Transport	53.4	100.2	213.8	7.0	9.0	10.6	5.9	7.1	6.5	2.0	2.7	4.4	4.9	5.4	5.8	2.7	4.5	3.6	26,208	36,811	48,572	3.1	2.6	2.8
Other services	222.3	332.4	612.0	29.3	29.8	30.2	3.7	5.7	4.7	11.4	15.8	27.3	27.6	31.2	36.0	3.0	5.1	4.1	19,536	21,094	22,381	0.7	0.5	0.6

Source Calculated from UNSD and ILO

Table 3.A5 Output, employment and labour productivity by sector—Latin America

Region/sector	GVA (constant 2005 USD, billion)			GVA (% total GVA)			GVA (annual growth, %)			Employment (million)			Employment (% total employment)			Employment (annual growth, %)			GVA per worker (constant 2005 USD)			GVA per worker (annual growth, %)		
	1991	2002	2013	1991	2002	2013	1991–2002	2002–2013	1991–2013	1991	2002	2013	1991	2002	2013	1991–2002	2002–2013	1991–2013	1991	2002	2013	1991–2002	2002–2013	1991–2013
Caribbean	125.3	179.1	219.2	100.0	100.0	100.0	3.3	1.9	2.6	11.7	13.9	16.5	100.0	100.0	100.0	1.6	1.5	1.6	10,736	12,876	13,315	1.7	0.3	1.0
Agriculture	7.1	6.9	8.6	5.7	3.8	3.9	-0.3	2.0	0.9	3.0	3.3	3.6	26.1	23.7	21.8	0.7	0.7	0.7	2328	2078	2387	-1.0	1.3	0.1
Mining & utilities	6.9	9.4	10.5	5.5	5.2	4.8	2.9	1.1	2.0	0.2	0.2	0.3	1.6	1.4	1.6	0.1	3.3	1.7	36,902	49,568	39,059	2.7	-2.1	0.3
Manufacturing	33.8	49.8	53.1	27.0	27.8	24.2	3.6	0.6	2.1	1.4	1.5	1.4	11.9	10.9	8.6	0.8	-0.6	0.1	24,396	32,844	37,511	2.7	1.2	2.0
Construction	7.5	9.1	11.4	6.0	5.1	5.2	1.8	2.0	1.9	0.7	0.8	0.9	5.7	5.4	5.3	1.2	1.3	1.2	11,270	12,045	13,020	0.6	0.7	0.7
Commerce	19.3	26.7	34.2	15.4	14.9	15.6	3.0	2.3	2.6	2.1	2.7	3.5	17.8	19.4	21.1	2.4	2.3	2.4	9337	9863	9852	0.5	0.0	0.2
Transport	6.5	11.5	17.9	5.2	6.4	8.1	5.4	4.0	4.7	0.5	0.7	0.9	4.6	5.1	5.6	2.7	2.3	2.5	12,157	16,150	19,363	2.6	1.7	2.1
Other services	44.2	65.8	83.5	35.2	36.7	38.1	3.7	2.2	2.9	3.8	4.7	5.9	32.4	34.0	36.0	2.1	2.1	2.1	11,693	13,909	14,108	1.6	0.1	0.9
Central America	616.5	836.2	1137.0	100.0	100.0	100.0	2.8	2.8	2.8	40.8	54.0	69.5	100.0	100.0	100.0	2.6	2.3	2.5	15,114	15,497	16,361	0.2	0.5	0.4
Agriculture	28.3	34.8	43.3	4.6	4.2	3.8	1.9	2.0	1.9	11.4	11.1	11.9	27.9	20.6	17.1	-0.2	0.6	0.2	2488	3132	3637	2.1	1.4	1.7
Mining & utilities	79.7	106.1	118.3	12.9	12.7	10.4	2.6	1.0	1.8	0.3	0.5	0.7	0.6	0.9	1.0	5.4	4.1	4.7	306,586	229,175	164,293	-2.6	-3.0	-2.8
Manufacturing	105.2	150.5	184.1	17.1	18.0	16.2	3.3	1.8	2.6	6.5	9.2	10.3	15.9	17.0	14.8	3.2	1.0	2.1	16,220	16,401	17,930	0.1	0.8	0.5
Construction	51.9	63.6	82.3	8.4	7.6	7.2	1.9	2.4	2.1	2.0	3.2	4.7	5.0	6.0	6.8	4.3	3.6	3.9	25,594	19,709	17,372	-2.3	-1.1	-1.7
Commerce	106.1	144.8	206.5	17.2	17.3	18.2	2.9	3.3	3.1	10.6	14.7	18.9	26.0	27.2	27.2	3.0	2.3	2.7	10,013	9866	10,944	-0.1	0.9	0.4
Transport	37.2	66.8	118.3	6.0	8.0	10.4	5.5	5.3	5.4	1.6	2.4	3.4	4.0	4.4	4.9	3.5	3.2	3.3	22,707	28,059	35,039	1.9	2.0	2.0
Other services	208.0	269.7	384.3	33.7	32.2	33.8	2.4	3.3	2.8	8.4	12.9	19.6	20.6	24.0	28.3	4.0	3.9	3.9	24,779	20,857	19,572	-1.6	-0.6	-1.1
South America	1003.2	1294.2	2018.8	100.0	100.0	100.0	2.3	4.1	3.2	113.4	149.5	192.6	100.0	100.0	100.0	2.5	2.3	2.4	8843	8659	10,481	-0.2	1.8	0.8
Agriculture	59.3	85.0	116.7	5.9	6.6	5.8	3.3	2.9	3.1	27.4	29.4	27.4	24.2	19.6	14.2	0.6	-0.6	0.0	2164	2896	4264	2.7	3.6	3.1
Mining & utilities	101.6	142.5	195.1	10.1	11.0	9.7	3.1	2.9	3.0	1.6	1.5	2.3	1.4	1.0	1.2	-0.8	4.3	1.7	63,445	97,397	84,234	4.0	-1.3	1.3
Manufacturing	185.8	223.8	321.5	18.5	17.3	15.9	1.7	3.4	2.5	16.4	19.1	23.5	14.5	12.8	12.2	1.4	1.9	1.6	11,320	11,733	13,689	0.3	1.4	0.9
Construction	60.8	69.9	125.1	6.1	5.4	6.2	1.3	5.4	3.3	6.6	9.7	15.4	5.8	6.5	8.0	3.6	4.3	3.9	9241	7226	8145	-2.2	1.1	-0.6
Commerce	168.2	200.3	350.4	16.8	15.5	17.4	1.6	5.2	3.4	23.9	33.4	45.8	21.1	22.3	23.8	3.1	2.9	3.0	7040	6000	7643	-1.4	2.2	0.4
Transport	71.9	106.3	184.3	7.2	8.2	9.1	3.6	5.1	4.4	5.0	8.2	12.4	4.4	5.5	6.5	4.6	3.9	4.2	14,345	12,992	14,836	-0.9	1.2	0.2
Other services	355.5	466.4	725.3	35.4	36.0	35.9	2.5	4.1	3.3	32.5	48.3	65.8	28.7	32.3	34.2	3.7	2.8	3.3	10,926	9649	11,026	-1.1	1.2	0.0

Source Calculated from UNSD and ILO

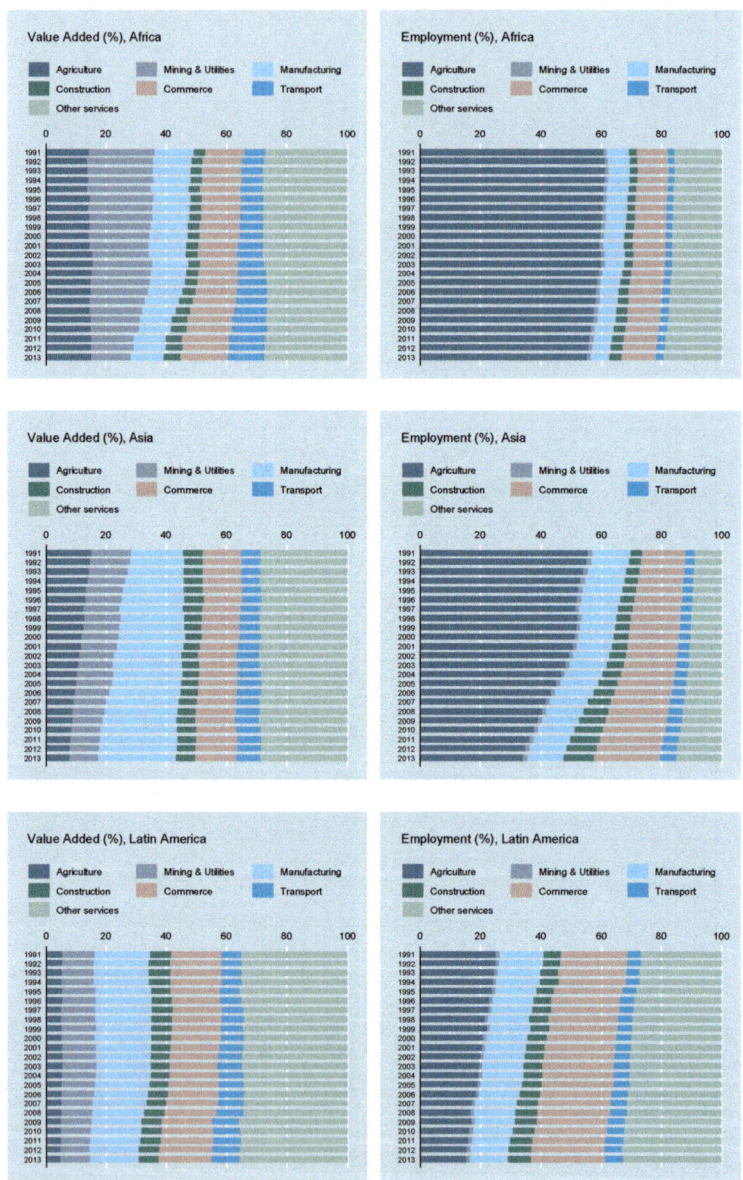

Fig. 3.A1 Structure of output and employment by region

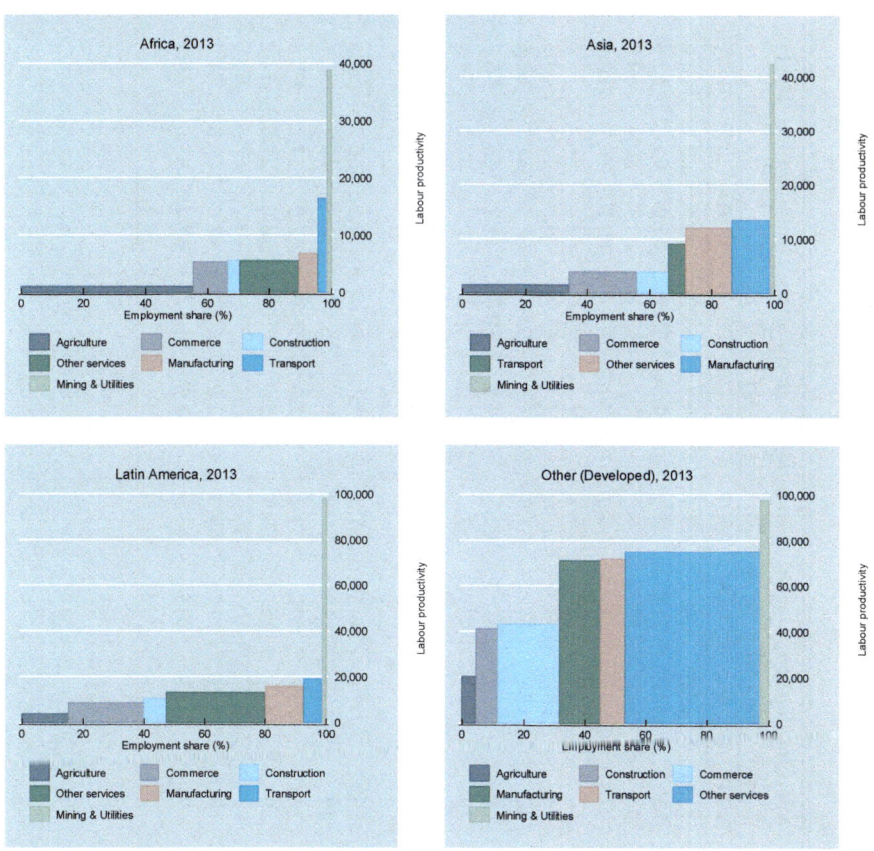

Fig. 3.A2   Labour productivity gaps, 2013

Table 3.A6 Demographics and employment rate

Region	Total population (millions)			Working-age population (15–64, millions)			Working-age population (% total population)			Employment rate (%)		
	1991	2002	2013	1991	2002	2013	1991	2002	2013	1991	2002	2013
World	**5343**	**6203**	**7072**	**3254**	**3946**	**4654**	**60.9**	**63.6**	**65.8**	**68.6**	**67.5**	**66.8**
Africa	**639**	**838**	**1097**	**335**	**457**	**611**	**52.4**	**54.6**	**55.7**	**61.9**	**61.8**	**63.6**
Eastern Africa	190	258	349	96	133	185	50.4	51.5	53.1	80.1	80.0	80.8
Middle Africa	72	99	136	37	50	71	50.8	50.7	52.1	69.5	70.1	70.0
Northern Africa	149	182	221	82	110	139	54.9	60.3	63.2	43.2	41.8	44.3
Southern Africa	43	53	60	25	33	39	57.6	63.1	64.4	44.0	44.9	44.3
Western Africa	185	246	331	96	131	177	51.9	53.2	53.3	61.3	61.1	62.5
Asia	**3099**	**3625**	**4108**	**1881**	**2339**	**2803**	**60.7**	**64.5**	**68.2**	**71.2**	**69.2**	**66.6**
Central Asia	51	56	64	29	34	43	57.3	61.2	66.3	62.7	62.0	64.1
Eastern Asia	1234	1351	1445	803	935	1056	65.0	69.2	73.1	81.1	79.2	76.0
South-Eastern Asia	458	547	628	272	350	420	59.5	64.1	67.0	72.0	71.3	73.1
Southern Asia	1217	1498	1749	698	914	1139	57.3	61.1	65.1	61.9	60.7	57.5
Western Asia	138	174	222	79	105	145	56.9	60.5	65.4	52.3	48.1	52.1
Latin America	**452**	**539**	**614**	**267**	**339**	**405**	**59.2**	**62.8**	**65.9**	**62.0**	**64.2**	**68.8**
Caribbean	33	37	40	20	23	26	60.9	63.0	65.4	58.0	59.3	62.2
Central America	118	144	167	67	87	107	56.7	60.2	63.9	61.2	62.4	65.0
South America	301	358	406	181	229	271	60.0	63.9	66.7	62.8	65.3	71.0
Other (Developed)	**1153**	**1201**	**1252**	**771**	**811**	**835**	**66.8**	**67.5**	**66.7**	**67.4**	**67.5**	**69.0**

Source Calculated from UNPD

Table 3.A7 Decomposition of GVA per capita growth—regions

Region/ period	Contribution from (percentage points)				GVA per capita growth (%)
	Within-sector productivity	Between-sector productivity	Changes in employ-ment	Changes in demogra-phy	
Africa (1991–2013)	**0.52**	**0.44**	**0.13**	**0.28**	**1.36**
1991–2002	−0.05	0.04	−0.02	0.36	0.33
2002–2013	1.10	0.84	0.28	0.19	2.41
Asia (1991–2013)	**3.74**	**1.10**	**−0.34**	**0.59**	**5.09**
1991–2002	3.39	0.58	−0.27	0.57	4.27
2002–2013	4.12	1.63	−0.36	0.54	5.92
Latin America (1991–2013)	**0.30**	**0.35**	**0.48**	**0.49**	**1.61**
1991–2002	−0.10	0.19	0.30	0.54	0.94
2002–2013	0.73	0.47	0.65	0.43	2.29
Other (1991–2013)	**1.05**	**0.26**	**0.11**	**−0.01**	**1.40**
1991–2002	1.36	0.33	0.00	0.10	1.80
2002–2013	0.68	0.23	0.21	−0.11	1.01

Table 3.A8 Decomposition of GVA per capita growth—Africa

Region/ period	Contribution from (percentage points)				GVA per cap-ita growth (%)
	Within-sector productivity	Between-sector productivity	Changes in employment	Changes in demography	
Eastern Africa (1991–2013)	**0.70**	**0.66**	**0.04**	**0.24**	**1.64**
1991–2002	−0.19	0.04	−0.01	0.19	0.03
2002–2013	1.65	1.25	0.10	0.29	3.28
Middle Africa (1991–2013)	**−0.08**	**0.83**	**0.04**	**0.11**	**0.89**
1991–2002	−2.40	0.91	0.08	−0.02	−1.44
2002–2013	2.25	0.78	0.00	0.24	3.27
Northern Africa (1991–2013)	**0.39**	**0.26**	**0.12**	**0.64**	**1.41**

(continued)

Table 3.A8   (contiuned)

Region/ period	Contribution from (percentage points)				GVA per capita growth (%)
	Within-sector productivity	Between-sector productivity	Changes in employment	Changes in demography	
1991–2002	0.06	0.28	−0.29	0.85	0.90
2002–2013	0.72	0.25	0.54	0.42	1.93
Southern Africa (1991–2013)	**0.64**	**0.10**	**0.03**	**0.51**	**1.28**
1991–2002	−0.79	0.22	0.19	0.84	0.46
2002–2013	2.04	0.01	−0.13	0.19	2.11
Western Africa (1991–2013)	**1.86**	**0.74**	**0.09**	**0.13**	**2.82**
1991–2002	1.10	0.12	−0.04	0.24	1.42
2002–2013	2.64	1.38	0.22	0.01	4.24

Table 3.A9   Decomposition of GVA per capita growth—Asia

Region/ period	Contribution from (percentage points)				GVA per capita growth (%)
	Within-sector productivity	Between-sector productivity	Changes in employment	Changes in demography	
Central Asia (1991–2013)	**0.67**	**0.41**	**0.11**	**0.67**	**1.86**
1991–2002	−2.95	−0.03	−0.10	0.59	−2.49
2002–2013	4.45	0.85	0.33	0.78	6.40
Eastern Asia (1991–2013)	**6.02**	**1.17**	**−0.37**	**0.65**	**7.47**
1991–2002	5.90	0.92	−0.23	0.61	7.21
2002–2013	5.84	1.78	−0.42	0.54	7.74
South-Eastern Asia (1991–2013)	**1.51**	**1.37**	**0.08**	**0.56**	**3.52**
1991–2002	0.97	1.37	−0.08	0.68	2.94
2002–2013	2.12	1.33	0.24	0.41	4.10
Southern Asia (1991–2013)	**3.05**	**0.76**	**−0.37**	**0.62**	**4.06**
1991–2002	2.41	0.31	−0.19	0.58	3.12
2002–2013	3.78	1.15	−0.52	0.61	5.01
Western Asia (1991–2013)	**1.00**	**0.70**	**−0.01**	**0.64**	**2.33**
1991–2002	1.13	0.52	−0.76	0.55	1.45
2002–2013	0.92	0.83	0.74	0.73	3.22

Table 3.A10 Decomposition of GVA per capita growth—Latin America

Region/ period	Contribution from (percentage points)				GVA per capita growth (%)
	Within-sector productivity	Between-sector productivity	Changes in employment	Changes in demography	
Caribbean (1991–2013)	1.06	−0.08	0.32	0.33	1.63
1991–2002	1.68	−0.01	0.20	0.30	2.17
2002–2013	0.46	−0.15	0.44	0.35	1.10
Central America (1991–2013)	−0.47	0.84	0.28	0.55	1.18
1991–2002	−0.84	1.07	0.17	0.55	0.95
2002–2013	−0.08	0.58	0.38	0.54	1.42
South America (1991–2013)	0.53	0.25	0.56	0.49	1.83
1991–2002	−0.19	0.00	0.36	0.57	0.74
2002–2013	1.30	0.46	0.77	0.40	2.93

Table 3.A11 Top-10 performers by (developing) region, 2002–2013

Region	Country	GVA per capita growth (%)	Contribution from (%)			
			GVA per worker		Employment rate	Demographic structure
			Within-sector	Between-sector		
Africa	NGA	5.1	2.5	2.6	0.1	−0.1
	ETH	6.9	3.5	2.5	0.3	0.7
	TZA	3.6	1.2	2.4	0.1	−0.1
	ZMB	3.2	1.5	1.7	0.1	−0.1
	UGA	2.4	1.4	1.4	−0.6	0.2
	GHA	4.7	2.7	1.3	0.4	0.4
	MRT	2.5	0.2	1.3	0.6	0.4
	TCD	4.3	3.3	0.9	−0.1	0.2
	CPV	3.2	0.4	0.9	0.3	1.7
	COD	3.3	2.3	0.8	−0.1	0.3
Asia	KHM	6.0	2.5	1.8	0.7	0.9
	VNM	5.4	2.8	1.7	−0.1	1.0
	LAO	5.9	3.2	1.7	−0.2	1.2
	AFG	5.3	3.3	1.6	0.0	0.5
	CHN	9.5	7.9	1.5	−0.5	0.6
	MDV	4.4	0.0	1.5	1.5	1.4
	IND	6.0	4.9	1.4	−0.8	0.6
	MNG	7.0	4.5	1.3	0.4	0.7
	IDN	4.3	2.6	1.2	0.4	0.1
	PNG	2.9	1.4	1.2	0.0	0.3

(continued)

Table 3.A11 (contiuned)

Region	Country	GVA per capita growth (%)	Contribution from (%)		Employment rate	Demographic structure
			GVA per worker			
			Within-sector	Between-sector		
Latin America	CHL	3.4	−0.3	1.4	1.9	0.4
& the	VEN	2.4	0.2	1.4	0.5	0.4
Caribbean	PER	5.0	2.2	1.3	1.0	0.5
	ECU	3.0	1.3	0.9	0.4	0.4
	HTI	0.6	−1.4	0.9	0.5	0.6
	BOL	2.7	0.7	0.9	0.6	0.6
	GTM	1.2	−0.7	0.7	0.7	0.5
	MEX	1.4	−0.1	0.7	0.3	0.5
	NIC	2.2	0.2	0.6	0.5	0.9
	BRB	1.0	−0.1	0.6	0.1	0.4

Note The table excludes countries with a negative GVA per capita growth rate. These are: Gabon (−1.0%), Guinea (−0.1%) and Yemen (−0.5%)

References

Chenery, H. (1960). Patterns of Industrial Growth. *American Economic Review, 50*, 624–653.

Chenery, H., & Taylor, L. (1968). Development Patterns: Among Countries and Over Time. *The Review of Economics and Statistics, 50*(4), 391–416.

Gollin, D., Lagakos, D., & Waugh, M. (2014). The Agricultural Productivity Gap. *The Quarterly Journal of Economics, 129*(2), 939–993.

Herrendorf, B., Rogerson, R., & Valentinyiet, A. (2014). Growth and Structural Transformation. In P. Aghion & S. Durlauf (Eds.), *Handbook of Economic Growth* (Vol. 2, pp. 855–941). Amsterdam, North Holland: Elsevier.

Kucera, D., & Roncolato, L. (2012). *Structure Matters: Sectoral Drivers of Growth and the Labour Productivity Employment Relationship* (ILO Research Paper 3). Geneva: ILO.

Kuznets, S. (1957). Quantitative Aspects of the Economic Growth of Nations: II. Industrial Distribution of National Product and Labor Force. *Economic Development and Cultural Change, 5*(Suppl. 4), 1–111.

Kuznets, S. (1966). *Modern Economic Growth*. New Haven: Yale University Press.

McMillan, M., & Harttgen, K. (2015). *What Is Driving the African Growth Miracle* (NBER Working Paper No. 20077).

McMillan, M., & Headey, D. (2014). Introduction—Understanding Structural Transformation in Africa. *World Development, 63,* 1–10.

McMillan, M., Rodrik, D., & Verduzco-Gallo, I. (2014). Globalization, Structural Change, and Productivity Growth, with an Update on Africa. *World Development, 63,* 11–32.

Shorrocks, A. (2013). Decomposition Procedures for Distributional Analysis: A Unified Framework Based on the Shapley Value. *The Journal of Economic Inequality, 11*(1), 99–126.

Timmer, M., de Vries, G., & de Vries, K. (2015). *Patterns of Structural Change in Developing Countries.* Groningen Growth and Development Centre, Research Memorandum 149.

UNCTAD. (2014). The Least Developed Countries Report 2014—Growth with Structural Transformation: A Post-2015 Development Agenda. New York and Geneva: United Nations.

World Bank. (2015). *Job Generation and Growth Decomposition Tool: Understanding the Sectoral Pattern of Growth and Its Employment and Productivity Intensity Reference Manual and User's Guide Version 1.0.* World Bank Group. Available via http://siteresources.worldbank.org/INTEMPSHAGRO/Resources/JoGGs_Decomposition_Tool_UsersGuide.pdf. Accessed mid-April 205.

4

Economic Regulation and Employment Intensity of Output Growth in Sub-Saharan Africa

Abidemi C. Adegboye, Monday I. Egharevba and Joel Edafe

Introduction

Availability of productive employment or "good jobs" is an essential aspect of modern economic existence, development and prosperity. This is because productive employment, that is widely accessible, is the quality road through which any improvement in economic performance could be translated into improved standards of living and guarantee of growth dividends to the poor (Golub and Hayat 2014; Khan 2008;

Prepared for the 17th Nordic conference on development economics 2018, 11–12 June 2018, Helsinki, Finland.

A. C. Adegboye (✉)
Department of Economics and Statistics,
University of Benin, Benin City, Nigeria

M. I. Egharevba · J. Edafe
Department of Finance and Economics,
Benson Idahosa University, Benin City, Nigeria

© The Author(s) 2019
A. B. Elhiraika et al. (eds.), *Governance for Structural Transformation in Africa*,
https://doi.org/10.1007/978-3-030-03964-6_4

101

World Bank 2005; International Labour Organization [ILO] 2003). Growth patterns that generate consistent and sustainable employment opportunities would, however, entail that:

1. the growth is accompanied by adequate structural transformation of the economy (Lewis 1954; McMillan and Harttgen 2014);
2. the growth occurs in all the sectors simultaneously in terms of productivity growth (Ranis and Fei 1961; Timmer et al. 2012);
3. demographic transition accompanies such growth processes (Fields 2012; Fuchs and Weyh 2014); and
4. there are institutional setups that facilitate labour absorption in the economy due to economic dualism (Agénor and Montiel 2008).

Apparently, a range of conditions need to be met in order for economic growth to yield employment and good jobs. Structural transformation that proceeds with effective demographic transition, with falling population and urban rates are critical for the growth–employment nexus. In particular, the fourth requirement highlights the role of government and its institutions in managing the growth–employment nexus, especially in economies with deep structural dualism and market imperfections.

Theoretical postulations about employment-enhancing growth that is based on effective factor reallocation have not been consistent with realities in SSA countries (Ajakaiye et al. 2016; Islam and Islam 2015; Pena 2013; Edwards 1988). In this region, respectable rates of economic growth in the past few decades have not been translated to similar rates of employment growth and transfer of workers to sectors with higher productivity. Indeed, the accompanying structural transformation of the economies, have actually resulted in productivity decline in the modern sectors (through increased informality). These have further weakened the ability of the sectors to generate more jobs (McMillan and Harttgen 2014; Agénor and Montiel 2008, p. 43).

Thus, the issue with growth in SSA countries is the inability to translate impressive growth rates to employment creation. Although available data on aggregate levels shows that unemployment (at 7.7% in

2014) is relatively not a critical issue in SSA (youth unemployment—at 11.8% in 2014—is however generally high), the case of productive employment opportunities is critical. Fields (2012, p. 202) aptly noted that "what the developing countries have is an employment problem rather than an unemployment problem". Though the labour force in the region is largely involved in some forms of activity, the jobs being performed do not guarantee their livelihood. For instance, World Bank (2012) expressed the peculiarities of the employment challenge to include the poor aspects of work people do, reallocation of labour to better jobs and generally creating new jobs. Indeed, some authors have stated that employment problems in SSA increased during the years of high economic growth (Krueger 1983; McMillan and Harttgen 2014; Page and Shimeles 2015).

Furthermore, deep segmentation in the region's labour markets may lead to irregularities that may not be self-adjusting (Krueger 1983; Agénor and Montiel 2008), requiring institutional regulations. The conditions of informal employment within the urban sectors in African economies have intensified in recent periods (Fields 2007; McMillan and Harttgen 2014). This has resulted from the surge in migrants from rural areas seeking for jobs in the urban areas. As the Harris and Todaro (1970) model shows, with persistently rising population, improvements in the urban or modern sectors may actually lead to reduction in overall employment in the country.

Thus, regulations and government involvement tend to play essential roles in facilitating employment during periods of economic growth. In pursuing employment enhancing growth, regulatory institutions in SSA countries could function in the areas of controlling excessive population growth, ensuring smooth factor reallocation and aiding balanced growth. In this direction, policies that regulate labour market and other economic activities are essential in aiding feasible employment outcomes given the structural bottlenecks in many SSA economies. These forms of institutional setups have been said to favour employment security.

Despite the attractiveness of regulations to enhance transitions in the growth–employment relationships for SSA economies, its use has been noted to also possess certain inhibitory abilities, especially on formal sector employment. As Henrekson (2014) noted, excessive regulations of the formal sector increases "incentives to circumvent the regulations" as demonstrated in several European countries through "increased self-employment, a larger underground economy, and greater reliance on temporary employment" (p. 13). It has therefore been argued that while regulations promote pro-poor growth, it could be an effective hindrance to formal sector employment activities (Ernst and Berg 2009).

In this study, we acknowledge the peculiarities of SSA economies with extensive dualities in labour and product markets, and ask the question whether employment resulting from output growth could be enhanced with adequate economic regulation in the region. We argue that "demand-side" factors of structural transformation and productivity changes (as shown in McMillan and Rodrik 2011; McMillan and Harttgen 2014) and "supply-side" factors of demographic transition alone do not provide an adequate explanation of the growth employment relationship for SSA. Although a number of research has presented both theoretical and empirical bases for labour and production integration within dualistic structures (Lewis 1954, 1958; Ranis and Fei 1961; Pasinetti 1981; Fields 2012), market segmentation could, in practice, present strong challenges with respect to job creation resulting from growth. Indeed, labour market and other economic institutions and regulatory processes play a key role in explaining international differences in labour market performance. We seek to show in this study that regulatory activities within African economies can provide the stimulating background for labour markets behaviour in the region.

Economic Performance and Employment in SSA

Overall economic performance in Sub-Saharan Africa (SSA) countries has been impressive since the late 1990s. The major reason often considered for the performance has been improved terms of trade due to commodity price increases and favourable domestic institutional environment that has been enhanced by nascent democracies in most of the countries (Iyoha and Oriakhi 2008; Golub and Hayat 2014;

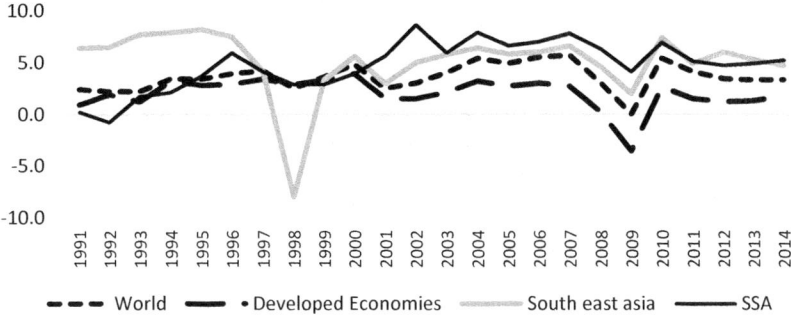

Fig. 4.1 Economic growth in SSA and other regions (*Source* Based on data from WDI)

UNCTAD 2008). Figure 4.1 shows the performance of the SSA economies in comparison with other regions of the world. It can be seen that between 2000 and 2010, SSA reported the highest growth rate of GDP among all the other regions and the rate has remained high since. In 2009 for instance, SSA recorded growth rate of 4.1% while global average growth rate for that period was 0.01%. It is therefore clear that the SSA region has performed well in terms of economic growth in the past two decades. A transpicuous reality from Fig. 3.1 is the well-defined pattern of growth performance that is in line with commodity price movements. Growth rate started to rise appreciably after 1998, marking the beginning of good fortunes in the international commodity market. This also buttresses the assertion about the strong effects of natural resource in economic fortunes in the SSA region.

Figure 4.2 shows the trend and movements in output and employment growth among the SSA sample from 1990 to 2014. There is evidence that the two variables grew at divergent rates in the 1990s but tended to move together after 2003. Remarkably, the closer correlation coincided with the period in which the continent's growth rate in GDP improved tremendously; note that the growth rates were higher on average and more stable from 2003. While employment growth was mostly negative before 2003, it was mostly positive after then (apart from 2009), reaching a maximum of 0.56 in 2005. It appears that stable and fast growing systems tend to exhibit better employment effects.

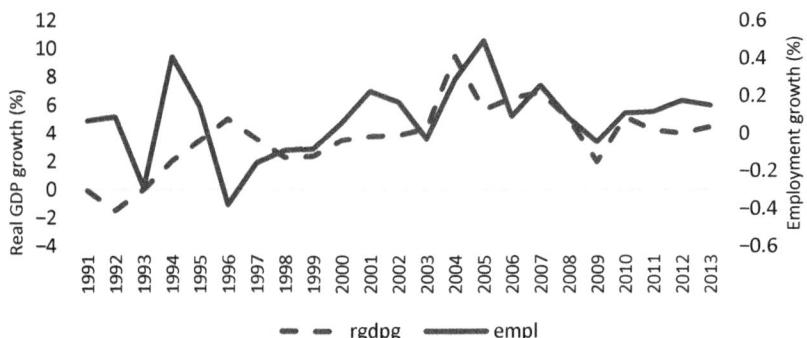

Fig. 4.2 Output growth and employment growth in SSA (*Source* Based on data from WDI)

The historical data thus shows that there is a basic positive relationship between employment growth and output growth. The broad-based economic upturn in Africa in the last decade and growing profitability have supported business owners to expand their workforce and investment. It should, however, be noted that employment growth trend line was below the GDP growth trend line for most of the period. This suggests that changes in employment were lower than changes in GDP growth in the region.

Sub-Saharan Africa countries have experienced much structural transformation since the 1960s. Table 4.1 provides information on individual countries and shows the largest sectors as part of GDP and the largest sectors in terms of total employment. The table is based on the study by Gong (2015) on the structure of economies in Africa. It takes the data on individual countries for an initial year (between 1960 and 1990) and a final year (between 2010 and 2014). The table shows how the economies have evolved over time from one sector to another in terms of employment and value-added output.

The observations from Table 4.1 indicate that in the initial year, there were only five countries from all African economies that had industry as the largest sector in their GDP and none of the countries had industry as the largest employment sector. In the final year, there were only eight countries that had industry as the largest sector in GDP and there is, again, no country that had industry as the largest sector in employment.

Table 4.1 Largest sectors in SSA economies (1960–1980—initial year and 1990–2015—latest year)

Largest sector in economies (initial year)	Agriculture	Industry	Services
Largest sector in GDP	Angola, Benin, Burkina Faso, Burundi, Cameroon, Central African Republic, Chad, Congo, Côte d'Ivoire, Djibouti, DRC, Ethiopia, Gambia, Ghana, Guinea, Kenya, Liberia, Malawi, Mali, Mozambique, Namibia, Niger, Nigeria, Rwanda, Sierra Leone, Senegal, Seychelles, Somalia, Sudan, Tanzania, Togo, Uganda, Zimbabwe	Equatorial Guinea, Eritrea, Gabon, Swaziland	Botswana, Cape Verde, Comoros, Mauritius, São Tomé and Príncipe, Zambia
Largest sector in total employment	Angola, Benin, Botswana, Burkina Faso, Burundi, Cameroon, Cape Verde, Chad, Congo, Côte d'Ivoire, DRC, Djibouti, Ethiopia, Equatorial Guinea, Eritrea, Ghana, Guinea, Kenya, Liberia, Mali, Nigeria, Namibia, Rwanda, Senegal, Sierra Leone, Sudan, Togo, Tunisia, Uganda, Zambia, Zimbabwe		Gabon, Lesotho, Mauritius, Swaziland, São Tomé and Principe

Table 4.1 (continued)

Largest Sector in Economies (final year)		
Largest sector in GDP	Central African Republic, Comoros, Guinea, Seychelles, Sierra Leone, Somalia	Angola, Congo, Djibouti, Equatorial Guinea, Eritrea, Ethiopia, Gabon, Swaziland	Benin, Botswana, Burkina Faso, Burundi, Cameroon, Cape Verde, Chad, Côte d'Ivoire, DRC, Gambia, Ghana, Kenya, Liberia, Libya, Malawi, Mali, Mauritius, Mozambique, Namibia, Niger, Nigeria, Rwanda, São Tomé and Príncipe, Senegal, Sudan, Tanzania, Togo, Uganda, Zambia, Zimbabwe
Largest sector in total employment	Burkina Faso, Burundi, Cameroon, Chad, DRC, Egypt, Equatorial Guinea, Eritrea, Ghana, Guinea, Mali, Mauritius, Nigeria, Rwanda, Senegal, Sierra Leone, Sudan, Togo, Uganda, Zimbabwe		Angola, Benin, Botswana, Cape Verde, Congo, Côte d'Ivoire, Djibouti, Ethiopia, Gabon, Kenya, Lesotho, Liberia, Namibia, São Tomé and Príncipe, Swaziland, Zambia

Source Adapted from Gong (2015, pp. 6–7)

In addition to the initial five countries, three countries—Angola, Congo and Djibouti—had joined the rank on countries with largest industry share in GDP. For most of the countries (including Nigeria), agriculture was the largest sector in term of both GDP and employment for the initial year, but services sector took over as the largest sector both in terms of GDP share and employment in the final year. Though the services sector had the largest employment share for only eight countries in the initial year, sixteen countries eventually had more people employed in the services sector in the final year.

Table 4.1 also highlights that though agriculture has remained the largest employment sector for a majority of the countries, its sectoral share GDP has declined over the years. The data in Africa has reinforced the evidence that the process of economic structural transformation has been moving employment and output from the agricultural sector to the services sector. While factors that affect the direction and pace of structural transformation of an economy may include demand and supply factors, demographic and geographic variables, organisational capabilities, institutions and policies have also contributed significantly to such changes (Gong 2015). It is now left to determine whether the movement of labour has been beneficial to the economies in order to grow employment. From the perspective of productivity of labour in the new sectors, McMillan and Rodrik (2011) noted that the movement has actually hindered productivity (and employment) growth in the region.

A major labour market characteristic in SSA is the economic nature of employment. According to Campbell (2013), this employment characteristic tends to explain the benefit of output growth in employment determination. Table 4.2 shows the economic nature of employment for the region. Own-account workers dominated labour market employment for the entire period. These are the self-employed individuals whose income and productivity levels have been generally low (Campbell 2013). Interestingly, employers (entrepreneurs) had the least share in total employment with a proportion of 1.5% in 2014. Considering that entrepreneurship is essential for structural changes and rising income (especially in the industrial sector), the nature of employment in SSA has tended to exhibit self-effacing characteristics.

Table 4.2 Economic nature of employment in SSA

Period	Wage and salary workers	Employers	Own-account workers	Contributing family workers
1991–1999	18.0	1.1	51.0	30.0
2000–2005	19.0	1.0	51.0	28.0
2006–2010	21.0	1.0	50.0	28.0
2011	21.3	1.4	49.6	27.7
2012	21.6	1.4	49.3	27.6
2013	21.7	1.5	49.1	27.7
2014	21.9	1.5	49.1	27.5

Source Based on data from ILO, Key Indicators of Labour Markets (KILM)

Wage and salary workers were the only employment group that experienced proportional increase between 1991 and 2014, from 18.0% of total employment to 21.9%. The prevalence of own-account workers (or self-employment) in the region is due to the nature of labour market, where high under-employment can be absorbed into the informal sector.

Benefits derived from employment are particularly expressed in the level of social and economic security inherent in such jobs. Figure 4.3 shows the types of employment in SSA and other regions in terms of the level of vulnerability. Vulnerability of employment indicates the level of security of jobs as well as social and economic stability such jobs

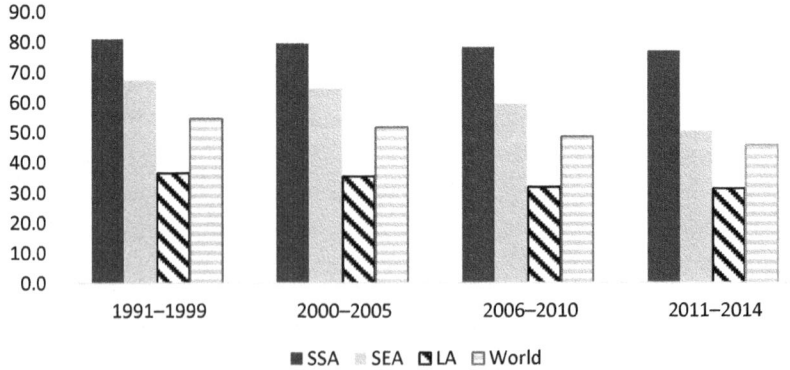

Fig. 4.3 Vulnerable employment (*Source* Based on data from ILO, Key Indicators of Labour Markets (KILM))

could provide. Vulnerable employment for the entire world economy, South-East Asia and Latin America are also reported. The chart shows that the SSA region (first bar) had more vulnerable employment than any other region over the period. The situation is actually precarious; since 1991, vulnerable employment has reached close to 80% of total employment secured in the region. Moreover, vulnerability does not appear to be slowing down over the period. The proportion of vulnerability of the many jobs being provided in the region remained constant. This is a demonstration of the fundamental issue in employment for the SSA region presented by Fields (2007, 2012) and Campbell (2013) that though employment activities are rampant in the region, the types of jobs provided are not economically viable. High vulnerability in employment is a natural consequence of the excess unproductive employment that pervades SSA economies.

Brief Review of Literature

Theoretical Basis for Growth and Employment

Much of the relationship between growth and employment has been widely studied based on variations of Okun's law. Indeed, the distribution of employment among agriculture, industry and service within countries is closely related to the level of real gross domestic product per capita (Fuchs 1980). In his work, Okun (1962) formalised a constant inverse relationship between the unemployment rate and growth in real output. This has been extended as a measure on which to evaluate how economic growth generates employment over time. For most of the studies, estimation of employment elasticities has been the main focus, while few studies have employed decomposition and other methods. Schalk and Untied (2000) discussed the link between employment and growth with a special focus on the German economy. They estimated Okun equations and concluded that Okun's law is a valid approximation.

Empirical research has identified a number of channels through which the equilibrium rate of unemployment and the process of economic growth could potentially affect each other even in the very long term. Calmfors and Holmlund (2000) and Landmann (2004) have investigated the following:

i. *The capitalisation effect.* More rapid growth raises the rate of return on hiring and may thereby lower equilibrium unemployment.
ii. *Creative destruction.* If economic growth brings about structural change, more rapid growth raises the rate of job destruction and may thereby raise frictional and structural unemployment.
iii. *Biased technological change.* If the technological change affects the structure of labour demand, favouring skilled labour at the expense of the unskilled, if wage differentials are rigid and if the structure of labour supply is slow in responding to changing skill requirements, then more rapid growth may raise equilibrium unemployment.
iv. *Joint determination of unemployment and growth.* The same political and institutional framework that shapes the operation of the labour market may also affect the dynamism of economic growth (Scarpetta et al. 2002).

Employment Elasticity of Growth

Employment elasticities are econometric estimations of the partial correlation relationships between output growth and employment growth in an economy (Kapsos 2005; Pattanaik and Nayak 2011). This can also be extended employment and demographic and other factors that determine employment in an economy. In general, estimation of employment elasticities is generally referred to as indirect analysis of the employment problem (Fuchs and Weyh 2014; Slimane 2015). It is used to show a historical perspective on employment intensiveness of recorded economic growth, and the extent to which any production increase leads to changes in quantity of employment (Anderson 2015). From another perspective, elasticities of this form could be regarded as measures of labour absorption in an economy.

As demonstrated in Kapsos (2005), Pattanaik and Nayak (2011) and Anderson (2015), the methodology adopted in estimating employment elasticities or indirect effects of economic growth on employment is to specify an employment equation with only output as the explanatory factor:

$$E_i = f(Y_i) \tag{4.1}$$

where E is employment and Y is output. More appropriately, the equation is estimated in log-linear form such that the coefficient of Y in the model represents the given elasticity.

Many studies have adopted the elasticities analysis to estimate the employment effects or employment intensity of growth both for single country and country group cases. For instance, Kapsos (2005) provided comprehensive employment intensities for 160 countries for the period 1991–2003 and was able to distinguish the pattern of employment intensities among different income groups. Other studies have localised the analysis to single economies (Pattanaik and Nayak 2011; Basu and Das 2015; Mkhize 2016).

Kapsos (2005), who presented an in-depth estimation of employment elasticities of growth highlighted two basic shortcomings of elasticities analysis. First, specified equations used for elasticity reveal that the current methodology utilised to produce employment elasticities only takes into account information pertaining to historical employment and output growth. The estimated employment elasticities may suffer from omitted variable bias (see Greene 2011) as no other variables that may influence either employment performance or overall economic performance are controlled for in this simple model used for estimating elasticities. To internalise this issue, the results of employment elasticity estimates are interpreted as "evidence of correlation rather than of causality" (Kapsos 2005, p. 5).

The second issue is that of relatively rapid swings in GDP performance within a country that may lead to large degree of volatility of employment elasticities from one period to the next. To address this issue, the elasticity estimations are broken down into multi-year periods spread over the entire sample period. This helps to smooth out annual fluctuations in elasticity estimates and also provides strong indications about the occurrences of any structural changes in employment over time. The elasticity estimates will also show whether the sectors with the highest growth rates are actually the ones churning out more jobs or not.

One of the earlier and most extensive studies on employment elasticity of growth for a panel of countries was conducted by Kapsos (2005). In the study, he estimated country, regional and global estimates of the employment intensity of economic growth over the period 1991–2003 for general employed population as well as different demographic groups. From data available for 160 economies, Kapsos estimated point elasticities and also extended to the determinants of such elasticities. Surprisingly, the study found that the most employment-intensive growth was registered in Africa and the Middle East when other macroeconomic factors were controlled for. The results from the study also suggested that employment elasticities were positively related with the share of services in the economy, and negatively related with inflation and taxes on labour. In contrast, no statistically significant relation was found between employment elasticities and (i) employment protection regulations and (ii) measures of globalisation and export orientation.

Döpke (2001), presented employment intensities for European and other selected advanced economies. He estimated various versions of Okun's law and analysed the long-run relationship between (log) employment and (log) GDP for single countries, a using time-series approach. He adopted the error correction method in order to combine short-term effects on employment with long-run impacts derived from the cointegration equation (DOLS). His result showed that lower real labour costs, greater labour market flexibility and less exchange rate volatility had significant impacts on employment elasticities. In the same direction, Mourre (2004) estimated employment elasticities for the Euro area based on the CES production function and segregating data for different periods. The results from the estimations showed that lower real labour costs tended to increase employment elasticities in the Euro area. He also found that job intensity of growth has been highest in the service sector.

Slimane (2015) assessed the determinants of cross-country variations in employment elasticities, focusing particularly on the role of demographic and macroeconomic variables. Long-term employment–GDP elasticities were estimated using an unbalanced panel of 90 developing countries from 1991 to 2011 using a two steps estimation strategy. The study finds that employment elasticities tended to be higher in more advanced and closed countries. In terms of policy directions, the study showed that macroeconomic policies aimed at reducing macroeconomic (price) volatility had significant effects in increasing employment elasticities. Moreover, the study found that countries with a larger service sector and a higher share of urban population exhibited higher employment elasticities of growth.

Basu and Das (2015) investigated the phenomenon of jobless growth in India and the United States by presenting employment elasticities for the two countries. Using employment and output data, the level and change of aggregate employment elasticity were decomposed in terms of sectoral elasticities, relative growth and employment shares. The results showed that the agricultural sector was the key determinant of both the level and change of aggregate elasticity for a long time in India. For the United States, services and manufacturing sectors were shown to be the most important determinants of the levels and changes, respectively, in aggregate employment elasticity.

Studies with a particular focus on SSA (both as a panel and individual countries) varied. Bbaale (2013) investigated the relationship between economic growth and employment in Uganda for the period 2006–2011. Adopting the Job Generation and Decomposition (JoGGs) Tool of the World Bank for the analysis, they found that agricultural sector registered the greatest dampening effect on overall value added per person and to the share of the employed in the population of working age by 31 and 6.5%, respectively. Their results also showed that the manufacturing sector contributed negatively to change in total employment rate by 0.2% but positive contributions to the employment rate and per capita GDP were observed in the services and industrial sectors.

Page and Shimeles (2015) investigated the disconnect between economic growth and poverty reduction in Africa. They argued that the disjoint could be linked to inadequate good jobs resulting from the growth in the region. The study found that since structural transformation (in terms of the relative growth of employment in high productivity sectors) did not contribute to economic growth in the region, the fastest growing economies exhibited the least responsiveness of employment to growth.

Akinkugbe (2015) in a study for Zambia found that while employment elasticities were positive and significant for most sectors of the economy during the period 1990–2008, the mining, and the finance, insurance and business services sectors recorded negative elasticities. This implied the declining propensities to generate employment over the two-decade period by the mining and finance sectors. Ajilore and Yinusa (2011) explored the employment intensity of sectoral output growth in Botswana. They found that the Botswanan economy exhibited low labour absorptive capacity at the aggregate and at sectoral decompositions. Mkhize (2016) investigated sectoral employment intensities in eight non-agricultural sectors of the South African economy in the period 2000Q1–2012Q2. They found that that total non-agricultural employment and GDP did not move together in the long run, implying that jobless growth occurred in South Africa during the period in their review.

For Nigeria, Ajakaiye et al. (2016) examined the relationship between growth and employment using the Shapley decomposition approach, complemented with econometric estimation of the country's employment intensity of growth. Their findings revealed that Nigeria's growth "over the last decade had been 'jobless' and sustained largely by factor reallocations rather than productivity enhancement".

Economic Regulations and Employment Elasticity of Output

Regulations and other institutional factors have been shown to exert level effects on both economic growth and the outcomes of growth. For instance, the role of active and effective institutions was noted to have both direct and indirect linkages with the inputs as well as outcomes of the growth processes. The general idea can be illustrated as follows (Sorensen and Whitta-Jacobsen 2010):

Quality of institutions and social infrastructure
↓
Propensity to save and invest, to educate and ability to turn inputs into output, A in the standard production function
↓
Output and income per worker (productivity outcome)

The causality indicated by the second arrow is exactly the content of the Solow-type model with human capital having the overall conclusion that the basic parameters of human and physical capital are decisive for productivity growth. The first arrow represents the idea that the quality of institutions affects these basic parameters. Putting it all together implies a positive influence of the quality of institutions on workers' productivity and effective employment. Ernst and Berg (2009) also presented the relevance of institutions and policies of the labour market as instrumental in improving social justice and, as such, can be an effective tool in promoting pro-poor employment.

Models and Methods

Estimation of Employment Intensity (Elasticity) of Growth

The theoretical linkage between output and the employment behaviour in an economy is often demonstrated by considering that employment, productivity and aggregate output are all endogenously determined (Rifkin 1994; Pissarides and Vallanti 2004; Landmann 2004; Agénor and Montiel 2008). The three variables are linked by the so-called "fundamental identity" (Rifkin 1994; Landmann 2004):

$$\text{output} = \text{employment} \times \text{productivity} \tag{4.2}$$

which, for small rates of change, can approximately be translated into

$$\text{output growth} \sim \text{employment growth} + \text{productivity growth}. \tag{4.3}$$

Econometric estimation of employment elasticities shows how employment in an economy changes as output also changed. It is an indicator of the level of responsiveness of employment to economic growth. When sectoral elasticities are computed, they show the absorptive capacities of each sector in terms of employment generation (Basu and Das 2015). The methodology that will be adopted for the elasticity analysis in this section is based on the original panel study by Kapsos (2005) and applied by Islam and Islam (2015) and Anderson (2015). The baseline model for elasticity is specified as:

$$lnE_{it} = \alpha + \beta_1 lnY_{it} + \sum_{i=1}^{n} \beta_{2i} lnY_{it} \times D_i + \sum_{i=1}^{n} \beta_{2i} D_i + \mu_{it} \quad (4.4)$$

where lnE is the log of employment, lnY is the log of real output for country i in year t, D is a country dummy variable and u is the random error term. Differentiating (partially) Eq. (4.4) with respect to Y gives us the output elasticity of employment for the economy as:

$$\frac{\partial E_{it}}{\partial Y_{it}} \left(\frac{Y_{it}}{E_{it}} \right) = \beta_1 + \sum_{i=1}^{n} \beta_{2i} \times D_i \quad (4.5)$$

Based on this econometric method, $\beta_1 + \beta_2$ represents the change in employment associated with a differential change in output for a particular economy. For instance, if $\beta_1 + \beta_2$ is 0.6 in an economy, then every 1 percentage point of GDP growth is associated with employment growth of 0.6 percentage points.

For the sake of the current study where structural issues and labour markets are relevant, differences in the employment–output relationship among different subsets of the population will be estimated. Thus, eleven (11) separate elasticities will be calculated for each of the countries in the sample. The first seventeen elasticities correspond to different demographic groups including the total employed, by sex (females and males), by age group (youth), in terms of formality (wage/salary, employers and own account), by class (extremely poor and poor) and by vulnerability of employment. Equation (4.4) above will be used to generate the seventeen elasticities. For these estimates, E_{it} represents employment for the respective group while Y_{it} represents total GDP. It should be noted that GDP data is not available for each of the demographic groups in the study, hence total GDP was used in the calculation of each of the elasticities.

Due to the endogeneity between employment and output, the elasticity equations are estimated using an instrumental variable technique. In particular, the Two Stage Least Squares technique is adopted for the estimation and the first lag of output is used as instrument in the estimation. Behar (2012) and Crivelli et al. (2012) have argued that a cointegration relationship exists between output and employment which suggests that the lag of employment should be included in estimating the relationship. This pattern of estimation has however been shown to be suited particularly for estimating short-run elasticities while the long-run outcomes are similar to the estimates using our model (Eq. 4.5).

Regulation, Structural Transformation and Employment Elasticities

In order to determine how economic regulation and other factors affect employment elasticities, a model that specifies the determinants of the employment elasticities is estimated. In carrying out this estimation, the study follows the propositions by Slimane (2015) and Kapsos (2005). The model for estimating the determinants of employment elasticity of growth is specified for a panel data form as:

$$\xi_{it} = \Omega_{it} + \delta R_{it} + \lambda S_{it} + \pi X + \psi_{it} \qquad (4.6)$$

where ξ is the estimated employment elasticity, R represents the regulation variables, S denotes structural variables and X denotes the other variables included in the model, and δ, λ, π are the coefficients of interest. Each of the regressors, as described in the model, will be obtained by taking average samples over each of the multi-year period for each of the countries. Since data used will cover 1991–2014, three multi-year periods will be used in the estimations. These are 1991–1999, 2000–2009 and 2010–2014.

Apart from the advantage of the multi-year period stated above, the disaggregation of the periods is aligned with certain regional economic occurrences that remarkably affected SSA countries. 1991 to late 1990s was the era of low commodity prices, accompanied by a poor economic performance for most of the countries in the region. It also marked the period when economies in the region began to make some improvements. The 2000s marked the period of high growth rates and large output in most of the SSA countries, while the period after 2009 was like a peak period for African economic performance (Gong 2015). The model in (4.6) above also gives an indication concerning the rate of adjustment of the labour market to structural and demographic factors in the SSA region.

Variables in the Model

The factors that affect employment elasticity of output is usually categorised into structural, macroeconomic, demographic and policy/institutional. Though the focus of the study is on the effects of institutional variables that are related to economic regulation, the other two broad factors are also taken into account. In particular, structural factors are critical in explaining the relationship in the study since it provides the background for assessing factor reallocation and productivity changes. Demographic factors are also important in describing the supply side of the labour market. Both structural and demographic factors can also interact with regulatory factors to determine the output-employment nexus.

Economic regulation in this study is defined as the ability and effectiveness of the government to control markets and production activities in the economy. From the perspective of this study, the focus of such regulations is on labour market activities. Regulations are conceived to be subsumed within legal systems of the economy or institutional wage-bargaining systems or obligations towards employees that are imposed on employers. Such measures could alter the pattern of employment being generated, impose limits on innovative firm growth or outrightly reduce employment growth (Henrekson 2014).

The variable is based on estimates provided by the Fraser Institute's Economic Freedom of the World (EFW) database. The database provides composite measures of overall economic freedom and economic freedom indicators in five areas, including size of governments, legal system and property rights, sound money, freedom to trade internationally and regulation. The regulation indicator is further decomposed into credit market regulation, labour market regulation and business regulation. For the purpose of this study, four indicators are used to measure economic regulation, namely, the overall index of economic freedom, indicator of size of government, indicator of legal and property rights and labour market regulation. In terms of its effects on employment elasticity of output, it is expected that the regulatory measures would have varying effects. For instance, more regulation is expected to limit overall employment over time. This is because though regulation may promote employment of the poor, continued and excessive regulations may reduce formal sector employment in the long run. Since most economies are seeking to boost formal employment in SSA region, more regulations could hinder overall employment growth.

Another indirect regulation factor included in the model is the share of government consumption in total GDP. Though this variable is structural in nature, the public sector is critical in labour market implications of structural changes in SSA economies. Its role is extensive both in influencing labour market conditions through wage control in the formal sector (as in Harris and Todaro 1970) and through direct participation in production and employment process (Kuznets 1973). Although privatisation and increased private sector participation is a major indicator of structural changes, there has been clear evidence that wage employment is positively correlated with the size of government (Armah et al. 2014). However, it has been shown in the H-T model that higher wages in the urban sector do not have to be a result of legislation only. Stiglitz (1974) has provided a number of "efficiency wage" factors that could realistically cause such differentials. In our model, we consider that FDI inflows and desire for internationalisation could cause urban firms to raise wages. To account for this, the FDI–GDP ratio is included as a determinant of employment elasticity.

Like in basic models (e.g. Kapsos 2005; Anderson 2016), three structural variables are included, namely, the respective shares of agriculture, industry and services in total output (measured in value-added terms). It is expected that a widening services sector world facilitate ease of absorption of labour—whatever the type—when output rises. This is because of the capacity of the sector to create both formal and informal employment to a rising labour in the modern sector. Thus, the effect of the share of services in total output is expected to be positive, while that of the industrial sector is not determined *apriori*. The share of agricultural sector in output is not included in the estimation, implying that the coefficients of the other share variables are interpreted in relation to agricultural sector share.

Three demographic variables are used in the model, including average annual growth in labour force, population density and proportion of population in urban areas. Two of the variables are founded on previous empirical evaluation (Kapsos 2005; Fuchs and Weyh 2014) while the rate of urbanisation is an additional factor proposed in this study based on the theoretical framework on the Harris-Todaro model and in Chenery and Syrquin (1986). The theoretical presentation proposes that gap in output is closely related to how output growth yields employment levels, hence volatility of output growth is included in the model. Given the roles of investment spending in determining the size of production and output in an economy, the investment rate is also included in the model in line with the argument in Anderson (2016). Together there are twelve explanatory variables that will be included as the factors that determine employment elasticity for the SSA region.

In estimating Eq. (4.6), the presence of heteroskedasticity must be taken into account since the dependent variable is itself estimated (Lewis and Linzer 2005; Anderson 2016). A weighted Generalised Least Squares estimation technique is, therefore, better suited to produce unbiased and consistent estimation. In this direction, the Feasible Generalized Least Squares (FGLS) technique is used for estimating the elasticity determinants equations. The estimations used data for 37 Sub-Saharan Africa countries for the period 1991–2014 based on data availability. Further data definitions and sources are reported in the appendix.

Empirical Analysis

Data Description

We begin the empirical analysis by reporting the estimated employment elasticities for the subperiods in the sample for each of the groups. The average growth rates of GDP, total employment and productivity are also reported along with the elasticities. As expected, elasticities were higher during the period when growth rate was highest (2010–2014). This indicates that the rate of responsiveness of employment to output growth generally increases when output growth rises. Elasticity of total employment was low during the 1991–1999 period and the standard deviation was also high, suggesting that the elasticities were generally unstable during the period. Both male and female employment elasticities are similar in trend to that of total employment with female elasticity slightly higher than that of total average. Youth employment elasticity is however much lower than the average for each of the subperiods. Though the rate was similar to the overall employment rate in the initial period, youth employment elasticity did not rise as rapidly as the total (or male and female) level over the next periods. This underscores the challenge of rising youth unemployment in the SSA region (Table 4.3).

In terms of status in employment, wage employment was higher than that of total employment level over the entire period and it rose drastically between the 1991–1999 and 2010–2014 periods. Apparently, economic growth in the region has effectively favoured wage employment, perhaps through government employment programmes or expansion of private sector activities (often caused by the inflow of foreign firms). Since institutional background in a country is a major factor considered by foreign firms, the large wage employment elasticity of output suggests that improved institutions may have had indirect positive impacts on the elasticity through attracting foreign firms into the countries. The elasticity of self-employment, on the other hand, remained virtually constant at 0.24 over the entire period. The rise in output growth did not change the responsiveness of the employment group over time.

Table 4.3 Employment elasticities

Employment elasticity	1991–1999 Mean (Std. dev)	2000–2009 Mean (Std. dev)	2010–2014 Mean (Std. dev)
Total employment elasticity	0.16 (0.20)	0.36 (0.21)	0.45 (0.21)
Demographic roups			
Male employment	0.16 (0.20)	0.34 (0.21)	0.45 (0.21)
Female employment	0.17 (0.21)	0.39 (0.22)	0.46 (0.22)
Youth employment	0.16 (0.20)	0.30 (0.21)	0.38 (0.21)
Status in employment			
Wage employment	0.18 (0.19)	0.58 (0.22)	0.62 (0.22)
Self	0.25 (0.23)	0.24 (0.22)	0.25 (0.22)
Economic status			
Extreme poor	0.09 (0.26)	−0.02 (0.25)	−0.15 (0.25)
Poor	0.17 (0.21)	0.57 (0.25)	0.59 (0.24)
Middle class	0.22 (0.21)	1.03 (0.29)	1.11 (0.24)
Vulnerable employment	0.14 (0.23)	0.23 (0.24)	0.30 (0.24)
Non-vulnerable employment	0.18 (0.19)	0.57 (0.22)	0.64 (0.22)
GDP growth rate	3.77	4.92	5.01
Employment growth	2.90	2.90	2.90
Productivity growth	1.12	2.01	2.31

Source Author's computations

For the elasticities based on employment by economic groups, the extreme working poor group appears to have declined with output growth over the period, suggesting that with every increase in real GDP by 1%, the number of extreme working fell by 0.02% for the 2000–2009 period and 0.15% for the 2010–2014. Thus, output growth is seen to be gaining momentum in reducing the number of working extreme poor in the SSA region. The elasticity for the poor has remained positive irrespective of the growth rate of real GDP over the period; indeed, the elasticity is rising, indicating that output growth tends to generate more working poor in the region. The conditions of the employment in the services sector (low productivity and low wages) where more labour has migrated in recent decades suggests that working poor would be on the increase with output growth (Agénor and Montiel 2008). The working middle class also has a positive and very high elasticity across the period. The value of the elasticity suggests that productivity of this set of workers actually drops following any growth in output. The results also show that non-vulnerable employment elasticity is always larger than vulnerable elasticity as shown in the averages across the periods. Anderson (2016) found a similar result and argues that output growth tends to reduce vulnerable employment and increase non-vulnerable employment over time.

The descriptive statistics of the data used in the estimations are presented in Table 4.4. The share of services in total output (in value added) has dominated sectoral distribution over the entire period, with agricultural sector share taking the rear. Surprisingly, data from ILO shows that agricultural sector still employs more workers than any other sector in many of the countries in SSA. The low share of the sector suggests the weak productivity of the sector since 1991 in the SSA region. GDP growth volatility was quite high between 1991 and 1999 considering the coefficient of variation value of 2.17 for GDP growth rate. The volatility has stabilised since 2000 and the coefficient of variation only averaged 0.34 during the 2010–2014 period. Urban population rate is high and Grant (2012) has suggested that it is one of the highest in the world. Population density and labour force growth rate have also increased over the period. The demographic factors in the region have tended towards unsustainability in terms of employment generation over time. The share of government consumption in GDP was 15% on average across the periods, suggesting a relatively large government size, FDI rate is low, reaching only 6.21% of GDP in 2010–2014 period and investment to GDP ratio was over 30% in 2010–2014 period. Thus, domestic investment is seen to play strong roles in output levels across the region, while foreign investment has less roles.

Table 4.4 Descriptive statistics of determinants of employment elasticities

	1991–1999		2000–2009		2010–2014	
	Mean	Std. dev.	Mean	Std. dev.	Mean	Std. dev.
Share of agriculture (%)	27.82	15.44	26.50	16.03	24.47	15.93
Share of industry (%)	26.76	17.68	27.60	17.14	26.97	15.16
Share of services (%)	44.91	12.13	45.95	12.37	48.85	13.94
GDP growth volatility (%)	2.17	3.23	0.89	0.97	0.34	0.74
Proportion of urban population (%)	32.39	13.99	35.89	14.88	39.10	15.52
Population density	66.44	98.59	82.10	114.54	97.27	127.95
Labour force growth rate (%)	2.95	1.39	2.84	1.42	3.02	1.33
FDI to GDP ratio (%)	3.28	13.78	4.30	7.48	6.21	9.63
Share of govt. consumption in GDP	15.68	7.39	14.52	6.14	15.41	5.89
Investment to GDP ratio (%)	25.12	36.96	26.87	41.86	30.56	44.87
Trade openness (%)	70.93	55.83	75.86	44.95	78.01	28.79
Lrent	14.01	15.41	14.38	12.95	15.58	13.35
Economic freedom index	4.87	0.94	5.85	0.88	6.19	0.76
Labour market flexibility	5.03	1.76	5.92	1.54	6.18	1.62
Legal system	4.40	1.30	4.22	1.38	4.50	1.20
Govt participation in economic activities	5.37	1.17	6.33	1.28	6.29	1.16

Source Author's computations

For the economic regulation variables, average index of economic freedom increased tremendously within the sample period. Given that a score of 10 represents total or perfect economic freedom, the score of 6.18 for the 2010–2014 period suggests large improvements in economic freedom. It also shows that governments in the SSA region are loosening control and strong regulations over economic activities. Two of the main areas where economic regulations have slacked are government direct participation in economic activities and labour market regulations with scores of 6.29 and 6.18 respectively for the 2010–2014 period. As the economies evolve, governments appear to be allowing more freedom of economic activities in the region. While this may be good for formal sector activities and employment, the effect on informal sector may be less than desirable, since effective controls and regulations are necessary for pro-poor economic activities (Ernst and Berg 2009).

Econometric Results

The results of the estimated employment elasticity determinants equation are reported and analysed in this section. The elasticities for the 37 countries in the three subgroups were pooled to obtain a total of 111 observations that were used to estimate the relationships. Three estimations were conducted for the observations. The first used only the economic freedom index to represent the regulation effects while all other variables were included in estimating the elasticity equations for each group. The second estimation used the three composite measures to represent economic regulation. The third estimation interacted the economic freedom index with structural, macroeconomic and demographic variables while still retaining the three composite measures.

In Table 4.5, the result of the estimated equation using economic freedom index alone is reported. Economic freedom index has a significant positive impact on elasticities for each of the groups except self-employment, extreme working poor and vulnerable employment. This result shows that more freedom in economic activities or less regulation has an overall positive impact on employment elasticities for most sectors in the economy. Less regulation also has a negative impact on self-employment, extreme working poor and vulnerable employment. This implies that with less regulation, the proportion of extreme working poor tends to fall significantly following growth in real GDP at any given period. The effect of regulation on employment elasticities of self-employment and vulnerable employment are however not significant, though it suggests that less regulation tends to reduce self-employment, and by extension, informal employment. This is what Henrekson (2014) also showed in his study of European economies by reporting that excessive regulation tends to increase informalities in the labour market.

The other variables also contribute to explaining employment elasticities in the region. The log of government size has a positive impact on youth employment elasticity, extreme working poor elasticity and vulnerable employment elasticity. Apparently, though government spending improves growth in youth employment when output grows, it also increases the proportion of extreme working poor and vulnerable employment. This outcome is rather surprising since government spending has been shown to lead to more vulnerable employment yield from any output growth. This calls for adequate and proper channelling of government spending patterns that tend to address unemployment issues directly.

Interestingly, the shares of industry and services, relative to that of agriculture have significant negative impacts on employment intensities for all groups. This result is at variance with findings from Kapsos (2005), Anderson (2016) and Slimane (2015). In these studies, the share of services, in particular, had strong positive impacts on employment elasticity of growth, especially at the aggregate levels. The peculiar outcome from our study may be found in the fact that none of the studies focused on Africa in estimating the employment–output relationships, given that the structure and systems operating in the African region are peculiar. First, the role of labour productivity growth is critical in ensuring sustained employment outcomes when sectoral shares increase (ECA 2015; Rodrik 2016; Diao et al. 2017). When productivity levels are low, economic sectors may find it difficult to increase employment even when output rise. Second, Saget (2000) has noted the debilitating effects that the low quality of data on GDP has had on

Table 4.5 Determinants of employment elasticity with economic freedom index

Variable	templ	yemply	Wage	Self	xtrpoor	Poor	vempl	nvempl
Constant	−0.13	0.15	−1.18	1.01***	1.47***	−0.29	0.61*	−1.25**
Economic freedom index	0.08***	0.05***	0.15***	−0.03	−0.11***	0.12***	0.02	0.15***
Log govt size	0.16	0.16*	0.10	0.16*	0.31**	0.14	0.19*	0.11
Log share of industry	−0.40***	−0.42***	−0.17	−0.46***	−0.50***	−0.45***	−0.52***	−0.19
Log share of services	−0.57***	−0.57***	−0.34*	−0.67***	−0.55***	−0.59***	−0.72***	−0.34*
Log investment rate	−0.06	−0.07	−0.07	−0.02	−0.05	−0.07	−0.04	−0.07
Log rent	0.02	0.02	0.06*	−0.01	−0.01	0.06*	0.01	0.06
Log trade open	0.31**	0.26**	0.43***	0.11	0.07	0.27*	0.18	0.45***
Growth volatility	−0.01**	−0.01*	−0.02***	0.00	0.01	−0.02**	−0.01	−0.02***
Log FDI rate	0.06*	0.06*	0.06	0.05	0.06	0.09**	0.07**	0.06
Labour force growth	0.19***	0.20***	0.14***	0.19***	0.21***	0.20***	0.22**	0.15***
Log population density	0.05**	0.05*	0.08**	0.04*	−0.03	0.08**	0.05	0.08**
Log urban rate	0.04	0.00	0.09	0.02	−0.24	0.16	0.04	0.10
R-squared	0.58	0.58	0.57	0.55	0.58	0.56	0.58	0.59
Adjusted R-squared	0.53	0.53	0.52	0.49	0.53	0.51	0.52	0.54
F-statistic	11.47	11.42	10.96	9.95	11.18	10.37	11.12	11.74

Source Author's computations

Note *, ** and *** indicate statistical significance at 10%, 5% and 1% levels respectively

deriving reasonable and systematic relationship between employment and economic performance in many SSA countries. For these countries, the informal sector has grown significantly since the 1990s (especially in services) and it has been difficult to fully account for their output in national accounts (Kamgnia 2005), thereby leading to lower estimates of the employment output relationships.

Growth volatility in the result has negative coefficients for each of the groups, suggesting that business cycles play strong roles in determining employment elasticities. Especially for the employment outcomes that are not related to informalities and vulnerability, volatility in output had significant negative impacts. The impacts are not significant for the informal sector employment (self-employment) and vulnerable and extreme poor employment, implying that informal and vulnerable employment do not have a strong link with economic performance. Surprisingly, two demographic variables (population density and labour force growth) have significant positive impacts on most of the employment elasticities. FDI rate has significant positive impacts on each of the employment elasticities by demographic groups and surprisingly on vulnerable employment. Also, the FDI rate has a weak impact on wage employment across the periods.

In the next series of analysis, we consider the results of the model with the three composite measures of economic regulations as shown in Table 4.6. In the result, labour market flexibility has significant positive impacts on the elasticities of total, male and female employment, as well as the poor and middle class in employment and non-vulnerable employment. This implies that a 1% improvement in labour market flexibility will lead to a 0.02% increase in total employment after any 1% rise in output. The effect of such improvement in labour market flexibility on non-vulnerable employment is double that of total employment. Indeed, the results for each of the employment group suggests that when labour markets are more flexible, employment at all levels tend to respond positively to output growth among countries in the SSA region. Crivelli et al. (2012) and Bernal-Verdugo et al. (2012) also found that labour market flexibility improves employment and reduces unemployment irrespective of the economic grouping of a country.

Table 4.6 Determinants of employment elasticities with composite regulation measures

Variable	templ	yempy	Wage	Self	xtrpoor	Poor	vempl	nvempl
Constant	−0.10	0.21	−0.80*	0.82*	1.11**	0.02	0.56*	−0.85*
Labour market flexibility	0.02*	0.01	0.04	0.00	−0.01	0.03**	0.01	0.04**
Legal system	0.00	−0.01	0.00	−0.01	−0.04**	−0.02	−0.02**	0.00
Govt participation	0.04***	0.03**	0.06**	0.01	0.00	0.05***	0.04**	0.06**
Log govt size	0.28**	0.26**	0.27*	0.19*	0.32**	0.32***	0.30***	0.28*
Log share of industry	−0.44***	−0.46***	−0.24*	−0.46***	−0.47***	−0.52***	−0.54***	−0.26**
Log share of services	−0.54***	−0.58***	−0.36*	−0.68***	−0.58***	−0.58**	−0.74***	−0.36*
Log investment rate	−0.08	−0.08	−0.11	−0.02	−0.05	−0.11	−0.05	−0.11
Log trade open	0.27**	0.23**	0.35**	0.12	0.10	0.19	0.15	0.37**
Growth volatility	−0.02**	−0.01**	−0.03***	0.00	0.01	−0.02**	−0.01	−0.03***
Log FDI rate	0.08**	0.07**	0.11***	0.02	0.00	0.14***	0.06**	0.12**
Labour force growth rate	0.19***	0.20***	0.15***	0.19***	0.20***	0.21***	0.22***	0.16***
Log population density	0.05*	0.04*	0.07**	0.03	−0.05	0.06*	0.03	0.07**
Log urban rate	0.07	0.02	0.13	0.01	−0.26**	0.20*	0.05	0.14
R-squared	0.57	0.59	0.49	0.57	0.49	0.52	0.61	0.51
Adjusted R-squared	0.51	0.53	0.43	0.51	0.42	0.46	0.55	0.44
F-statistic	9.15	10.59	7.27	9.84	7.04	8.20	11.43	7.64

Source Author's computations

Note *, ** and *** indicate statistical significance at 10%, 5% and 1% levels respectively

The index of government participation also has significant positive coefficients for each employment group, apart from extremely poor, where the coefficient is 0. This result indicates that less direct government participation in economic activities tend to promote employment yields from output growth. The coefficient of government participation measure ranged from 0.03 to 0.1, suggesting that reduction in direct government involvement in economic activities, perhaps through playing less active roles, would improve employment yields of output in the SSA region. For advanced economies, Bassanini and Duval (2009) and Flaig and Rottmann (2007) found this to be true. Unfortunately, most African governments do not have the capacity to act only passively in the labour market in order to guarantee sustained government involvement. For instance, Cazes and Verick (2010) noted that only Mauritius and South Africa among the SSA countries had an unemployment benefits scheme. The tendency, therefore, is for governments to perform more active roles in terms of job placement and employment stipulations, which tend to further worsen employment conditions in the economies over time.

Legal system and property rights, on the other hand, has only marginal effects on each employment elasticity. However, the two significant coefficients for this regulation variable are for elasticities extreme working poor and vulnerable employment which are negative. This outcome provides strong bases to show that strong institutions that guarantee judicial and legal qualities will ensure reduction in the share of extreme working poor in total employment, and it will also reduce vulnerable employment. Essentially, improved legal systems could encourage more focus on the poor and vulnerable and help generate growth patterns that lead to improvement in the access of this category of people to better jobs. Anderson (2016) found similar results for a group of developing countries.

Finally, we leave the composite regulation measures in the equation and interact economic freedom index with some structural, macroeconomic and demographic factors. The results are shown in Table 4.7. With the interactions, it can be seen that labour market flexibility has weak, but positive impacts on each employment elasticity, apart from extreme working poor, while the impacts of legal system and

Table 4.7 Determinants of employment elasticities with interaction terms

Variable	templ	yemply	Wage	Self	vempl	Poor	nvempl	xtrpoor
Constant	0.43	0.48	0.12	0.52*	0.61*	0.86**	0.08	0.29
Labour market flexibility	0.01	0.01	0.02	0.00	0.01	0.01	0.02	0.00
Legal system	-0.05**	-0.04**	-0.08***	0.01	-0.03	-0.10***	-0.08***	0.03
Govt participation	0.00	0.01	-0.02	0.04**	0.03	-0.02	-0.02	0.07*
Log govt size	0.21**	0.23**	0.11	0.25**	0.30**	0.19	0.13	0.46***
Log share of industry	-0.73	-0.85	-0.36	-1.01*	-0.84	-1.05	-0.40	-1.27*
Log share of services	-0.27	-0.42	0.15	-0.75	-0.80	-0.05	0.14	-1.05
Log investment rate	-1.19**	-1.17**	-1.54**	-0.85*	-1.04**	-1.60**	-1.45**	-1.10*
Log trade open	1.07	1.30*	1.10	1.26	1.27*	1.26	1.10	1.80*
Growth volatility	-0.01	-0.01	-0.02**	0.00	0.00	-0.01*	-0.02**	0.01
Log FDI rate	0.20	0.11	0.57**	0.00	0.02	0.51*	0.51*	0.00
Labour force growth rate	0.19***	0.19***	0.15***	0.17***	0.21***	0.20***	0.16***	0.17***
Log population density	0.04	0.04	0.04	0.05*	0.03	0.04	0.04	-0.02
Log urban rate	-0.32	-0.31	-0.66	0.16	-0.09	-0.52	-0.68	0.45
Industry × economic freedom	0.06	0.07	0.03	0.10	0.05	0.11	0.03	0.13
Services × economic freedom	-0.06	-0.03	-0.09	0.01	0.01	-0.10	-0.09	0.08
Investment × economic freedom	0.23**	0.22**	0.30**	0.17*	0.21*	0.31**	0.28**	0.22*
Trade openness × economic freedom	-0.15	-0.20	-0.14	-0.22*	-0.21	-0.20	-0.13	-0.32*
FDI rate × economic freedom	-0.03	-0.01	-0.10**	0.01	0.01	-0.08	-0.09*	0.01
Urban rate × economic freedom	0.07	0.06	0.14	-0.02	0.03	0.13	0.14	-0.12
R-squared	0.64	0.63	0.64	0.62	0.63	0.64	0.65	0.61
Adjusted R-squared	0.56	0.55	0.56	0.54	0.55	0.56	0.57	0.53
F-statistic	8.17	8.18	8.47	7.73	8.13	8.45	8.80	7.65
	111	111	111	111	111	111	111	111

Source Author's computations

Note *, ** and *** indicate statistical significance at 10%, 5% and 1% levels respectively

government participation are now staggered. In particular, legal systems have significant negative impacts on total employment elasticity as well as most of the subgroups, apart from extreme working poor and vulnerable employment. This shows that when overall economic regulation is taken into consideration, legal system quality tends to have an overbearing effect on employment levels in the region.

The results also show that when industry and services sectors interact with economic regulation, the impact of the sectoral shares on employment elasticities become mainly insignificant and mostly positive, especially for the industrial sector. This outcome has strong implication for the role of government and institutions in structural transformation to ensure adequate factor reallocations and employment effects. The results show that with less regulations, intersectoral integration and adjustments play little roles in ensuring employment benefits. This draws attention to the need for regulations and policies to guide sectoral interlinkages and adjustments during structural transformation, in order to achieve effective employment outcomes. When the sectors are left to market forces for adjustments as income grows over time, the resulting effects would not improve employment, but lead to more structural unemployment in the region. Pasinetti (1981) initial suggested this outcome for economies that experience rapid structural transformation and advocated a guided transformation of economies over time. For the SSA region, output growth has not favoured overall employment because structural transformation has reallocated capital (not labour) resources into the mining sectors which appear to be driving growth in most of the economies. Regulatory policies are needed to ensure that the labour factor is also catered for in the mining sector, and more importantly, that structural transformation boosts labour productivity in other sectors of the economy.

Conclusion

In this study, the impact of economic regulation on the employment elasticity of output growth was examined. Though structural changes coupled with demographic transitions are essential for employment-enhancing growth in an economy, the level of regulation based on institutional capacity of government could also provide strong background for analysing how growth affects employment. In particular, the nature of jobs being created in the growth process could be effectively influenced using regulatory and institutional measures. Though regulations could also act as a wedge to effective structural transformation and employment intensity of output, especially for the formal economy, the dualistic nature of Sub-Saharan Africa economies provides that additional policy stance would be required to guarantee adequate changes and integration in the sectors over time as output grows. It is believed that such enhancement function cannot be fully left to market forces to perform in dualistic economies.

The results from the study highlight the fact that there is a strong distinction between active regulation and institutional quality in terms of their effects on employment elasticities. Less economic regulation essentially enhances formal sector activities and employment, while the effects on informal and pro-poor employment are not straight-forward. Although overall regulation tends to improve both formal and informal sector employment, labour market flexibility tends to worsen informal sector employment. In the same vein, legal institutions appear to be pro-poor in terms of employment effects, while government participation has strong disincentive effects in improving employment elasticity of output growth in the SSA regions.

Interestingly, the results also showed that intersectoral integration and adjustments play little roles in ensuring employment benefits from output growth when regulations are minimal regulations. This calls for dexterity in balancing regulations to address structural bottlenecks that may prevent structural changes to result in employment growth, to ensure that the formal sector evolves and expands in terms of production and employment and to ensure that growth resulting from structural transformation favours the vulnerable in the society. The major policy implications of the results are that the establishment and sustenance of quality institutions in SSA, not mere focus on direct regulations, is the major means of attaining effective linkages between output growth and employment in the region.

Appendix

Variables in the Study

Variable	Explanation	Source
Total employment	Total number of individuals employed in the economy ('000)	ILO World Employment and Social Outlook database, 2016
Male employment	Total number of males in employment ('000)	ILO World Employment and Social Outlook database, 2016
Female employment	Total number of females in employment ('000)	ILO World Employment and Social Outlook database, 2016
Youth employment	Total number of youth in employment ('000)	ILO World Employment and Social Outlook database, 2016
Wage employment	Total number of individuals with wage employment	ILO World Employment and Social Outlook database, 2016
Self-employment	Total number of individuals that are self-employed	ILO World Employment and Social Outlook database, 2016
Extreme poor employment	Extreme poor in employment: The number of jobs that can make an individual to be in extreme poor group	ILO World Employment and Social Outlook database, 2016
Poor employment	Poor individuals in employment	ILO World Employment and Social Outlook database, 2016
Middle-class employment	Middle class in employment	ILO World Employment and Social Outlook database, 2016
Vulnerable employment	Workers typically subject to high levels of precariousness	ILO World Employment and Social Outlook database, 2016
Non-vulnerable employment	Workers typically not subject to high levels of precariousness	ILO World Employment and Social Outlook database, 2016
Share of agriculture (%)	Measured in GDP value added	UNCTAD World Investment Report database
Share of industry (%)	Measured in GDP value added	UNCTAD World Investment Report database

Variable	Explanation	Source
Share of services (%)	Measured in GDP value added	UNCTAD World Investment Report database
GDP growth volatility (%)	Coefficient of variation of GDP growth rate	Base data from World Bank World Development Indicators
Proportion of urban population (%)	Urban population as percentage of total population	World Bank World Development Indicators
Population density	Total pollution as proportion of total landmass	World Bank World Development Indicators
Labour force growth rate (%)	Year-on-year percentage change in labour force	World Bank World Development Indicators
FDI to GDP ratio (%)	Total FDI inflow as percentage of GDP	World Bank World Development Indicators
Share of govt. consumption in GDP	Total government consumption expenditure as percentage of GDP	UNCTAD World Investment Report database
Investment to GDP ratio (%)	Total investment expenditure as percentage of GDP	IMF World Economic Outlook database
Trade openness (%)	Import + export as percentage of GDP	World Bank World Development Indicators
Rent	Proportion of rent-seeking in an economy	World Bank World Development Indicators
Economic freedom index	Overall measure to indicate the level of economic freedom in a country. It is a composite of five indicators. All indicators are standardized on a 0–10 scale, with higher value of the indicator representing more economic freedom	Fraser Institute's Economic Freedom of the World (EFW) database
Labour market flexibility	A composite measure of labour maker flexibility and indicators of labour market flexibility in six policy areas: minimum wage; hiring and firing regulation; centralized collective wage bargaining; mandated cost of hiring; mandated cost of work dismissal and conscription	Fraser Institute's Economic Freedom of the World (EFW) database

Variable	Explanation	Source
Legal system and property rights	A composite measure of the effectiveness of legal system and adherence to property rights in a country. The indicator is standardized on a 0–10 scale, with higher value of the indicator representing better system	Fraser Institute's Economic Freedom of the World (EFW) database
Govt participation in economic activities	A composite measure of the rate of government participation and size in a country. The indicator is standardized on a 0–10 scale, with higher value of the indicator representing less government involvement	Fraser Institute's Economic Freedom of the World (EFW) database

References

Agénor, P., & Montiel, P. J. (2008). *Development Macroeconomics* (3rd ed.). Princeton University Press.

Ajakaiye, O., Jerome, A. T., Nabena, D., & Alaba, O. A. (2016). Understanding the Relationship Between Growth and Employment in Nigeria. In H. Bhorat & F. Tarp (Eds.), *Africa's Lions: Growth Traps and Opportunities for Six African Economies* (pp. 181–228). Washington, DC: Brookings Institution Press.

Ajilore, T., & Yinusa, O. (2011). An Analysis of Employment Intensity of Sectoral Output Growth in Botswana. *Southern African Business Review, 15*(2), 26–42.

Akinkugbe, O. (2015). Economic Growth and Sectoral Capacity for Employment Creation in Zambia. *International Journal for Cross-Disciplinary Subjects in Education, 6*(3), 2217–2223.

Anderson, B. (2015). *Macroeconomic Structure and the (Non-)Vulnerable Employment Intensity of Growth.* Institute for the Study of International Aspects of Competition (ISIAC). Available via https://web.uri.edu/isiac/files/wp15-1.pdf. Accessed 7 Aug 2016.

Anderson, B. (2016). Do Macroeconomic Structures and Policies Shape the Employment Intensity of Growth Differently for Women and Men? *Journal of Economic Issues, 50*(4), 940–962.

Armah, B., Keita, M., Gueye, A., Bosco, V., Ameso, J., & Chinzara, Z. (2014). Structural Transformation for Inclusive Development in Africa: The Role of Active Government Policies. *Development, 57*(3–4), 438–451.

Bassanini, A., & Duval, R. (2009). *Employment Patterns in OECD Countries: Reassessing the Role of Policies and Institutions.* OECD. Available via https://www.oecd-ilibrary.org/economics/employment-patterns-in-oecd-countries_846627332717. Accessed 11 Aug 2017.

Basu, D., & Das, D. (2015). *Employment Elasticity in India and the U.S., 1977–2011: A Sectoral Decomposition Analysis.* Available via https://scholarworks.umass.edu/econ_workingpaper/190/. Accessed 7 Aug 2016.

Bbaale, E. (2013). Is Uganda's Growth Profile Jobless? *International Journal of Economics and Finance, 5*(11), 105–123.

Behar, A. (2012). *A Template for Analyzing and Projecting Labor Market Indicators.* IMF. Available via https://www.imf.org/external/pubs/ft/tnm/2012/tnm1201.pdf. Accessed 13 Aug 2017.

Bernal-Verdugo, L. E., Furceri, D., & Guillaume, D. (2012). Labor Market Flexibility and Unemployment: New Empirical Evidence of Static and Dynamic Effects. *Comparative Economic Studies, 54*(2), 251–273.

Calmfors, L., & Holmlund, B. (2000). Unemployment and Economic Growth: A Partial Survey. *Swedish Economic Policy Review, 7,* 107–153.

Campbell, D. (2013). The Labour Market in Developing Countries. In S. Cazes & S. Verick (Eds.), *Perspectives on Labour Economics for Development* (pp. 7–38). Geneva: International Labour Organization.

Cazes, S., & Verick, S. (2010). *What Role for Labour Market Policies and Institutions in Development? Enhancing Security in Developing Countries and Emerging Economies.* ILO. Available via http://www.ilo.org/wcmsp5/groups/public/—ed_emp/—emp_elm/—analysis/documents/publication/wcms_150629.pdf. Accessed 7 Aug 2016.

Chenery, H. B., & Syrquin, M. (1986). Typical Patterns of Transformation. In H. B. Chenery, S. Robinson, & M. Syrquin (Eds.), *Industrialization and Growth: A Comparative Study* (pp. 37–83). London: Oxford University Press.

Crivelli, E., Furceri, D., & Toujas-Bernate, J. (2012). *Can Policies Affect Employment Intensity of Growth? A Cross-Country Analysis.* Washington, DC: IMF.

Diao, X., Harttgen, K., & McMillan, M. (2017, January). *The Changing Structure of Africa's Economies.* National Bureau of Economic Research (NBER) (Working Paper No. 23021). Available via https://www.nber.org/papers/w23021. Accessed 3 Jul 2017.

Döpke, J. (2001). *The Employment Intensity of Growth in Europe.* Kiel Institute for the World Economy. Available via http://citeseerx.ist.psu.edu/viewdoc/download?doi=10.1.1.570.8411&rep=rep1&type=pdf. Accessed 27 Apr 2016.

ECA. (2015). *The Demographic Profile of African Countries.* Addis Ababa: Economic Commission for Africa.

Edwards, S. (1988). Terms of Trade, Tariffs, and Labour Market Adjustment in Developing Countries. *World Bank Economic Review, 2,* 165–185.

Ernst, C., & Berg, J. (2009). The Role of Employment and Labour Markets in the Fight Against Poverty. In OECD (Ed.), *Promoting Pro-Poor Growth: Employment* (pp. 41–67). Paris: OECD.

Fields, G. S. (2007). *Dual Economy.* Retrieved 23/09/2016, from Cornell University, ILR School site: http://digitalcommons.ilr.cornell.edu/working-papers/17/. Accessed 14 Aug 2016.

Fields, G. S. (2012). *Working Hard, Working Poor.* New York: Oxford University Press.

Flaig, G., & Rottmann, H. (2007). *Labour Market Institutions and the Employment Intensity of Output Growth. An International Comparison.* CESifo. Available via https://www.cesifo-group.de/DocDL/cesifo1_wp2175.pdf.

Fuchs, V. R. (1980, June). *Economic Growth and the Rise of Service Employment.* National Bureau of Economic Research (NBER) (Working Paper No. 486). Available via https://www.nber.org/papers/w0486. Accessed on 12 Aug 2016.

Fuchs, M., & Weyh, A. (2014). *Demography and Unemployment in East Germany: How Close Are the Ties?* IAB. Available via http://doku.iab.de/discussionpapers/2014/dp2614.pdf.

Golub, S., & Hayat, F. (2014). *Employment, Unemployment, and Underemployment in Africa.* UNU-WIDER. Available via https://www.wider.unu.edu/sites/default/files/wp2014-014.pdf.

Gong, X. (2015). African Economic Structural Transformation: A Diagnostic Analysis. *Journal of African Transformation, 1*(1), 1–22.

Grant, U. (2012). *Urbanization and the Employment Opportunities of Youth in Developing Countries.* UNESCO. Available via http://unesdoc.unesco.org/images/0021/002178/217879E.pdf.

Greene, W. H. (2011). *Econometric Analysis* (7th ed.). Prentice Hall.

Henrekson, M. (2014). *How Labor Market Institutions Affect Job Creation and Productivity Growth.* IZA. Available via https://wol.iza.org/articles/how-labor-market-institutions-affect-job-creation-and-productivity-growth/long. Accessed 20 Jul 2017.

International Labour Organisation. (2003). *Working Out of Poverty*. Report of the Director-General at the International Labour Conference 91st Session, Geneva, Switzerland. Available via https://www.ilo.org/public/english/standards/relm/ilc/ilc91/pdf/rep-i-a.pdf. Accessed 11 Apr 2016.

Islam, R., & Islam, I. (2015). *Employment and Inclusive Development*. London: Routledge Studies in Development Economics.

Iyoha, M., & Oriakhi, D. (2008). Explaining African Economic Growth Performance: The Case of Nigeria. In B. Ndulu, A. O. S. O'Connell, J.-P. Azam et al. (Eds.), *Country Case Studies. The Political Economy of Economic Growth in Africa, 1960–2000* (Vol. 2, pp. 621–659). Cambridge: Cambridge University Press.

Kamgnia, B. D. (2005). Growth–Employment Nexus: The Specificities in Africa. In L. Kasekende & O. Ajakaiye (Eds.), *Accelerating Africa's Development Five Years into the 21st Century* (pp. 40–78). Nairobi: African Economic Research Consortium.

Kapsos, S. (2005). *The Employment Intensity of Growth: Trends and Macroeconomic Determinants*. ILO. Available via https://www.ilo.org/wcmsp5/groups/public/@ed_emp/@emp_elm/documents/publication/wcms_143163.pdf. Accessed 7 Jul 2017.

Khan, A. R. (2008, July 10–11). *Employment in Sub-Saharan Africa. Lessons to be Learnt from East Asian Experience*. Paper presented at the Africa Task Force Meeting, Initiative for Policy Dialogue, Addis Ababa.

Krueger, A. O. (1983). Employment and Labor Markets in Less Developed Countries. In A. O. Krueger (Ed.), *Trade and Employment in Developing Countries, Volume 3: Synthesis and Conclusions* (pp. 10–29). Chicago: University of Chicago Press. Retrieved from http://www.nber.org/chapters/c8762. Accessed 12 May 2016.

Kuznets, S. (1973). Modern Economic Growth: Findings and Reflections. *The American Economic Review, 63*(3), 247–258.

Landmann, O. (2004). *Employment Strategy Papers Employment, Productivity and Output Growth*. Freiburg University Employment Trends Unit. Available via http://citeseerx.ist.psu.edu/viewdoc/download?doi=10.1.1.554.5378&rep=rep1&type=pdf.

Lewis, A. (1954). Economic Development with Unlimited Supply of Labour. *The Manchester School, 22,* 139–191.

Lewis, W. A. (1958). Unlimited Labour: Further Notes. *The Manchester School, 26*(10), 1–32. https://doi.org/10.1111/j.1467-9957.1958.tb00922.x.

Lewis, J. B., & Linzer, D. A. (2005). Estimating Regression Models in Which the Dependent Variable Is Based on Estimates. *Political Analysis, 13*(4), 345–364.

McMillan, M., & Harttgen, K. (2014). *What is Driving the 'African Growth Miracle'?* African Development Bank. Available via https://www.afdb. org/fileadmin/uploads/afdb/Documents/Publications/Working_Paper_- _209_-_What_is_driving_the_African_Growth_Miracle.pdf. Accessed 21 Apr 2016.

McMillan, M. S., & Rodrik, D. (2011). Globalization, Structural Change, and Productivity Growth. In M. Bachetta & M. Jansen (Eds.), *Making Globalization Socially Sustainable* (pp. 36–70). Geneva: International Labour Organization and World Trade Organization.

Mkhize, N. (2016). *The Sectoral Employment Intensity of Growth in South Africa*. Economic Research in South Africa. Available via https://econrsa. org/system/files/publications/working_papers/working_paper_631.pdf. Accessed 7 Aug 2017.

Mourre, G. (2004). *Did the Pattern of Aggregate Employment Growth Change in the Euro Area in the Late 1990s?* Frankfurt am Main: European Central Bank.

Okun, A. (1962). Potential GNP: Its Measurement and Significance. In *Proceeding of the Business and Economic Statistics Section* (pp. 98–104). Chicago: American Statistical Association.

Page, J., & Shimeles, A. (2015). Aid, Employment, and Poverty Reduction in Africa. *African Development Review, 7*(S1), 17–30. https://doi. org/10.1111/1467-8268.12136.

Pasinetti, L. L. (1981). *Structural Change and Economic Growth: A Theoretical Essay on the Dynamics of the Wealth of Nations*. Cambridge: Cambridge University Press.

Pattanaik, F., & Nayak, N. C. (2011). *Employment Intensity of Service Sector in India: Trend and Determinants*. 2010 International Conference on Business and Economics Research 1.

Pena, X. (2013). *The Formal and Informal Sectors in Colombia: Country Case Study on Labour Market Segmentation* (Employment Working Paper No. 146). Geneva: International Labour Office.

Pissarides, C. A., & Vallanti, G. (2004). *Productivity Growth and Employment: Theory and Panel Estimates*. Centre for Economic Performance. Available via http://eprints.lse.ac.uk/2189/.

Ranis, S., & Fei, J. C. (1961). A Theory of Economic Development. *The American Economic Review, 51*, 533–558.

Rifkin, J. (1994). *The End of Work*. New York: Tarcher/Putman.

Rodrik, D. (2016). Premature Deindustrialization. *Journal of Economic Growth, 21*(1), 1–33.

Saget, C. (2000). Can the Level of Employment Be Explained by GDP Growth in Transition Countries: Theory Versus the Quality of Data. *Labour, 14*(4), 623–644.

Scarpetta, S., Hemmings, P., Tressel, T., & Woo, J. (2002). *The Role of Policy and Institutions for Productivity and Firm Dynamics: Evidence from Micro and Industry Data.* Organisation for Economic Co-operation and Development. Available via https://www.oecd-ilibrary.org/economics/the-role-of-policy-and-institutions-for-productivity-and-firm-dynamics_547061627526. Accessed 20 Jul 2015.

Schalk, H. J., & Untied, G. (2000). *Wachstum und Arbeitslosigkeit. Friedrich Ebert Stiftung.* Available via http://www.gefra-muenster.de. Accessed 4 May 2016.

Slimane, S. B. (2015). The Relationship Between Growth and Employment Intensity: Evidence for Developing Countries. *Asian Economic and Financial Review, 5*(4), 680–692.

Sorensen, P. B., & Whitta-Jacobsen, H. (2010). *Introducing Advanced Macroeconomics: Growth and Business Cycles* (2nd ed.). Berkshire, UK: McGraw-Hill Higher Education.

Stiglitz, J. E. (1974). Alternative Theories of Wage Determination, and Unemployment in LDCs: The Labour Turnover Model. *Quarterly Journal of Economics, 88*(2), 194–227.

Timmer, P., McMillan, M., Badiane, O., Rodrik, D., Binswanger-Mkhize, H., & Wouterse, F. (2012). *Patterns of Growth and Structural Transformation in Africa: Trends and Lessons for Future Development Strategies.* IFPRI Thematic Research Note 2.

United Nations Conference on Trade and Development (UNCTAD). (2008). *Globalization for Development: The International Trade Perspective.* UNCTAD, New York and Geneva.

World Bank. (2005). *World Development Report 2006: Equity and Development.* Washington, DC: World Bank, New York: Oxford University Press.

World Bank. (2012). *World Development Report 2013: Jobs.* Washington, DC: World Bank.

5

Governance in the Mineral Dependent Economy: The Case of Botswana

Ita M. Mannathoko

Introduction

Background

In mineral dependent economies, structural transformation is often an ongoing priority necessitated by the need for risk mitigation. This is usually pursued through efforts to diversify sources of national income, foreign exchange and jobs. Such transformation is essential to sustainable growth and job creation in these economies. The experience in mineral resource-rich countries has shown that neither the creation of special

---

This is an update and significant expansion (broader coverage with cointegration analysis and an error correction model; use of log values rather than levels; use of R-studio rather than Excel) of an earlier 2014 paper presented in Gaborone at a Frederich-Ebert-Stufig/Botswana Institute of Development Policy Analysis Conference titled: *Are Diamonds Forever? Prospects for a Sustainable Development Model for Botswana.*

I. M. Mannathoko (✉)
Gaborone, Botswana

© The Author(s) 2019
A. B. Elhiraika et al. (eds.), *Governance for Structural Transformation in Africa*,
https://doi.org/10.1007/978-3-030-03964-6_5

145

resource or revenue stabilisation funds, nor the implementation of rigid fiscal rules can fully protect the countries from the negative impact of external shocks and commodity price fluctuations (IMF 2013b). This makes diversification an imperative in such countries. The IMF points to existing research that provides evidence that diversification can significantly reduce countries' vulnerability to external shocks and provide a more robust basis for sustained, broad-based, long-term growth.

Achieving diversification, however, is difficult and requires sustained strong economic governance in an environment that is continually susceptible to Dutch disease pressures, such as wasteful spending of mineral receipts, anti-competitive real exchange rate appreciation or rent-seeking behaviour. The literature on the influences of mineral dependency on the quality, effectiveness and impact of government implies that the standard, macroeconomic policy/Dutch disease list of considerations for a mineral dependent economy are not enough, and that to this list should be added the need to sustain government systems that measure, monitor and give ongoing priority to government effectiveness. This thinking suggests that mineral dependent economies more than other economies, will only grow their non-mineral tradable economy over time as quickly (or slowly) as the effectiveness and quality of their government allows, due to the types of incentives they face. This paper investigates how this proposition plays out using a case study.

While there is ample literature on prudent governance and fiscal rules for mineral resource management—with recommendations that focus on reforming fiscal and monetary policy to help avert Dutch disease tendencies (e.g. Collier 2011; Elbadawi and Nandwa 2011), unlike that literature, this paper undertakes a case-study in order to gain specific evidence and a deeper understanding of the extent and nature of the influence of ongoing mineral dependency over time, on the quality of governance. From this study, the paper will then be better positioned to suggest ways at the micro-level for government to overcome pitfalls related to mineral dependency, which can derail good governance. It will, therefore, be able to provide recommendations that are additional to the standard prescriptions of macroeconomic policy reform.

The paper draws lessons from Botswana, a long-standing mineral dependent economy in Africa. Botswana is well known as an African economic success story. Its rapid growth has been the focus of many scholars. It experienced GDP per capita growth of 13% per annum in the years 1980–1989 (Mpabanga 1997), due to production from new diamond mines. Growth over four decades surpassed even that of the Asia-Pacific tigers (Leith 2005). Botswana is also one of the oldest successful multiparty democracies in Africa—though only one political party has ever won elections. Its growth success and political stability have been attributed to indigenous democratic institutions and limited colonial influence, alongside wise leadership since independence, a government reliant on technocrats rather than politicians for economic governance, and prudent economic policy (Harvey and Lewis 1990; Mpabanga 1997; Owusu and Samatar 1997; Samatar 1999; Acemoglu et al. 2003; Leith 2005; Beaulier and Subrick 2006; Iimi 2006). In more recent years, however, there has been a shift in both growth and governance performance. With sustained declines in capital, labour and total factor productivity growth over the two and a half decades to 2010, there is now general recognition that the public-sector driven capital-deepening growth model that Botswana depended on for so long has run its course (IMF 2013a).

Hillbom (2008) also found, based on a structural analysis, that Botswana's success was one of premodern growth without development. The research concluded that though the country had grown rapidly, it had not yet experienced 'modern economic growth' characterised by structural change in patterns of production, and in social and political institutions. Premodern growth without development allows for significant poverty rates and very unequal resource and income distribution to prevail in the midst of plenty—characteristics which hold for Botswana.

Sustaining good governance and in particular, government effectiveness, is important if the country is to achieve the broad-based private sector development outside of the mining sector, needed to achieve the national goal of economic and export diversification. This paper uses a time-series cointegration model to explore the long-run influence in Botswana that dependence on mining has had on the quality of governance (proxied by government effectiveness). The paper then constructs a dynamic error correction model to also determine the immediate factors that can be addressed to help improve government effectiveness.

The Literature and Botswana's Experience

Resource Dependency and Government

The effects of mineral dependency are well documented in the literature and there is wide practical experience from numerous countries.[1] A formal economic model dealing with mineral dependency (and Dutch Disease) was developed in 1982 by W. Max Corden and J. Peter Neary. The model addressed macroeconomic considerations. It also showed among other things, that while technological growth tended to be more in non-mining traded goods and service sectors,[2] mineral dependency tended to lead to this sector being neglected or stifled over time, overshadowed by the mining sector. This resulted in overall technological growth in the mining-dependent economy lagging behind that seen elsewhere. As long-term sustainable growth is determined by technological growth which enhances productivity, this would be a concern. Less technological growth would result in the country's comparative (and competitive) advantage in the traded goods and services sectors shrinking, leading to firms avoiding or disinvesting in non-mining traded goods and services sector over time. Mining dependent governments, therefore, needed to take deliberate and specific measures to guard against deindustrialisation. The Corden-Neary model addressed the macroeconomic considerations that led to deindustrialisation, but did not deal with the specific issue of government effectiveness over time in a mining dependent economy. This paper will

---

[1]Sixteenth Century Spain—Large inflow of gold and other wealth into Spain from the Americas, Australian gold rush—Documented by Cairns in 1859, Netherlands in the 1960s, Norway—oil boom in the late 1970s, '80s and early '90s, Mexico—oil boom in 1970s, early 1980s, Australia—mineral commodities (current), Russia—oil, natural gas (current), Canada—oil (current), oil sands in the province of Alberta and Saskatchewan, Nigeria and Zambia—with large natural-resource endowments; up until recent years, economic management inadvertently created serious impediments to domestic investment and growth. More recently, see Elbadawi et al. (2007).

[2]Traded goods and services are those that are exportable, and as such are either sold to the domestic market (often substituting for imports) or exported. In the Botswana context, these goods and services are critical to sustainable, long-term growth because of the demand limitations imposed by the smallness of the Botswana market.

focus on that latter aspect of mining dependency, exploring whether the different financial incentives a mining dependent government faces influence its effectiveness and by extension its ability to promote sustainable non-mining private sector growth.

The literature also discusses the implications of sources of revenues. The presence of a consistent connection between citizen influence on government and governance quality; and between the way in which a government is financed and how well it governs is an old idea (Rudolph Goldscheid 1917; Schumpeter 1918; see also Moore et al. 1999). The modern version of this thinking posits that in most governments, the dominant income sources are (a) broad taxation, (b) surpluses from natural resource exports and (c) borrowing from capital markets and other governments—including development aid; and that when governments are not mining-dependent and instead rely heavily on broad taxation, this tends to promote accountability to taxpayers—especially to the non-mining private sector that needs to grow rapidly for diversification to occur.

When the government leadership and administration earn their income from a broad base of taxpayers, they are incentivised to be accountable to them; to deliver effectively on agreed government services and development programs. However, when the link between government income and the people is broken, and the government has an alternative primary source of income such as mining receipts, the influence of the people and the non-mining private sector on government behaviour is reduced. Government, in the absence of meaningful pressure from the private sector and the public (via broad-based revenues) for quality, efficiency and effectiveness, only has to focus on pleasing the mining sector and can get by doing the minimum required elsewhere (e.g. ensuring adequate social welfare for the poorer majority who comprise the bulk of the electorate).

Governments that rely heavily on surpluses from natural resource exports thus operate in a context where the link between government income and the non-mining private sector and public is broken over an extended period. Table 5.1 provides a schematic of how mineral dependency changes the financial incentives that governments face. It becomes harder to hold a government to account when it is strongly

Table 5.1 The mineral dependent economic structure distorts the performance incentive faced by the government

Type of revenue source	Extent to which the revenue source is 'earned' by the state in terms of organization effort	Incentive for state accountability to the electorate	Ability of economic climate to guide government
Board taxation of citizens	High (State focuses on collecting revenues and electorate typically will monitor delivery by the state against election promises)	High (Electorate typically not understanding of taxation without representation)	High (Business sector is an important source of income—and the state experiences similar economic conditions to the private sector)
Surpluses from export of natural resource products	Low (The State does not need to exert any public sector organizational effort that will ensure effective public service delivery, in order to safeguard its income source)	Low (The state relies on the mineral export for its revenue—not on the electorate—therefore it is not readily held to account on delivery)	Low (State's economic climate follows that of its principal income source—the mining sector. It may even run surpluses when the non-mining economy is in recession, and so is often out of touch with public and the private sector)

Source Adapted from Mick Moore, *Taxation and the Quality of Governance*, Institute of Development Studies (2007)

dependent for its revenues on a mineral resource that it mines jointly with external (international) corporations.

A 1999 University of Sussex paper assessed the experience of sixty-one governments.[3] The cross-country analysis determined factors

---

[3] *Polity Qualities: How Governance Affects Poverty*, Mick Moore, Jennifer Leavy, Peter Houtzager and Howard White; The Institute of Development Studies at the University of Sussex, Brighton BN1 9RE UK, September 1999.

influencing the efficiency with which national political-economic systems converted material resources (GNP per capita) into human capital (longevity and human competencies; education, literacy). Statistical analysis suggested that national political-economic systems generally converted material resources into human development most effectively when:

i.   The government was not highly dependent on mineral resources for revenue (result significant at 0.1% level). The extent to which governments were financially independent of their own citizens was significantly and negatively correlated with the efficiency of conversion of material resources into human capital. Governments that didn't depend significantly on a broad segment of citizens' taxes to finance them, tended to be inefficient when converting material resources into human development;

ii. Government institutions rated lower from the perspective of international investors and lenders (result significant at 2% level). A composite measure of the quality of government institutions used by international investors and lenders was significantly and negatively correlated with the efficiency of conversion of material resources into human capital. This suggested that countries whose institutions focused mainly on attracting international investors and less on supporting their own, tended to perform less favourably at converting material resources into human development and

iii. The population was dense (result significant at 2% level). It was easier and cheaper to build human capital (health and capacities) in densely clustered populations. Clusters allow for economies of scale and facilitate linkages between economic agents for the development of capacities.

This and other analyses support the general proposition that governments that are dependent on mineral receipts (mined together with international companies) rather than on the mass of their citizens for critical financial resources are less likely to treat their citizens and the indigenous private sector well. Moore's proposition is essentially that states with broad taxation will tend towards more accountable, representative government; while those dependent on a narrow income source, are more likely to become less accountable and less representative over time. In Moore's view, government effectiveness has three aspects that complement and reinforce one another: (i) the responsiveness of government to citizens, i.e. an orientation to meeting citizens' needs; (ii) the accountability of government to citizens and (iii) the capability of governments to determine and respond to citizens' needs and wants, which includes the government's organisational capacity to arrive at effective policies, and capabilities to deliver the required public services efficiently and effectively.

Overall, the Dutch Disease and mineral dependency literature suggests that the distorted incentive structure arising from mineral dependency is likely to encourage complacency, inefficiency and rent-seeking behaviour in government when it deals with the public and the non-mining private sector. Mineral dependency can thus lead to erosion of governance, as institutions and decision-making are undermined by these behaviours. The literature implies that accountability has to be guarded, and implementation properly managed and monitored and that strong and competent managers and systems are needed on an ongoing basis to ensure that service delivery is strong and remains so.

Botswana's Experience

Diamond mining in Botswana started in the 1970s though Botswana only became a significant world producer after 1982 following the opening of the Jwaneng Diamond Mine. With the discovery of diamonds and the coming on-stream of the Orapa and Jwaneng mines, the Botswana government was wary of the potential economic pitfalls associated with mineral dependency, and put in place systems to avoid these pitfalls.

Numerous World Bank and IMF reports confirmed that with respect to macroeconomic management, the government averted boom-bust spending patterns through the use of national development plans as a disciplining tool; this ensured that expenditure was consistent with plans and was smoothed out over time. The government was also relatively successful in establishing effective buffers for revenues. A managed exchange rate regime was also used to contain the erosion of non-mining sector competitiveness and avoid an overvalued Pula relative to the non-mining productive sector.

The government limited opportunities for rent-taking through its hands-off approach to the management of Debswana (the diamond mining company) and through internal safeguards to counteract rent-seeking.[4] However, performance indicators now show that over time, there has been erosion in the efficiency of spending, in implementation capacity and in non-mining sector competitiveness. The challenge that the Botswana government faced was in sustaining early management systems that worked, and maintaining the effective use and enforcement of checks and balances, and of financial safeguards. The quality of management in government structures, its understanding of how the overall mining-dependency system works and its ability to guard against complacency in order to avoid the erosion of effective government, became increasingly important over time. Some analysts, however, suggest that the previous critical mass of officials driven by excellence and a public service motivation has been eroded over time (see also Jaimovich and Rud 2009 model on rent-seeking).

Various authors have commented on these issues. Some noted the importance of political economy influences. In 1984, Nimrod Raphaeli, Jacques Roumani and A.C. MacKellar wrote that:

---

[4]The term "rent" in rent-seeking is short for "economic rent" and refers to what a government earns without any effort. In Botswana's case, revenues from diamonds are not earned through government effort. Government does not have to exert that much effort at expanding the economic base off which it earns tax revenue. History shows us that around the world bureaucrats and people in authority have sometimes maneuvered to position themselves to access "rents" or to create situations where they can be paid unearned income (bribed). Where government officials have discretion in applying government regulations, individuals are often willing to pay bribes to officials to circumvent the rules in order to counter delays and inefficient service. These rent-seeking activities have been shown to exact a heavy economic and social toll. They are illegal and represent a corrupting influence (Mauro 1997).

Public sector management in Botswana rests on two pillars: democracy and pragmatism. The democratic nature of the Government of Botswana allows not only an open dialogue of policy making but ensures a remarkable degree of accountability of the bureaucracy to, and control by, Parliament. Pragmatism reflects a dedication to a profound, yet basically simple, principle that ends should be dictated by realistic means and not by ideological fervor. Commitment to economic and social development is a way of life, not a slogan....

Public sector management is performed in Botswana with commendable attention to detail, discipline and dedication by the civil service. Planning and budgeting remain under the domain of a unified Ministry of Finance and Development Planning (MFDP) ensuring a considerable measure of integration and cohesiveness between them. The National Development Plan is a consensus plan, reflecting different levels of consultations with various constituents. There is a dialogue at all levels both with regard to the plan and the budget until agreement is reached on realistic levels of expenditures.

A decade and a half later, some government practitioners began to highlight the growing challenge to government effectiveness faced by Botswana due to mineral dependency. Modise Modise (then Deputy Permanent Secretary, MFDP) concluded in his 1999 UNCTAD paper *"Managing Mineral Revenues in Botswana"*[5] that:

the higher the economic rent the country faced, and the longer the mineral reserves are expected to last, the less the pressure for the country to adopt viable and sustainable policies for the use of revenues. A higher world market share of the natural resource also tended to make the producer country complacent.

Ensuring optimal use of mineral receipts without succumbing to popular pressures was a challenge:

---

[5]Published by UNCTAD in 1999 in *Development Policies in Natural Resource Economies*, edited by Jorg Mayer, Brian Chambers and Ayisha Farooq.

In the management of large mineral revenues, the best strategy is one that is in-keeping with long term sustainable economic development. Mineral revenues should be used to develop the productive base of the economy, in other words converting natural mineral assets into other kinds of long-term assets such as viable technologies, physical and social infrastructure, as well as human capital. ... In poor developing countries, pressures to finance current consumption to address poverty are immense. Development of prestige projects, which are highly conspicuous, give a false sense of developmental success.....Whilst supplying the poor with consumption goods and basic necessities using such revenues can temporarily alleviate the plight of the poor, this is not a long term solution to poverty. Some analysts argue (however) that using such revenues for social safety nets for those who cannot be productively employed is justified.

Modise Modise also observed that through its mineral receipts, government influenced the economy in numerous ways, such as in investment spending, in savings and in the rapid increase in government jobs and wages[6] which crowded out private sector jobs and increased the price level, in addition to fuelling household credit expansion:

Some of the effects of mineral revenues on consumption and investment can be deduced from the General Government share of GDP, national savings and commercial bank credit. The share of General Government in GDP has remained relatively stable. It accounted for 15.4% in 1995/96 and 16.3% in 1998/99. This is a fairly high proportion of public consumption by international standards. Government also has disproportionately large shares in national savings and investment, on account of mineral revenues.... The share of household credit in total commercial bank credit rose from 47% in 1998 to 50% in 1999 compared to a share of 32% in 1991; while the share of credit to business has been declining. The rapid increase in household credit expansion was mostly in response to the substantial rise in public sector salaries in 1998.... The growing share of credit to the households, with a higher propensity to consume, is worrisome. If this continues, it will compromise investment and consequently economic growth and sustainable economic development.

---

[6]The amount going to public and parastatal remuneration in Botswana, as a share of GDP, was almost three times the OECD average.

The importance of improving government's implementation capacity and of investment in technology and in labour force capabilities was also noted:

> Botswana should spare no effort in improving project implementation and selecting projects with high economic returns. Remaining bottlenecks impeding private sector development should be speedily removed. ... Botswana should have a well developed and aggressive human resources development strategy focusing on professional and technical skills, especially information technology. Unless these needs are addressed, they will seriously undermine development of high technology industries. Without IT skills and infrastructure, the country cannot go far in this era of digital technology. The people are the country's greatest assets; investment in human resources development and technology will make the country better placed for more innovative and productive additional engines of economic growth that are a sine qua non for sustainable economic diversification.

While some of the things Modise Modise proposed in his 1999 and 2000 papers were done in subsequent years, it would appear that the reforms were not implemented as an integral part of a well-defined sustained non-mining private sector development strategy, consequently professional and technical skills were developed in a vacuum, resulting in a job-skills mismatch in later years.

In 2000, analysts commended Botswana's strong fiscal management record, but noted emerging weaknesses, including concerns regarding fiscal discipline in the face of rising expenditures.

J. Clark Leith (2000):

> While government was successful in implementing a macroeconomic planning process, it was somewhat less successful in three important dimensions of expenditure policy: (1) consistently maintaining overall macroeconomic balance; (2) achieving the optimal share of government expenditure in the economy; and (3) maintaining an appropriate balance in the composition of government expenditure. ..... With ample funds in the bank (from mining receipts), and in the absence of specific restraining influences, it was all too easy for government to give into demands

for particular expenditures of one kind or another. Gradually the ratio of government expenditure to GDP grew, becoming one of the highest in Africa – higher even than countries which have garnered a reputation for indiscipline. Indeed, Botswana's ratio of central government expenditure to GDP ...(was) substantially in excess of the average of high income countries.

Leith cited some instances of waste and noted the scale of spending of mineral rents on the military:

The category "general public services", including government transport, buildings, police and the courts, certainly contained some waste, but did not take on an ever-expanding share of government expenditure as so often happened elsewhere. ....The magnitude of the military expenditure is also notable. In the 1970s Botswana was ill equipped to stand up to the hostile regimes which surrounded it in South Africa, South African controlled Namibia, and the UDI regime in Rhodesia.... Botswana's investment in its military escalated. The result was that, in the first half of the 1990s, Botswana's military expenditure, as a proportion of GDP became one of the highest reported in Africa.

Leith's positive and negative assessments were reinforced by other analysts. Glenn-Marie Lange and Matthew Wright (2002) wrote:

Botswana is an excellent model for resource-rich economies, escaping the 'resource curse' through prudent macroeconomic management. It devised its own rule-of-thumb for reinvestment of mineral revenues to offset depletion, the Sustainable Budget Index (SBI), which requires that all mineral revenues be reinvested. ...

The SBI, with its strong bias toward reinvestment, has served Botswana well in the past, but .... there is evidence that not all of public sector investment has been productive, and that a better allocation of mineral revenues might improve the sustainability of the economy. ... there are no criteria for allocation of mineral revenues, or evaluating a given allocation..... Closer examination reveals that less of the revenues have been used for productive investment than the SBI would indicate.

Some capital account spending does not add to productive capacity ....(and) though not quantifiable, there is a tendency toward 'monuments', which are not productive. Some of the investments may even be harmful, leading to the depletion of other natural capital. .... The process of approving development projects is not subject to close economic scrutiny.

At this point, as seen in Fig. 5.1 which shows the percentile ranking for different indicators (0 being the lowest performer and 100 being the highest), measures taken to improve various aspects of governance were reflected in possible influences on government effectiveness such as control of corruption or voice and accountability. Both improved significantly in 2003 and 2004 respectively. However, after 2004, subsequent deterioration in these indicators was matched by deterioration in government effectiveness.

Some analysts have also noted the adverse impacts of mineral dependency on income equity, job creation and on total

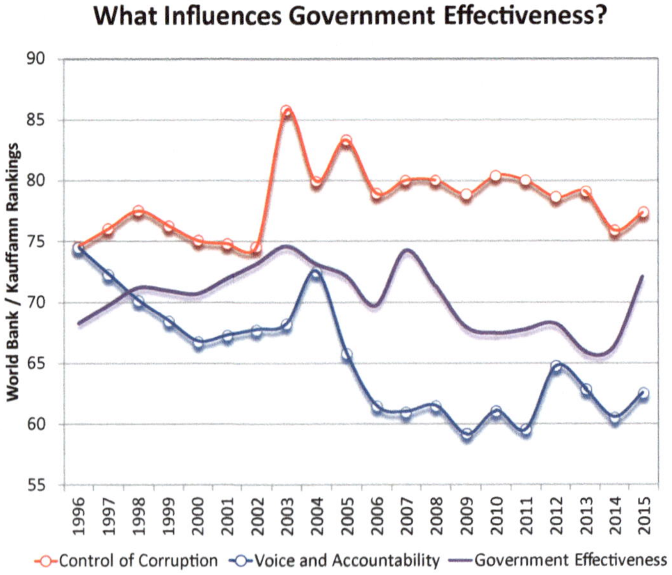

Fig. 5.1   Governance Indicators in Botswana

factor productivity. Back in 1986, a World Bank Report titled *Public Expenditure and Development in Botswana* had indicated that:

> In order to cope with the increasing pressures associated with income disparities and high population growth, in the short and medium term Botswana must work to *expand the capabilities of existing production activities*. For the much longer run Botswana will need to continue laying the basis for industrialization.

This advice still remains valid today, almost thirty years later.

J. Clark Leith (2000) observed that with the focus on discovery and mining of diamonds, alongside population growth at about 3.5% per annum, Botswana was not able to create enough jobs to absorb all new entrants to the labour force and the result was growing unemployment:

> Data from the censuses and the 1993/94 HIES[7] provide numbers which suggest a serious and growing unemployment problem. The 1991 census reported an unemployment rate of 14% and the 1993/94 HIES revealed a rate of 21% (NDP8 page 55).

Private sector job creation was being crowded out by government pay levels:

> The crowding out of private formal sector employment, via more rapid growth of government wages and salaries, stands in contrast with the crowding out mechanisms typically found elsewhere... In the 1990s the phenomenon of youth unemployment (also) began to emerge. The ranks of junior and senior secondary school leavers were growing much faster than demand for labor with those skills. Unemployment stood at 41% for the 15-24 age group, compared to the total unemployment rate of 21% reported for the labor force as a whole. At the same time, the structure of wages and salaries remained heavily influenced by the public service.

---

[7]Household Income and Expenditure Survey.

Leith also found that after diamond production peaked in the mid-1980s, total factor productivity estimates dropped sharply for the economy. This suggests that the sizeable investment in health and basic education may have been uninformed, "in a vacuum"; as investments geared towards the productive sector in industry-related capabilities in the labour force, and in technology fell short (notwithstanding the World Bank's 1986 advice to bolster these). Leith wrote that:

> Calculation of total factor productivity, TFP is by no means an exact science, but the Botswana data do permit it for the period 1974/75 to 1994/95. The calculations … reveal a TFP growth for Botswana over the two decades running at 2.2%, which is similar to that calculated for the very fast growing Asian countries over somewhat longer periods. However, when the data are broken into the earlier and the later decades, they reveal a marked change. TFP growth drops from a rate of 4% for the earlier decade to 0.5% for the later decade. Thus, the rapid growth of output masked a substantial fall in productivity growth.

Other analysts have commented on low *public* sector productivity and weak implementation capacity. The Botswana Institute of Development Policy Analysis, BIDPA (2004) policy brief on public sector reform initiatives noted that:

> (Public sector) reforms appear to have been influenced by the realization that, in spite of the country's relative success in economic terms, its public sector performs poorly. Official statements, including the National Development Plans (NDPs), annual budget speeches and the Vision 2016 document, identify low public sector productivity and weak implementation capacity as the major factors that constrain the realization of public policies that are otherwise clear and comprehensive.

> The Privatization Policy for Botswana (2000) acknowledged that the public sector had grown too large and cumbersome for efficient management and required re-orientation towards facilitation and regulation, rather than direct provision.

Recent studies conducted by BIDPA… reveal fundamental structural and organizational problems that constrain effective and efficient implementation of rural development. These include lack of clarity of functions, roles and responsibilities between central government and local government councils, ignorance of policy objectives, strategies and expected outcomes by line officers, and general lack of human capacity and skills. … The 2003 study on decentralization initiatives also revealed the recipients' perceptions of low effectiveness, inefficiency and inadequacy of coverage of public services delivered by local government councils and land boards. Additionally, a customer satisfaction survey of the public service conducted in the last quarter of 2003 for the Directorate of Public Service Management (DPSM) identified citizens' perceptions that the public sector in Botswana performs poorly in terms of effectiveness, efficiency and responsiveness to public demands.

Government practitioners made similar observations. The Public Service Reforms Coordinator E. Magosi (2006) noted that:

The government performance system was brought in because there were serious problems in the delivery of government services to Botswana citizens. There are four primary problem areas:

- Firstly, we had the plans and resources, but we could not deliver on the promises that the government made;
- Secondly, the public service had become so insensitive that civil servants were "the masters" instead of "the servants". The Director-Generals, Directors and Supervisor's offices were no-go areas to the public. The public did not know where to go and who to contact when they had problems. Citizens did not think they were getting their money's worth;
- Thirdly, we needed to align planning with the budgeting process[8]; and
- Lastly, we had to ensure that there is effective performance in delivery by the whole organization and individuals.

---

[8]It is worth noting here that over a decade earlier, in 1984 World Bank staff (Nimrod Raphaeli, Jacques Roumani and A. C. MacKellar) had commended Botswana for the effectiveness of its fiscal management system in which "planning and budgeting remain(ed) under the domain of a unified Ministry of Finance and Development Planning ensuring a considerable measure of integration and cohesiveness between them." The bullet is puzzling, therefore, unless internal restructuring between 1984 and 2006 weakened or removed the alignment between planning and budgeting.

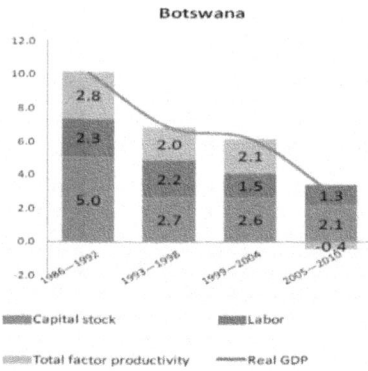

Fig. 5.2 Total factor productivity's contribution to growth (*Source* Parulian, Friska (2013) IMF, IMF Staff calculations)

In 2013, the International Monetary Fund also weighed in on declining productivity concerns. A "selected issues" paper on Botswana sought to determine the main contributors to growth over time and expressed concern at the trend calculated for total factor productivity's contribution (Fig. 5.2).

As seen in Fig. 5.2, capital stock (the medium grey shade) has always been the largest input in the growth function, while the labour input (dark grey shade) has been much less. Of particular concern is the fact that total factor productivity's contribution to growth (light grey shade) has seen substantial decline since the end of the 1990s.

The Model and Data

Potential Determinants of Government Effectiveness

The literature identifies numerous factors influencing effective governance. As seen in the above literature review, mining dominance can be an adverse influence on government performance, especially in areas such as effective human capital development (essential for productivity and long-term growth). Even if there is high investment in human capital, the quality of that investment may be suboptimal, undermining productivity outcomes. Other factors likely to be pertinent to government effectiveness in the mineral dependency context are also considered below.

Participation of citizens in governance: As seen in the literature discussed above (Schumpeter, Moore and others), the government's over-reliance on mineral revenues from taxes, royalties and dividends tends to marginalise the role that broad-based citizen participation plays in incentivising effective government performance. Based on this reasoning, it is likely that if significant, citizen participation will be a positive influence on government effectiveness.

Size of government: Garcia-Sanchez et al. (2013) estimated government effectiveness using a 202-country, panel data dependence model. They found that government effectiveness was explained initially by the organisational environment related to the level of economic development and the educational level. They also found that based on a country's income distribution, factors such as government size and gender diversity could also affect government effectiveness. Cross-country panel analysis such as this provides some insight into what factors might generally influence government effectiveness, but it does not confirm specifics with regard to an individual country. Since Botswana was classified as middle income for the period considered in this study, and its educational status did not change much either, those two variables are unlikely to help us estimate government effectiveness in Botswana. Instead, I will explore whether government size influences government effectiveness.

Quality of regulation: Some authors have also looked at the impact of regulatory systems on government effectiveness. An OECD (2000) study, Reducing the Risk of Policy Failure: Challenges for Regulatory Compliance, looked at the impact of regulatory failure (specifically inadequate compliance), on government effectiveness. In the case of Botswana, data on regulatory compliance was not available; however, while it is unlikely to capture regulatory compliance, the paper will explore whether the indicator "quality of regulation" which measures perceptions of the ability of the government to formulate and implement sound policies and regulations that permit and promote private sector development, can nevertheless help to explain government effectiveness.

Control of corruption: Various studies have shown that the control of corruption contributes to government effectiveness. Study of the causes and consequences of corruption has a long history in economics, going back fifty years to seminal contributions on "rent seeking". These studies showed that in addition to stealth of public funds, corrupt public sector practices, which are illegal activities by government and government agency officials, reduced the economic efficiency of governments. Mauro (1997) reviewed empirical studies that used cross-country regressions to determine the strength of the links between corruption and its causes and consequences. He presented evidence on how corruption influenced governments' choices regarding what to spend their money on—often to the detriment of the economy, and how it discouraged productive investment and limited economic growth to a significant extent. He noted that resource-rich economies may be more likely to be subjected to extreme rent-seeking behaviour than resource-poor ones. Various corruption channels were highlighted by Mauro.

First, corrupt government officials often influenced government expenditures away from the public welfare objective, towards opportunities for extorting bribes. Large projects whose exact value was difficult to monitor presented lucrative opportunities for corruption, making it easier to collect substantial bribes—"facilitation fees", for example on large infrastructure projects or high-technology defence systems; Second, the allocation of public procurement contracts through a corrupt system often led to lower quality infrastructure and public services; Third, in corrupt systems, businessmen often found that an up-front bribe was "required" before an enterprise could be licensed (for example) and that afterwards corrupt officials might lay claim to part of the proceeds from the investment. Businessmen, therefore, interpreted corruption as a species of tax—though of a particularly pernicious nature. This "tax" diminished the private sector incentive to invest.

More recently, econometric analysis of a panel of 52 middle-income countries (Iqbal and Daly 2014) confirmed that government rent-seeking activities retarded economic growth, while reduced corruption was growth enhancing. Thus the relationship between control of corruption and government effectiveness will be explored.

The reasoning behind population density affecting government effectiveness (Moore) also makes sense in the Botswana context; however, it has not been possible to gather meaningful time series data on population density for the period under consideration, so this will not be explored.

The Model

Based on the foregoing, the model investigated is one where government effectiveness in the economy is a function of its mineral dependency, control of corruption, the voice and participation of its citizens, regulatory quality and the size of government. It has not been possible to secure an adequate set of annual productivity time series, so this variable is not reflected in the model.

Government effectiveness is given by:

$$GE_t = \alpha_t + \beta^1 MD_t + \beta^2 CC_t + \beta^3 CP_t + \beta^4 RQ_t + \beta^5 SG_t + \varepsilon \quad (5.1)$$

where:

GE is government effectiveness, MD is mineral dependency, CC is control of corruption, CP is citizen participation, RQ is regulatory quality and SG is the size of government.

With respect to the data series used, government effectiveness is represented by the indicator of the same name published in the Worldwide Governance Indicators.[9] It captures perceptions of the quality of public services, the quality of the civil service and the degree of its independence from political pressures, the quality of policy formulation and implementation and the credibility of the government's commitment to such policies.

Mineral dependency is represented by the share of mining in gross domestic product (GDP). The series is calculated using real values of mining GDP and total GDP.

---

[9]See Daniel Kaufmann, Aart Kraay and Massimo Mastruzzi (2010). *The Worldwide Governance Indicators: A Summary of Methodology, Data and Analytical Issues*, World Bank Policy Research Working Paper No. 5430. http://papers.ssrn.com/sol3/papers.cfm?abstract_id=1682130.

The control of corruption series is taken from Worldwide Governance Indicators and reflects perceptions of the extent to which public power is exercised for private gain, including both petty and grand forms of corruption, as well as "capture" of the state by elites and private interests.

Citizen participation is represented by the voice and accountability series in Worldwide Governance Indicators and captures perceptions of the extent to which a country's citizens are able to participate in selecting their government, as well as freedom of expression, freedom of association and a free media.

The regulatory quality series is also taken from Worldwide Governance Indicators and measures perceptions of the ability of the government to formulate and implement sound policies and regulations that permit and promote private sector development.

Size of government is represented by government's share in total GDP. The series is calculated using real values of government and total GDP.

Time Series Characteristics of the Data

I first establish whether the data for each of the variables used in the government effectiveness Eq. (5.1) has characteristics similar to a random walk (i.e. is the first order of integration) as expected. Given that the various series reflect economic patterns and none of the variables are rates of change, the general expectation is that they should all follow or be similar to a random walk pattern. To confirm this, I use R-Studio to test for the stationarity (order of integration) of each of the variables in the government effectiveness equation and for cointegration (a long relationship) of this dependent variable with each of the independent variables in Eq. (5.1). The stationarity tests used are the Phillips-Perron (PP) and Augmented Dickey-Fuller (ADF) unit root tests (e.g. see Banerjee et al. 1993).

Stationarity Tests

The results of the unit root (stationarity) tests on all the variables are given in Annex I Table 5.A1, with all variables represented in natural logs. The unit root test statistics in the table are compared with their corresponding critical values at the bottom of the table. For the ADF test, a test statistic that is less (more negative) than the critical value confirms that the tested values are stationary and the series is I(0). Likewise, in the PP test, a value that is less (more negative) than the critical value indicates a rejection of the null hypothesis that the series has a unit root (rejection of stance that it is non-stationary). These comparisons show that both the PP and ADF tests reject stationarity of each of the series where the values are levels, but confirm stationarity of the first differenced values of these series, confirming that the variables are all integrated of order 1, i.e. I(1). The only caveat is with respect to control of corruption where the PP test suggests stationarity of the level (with intercept) at the 5% level of significance; however, stationarity of the level is rejected even at 10% by the more reliable ADF test and by the Zivot-Andrews test which allows for structural breaks in the level or trend of the series or both. Since evidence of stationarity was not convincing, the level was differenced and stationarity of the differenced control of corruption series confirmed. Thus all the variables are confirmed as integrated of order 1.

Estimation and Analysis of Results

Having established the order of integration of each variable in the model, it is then possible to find out if there is a long-run (cointegrating) relationship between the dependent variable and any of the independent variables in the model. Cointegration confirms the presence of a valid long-run relationship between variables. For cointegration to be possible, the two variables being tested must be integrated of the same order. If there is a cointegrating relationship, then the residuals from the relationship can be used to construct a dynamic error correction model, where changes in explanatory variables help to explain changes in government effectiveness with the annual adjustment towards long-term equilibrium captured by the error correction term.

Long-Run Relationships and the Government Effectiveness Model

When testing the natural log values of all the variables for a long-run relationship with government effectiveness, the results showed only mineral dependency to be cointegrated with government effectiveness at 95% confidence (i.e. 5% significance) in one test and at 90% confidence in two others (Table 5.2). So we can be reasonably confident that government effectiveness is cointegrated with mineral dependency. In Table 5.2, the Johansen test results (using 2 lags) confirm cointegration for government effectiveness and mineral dependency. The Johansen test has two forms: the trace test and the maximum Eigen-value test. The trace test has the null that the number of linear combinations that is cointegrated $K=0$, so rejecting the null means there is at least one cointegration relationship. In the Eigen test, rejecting the null $K=0$ implies there is just one (it confirms just one) cointegrating relationship. As seen in Table 5.2, the Johansen Eigen test confirmed cointegration at the 5% significance level, while the Johansen trace test, as well as the Phillip-Perron test, confirmed it at the 10% significance level. Thus a long-run relationship between government effectiveness and mineral dependency is confirmed.

None of the other variables: control of corruption, citizen participation, size of government or regulatory quality were cointegrated with government effectiveness in Botswana. Control of corruption was however, a significant explanatory variable in the static model, alongside mineral dependency, even though it has no cointegrating relationship.

Having determined that there is a long-run relationship between government effectiveness and mineral dependency, Eq. (5.1) was then estimated with only the statistically significant influences on government effectiveness being retained. This gave the following static model:

In Table 5.3, the static regression's coefficient of determination, R^2 suggests that mineral dependency, together with control of corruption explains about 75% of government effectiveness in the long run. The equation standard error of 0.019 supports its overall validity. The Durbin-Watson statistic of 2 confirms the statistical independence of

Table 5.2 Cointegration regression and test results for government effectiveness

Regression	Long-run coefficient	R^2	t-value	Equation DW	Residual ADF[a]	Residual Phillips-Perron	Johansen-Procedure Trace	Eigen
Government effectiveness vs								
Mineral dependency (real mining GDP/real GDP)	0.055 (0.02)	0.35	3.1	1.32	−2.64 [−3.24]	−2.89* [−2.65](−3.03)	**19.92*** [**17.85**]	**16.79**** (**15.67**)
Size of government (real govt. GDP/real GDP)	0.17 (0.11)	0.12	1.6	0.90	−2.50 [−3.24]	−2.51c [−2.65]	3.74t [5.42] $r=1$	2.05 [7.52]
Control of corruption	0.23 (0.22)	0.05	1.0	0.72	−2.35 [−3.24]	−2.25b [−3.28]	4.62t [5.42] $r=1$	4.64 [5.87]
Regulatory quality	0.10 (0.17)	0.02	0.6	0.78	−2.18 [−3.24]	−2.14c [−2.65]	2.78 [7.52] $r=1$	2.78 [7.52]
Citizen participation (voice and accountability)	0.18 (0.11)	0.12	1.6	0.82	−2.24 [−3.24]	−2.46c [−2.65]	5.14t [5.42] $r=1$	5.28 [7.52]

[a]Lag selection is achieved according to the Akaike "AIC" or the Bayes "BIC" information criteria

Note All variables are expressed as natural logs. Standard errors are in parentheses. For unit-root tests on residuals, critical values are shown in normal parentheses at 5%, and in box parentheses at 10%. For the ADF lag selection is achieved according to the Akaike "AIC" or the Bayes "BIC" information criteria with the best result shown in this table. The mineral dependency Johansen-Procedure results shown are for the null $r=0$ in a trace test without a linear trend and constant. If the test is done with a linear trend in the shift correction, then the null is rejected again, this time for both $r=0$ and $r<=1$ at 10% and almost so at 5%. The equation Durbin-Watson statistic, DW is a rough check. When zero or near-zero, then stationary residuals are unlikely

Key for superscripts c denotes "with constant" (intercept), *t* denotes "with trend", *b* denotes "with both"

Significance codes *** = 0.01, ** = 0.05, * = 0.1

Table 5.3 The long-run government effectiveness model

Government effectiveness$_t$ = 1.95 + 0.06 (mineral dependency$_{t-1}$) + 0.36 (corruption control$_t$) + ε		
	(3.42)*** (6.59)****	(3.63)***

R^2 = 0.75,   Adjusted R^2 = 0.72,   DW = 2.0,   S.E. = 0.019, $F(2,$ 16) = 23.65
p-value = 0.0000016, t-values in parentheses
Significance codes **** = 0.001, *** = 0.01, ** = 0.05, * = 0.1

the errors (no serial correlation). The t-test determines whether the coefficient for each independent variable is useful—that is whether the variable is significant in estimating government effectiveness. The t value for each variable needs to be higher than the critical value of t, for this to hold. This is the case for both the explanatory variables shown. Mineral dependency (or mining dominance) is strongly significant at the 0.1% level of significance, while control of corruption (and the constant). is significant at the 1% level. The F statistic is used to determine whether these results occurred by chance. The F-test shows that this probability, p = 0.0000016, is very low—therefore the regression equation is useful in estimating government effectiveness.

All explanatory variables are of the expected sign: control of corruption is positive as expected, since increased control over corruption supports more efficient resource use and better quality services; and mining dominance is positive, implying that Botswana's government systems relied on strong mining income to be effective. As mining's share in GDP declined, however, so did government effectiveness suggesting that either (a) government set up systems reliant on mining income to be effective (systems where mining's ample financing of human and physical capital accumulation may have compensated for lack of effectiveness in services to the non-mining sector) and where a non-binding budget constraint may have covered for laxity or (b) government restructuring over the years intended to deal with declining mining income, resulted instead in reduced government effectiveness; or both.

As all the variables are in natural logarithms, the coefficients shown for explanatory variables are elasticities. Taking this into account in interpreting impacts, a 10% increase in mineral dependency (other things held constant) leads to a 0.6% improvement in government effectiveness. Likewise, a 10% improvement in the control of corruption, other things held constant, leads to a 3.6% improvement in government effectiveness.

A Dynamic Error Correction Model for Government Effectiveness

The stored residuals from the cointegrating regression are used as the error correction series in a dynamic equation that investigates how changes in explanatory variables impact government effectiveness in the short run. The error correction specification is said to be one of the most efficient dynamic representations in that it encompasses all other dynamic specifications (see Engle and Granger 1987).

The error correction term is incorporated in a statistically consistent model that relates annual changes in the Botswana government's effectiveness to annual changes in other variables. By including the error correction term (which represents adjustment towards the long-run equilibrium), the model links the short-run change in government effectiveness to the long-run relationship that exists between government effectiveness and mineral dependency. The error correction term measures the feedback mechanism—where the long-term relationship feeds back into the change in government effectiveness seen each year. Thus both short-run and long-run information is provided in the same model.

Initially, an over-parameterised equation was constructed, with the (stationary) first difference of government effectiveness as the dependent variable and the (stationary) differences of all the other variables in Eq. 5.1(with one lag) as explanatory variables. A variable-by-variable investigation (including lags), then provided guidance on the appropriate selection of variables and lags to be retained in the dynamic model. Insignificant variables were deleted. The dynamic model also includes a lagged error correction term EC_{t-1}, and a constant term and a trend term. R-Studio output for the period 1996–2015 is shown in Table 5.4.

Table 5.4 Dynamic error correction model for government effectiveness

Regression model	Coefficient	Standard error	t-value
Change in government effectiveness as a function of:			
Change in control of corruption$_{t-1}$ (lag 1)	0.250	0.122	2.050**
Change in citizen participation$_t$	0.252	0.121	2.000**
Error correction term$_{t-1}$ (ec$_{t-1}$)	−0.800	0.205	−4.076****

Note Standard errors are in parentheses; $R^2 = 0.60$, Adjusted $R^2 = 0.53$, SE = 0.02, $F(3,16) = 8$
F-test p-value: 0.0018, DW = 1.2, Akaike criterion: dropped from −129.80 in the initial over-parameterised regression to −141.77 in the final model
Significance codes $^{****} = 0.001$, $^{***} = 0.01$, $^{**} = 0.05$, $^{*} = 0.1$

The over-parameterised dynamic equation was simplified in a way that improves the goodness of fit of the model so that as variables were reduced, model parsimony was achieved. An information criterion (the Akaike criterion), which shows progressive model parsimony (as it becomes more negative), was used to guide the process. Thus differenced variables in the dynamic version of Eq. (5.1) were eliminated and the dynamic version of Eq. (5.1) reduced to Eq. (5.2) below where changes in government effectiveness are given by the error correction adjustment, changes in control of corruption and changes in citizen participation:

$$\Delta GE_t = ec_{t-1} + \gamma^2 \Delta CC_{t-1} + \gamma^3 \Delta CP_t + \varepsilon \qquad (5.2)$$

Estimates from the regression based on Eq. (5.2) are given in Table 5.4.

The model has a good fit with highly significant explanatory variables and a low regression standard error. The Durbin Watson statistic confirms that there is no autocorrelation in the residuals.[10] The low F-test

---

[10]The Durbin-Watson test statistic tests the null hypothesis that the residuals from the regression are not autocorrelated. A value near 0 indicates positive autocorrelation, near 2 indicates no autocorrelation and near 4 indicates negative autocorrelation. For the critical values, the regression has no lagged dependent variable, and there is no constant term, so the applicable table by Durbin (Farebrother Tables) is used. The lower bound for the dynamic error correction model is 0.694 while the upper bound is 1.41 at the 1% level of significance. The test statistic of 1.2 is close enough to the upper bound that it is acceptable, in this context, not to reject the null, so we can conclude that it is likely that there is no autocorrelation.

probability of 0.0018 confirms that the regression is useful in explaining changes in government effectiveness. A plot of the regression residuals (see Annex III) does not show growing values over time, confirming that there's no heteroskedasticity.

In the short run, the dynamics in the parsimonious dynamic model show that out of all the variables in the initial model (Eq. 5.1) including the constant, only changes in control of corruption and citizen participation influence the change in government effectiveness, while mineral dependency has a strong long-term influence. All the variables have the expected signs; increasing control of corruption and increasing citizen participation as expected by the literature, both lead to improvements in government effectiveness. Thus the results show that last year's decline in control of corruption and this year's decline in citizen voice and government accountability, both lead to a decrease in government effectiveness.[11] The combined effect of both the variables and the annual adjustment towards long-run equilibrium is to explain 60% of changes in government effectiveness.

Of note in the equation is the strongly significant, negative error correction term. This term estimates the feedback in the current year from last year's disequilibrium from the long-run government effectiveness relationship. The coefficient gives the speed of adjustment—which is quite fast. The results suggest that over the course of a year up to 80% of last year's disequilibrium feeds back into the current change in government effectiveness guiding it towards the long-run level of government effectiveness. The coefficients (elasticities) on the other (differenced) terms, on the other hand, provide an indication of short-run influences on government effectiveness within a given year; with a 10% increase in improvements in control of corruption or in citizen participation (other things held constant) leading to a 2.5% increase in improvements in government effectiveness in each case.

---

[11]The literal interpretation given the data used, is that perceived improvements or deterioration in government effectiveness are influenced by changing perceptions regarding the control of corruption and voice and accountability. So if government is able to improve the control of corruption and of voice and accountability enough to improve perceptions of both on a sustained basis, this will enhance government effectiveness.

Conclusions and Policy Implications

The results of the analysis establish that mining dominance in Botswana has had a long-term influence on government effectiveness, where the effectiveness of governance systems has been dependent on strong mining sector receipts. Due to its entrenched reliance on mineral export receipts, Botswana has struggled to achieve the type of structural transformation envisaged in its early economic diversification strategies, which sought the sustained rapid expansion of non-mining exportable goods and services, which would, in turn, generate foreign exchange and government revenues after diamonds and significantly reduce double-digit unemployment.

Conclusions

The findings in this paper confirm that there is a statistically significant underlying relationship between mineral dependency and government effectiveness in the long run with the latter relying on the former. In the short-term, meanwhile, even though the short-term adjustment back towards the long-term mineral dependency relationship dominates, increasing the pace at which improvements are attained in the control of corruption and citizen participation (embodied in voice and accountability data) also makes a significant contribution, accelerating improvements in government effectiveness. Thus while government effectiveness in Botswana relied to some extent on mineral receipts in the past; going forward, as mineral receipts decline, a rapid pace of improvements in control of corruption and voice and accountability can help to recoup government's effectiveness. Put differently, while corruption and lack of accountability have hampered government's service delivery and general effectiveness, quickly addressing these two main issues will help the government recover its effectiveness even with declines in mining receipts.

The dynamic error correction model shows that the influence from the preceding year's mineral dependency feeds back rapidly into current changes in government effectiveness on an annual basis as the system adjusts towards the long-run level of government effectiveness. In addition, changes in the control of corruption in the preceding year and in citizen participation (represented by voice and accountability data) in the current year both have a significant and positive impact on the improvement or deterioration of government effectiveness. Thus, for example, an escalation of the increase in corruption in the previous year and of the current year's decline in citizens' voice and government accountability will each escalate the current year's deterioration in government effectiveness; and vice versa.

The review of developments in Botswana illustrated how in recent years, as mining dominance receded, the absence or mismatch of requisite capabilities, both in government and in the non-mining private sector, to sustain development, became more evident. That discussion alongside Fig. 5.1 and the charts in Annex III reveal that signs of weakening in government effectiveness have been there since the early 2000s after mining's dominance in GDP passed its peak and again since the 2007 global crisis. As the buffer of excess mining receipts declined over time, government effectiveness followed suit, with weaknesses showing up in poor government service delivery, weak implementation and inadequate measures to support non-mining private sector development. The mining-dominated economic structure has thus worked against sustaining the type of government effectiveness required to achieve diversification goals and sustainable growth.

A more effective government will need to be better equipped to implement reforms and programs needed to achieve diversification goals, empowering Botswana to produce more and different non-mining products. As these products require capabilities (diversified economies have more capabilities and so are able to make more products—see Hausmann 2010), a more effective government will be able to achieve visible, meaningful and relevant improvements in the quality of education and labour force skills outcomes, given the enormous financial investment (from mineral rents) that has gone into the education sector. The fact that Botswana wishes to graduate from the "poor economy" model that is dependent on mining because of a lack of capabilities in its people, to the model of a middle-income economy with many capabilities enabling it to produce different and more complex products, means that an effective government has to be able to use mineral rents to grow the requisite capabilities in its people—capabilities that were initially identified by the World Bank in 1986 when it noted the country's over-reliance on expatriate ownership and management *of enterprise*. Such capabilities are needed along value chains, to match the productive private sector's expansion needs and to match ongoing advances in technology. Active attention to value chains has only just begun three decades after the World Bank report, while the approach to addressing capabilities relevant to non-mining industry still needs work.

Policy Implications

Declines in government effectiveness have to be reversed; regardless of whether or not the mining sector and mining revenues make a comeback in the future. This requires a shift in internal incentives and motivations. Continued reliance on mining for growth and the financing of government, without a correction of the adverse internal incentives, and constrained systems and capabilities in government, will mean government effectiveness remains elusive. This, in turn, will stifle diversification and sustainable growth goals, result in wider income disparities, and contribute to youth underemployment and the high level of unemployment overall.

Consideration should be given to correcting incentives faced by government officials so that they are in tandem first, with the welfare of economic sectors engaged in the production of exportable non-mining goods and services, and second with the Botswana public they serve. This entails correcting government's organisational effort so that it is directed at the relevant non-mining private sector growth and development; strengthening and safeguarding accountability systems and re-strengthening management and operational systems to counter the adverse effects of mining dependence (see Annex II for details).

On control of corruption, given that Botswana's global rankings are now at the lowest levels seen since 2003, beefing up the capacity, authority, trustworthiness and effectiveness of anti-corruption systems and entities (covering both prevention and cure of corruption), is paramount. The government also needs to be seen to act on perceptions of corruption and to visibly enforce penalties for bribery, rigged projects and failure to comply with the required international best practice. This could have a sizable positive impact on the government's effectiveness and therefore on the quality of governance. It is no longer enough for Government to just say it has zero tolerance for corruption; it has to be seen to consistently demonstrate and enforce zero tolerance for corruption.

Even more than the control of corruption, Botswana's voice and accountability rankings dropped dramatically after 2004. Government effectiveness will also benefit by speeding up measures to improve citizen participation. This will entail measures to protect the robustness of democratic institutions and the independence of the three arms of government; it will require practices that acknowledge public concerns and enhance public trust in election systems and a government that shows leadership in actively and openly supporting freedom of expression, freedom of association and a free media.

For human capital investments by government to be relevant and effective, they need to visibly enhance productivity, skills and capabilities in the labour force. The Botswana government has to be able to address the capabilities gap in the existing labour force directly, through industry-based training of firms. The requisite capabilities needed now have to be developed by doing, not behind a classroom desk: for example, (a) setting up modern model factories or model firms and using them to train practitioners in the sector and along value chains and (b) facilitating the adoption of new approaches and technologies and adapting competitive technologies jointly with relevant private sector entities.

All the above measures would help to strengthen government effectiveness and do so in a more sustainable manner than continued reliance on mineral receipts.

Annex I

Table 5.A1 Unit root tests for order of integration

Variable (natural logs)	ADF statistic (level)	ADF statistic (1st diff.)	Phillips-Perron statistic (level)	Phillips-Perron statistic (1st diff.)	Variable's order of integration
Government Effectiveness vs:	−2.2244	−3.4559***	−2.3829	−3.4379[b]**	I(1)
Mineral dependency (real mining GDP/ real GDP)	−2.3841	−2.1224**	−2.2414	−5.0110***	I(1)
Size of government (real govt. GDP/real GDP)	−2.2816	−2.9279***	−2.4831	−4.4360***	I(1)
Control of corruption	−1.4397	−3.0823***	−3.1489**	−7.3555***	I(1)
Regulatory quality	−3.1871	−2.6221**	−1.8795	−3.8082**	I(1)
Citizen participation (voice & accountability)	−2.0390	−3.2403***	−2.3584	−4.6300***	I(1)
Critical values at 5%:	−3.60	−1.95	−3.67	−3.04[b]/−3.69[c]	

Note Sample: 1996–2015, 2 lags; For the ADF lag selection is achieved according to the Akaike "AIC" or the Bayes "BIC" information criteria with the best result shown in this table

Key for superscripts c denotes "with constant" (intercept), t denotes "with trend", b denotes "with both constant and trend"

Significance codes *** = 0.01, ** = 0.05, * = 0.1

Table 5.A2 Cointegrating regressions for government effectiveness

Cointegrating regression for Model 1 (mineral dependency*)*
Government effectiveness = 0.055 (mineral dependency) + 4.07
(0.02)   (0.06)
$R^2 = 0.35$, $F(1,18) = 10$, t(mineral dependency) = 3.12 (significant at 1%), constant significant at 0.1%, DW = 1.32

Cointegrating regression for Model 2 (mineral dependency and control of corruption)
Government effectiveness = 0.086 (mineral dependency) $_{t-1}$ +0.46 (control of corruption) + 1.95
(0.01)   (0.13)   (0.57)
$R^2 = 0.75$, $F(2,16) = 23$, t(mineral dependency) = 6.59 (significant at 0.1%), t(control of corruption) = 3.63 (significant at 1%), constant significant at 1%, DW = 2.06

Note In Model 1, the Durbin-Watson statistic of 1.3 falls above the upper bound of 1.147 in the Savin and White (DW) tables at the 1% significance level. This confirms that there is no autocorrelation in the residuals. Model 2 results for the Johansen (vector cointegration) procedure confirmed cointegration only at the 10% level of significance for the trace type test with a linear trend and shift correction. Model 1 had stronger cointegration results and so it is treated as the valid cointegrating regression and its residuals are used in the error correction model. When model 2 residuals were substituted in the error correction model, the model test results were similar

Model 2: Values of Johansen test-statistic (bold) and critical values of test

	Test	10pct	5pct	1pct
$r<=1$	**6.29**	5.42	6.79	10.04
$r=0$	**15.15**	13.78	15.83	19.85

Annex II: Policy Implications—Details

Correcting incentives faced by Government officials through accountability

The fortunes (welfare) of government officials and politicians should move in tandem with those of the Botswana they serve;

- An adverse economic climate for people in the non-mining sector should correspond to an adverse "economic climate" for public servants.
- Losses and waste of public resources impact Botswana negatively; they should impact the responsible parastatals, officials and ministers in public agencies, likewise.
- Non-performance and poor service delivery by the public sector impacts Botswana negatively; they should impact the responsible parastatals, ministers, managers and officials likewise.
- Loopholes and corruption impact Botswana negatively; they should impact the responsible parastatals, ministers, managers, officials and politicians likewise.

Correcting Government's organisational effort

Organisational effort should be directed at domestic non-mining business sector growth and development:

- Ministry, Central Bank and other Parastatal efforts should focus as much on improving the welfare of Botswana by growing the domestic business sector as on attracting foreign investors;
- Develop firm capabilities and more products. Focus to date has been on competitiveness policy, which is about improving the quality of what already exists—but if you don't have much by way of products to start with, then part of the mileage you would get out of a competitive environment is lost. In Botswana it is clear that more non-mining products are needed. Attention is being given to mineral beneficiation, however, given the poor connectedness of mining to the non-mining economy, the standard corrective measure of adding value to the raw materials—though beneficial, is not enough to diversify the economy. Mining has limited linkages and limited downstream scope. Progress in diversification beyond mining can be made by advancing in repeated short spurts to other products similar to or associated with those non-mining products already produced, along a well-defined value chain (Norway, Australia and Chile provide examples). Government has to be committed to providing the public inputs and unbiased price environment needed to support non-mining production and to build relevant capabilities in the current working population (not just in students). Innovation should be used to accumulate and enhance relevant capabilities useful for the diversification program looking forward.
- Ensure microeconomic policies target and serve local businesses efficiently—not just mining and foreign investors.
- Ensure macroeconomic policies are appropriate to non-mining private sector growth (avoid Dutch Disease tendencies).

Strengthening and safeguarding accountability systems

- Use technical team decisions for high-cost expenditure activities and remove discretionary powers and veto powers of senior officials and ministers.

- Reinstate the appropriate checks and balances to counter rent-seeking and enforce them.
- Eliminate personal and institutional conflicts of interest and take immediate corrective action to remove such conflicts when they arise.
- Act in response to perceptions of corruption (for example, by suspending officials who are being investigated). This is essential because perceptions of corruption that are not acted on embolden those that are already corrupt and attract more corrupt agents; as much as confirmed corruption itself does.
- Implement best practice used in comparable countries without qualifying and amending to maintain status quo.

Strengthening management and operational systems

- Build stronger managers. Have formalised compulsory management training of top global ranking, for current and upcoming managers (including Ministers if they are expected to manage), track and systemise the use of skills taught and rebuild stronger program and project management systems. Efficient and effective project and program management and implementation are critical. Efficiency monitoring is also important to avoid waste and the dissipation of resources and efforts, on low priority, low impact spending.
- Do not allow complacency to weaken or remove systems that work; or to remove or ignore checks and balances. For example, in the past use of social cost-benefit analysis where possible was mandatory, to assess expected project impacts on output/GDP or public welfare and prioritise efforts and procurement around the highest impact projects. While this is a critical task, it is no longer mandatory. However, the return on government spending must be measured, and consistently improved—a challenge—but especially critical.
- Build systems and know-how within government, for private sector development. The World Bank Group's International Finance Corporation (IFC) has numerous systems and mechanisms geared to this very purpose and could be a valuable partner in developing government officials' capabilities in this regard.

- Safeguard and perpetuate institutional memory. Accumulated knowledge resides in the heads of employees; once they go that knowledge is lost forever unless safeguards address this. Many corporations and countries use people who excelled in a given job, or in the same type of work, to serve on a fixed contractual basis as Advisors and mentors to new management incumbents, in order to pass on knowledge, avoid costly mistakes and sustain institutional memory. A post-contract bonus can be dependent on how well the incumbent delivers over the year after the Advisor leaves. Government systems have to be well entrenched and robustly structured—enough to ensure that newcomers do not drop the ball or reinvent the wheel due to ignorance of internal systems and processes, the rationale behind them and of past lessons. A new generation of officials is entering the civil service (as the first two generations leave or retire)—and maybe consideration should be given to requiring A or B grades on a compulsory civil service best-practice exam for incumbents and new entrants.

Annex III: Charts of Variable Levels

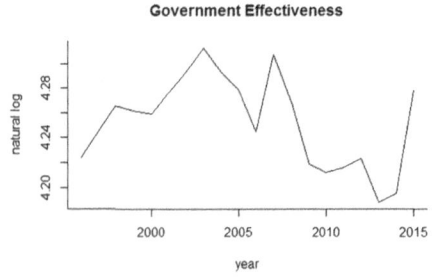

Government Effectiveness

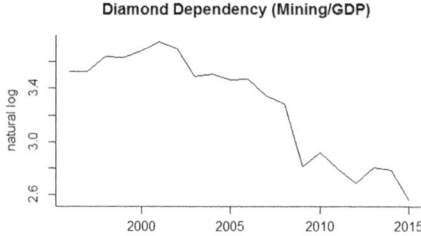

Diamond Dependency (Mining/GDP)

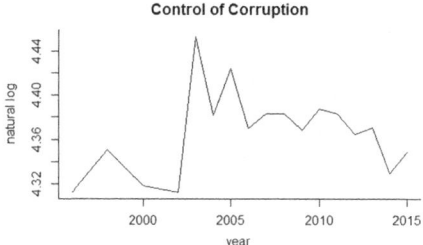

Control of Corruption

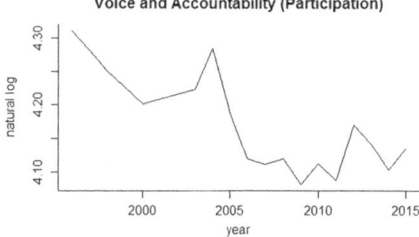

Voice and Accountability (Participation)

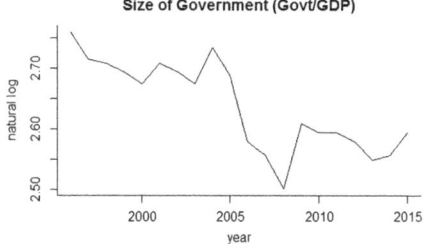

Size of Government (Govt/GDP)

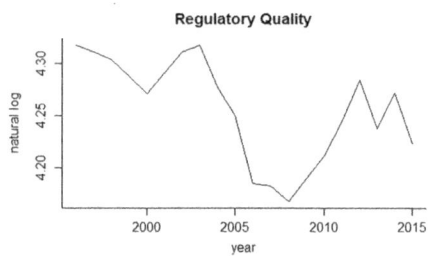

Charts of Model Residuals
Cointegration model

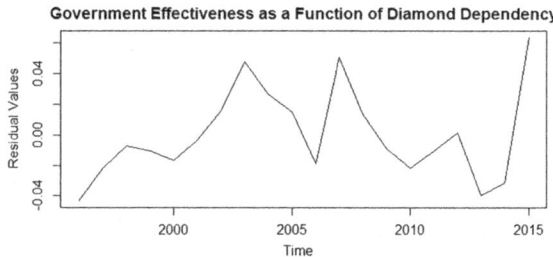

Dynamic error correction model

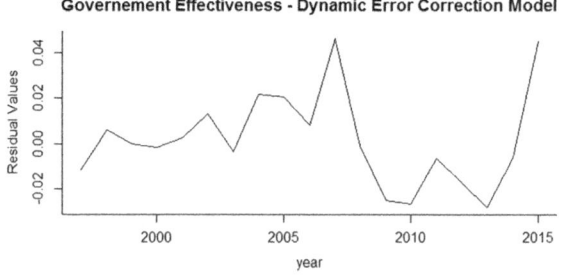

References

Acemoglu, D., Johnson, S., & Robinson, J. (2003). An African Success Story: Botswana. In D. Rodrik (Ed.), *In Search of Prosperity: Analytic Narratives on Economic Growth* (pp. 80–119). Princeton: Princeton University Press.

Banerjee, A., Dolado, J., Galibraith, J. W., & Hendry, D. F. (1993). *Cointegration, Error-Correction, and the Econometric Analysis of Non-stationary Data*. Oxford: Oxford University Press.

Beaulier, S., & Subrick, R. (2006). The Political Foundations of Development: The Case of Botswana. *Constitutional Political Economy, 17*(2), 103–115.

Botswana Institute of Development Policy Analysis, BIDPA. (2004). *Public Sector Reforms*. Gaborone: Botswana Institute of Development Policy Analysis, BIDPA.

Collier, P. (2011, March 28–30). *Role of the State in Natural Resources Exploration and Exploitation*. Paper presented at Natural Resource Management in Sub-Saharan Africa: Consequences and Policy Options for Africa, African Economic Research Consortium Senior Policy Seminar, Maputo.

Elbadawi, I. A., & Kaltani, L. (2007). *The Macroeconomics of Oil Booms: Lessons for SSA*. Washington, DC: Development Economic Research Group, World Bank.

Elbadawi, I. A., & Nandwa, B. (2011). *Managing Savings/Investment Decisions in Resource-rich Countries*. United Arab Emirates: Economic Policy and Research Institute.

Engle, R. F., & Granger, C. W. J. (1987). Co-Integration and Error Correction: Representation, Estimation, and Testing. *Econometrica, 55*(2), 251–276.

Garcia-Sanchez, I. M., Cuadrado-Ballestros, B., & Frias-Aceituno, J. (2013). Determinants of Government Effectiveness. *International Journal of Policy Administration, 36*(8), 567–577.

Goldscheid, R. (1917). *Staatssozialismus odor Staatskapitalismus* [State Socialism or State Capitalism]. Vienna: Brüder Suschitzky.

Harvey, C., & Lewis, S. R., Jr. (1990). *Policy Choice and Development Performance in Botswana*. London: Macmillan in Association with the OECD Development Centre.

Hausmann, R. (2010). *Diversification: Why and How?* Available via https://www.imw.fraunhofer.de/content/dam/moez/de/documents/Knowledge_Economy_Forum_9.pdf. Accessed 12 Oct 2011.

Hillbom, E. (2008). Diamonds or Development: A Structural Assessment of Botswana's Forty Years of Success. *Journal of Modern African Studies, 46*(2), 191–214.

Iimi, A. (2006). *Did Botswana Escape from the Resource Curse?* International Monetary Fund. Available via http://www.imf.org/external/pubs/ft/wp/2006/wp06138.pdf. Accessed 10 July 2009.

IMF. (2013a). *Botswana: 2013 Article IV Consultation.* Washington, DC: International Monetary Fund.

International Monetary Fund. (2013b). *Botswana Article IV Consultation* (IMF Country Report No. 13/296). Washington, DC: International Monetary Fund.

Iqbal, N., & Daly, V. (2014). Rent-Seeking Opportunities and Economic Growth in Transition Economies. *Journal of Economic Modelling, 37*(C), 16–22.

Jaimovich, E., & Rud, J. P. (2009). *Excessive Public Employment and Rent-Seeking Traps.* Collegio Carlo Alberto. Available via http://www.carloalberto.org/assets/working-papers/no.118.pdf. Accessed around July 2014.

Lange, G.-M., & Wright, M. (2002). *Sustainable Development in Mineral Economies: The Example of Botswana.* CEEPA. Available via https://ageconsearch.umn.edu/bitstream/18019/1/dp020003.pdf. Accessed 3 Mar and 23 May 2014.

Leith, J. C. (2000, June 6–8). *Why Botswana Prospered.* Paper presented at Canadian Economics Association Thirty-Fourth Annual Meetings, University of British Columbia, Vancouver.

Leith, J. C. (2005). *Why Botswana Prospered.* Montreal and Kingston: McGill-Queen's University Press.

Magosi, E. (2006). Botswana Develops a Strategy for Better Delivery. *Service Delivery Review, 4*(3), 78–80.

Mauro, P. (1997). *Why Worry About Corruption?* Economic Issues 6. Washington, DC: International Monetary Fund.

Modise, M. D. (1999). Managing Mineral Revenues in Botswana. In J. Mayer, B. Chambers, & A. Farooq (Eds.), *Development Policies in Natural Resource Economies.* New York and Geneva: UNCTAD and Edward Elgar.

Modise, M. D. (2000, November 7–9). *Management of Mineral Revenues: The Botswana Experience.* Paper presented at UNCTAD Workshop on Growth and Diversification in Mineral Economies, in Cape Town.

Moore, M. (2004). *Revenues, State Formation and the Quality of Governance in Developing Countries.* Brighton, UK: Institute of Development Studies at the University of Sussex.

Moore, M., Leavy, J., Houtzager, P., & White, H. (1999). *Polity Qualities: How Governance Affects Poverty*. The Institute of Development Studies at the University of Sussex. Available via https://opendocs.ids.ac.uk/opendocs/handle/123456789/3422. Accessed 30 Aug 2014.

Mpabanga, D. (1997). Constraints to Industrial Development. In J. S. Salkin, et al. (Eds.), *Aspects of the Botswana Economy Selected Papers* (pp. 369–387). Oxford: James Currey.

OECD. (2000). *Reducing the Risk of Regulatory Failure: Challenges for Regulatory Compliance*. Available via http://www.oecd.org/regreform/regulatory-policy/1910833.pdf. Accessed around July 2014.

Owusu, F., & Samatar, A. I. (1997). Industrial Strategy and the African State: The Botswana Experience. *Canadian Journal of African Studies, 31*(2), 268–299.

Parulian, F. (2013). Sustaining Growth and Enhancing Economic Diversification in Botswana, in IMF Country. Report No. 13/296. International Monetary Fund, Washington, DC.

Raphaeli, N., Roumani, J., & MacKellar, A. C. (1984). *Public Sector Management in Botswana: Lessons in Pragmatism*. World Bank. Available via http://documents.worldbank.org/curated/en/656071468767953036/pdf/multi-page.pdf. Accessed 3 June 2008.

Samatar, A. I. (1999). *An African Miracle: State and Class Leadership and Colonial Legacy in Botswana Development*. Portsmouth: Heinemann.

Schumpeter, J. A. (1954). English translation In Hickel (1976) of "The Crisis of the Tax State" written in 1918. *International Economic Papers, 4,* 5–38.

6

Can Export Promotion Agencies Stem the Deindustrialisation in Sub-Saharan Africa?

Isaac Marcelin and Malokele Nanivazo

Introduction

The lack of financing mechanisms and technological progress has left many developing countries unable to sustain and expand their capabilities to set successful industrialisation schemes in motion. This problem is more acute in sub-Saharan Africa (SSA), owing to (1) a shortage of capital for manufacturing and technological build-ups, (2) a relatively low-level human capital development and (3) a production process highly focused on primary commodities—consequences of abundant natural resources (UNECA 2011). Industrialisation appears not only to have bypassed the African continent, but there is also evidence of deindustrialisation in the region (Wells

I. Marcelin (✉)
School of Business, Management and Technology,
University of Maryland Eastern Shore, Princess Anne, MD, USA
e-mail: imarcelin@umes.edu

M. Nanivazo
Visiting Scholar, Department of Economics, University of Kansas,
Lawrence, KS, USA
e-mail: malokele.nanivazo@aaawe.org; nanivazo@ku.edu

© The Author(s) 2019
A. B. Elhiraika et al. (eds.), *Governance for Structural Transformation in Africa*,
https://doi.org/10.1007/978-3-030-03964-6_6

and Thirlwall 2003). Inasmuch as manufacturing (exporting) firms have to incur substantial upfront costs that cannot be funded out of their cash flows or accumulated reserves (Chor and Manova 2010), SSA firms' ease of access to external capital is necessary for the development, production and export of manufactured goods to sustain the development process.

Export promotion agency (EPA), a structure implementing a wide range of policies promoting manufacturing and exports, has gained traction in policymaking around the world. By 2011, as many as 116 countries had already established EPAs to cope with issues such as a lack of capital and export-related supports to (prospective) exporting firms. Some promote specific industries while others provide targeted loans and matching grants (Spence 2008). Some offer guarantees and insurance to export-oriented firms to bolster their creditworthiness in the private market (Belloc and Di Maio 2011); while others play a crucial role in easing market tensions particularly when credit is limited or traditional lending channels adopt stricter standards by making smaller loans with widened interest spreads, higher collateral and shorter maturities. Many offer protection against credit, political, country and legal risks by allowing exporters to access buyers in environments marked by heightened systemic and counterparty risks. With export-related risks insured, lenders should be more willing to increase borrowers' credit limits and relax financing conditions.

By the turn of 2011, at least 28 SSA countries had implemented an EPA and made it an integral part of their strategy to boost their manufacturing sector. Whether the policy has slowed down deindustrialisation in SSA by increasing production and export of manufactured goods remains an inquiry of empirical interest. We believe this is an important policy question for the SSA region, which has traditionally stagnated in terms of industrialisation and manufacturing exports. Trade promotion policies aimed at enhancing the manufacturing sector should have broad impacts on manufacturing value added (MVA) as a per cent of GDP and exports related outcomes.

Despite interests shown by policymakers in the many functions of EPAs, the link between EPAs and the manufacturing sector's performance is yet to be investigated. This study intends to fill this gap by addressing two related questions: first, has EPAs' policy of targeting the manufacturing sector been successful at slowing down deindustrialisation in SSA and second: Are SSA's Export Promotion Zones (EPZs) more effective in EPA countries? We hypothesise that if EPAs enable SSA's firms to foray into foreign markets, this should be reflected in these countries exports performance. Equally, if EPAs are successful in slowing down the deindustrialisation of the region, this should be observed in the manufacturing sector value added as well as in manufacturing as a per cent of GDP. Addressing these questions may help facilitate the crafting of policy interventions mitigating the effects of deindustrialisation and may also help evaluate the effectiveness of EPAs as an industrial policy.

We analyse the effect of EPA on SSA countries in general; next, employing synthetic control methods, we use the case of South Africa to illustrate the effect of the policy on deindustrialisation and export outcomes. We find that MVA as a per cent of GDP grows significantly as a result of EPAs implementation. In particular, MVA as a share of GDP is about 7.5% higher for South Africa compared to its synthetic counterpart. EPAs appear to play a vital role, at least, in stemming the deindustrialisation process in SSA. The results have several policy implications in terms of providing financial and human resources for these entities in countries where the policy has already been adopted and for its adoption in countries without the agency while industrialisation and exports are weak. A well implemented EPA in such countries could help boost both manufacturing and exports.

The remainder of the paper is organised as follows. "Literature Review: SSA, EPAs and Deindustrialisation" reviews the extant literature. "Data Analysis" discusses our approach to the data along with some descriptive statistics. "Empirical Specification" presents our methodological approach. "Results" discusses the empirical results, while "Conclusion and Policy Recommendations" concludes with policy implications.

Literature Review: SSA, EPAs and Deindustrialisation

EPA,[1] an outward-looking export-oriented policy set up in advanced economies in the wake of the creation of the International Trade Centre (ITC) in the mid-1960, has been adopted in many SSA countries

---

[1]Often referred to as Trade Promotion Organisation (TPO)

with the stated objectives of providing vital services and resources to (potential) manufacturing and exporting firms to increase manufacturing exports, employment, growth and macroeconomic performance. To succeed internationally, industrial firms need to sharpen their business and marketing skills, learn about market environments, business opportunities, quality and costs control and production efficiency. Weaknesses in these areas may amplify losses in the manufacturing sector. Keesing and Singer (1991) underscore that manufactured products for export to developed countries are generally quite different from anything produced for local markets and that exporters need to meet buyers' specifications and exported goods need to be ready for end users.

Through EPAs, recipient firms are provided with (1) export service programs (seminars for potential exporters, export counselling, how-to-export handbooks and export financing) and (2) market development programs, such as dissemination of sales leads to local firms, participation in foreign trade shows, preparation of market analysis and export letters (Kotabe and Czinkota 1992; Lederman et al. 2010). While EPAs have been pursued in some SSA countries, there has been a significant decline in industrialisation in the region marked by staggering economic losses in terms of employment and outputs, plants shut down and disappearance of industries in these economies. Behind this decline lurks the question of whether EPAs can effectively reverse the deindustrialisation process.

Kotabe and Czinkota (1992) lament the limited empirical evidence available on the appropriateness of public assistance to exporters and how adequately state export promotion activity is allocated among firms in different stages. Pangestu (2002) advocates for the economic case of government intervention, which rests on the need to correct for market failures resulting from externalities, missing markets or other market failures while taking into account potential spillovers on other sectors in the economy. Spence (2008) recommends that (1) export promotion programmes (EPPs) should be temporary, (2) evaluated critically and quickly abandoned should they underachieve the expected results and (3) remain agnostic about which industries to promote. The author agrees with Bhagwati (1988) and Nogués (1990) who assert that EPAs are not a superior substitute for other key supportive ingredients, such as education, infrastructure and responsive regulations.

There is a broad agreement that government intervention in export promotion is due to asymmetric information problems as well as other market failures. These include externalities associated with the gathering of foreign market information on consumer preferences, business opportunities, quality and technical requirements, which private firms will not share with competitors (English and Wulf 2002; Gil et al. 2008; Lederman et al. 2010; Belloc and Di Maio 2011). In an earlier study, Panagariya (2000) argues that adverse selection and moral hazard problems can lead to thinning of the market for credit insurance but that is not a case for government intervention. Pangestu (2002) argues that industrial policy often has multiple objectives, including short-term employment, increased output, more even income distribution, more equal regional distribution of economic activity and enhanced technological capacity. Chor and Manova (2010) highlight that in response to limited export opportunities, manufacturing plants around the world have scaled down production and employment.

Whereas Martincus et al. (2012) state that EPAs are better endowed in terms of personnel specialised with marketing expertise and are, therefore, a priori, in a better position to alleviate the specific information problems associated with exports of new products; Keesing and Singer (1991) argue that in developing countries with no more than partly satisfactory policies towards manufactured exports; EPAs manned by public officials have nearly always proved unsatisfactory in providing practical information, assistance and support services for expanding manufacturing exports. While Trindade (2005) and Mah (2011) note that South Korea has achieved significant economic progress, raising its economic stature from one of the most impoverished nations to an advanced economy because the Korean government has provided many types of export incentives to various industry sectors; Stein (1992) underscores that exports in Africa were hurt by the absence of subsidies that would offset the incentives to sell in protected domestic markets; and that the future of Africa will require some form of industrialisation to augment living standards.

Export Processing Zones (EPZs) and Deindustrialisation

Export Processing Zones (EPZs) are policy arrangements whereby exporting firms locate their manufacturing plants inside an in-bond, common physical space and benefit from a set of fiscal incentives in exchange for their commitment to produce and/or transform goods for the external market (Melo 2001). EPZs or Free Trade Zones (FTZs) and other forms of Special Economic Zones (SEZs) are demarcated geographical areas within a country's national boundaries where the regulation of firms' activities and the dedicated policies are differentiated from those applied to firms outside the zone, and designed to creating a policy environment and associated infrastructures that are exporter friendly, for both domestic and foreign producers (Farole 2010). Although Di Maio (2009) argues that EPZs often have a positive effect on exports, Rodrik (2004) warns that when the policy fails to effectively boost exports, it can be characterised as a "silly policy" consisting in subsidising foreign investors through transfers from poor countries' taxpayers to rich countries' shareholders.

Studying the effects of EPZs for a set of African countries, Helleiner (2002) reports that the policy was not an important contributor to non-traditional export success, except in the dramatic case of Mauritius where its contribution was dominant and influent. The author argues that other constraints evidently limited EPZs' attraction to investors in four other African countries, each of which experimented with EPZs (albeit somewhat hesitantly) with, at least so far, only very limited effect. Similarly, English and Wulf (2002) find that attempts to use EPZs in Africa have, except in Mauritius, been much less successful than elsewhere due to Africa's lack of adequate infrastructure and services to support the business community. Nevertheless, the authors argue that where countrywide reforms are difficult to implement, EPZs can be a useful instrument in the development arsenal of governments. They can confront large reform agendas since they only create the preconditions for efficient export production in a small geographic region, as opposed to pursuing reforms and undertaking investment on an economy-wide basis. Belloc and Di Maio (2011) point out that EPZs are a viable (second best) policy in the presence of economy-wide weak-nesses but impediments to national policies.

Fiscal Incentives Through EPAs

EPAs are ubiquitous and through them most governments intervene with policies ranging from providing infrastructure support to offer-ing direct export subsidies, such as reduced tax rates to exporting firms earnings, favourable insurance rates, advantageous financial conditions or variations in the exchange rate (Belloc and Di Maio 2011). Most SSA countries incorporate fiscal incentives in their industrial policy toolkit. Other incentives operate through tariffs, export subsidies, quo-tas and other non-tariff barriers (UNECA 2011).

Kenya and Malawi have utilised EPZs as a key industrial instrument by reducing or eliminating taxes on manufacturing bonds (Belloc and Di Maio 2011). Other successful fiscal incentive schemes for industrial development in SSA include the experiences of Lesotho, South Africa, Ghana and Kenya. Specifically, UNECA (2011) states that looking at its geographical and economic conditions, one would conclude that Lesotho is condemned to stay out from international trade; however, government intervention made a difference in this situation when, in the early 2000s, it took a series of actions to support the industriali-sation of the apparel sector including providing subsidies for starting new firms. Appendix presents some SSA countries, which have imple-mented tax exemptions and deductions schemes to support exporting/ manufacturing firms.

EPAs, Access to Finance and Manufacturing Expansion in SSA

One of the most fundamental roles of EPAs in industrial development involves facilitating industrial firms' access to external finance: The most significant hurdles facing many manufacturing firms, highly cap-ital and external finance dependent. Obtaining external finance allows these firms to acquire fixed assets and technology necessary to operate and grow. Lack of finance is a more pointed problem in SSA where financial markets are underdeveloped and credit is rare and costly. Nonetheless, EPAs are set with the stated objective of promoting foreign trade and alleviating financial sector constraints in providing necessary financial products to domestic firms involved in foreign trade (Chauffour et al. 2010).

English and Wulf (2002) emphasise that export finance is a major inhibitor to exports in many low-income countries. Belloc and Di Maio (2011) note that one of the most important obstacles to industrial development is a weak financial market, in which producers may face credit constraints and experience difficulties in finding necessary resources to finance investment. Thus, by facilitating financing to manufacturing firms, SSA's EPAs may play an important role in sustaining industrialisation since commercial banks in the region have a propensity to steer away from financing many types of activities. Malouche (2009) finds that (1) in Sierra Leone commercial banks prefer to invest in government securities and (2) in Ghana most institutions providing export finance tend to be undercapitalised, while (3) in Kenya, Ghana and South Africa, exporters seem to be most constrained by reasons related to the method of payment used, industry and firm's size. Thus, SSA's EPAs may play an important role in mediating trade and supplier credits and working capital financing for manufacturing activities.

When credit is tight or unavailable, industrial firms may find it difficult to maintain their operations and may, therefore, curtail their production, further hindering their export capabilities, employment and growth. Tight credit markets imply that capital intensive firms may face increasing interest payments, thus limiting their ability to replace industrial depreciation and making it more difficult to sustain their growth. As a result, those firms would more likely miss their production and export targets. Government financial supports to manufacturers and exporters include direct subsidies or facilitating access to financing industrial investment and production which take the form of: (1) subsidising exporting firms' borrowing costs, (2) providing credit insurance coverage to manufacturers to access private credit markets and/or

(3) providing direct financial assistance to (potential) exporting firms. However, UNECA (2011) points out that subsidised export financing has given rise to a number of disputes in the WTO, including cases against developing countries.

One of the reasons often cited for the government to intervene in easing financial constraints for manufacturing firms includes agency problems, pervasive in incomplete markets. Belloc and Di Maio (2011) argue that in the absence of perfect capital markets, the private cost of capital may turn out higher than the social one, and private risk evaluation by firms may be distorted; thus, government interventions may be aimed at subsidising credit and competition in the credit market in the former case, and facilitating information transmission and providing credit insurance in the latter. English and Wulf (2002) maintain that although ensuring the availability of trade finance is a matter that needs to be left to the private sector, governments can use various mechanisms to promote access to finance, especially for smaller firms. However, Chauffour et al. (2010) claim that EPAs can potentially undermine the development of the financial sector. They argue that the presence of such institutions may discourage private banks from developing export-related financial products or may delink certain types of activities or borrowers from the commercial banking system if their influence becomes large.

In addition, the prospects for manufacturers' supply expansion may be limited by the lack of finance or the inexistence of market mechanisms allowing the creation of financial products through which market participants would show commitments for long-term financing. We hypothesise that the present allocation of investible funds in SSA may not have facilitated the expansion of manufacturing firms into foreign markets and that EPAs' financing facilities for manufacturers should have a positive impact on industrialisation. Consequently, our theory is that SSA industrialisation is not independent of credit availability and its costs in the region; and the decline in SSA industrialisation may be a reverberation of limited access to finance; thus, SSA's EPAs should positively contribute to redress these failures; and this contribution can be captured in MVA and manufacturing as a per cent of GDP.

EPAs, Insurance and Market Expansion

Export credit insurance is perhaps one of the most fundamental functions performed by EPAs: A function that is likely to have important impacts on industrialisation. EPAs shield exporting firms by affording them insurance or protection against losses arising from default, insolvency and bankruptcy of their foreign buyers. This is particularly important given that buyers and sellers in international trade are of different jurisdictions and legal regimes and that the seller's judicial system has no jurisdiction on the buyer to enforce compliance with sale agreement or payment of merchandises purchased and delivered by the seller, i.e. to coerce an international buyer tempted to renege on import contracts.

Moreover, where business and country risks are covered through EPAs, manufacturers may have easier access to bank financing. Another important effect may be the reduction in volatility of manufacturers' cash flows making their capital budgeting and financial forecast more reliable and the financing of their industrial expansion less uncertain. EPAs offer, inter alia, (1) insurance against war, social unrest, currency inconvertibility and exchange rates volatility; this protection extends to deferment of payments and payment collection and (2) insurance for banks in providing working capital and finance exports to manufacturers. Deferment of payments is a corollary of lags between payments and period freight resulting in a need for working capital financing—a characteristic of competitive markets where the exporter is unable to request pre- or down payments from their international buyers. In this regard, to avoid depletion of cash, and/or interruptions in operations, exporters can mobilise funding either directly through financial institutions or through EPAs' direct subsidies or serving as guarantor of claims arising from foreign export sales.

When credit risk is insured, internationally oriented SMEs with limited collateral should have easier access to capital to support their production targets. Protection against credit, political, country and legal and counterparty risks allows domestic industrials to access markets, which were either unappealing or inaccessible, thus boosting industrial production and export capacities. Therefore, through EPAs, the public sector fulfils a basic function required by entrepreneurs: That of reducing risk in the investing environment; and more importantly, in this case, this function is operational across borders. Clearly, an EPA has the potential to serve as an industrial incubator, especially, in countries with backward financial markets.

Data Analysis

To estimate the effects of EPAs on manufacturing exports, we collect data from various sources. The main dataset is the World Development Index (WDI), tabulated by the World Bank. All of the macro variables are extracted from the WDI from 1960 through 2012. Initial data on EPAs collected from Lederman et al. (2010) are updated using data from the ITC. The ITC provides a wealth of data on every country with an EPA or a TPO including the coordinates of the agency's representatives.[2] Gabon appears to have implemented the first EPA (POMOGABON) in SSA in 1964 followed by Ghana, Burkina Faso and Nigeria in the 1970s. One of the main challenges to evaluating the impacts of those early EPAs is that data availability over these periods is very precarious. Table 6.1 presents two groups of countries (1) with and (2) without an EPA.

We start out with the hypothesis that there is no difference in manufacturing outcomes in EPA and in non-EPA countries. Table 6.2 shows some baseline descriptive statistics for the two sets of countries—EPA and non-EPA adopters. The values are averages over the study period, 1980 through 2016. The last column of the table presents some tests statistics, i.e. means test differences between EPA and non-EPA countries. There are some entanglements in terms of the EPA effect since averages for EPA countries include the pre-EPA period. Therefore, an insignificant means test difference provides insufficient information to fail to reject the hypothesis of equality of means between EPA

---

[2]The ITC refers to EPA as TPO or Trade Promotion Organisation.

Table 6.1 List of EPA and non-EPA countries

EPA country	Agency's name	Year	Non-EPA
Benin	Benin Agency for Trade Promotion (ABePEC)	2007	Angola
Botswana	BEDIA	1997	Cameroon
Burkina Faso	ONAC	1974	Central African Rep
Burundi	Agence de Promotion des Échanges Extérieurs (APEE)	1989	Chad
Cape Verde	Center for Tourism, Invt. and Export Promotion (PROMEX)	1991	Comoros
Congo	CCCE	2006	Dem. Rep. of Congo
Cote-d'Ivoire	APEX-CI	1996	Equatorial Guinea
Ethiopia	Ethiopian Export Promotion Agency (EEPA)	1998	Eritrea
Gabon	PROMOGABON	1964	Guinea
Gambia	Gambia Investment and Export Promotion Agency (GIEPA)	2001	Guinea-Bissau
Ghana	GEPC	1969	Liberia
Kenya	Export Promotion Council	1992	Madagascar
Lesotho	Trade Promotion Unit	1978	Mali
Malawi	MEPC	1971	Mauritania
Mauritius	Enterprise Mauritius	2006	Sao Tome Principe
Mozambique	IPEX	1990	Somalia
Namibia	Offshore Development Company	1996	Sudan
Niger	ANIPEX	2004	Swaziland
Nigeria	Nigerian Export Promotion Council (NEPC)	1977	Togo
Rwanda	RIEPA	1998	
Senegal	ASEPEX	2005	
Seychelles	SIBA	1995	
Sierra Leone	SLEDIC	2004	
South Africa	Trade and Investment South Africa (TISA)	2009	
Tanzania	Board of External Trade	1979	
Uganda	Uganda Export Promotion Board	1996	
Zambia	EBZ	1985	
Zimbabwe	ZimTrade	1998	

This table presents the list of SSA countries where an EPA has been adopted and those where the policy has not been adopted as well as the year of EPAs' adoption. Initial data on EPAs have been collected from Lederman et al. (2010) and updated using the International Trade Centre (ITC) database

Table 6.2 Descriptive statistics for EPA and non-EPA countries

Variables	EPA countries	Non-EPA countries	Mean differences
Annual GDP growth (%)	3.73	3.56	0.16 [$t=0.44$]
Per capita GDP (in USD)	1713.41	1569.51	143.90 [$t=1.15$]
Growth in per capita GDP	1.23	1.06	0.21 [$t=0.57$]
Import as a share of GDP	35.83	36.46	−0.64 [$t=-0.56$]
Import growth (%)	7.42	4.85	2.57** [$t=2$]
Export as share of GDP	27.14	28.89	−1.75* [$t=-1.77$]
Export growth (%)	7.63	5.33	2.30* [$t=1.68$]
Export volume index	203.30	124.43	78.87** [$t=2$]
Export value added (mil USD)	291.25	208.11	83.14 [$t=1.49$]
Export unit value added index	148.48	134.03	14.45** [$t=2.39$]
Industry value added growth	4.25	3.80	0.45 [$t=0.56$]
Manufacturing value added (mil USD)	4720	3370	1350* [$t=1.78$]
Manufacturing value added (growth)	3.71	3.89	−0.19 [$t=0.26$]
Manufacturing value added as share of GDP	12.85	12.20	0.65 [$t=1.50$]
Trade as a share of GDP	62.97	65.36	−2.39 [$t=-1.24$]

This table presents a summary of descriptive statistics for EPA and non-EPA countries. The variables are as defined in detail in the WDI database. The data is extracted from the World Bank's World Developing Indices (WDI). The values are averages for the two groups of countries over 1980 through 2016. The last column presents a means test difference between EPA and non-EPA countries; t-statistics are presented in squared brackets;
***, **, * represent 1, 5 and 10% level of significance, respectively

and non-EPA countries. Dehejia and Wahba (2002) and Baser (2006) perform a difference of means test on the covariates across the treatment and comparison groups using the pooled-variance t test in the pre-treatment period. Importantly, we observe that sub-Saharan EPA countries display dissimilar characteristics with non-EPA countries on various dimensions.

EPA countries present higher annual growth rate along with per capita growth rate than their non-EPA counterparts. Surprisingly, EPA countries' growth rate in import is about 2.57% higher than that of their non-EPA counterparts and is statistically significant at the 5% level of significance. Importantly, exports grow faster in EPA countries, about 2.3%, than in non-EPA countries. The higher growth rate in export is statistically significant at the 10% level of significance. This is prima facie evidence of the effect of EPA coupled with firm's internationalisation programmes channelled through fiscal incentives. A priori, this suggests that such schemes may at least stem the deindustrialisation process in the region. Similarly, the export volume index is significantly higher in EPA countries compared to non-EPA adopters. More specifically, the average EPA country witnesses a higher export volume index of 78.87. This implies that production of some types of tradable goods and/or services is significantly higher in EPA countries and is statistically significant at least at the 5% level.

Derived as the difference between GDP (in USD) and taxes receipts on production net subsidies, the average exports value added for EPA countries is higher than that of non-EPA adopters by about USD$83.14 million. The export value index or export/import unit value index (EUVI and IUVI), which captures variations in the price level of exported and imported goods over a time period relative to the base period is significantly higher for EPA countries. In particular, the EUVI is about 14.45 points higher in EPA countries and is statistically significant at least at the 5% level.

Manufacturing value added (MVA), a measure of manufacturing output as share of GDP or the value added of the manufacturing sector's output, proxy for industrialisation, is significantly higher for EPA countries compared to their non-EPA counterparts. In particular, MVA is approximately USD$1350 higher, on average, in EPA countries compared to their non-EPA counterparts and is statistically significant at least at the 10% level. Nevertheless, trade as a share of GDP is lower in EPA countries compared to their non-EPA adopters. Overall, MVA, export growth, export value added and export unit value index provide strong support for the economic case for establishing EPA and adopting export promotion schemes. These statistics provide prima facie evidence that manufacturing and exportable products can be produced profitably in SSA. Governments need to implement institutions to accompany firms to acquire capital and technologies to boost the industrial sector. The manufacturing sector is rife with externalities that warrant fiscal incentives or subsidy schemes, which can help firms defray upfront costs hampering investments, employment, trade and growth.

Assuming that the EPA and non-EPA countries are independent and normally distributed, we perform a variance ratio test for the difference between the two groups.[3] We perform the F test for the ratio of two variances, S_1^2/S_2^2, for each of the exports and manufacturing outcomes at baseline by formally testing the null hypothesis $H_0 : \sigma_1^2 - \sigma_2^2 = 0$. For each test statistic, the first sample is defined as the one with the larger sample variance. The statistics in Table 6.3 show insufficient support to reject the hypothesis of equality of variance for all of the variables except MVA to GDP ratio and the export value index, marginally significant at the 10% level. We follow Baser (2006) by comparing the difference of means as a percentage of the average standard deviation as well as the per cent reduction of bias in the means of the covariates in both groups before and after matching. Table 6.3 breaks down exports and the other trade related variables between treatment (EPA) and control (non-EPA) countries. Importantly, we observe that sub-Saharan EPA countries display similar characteristics with non-EPA countries during the pre-treatment period. In other words, before implementing evaluation strategy, EPA and non-EPA countries were similar with respect to manufacturing, exports and the various trade related outcomes.[4]

---

[3]Performing the test for the difference between the two variances is important to determining whether to carry out a pooled-variance t test (which assumes equal variances) or the separate variance t test (which assumes unequal variance).

[4]The evaluation literature stresses the importance of similar outcomes in pre-matching for both groups (see Ashenfelter 1978; Ashenfelter and Card 1985; Card and Sullivan 1988; Heckman et al. 1998).

Table 6.3 Summary statistics for EPA and non-EPA countries

	Control			Treatment			Tests statistics	
	Mean	Variance	N	Mean	Variance	N	Variance ratio test	t
Exports/GDP	33.52	371.11	18	26.05	348.12	27	1.066	1.30
Exports growth	14.30	595.04	13	11.34	318.75	20	1.867	0.41
Industry value added/GDP	26.56	194.70	17	23.84	182.09	26	1.069	0.64
Manufacturing exports/exports	14.92	317.37	10	15.61	337.22	17	1.062	−0.095
Manufacturing value added/GDP	11.02	88.69	13	11.18	32.79	24	2.703	−0.064
Trade/GDP	82.64	1268.4	18	64.56	907.62	27	1.398	1.77
Exports value index	4.74	1.098	12	4.77	0.53	22	2.069	−0.088
Exports volume index	4.65	0.648	12	4.46	0.54	22	1.231	0.68
Exports capacity to import	25.47	5.023	13	25.09	5.41	20	1.082	0.47
Exports revenues (USD)	19.42	3.929	18	20.17	3.95	27	1.010	−1.24
Industry value added (USD)	19.30	3.579	17	20.01	3.12	26	1.140	−1.25
Manufacturing value added (USD)	18.77	2.739	13	19.32	3.23	24	1.176	−0.88

This table presents some descriptive statistics on the exports and manufacturing variables at their baseline levels. Except for the variables deflated by GDP, all other variables are in natural log forms. A variance ratio test is performed to determine whether the means of the control and treatment groups can be tested assuming equal variances. The t statistics are reported for the tests of equality of the means at baseline

Empirical Specification

Estimating the effect of EPAs on deindustrialisation is not straightforward because it requires determining how countries with EPAs would have performed in the absence of the agency. Spence (2008) argues that EPAs' impact is hard to prove due to lack of counterfactuals. This effectively casts doubt on whether high growth potential industries (such as manufacturing firms) would not have succeeded even without targeted incentives. To assess whether the policy has successfully contributed to slow down the deindustrialisation process of SSA, we need to compare manufacturing exports of SSA countries under treatment, i.e. those with an EPA with those of countries under no treatment, i.e. countries without an EPA. Abadie argues that traditional regression analysis techniques require large samples and many observed instances of the events, such as large policy intervention. Comparative case studies are based on the idea that the effect of an intervention on some variables of interest can be inferred from the comparison of the evolution of the variables of interest between the unit exposed to the event or intervention of interest and a group of units that are similar to the exposed unit but that were not affected by the event/intervention (Abadie and Gardeazabal 2003; Abadie et al. 2010). When the units of observation are a small number of aggregate entities, like countries or regions, no single unit alone may provide a good comparison for the unit affected by the intervention (Craig 2015).

Synthetic control methods (SCM) estimates the effect of aggregate interventions, i.e. interventions that are implemented at an aggregate level affecting a small number of large units (such as cities, regions or countries), on some aggregate outcome of interest (Abadie and Gardeazabal 2003; Abadie et al. 2010). Synthetic control models have been applied in a number of studies to address a variety of policy questions including measuring: the effects of catastrophic natural disasters on national economic growth (Cavallo et al. 2013); the impact of the Kobe Earthquake on Japan's GDP (DuPont and Noy 2012); the effects of wars of liberation on economic growth in African countries (Somé 2013); the impact of German reunification on economic growth in West Germany (Abadie et al. 2015); the impact of trade openness on economic growth in transition economies (Nannicini and Billmeier

2011); the impact of US state-level tobacco control programmes on tobacco consumption (Abadie et al. 2010) and the impact of reducing numbers of traffic police on traffic fatalities and injuries (DeAngelo and Hansen 2014). Explicitly, this estimator is a measure of the difference between the difference in manufacturing export after treatment (EPA implementation) as compared to before treatment (EPA implementation) manufacturing exports in countries where the agency has been implemented (see Martincus and Carballo 2008; Gertler et al. 2011).

Particularly using any of the twenty SSA countries which have yet to adopt EPAs, we assume that the adoption of the policy is a random event and that the outcomes in manufacturing for EPA countries move in tandem with those of non-EPA countries. Intrinsically, EPA and non-EPA adopters would have equal trends in exports, and in manufacturing regardless of EPAs, i.e. their (1) manufacturing exports, (2) manufacturing value added and (3) manufacturing as per cent of GDP patterns travel through a similar path over time and what differs is the EPA event that has occurred. This natural split offers a unique opportunity to assess the effects of EPAs on deindustrialisation in SSA applying synthetic control methods to generate the counterfactuals.

Results

This study estimates the effect of EPA implementation on manufacturing exports and other exports related outcomes for SSA using SCM—a strategy allowing self-selection into treatment. The SMC identifies an equivalent synthetic group of countries based on observed characteristic of countries in the control group. It estimates unbiased treatment effects for the treated. The synthetic matching estimator ensures that the treatment group is evaluated relative to a similar control group on a data-driven basis without need for extrapolation. More explicitly, the synthetic control methods of matching put forth in Abadie and Gardeazabal (2003) and Abadie et al. (2010) constructs a synthetic match for each country in the treatment group (i.e. countries with an EPA) by using the countries in the control group in such a way that the synthetic country has comparable outcomes to the treated county before

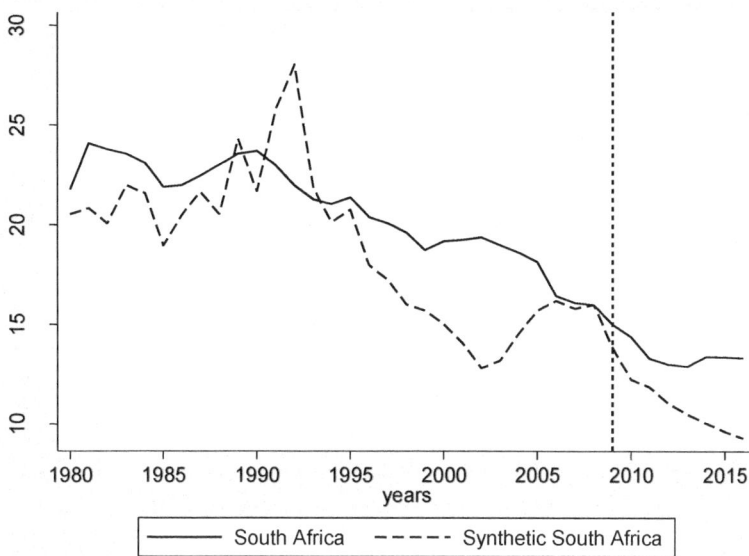

Fig. 6.1 South Africa and synthetic South Africa's paths of manufacturing value added

the EPA implementation. In this study, the SCM matches countries that are similar in terms of their manufacturing performance and other observable characteristics before the policy implementation.

Measured as a function of the difference between the treated country's performance and its synthetic counterpart following the policy implementation, the effect of EPA on the treated country for our sample involves several countries that have implemented the policy. Although we divide countries into EPA and non-EPA, after optimisation, using the SCM, we retain two cases: (1) South Africa and (2) Mauritius as the treated countries. In particular, Fig. 6.1 shows the paths between South Africa and synthetic South Africa in terms of manufacturing as a share of GDP. The figure shows that South Africa's manufacturing as a share of GDP was on the decline over the estimation period but remained substantially higher in the post-TISA—Trade and Investment South Africa implementation period. In particular,

South Africa witnessed about 7.5 percentage points higher manufacturing as a share of GDP compared to its synthetic counterpart. Mauritius experienced as much as 3 percentage points higher manufacturing as a share of GDP subsequent to the implementation of its EPA.

Table 6.4 presents the averages for South Africa and synthetic South Africa (composed of non-EPA countries) and Mauritius and synthetic Mauritius for export volume, export growth, export/import ratios, per capita GDP, industry value added and trade as a share of GDP. These predictors are averages over 1980 through 2016. In the case of South Africa, for instance, it can be observed that differences between treated and synthetic averages, for most of the predictors, except per capita GDP, total export and/or trade as a share of GDP, are very small and reach as low as 2.5%. Differences can be attributed to country's resource endowments and overall economic development. Greater differences are observed for per capita GDP and trade as a share of GDP.

In the cases of South Africa and Mauritius, the results suggest that pre-EPA manufacturing outcomes might have been a key motivation behind the adoption of the policy. They reinforce the notion that reasonable industrial outcomes can be achieved through appropriate industrial policies. Although the idea of implementing an EPA to provide exporting firms appropriate supports in the internationalisation process, the policy has achieved its objectives by supporting productivity, growth and exports, and that SSA countries that have not implemented the Agency might be missing out in terms of manufacturing (industrialisation) and growth. EPA's impacts appear to be strong along most of the trade, exports and manufacturing dimensions. Figure 6.1 suggests that EPA in South Africa has strengthened the country's export capacity and that these results may be extrapolated to other SSA countries with an EPA. Overall, the figure shows that although industrialisation has been on the decline in the region, the deceleration was slower in South Africa as the sector saw an uptick in the wake of TISA's implementation.[5] In terms of policy recommendation or as a matter of good practices, governments should keep private sector operators at arm's length to curb the incidence

---

[5]A similar graph for Mauritius is available upon demand.

Table 6.4 Predictors of manufacturing as a share of GDP and GDP growth

	Predictors	Treated South Africa	Synthetic South Africa
Panel A: South Africa			
Manufacturing as a share of GDP	Export volume	91.59	93.93
	Export growth	2.83	5.66
	Export to import ratio	1.11	0.83
	Per capita GDP	6382.80	2596.17
	Industry value added as % of GDP	35.18	31.64
	Manufacturing value added	19.22	18.68
	Total exports in million USD	79,800.00	16,000.00
	Trade as a share of GDP	52.47	69.57
GDP growth	Export volume	91.59	112.16
	Export growth	2.83	2.57
	Export to import ratio	1.11	1.12
	Per capita GDP	6382.80	4271.51
	Industry value added as % of GDP	35.18	45.84
	Manufacturing value added	19.22	12.87
	Total exports in million USD	79,800.00	39,000.00
	Trade as a share of GDP	52.47	73.09
Panel B: Mauritius			
Manufacturing as a share of GDP	Export volume	120.36	100.35
	Export growth	3.87	2.43
	Export to import ratio	0.92	0.90
	Per capita GDP	5693.88	1279.31
	Industry value added as % of GDP	18.32	19.36
	Manufacturing value added	0.32	0.46
	Total exports in million USD	112.89	146.09
	Trade as a share of GDP	121.33	62.74

(continued)

Table 6.4 (continued)

	Predictors	Treated South Africa	Synthetic South Africa
	Export volume	110.25	91.09
	Export growth	5.17	5.62
	Export to import ratio	0.91	0.84
GDP growth	Per capita GDP	5148.61	2515.76
	Industry value added as % of GDP	28.32	29.36
	Manufacturing value added	19.81	15.48
	Total exports in million USD	3090.00	8540.00
	Trade as a share of GDP	116.61	95.40

This table presents the predictors for manufacturing as a per cent of GDP for the treated country and the synthetic group. The variables are as defined in detail in the WDI database. The data is extracted from the World Bank's World Developing Indices (WDI). The values presented in the table are averages over the estimation period

of corruption, rent-seeking and other impediments to EPA. This is very important as exports drive growth and openness improves resource allocation (Harrison et al. 2010).

As Fig. 6.1 shows a rise in manufacturing as a share of GDP following TISA adoption, it raises the need for public policies seeking restructuring, diversification, internationalisation, financial development and/or fiscal schemes supporting local industries to stimulate industrialisation. However, Weil (1978) identifies two common shortcomings of such programs including (1) a lack of information about essential specific products and (2) inadequate financial resources (in Czintoza and Johnson 1981).[6] Ahmed et al. (2002) note that while a wide range of export promotion programs is available around the world to help firms

---

[6]Weil, F. A. (1978). 'Statement at hearings before the Subcommittee on International Finance of the Committee on Banking, Housing and Urban Affairs.' Export Policy Part 3, S Senate, 35th Congress, 2nd Session, Washington, DC, in Czintoza and Johnson (1981). See Marcelin and Mathur (2014, 2015, 2016) and Mathur and Marcelin (2014, 2015) for a detailed discussion on the effect of financial development.

penetrating export markets, government agencies need to do more to promote their role in developing external trade. While there is a burgeoning body of research inquiring into export promotion strategies in developing countries, it is rather limited in scope (see Milner 1990; Dominguez and Sequeira 1993).

Similar to MVA, the results show higher economic growth in South Africa and in Mauritius as compared to their synthetic group counterpart. In particular, we observe that in South Africa we observe about 3.6% higher growth of GDP compared to its synthetic counterparts as a result of TISA implementation. The results are consistent with our expectations that industrialisation drives economic growth. To further drive industrialisation a country that has implemented EPA may implement some of the many of the incentive schemes sustaining the manufacturing sector including drawbacks, duty deferral programs and standby agreements that eliminate restrictions on foreign direct investments in key sectors while establishing a level playing field in the traded sector. Since in addition to exporting, what to export matters (Dodaro 1991; Piñeres and Ferrantino 1997; An and Iyigun 2004; Hausmann et al. 2007); industrial policymaking has to be encompassing while targeting clusters of activities with high potentials.

Easier access to finance may facilitate the development of the industry sector—largely dependent on external finance to grow. Results illustrated in Fig. 6.1 point to broad effects of EPA in stemming the deindustrialisation in EPA adopters. Fisman and Love (2003) indicate that SSA countries with EPAs appear to partially leapfrog their weak financial structure to finance firms in high growth, manufacturing industries. Rajan and Zingales (1998) classify the manufacturing sector as high growth sector heavily dependent on external finance to thrive. There is abundant evidence that access to finance can boost growth (Levine et al. 1999; Marcelin and Mathur 2014, 2015). A lack of finance may slow down the industrialisation process, and by extension, economic growth.

Better resource allocation encourages investments in sectors requiring substantial external finance to grow by channelling savings to projects with higher expected returns (Marcelin and Mathur 2014). To promote industrialisation, EPA countries should provide incentives for activities supporting employment, income redistribution and growth. While sector-wide policies may have some appeal, EPA should also target activities with high spillover effects within the manufacturing or the traded sector. If governments provide fiscal incentives to high spillover activities, they may support interlinked activities or sectors. Although Keesing and Singer (1991) note that, poorly suited for providing production-related assistance and business services exporters need, developing countries' EPAs readily allow themselves to be deflected into policy, administrative or regulatory tasks that conflict with the provision of export support services; some of the weaknesses of SSA countries may be overcome where the policy has been successful in providing fiscal, financial and insurance services to firms in the region.

Many SSA countries regroup manufacturing firms under EPZs along with special regulatory regimes while granting them special customs duties and selective tariffs.[7] Farole (2010) reports that although several African countries launched EPZs or free zone programs in the early 1970s (Liberia in 1970, Mauritius in 1971 and Senegal in 1974), most African countries did not operationalise the programs until the 1990s or 2000s. Belloc and Di Miao (2011) emphasise that it is always recommended the EPZ not to be insulated from the rest of the economy and efforts be made to generate positive spillovers at an economy-wide level. As an important industrial policy, South Africa, Mauritius, along with other EPA countries in the region may consider regrouping clusters of manufacturing firms within EPZ zones. We note that, however, English and Wulf (2002) observe insignificant effects of EPZs in Africa while Farole (2010) reports that EPZs have been successful in Asia but highly disappointing in SSA.

In particular, we expect the joint effect of EPAs and EPZs on manufacturing firms' ability to add to GDP to be economically significant. Thus, EPZs can be more effective when adopted in conjunction with EPAs, which perhaps increase the focus on manufacturing firms.

---

[7]Appendix shows a list of countries with EPZs. Data on EPZs are obtained from Farole (2010). The table also presents some fiscal schemes and other industrial policies adopted in SSA.

Specifically, EPZs and EPAs provide a host of subsidies such as lower taxes and custom duty exemptions. They also shape regulatory policies and public goods provision that are better implemented in EPZs, often limited to a given geographic location (Belloc and Di Maio 2011). Overall, the results suggest that policies seeking at boosting the manufacturing sector may be an essential part of an effective development strategy. EPA and EPZ policies benefit the manufacturing sector with ramifications for economic growth.

Conclusion and Policy Recommendations

We investigate the effects of EPAs on manufacturing in SSA using two cases—South Africa and Mauritius, to illustrate the effect. Our results suggest that SSA countries that have not implemented EPAs might have missed out an opportunity to boost their manufacturing sector and thrive. EPAs have strong effects on manufacturing following their implementation. Jointly implemented with EPAs, EPZs can be beneficial to manufacturing activities as they reduce customs and trade regulatory burdens. Overall, EPAs appear to be an important tool for industrialisation. Thus, their funding and staffing are important features for their success and the sought after outcomes.

The main implication of this study is that non-EPA countries in SSA may improve their manufacturing and export positions by effectively adopting the policy. They should offer a host of fiscal incentives, such as tax breaks, direct subsidies and import tariff exemptions. From a financial standpoint, they may subsidise credit, provide matching grants, proceed with public sector equity infusion and credit insurance that covers credit, country and counterparty risks, or the bundling of all of these in export zones. They may assume certain tasks left out by financial intermediation in aiding manufacturing firms in overcoming certain hurdles to external finance. In other words, it is important for policymakers to orient EPAs towards facilitating credit for manufacturing firms. EPAs may also serve as guarantors for manufacturing firms to access credit to finance their expansion where collateral coverage is prohibitive. They may supply credit for working capital financing while extending coverage for exchange rate fluctuations to exporters to protect them against exchange rate losses and facilitating manufacturing firms' access to export finance from banks/financial institutions through increased working capital and trade finance. Both current and prospective EPAs may provide guarantees to lenders making loans to exporters operating in the manufacturing sector. Finally, with the backing of EPAs, interest rates can be negotiated for manufacturers and exporters. It is assumed that the effects of these policy prescriptions along with good governance of EPAs should improve SSA's manufacturing and trade landscapes.

Appendix

Export promotion policies: comparative table, selected SSA countries

	Botswana	Cameroon	I. Coast	Ghana	Kenya	Mauritius	Nigeria	Rwanda	Senegal	Uganda	Zimbabwe
Incentives for export activities	✓	✓	✓	✓	✓	✓		✓	✓	✓	✓
Export processing zones (EPZs)		✓	✓	✓	✓	✓	✓	✓	✓	✓	✓
Export promotion (manufacturing)	✓			✓	✓	✓	✓	✓			
Standardisation, Quality improvement for export	✓	✓	✓		✓			✓		✓	
Measures to attract FDI for export activities	✓		✓	✓	✓	✓		✓			✓
Facilitated credit for non-traditional manufacturing	✓		✓			✓			✓		
Selective tariff protection peak/high tariffs)	✓	✓		✓		✓		✓			
Utilisation of other trade instruments	✓			✓	✓						
Export duties to favour local manufacturing		✓						✓		✓	

Source Belloc and Di Maio (2011)

References

Abadie, A., & Gardeazabal, J. (2003). The Economic Costs of Conflict: A Case Study of the Basque Country. *American Economic Review, 93*(1), 113–132.

Abadie, A., Diamond, A., & Hainmueller, J. (2010). Synthetic Control Methods for Comparative Case Studies: Estimating the Effect of California's Tobacco Control Program. *Journal of the American Statistical Association, 105*(490), 493–505.

Abadie, A., Diamond, A., & Hainmueller, J. (2015). Comparative Politics and the Synthetic Control Method. *American Journal of Political Science, 59*(2), 495–510.

Ahmed, U. Z., Mohamed, O., Johnson, P. J., & Meng, Y. L. (2002). Export Promotion Programs of Malaysian Firms: An International Marketing Perspective. *Journal of Business Research, 55*, 831–843.

An, G., & Iyigun, F. M. (2004). The Export Skill Content, Learning by Exporting and Economic Growth. *Economic Letters, 84*, 29–34.

Ashenfelter, O. (1978). Estimating the Effect of Training Programs on Earnings. *Review of Economics and Statistics, 60*(1), 47–57.

Ashenfelter, O., & Card, D. (1985). Using the Longitudinal Structure of Earnings to Estimate the Effect of Training Programs. *Review of Economics and Statistics, 67*(4), 648–660.

Baser, O. (2006). Too Much Ado About Propensity Score Matching Models? Comparing Methods of Propensity Score Matching. *Value in Health, 9*, 377–385.

Belloc, M., & Di Maio, M. (2011). *Survey of the Literature on Successful Strategies and Practices for Export Promotion by Developing Countries, International Growth Centre.* International Growth Centre. Available via https://www.theigc.org/wp-content/uploads/2011/06/Belloc-Di-Maio-2011-Working-Paper.pdf. Accessed 14 Aug 2018.

Bhagwati, J. N. (1988). Export-Promoting Trade Strategy: Issues and Evidence. *The World Bank Research Observer, 3*(1), 27–57.

Card, D., & Sullivan, D. (1988). Measuring the Effect of Subsidized Training Programs on Movements In and Out of Employment. *Econometrica, 56*(3), 497–530.

Cavallo, E., Galiani, S., Noy, I., & Pantano, J. (2013). Catastrophic Natural Disasters and Economic Growth. *Review of Economics and Statistics, 95*(5), 1549–1561.

Chauffour, J. P., Saborowski, C., & Soylemezoglu, I. A. (2010). *Trade Finance in Crisis: Should Developing Countries Establish Export Credit Agencies?* World Bank. Available via https://openknowledge.worldbank.org/handle/10986/19946. Accessed 14 Aug 2018.

Chor, D., & Manova, K. (2010). *Off the Cliff and Back? Credit Conditions and International Trade During the Global Financial Crisis*. National Bureau of Economic Research. Available via http://www.nber.org/papers/w16174. Accessed 15 Aug 2018.

Craig, P. (2015). *Synthetic Controls: A New Approach to Evaluating Interventions*. http://eprints.gla.ac.uk/116324/. Accessed 15 Aug 2018.

Czintoza, R. M., & Johnson, J. W. (1981). Segmenting U.S. Firms for Export Development. *Journal of Business Research, 9*(4), 353–365.

DeAngelo, G., & Hansen, B. (2014). Life and Death in the Fast Lane: Police Enforcement and Traffic Fatalities. *American Economic Journal: Economic Policy, 6*(2), 231–257.

Dehejia, R., & Wahba, S. (2002). Propensity Score Matching Methods for Nonexperimental Causal Studies. *Review of Economics and Statistics, 84*(1), 151–161.

Di Maio, M. (2009). Industrial Policies in Developing Countries: History and Perspectives. In C. Mario, D. Giovanni, & J. S. Joseph (Eds.), *Political Economy of Capabilities Accumulation: The Past and Future of Policies for Industrial Development* (pp. 107–143). Oxford: Oxford University Press.

Dodaro, S. (1991). Comparative Advantage, Trade and Growth: Export-led Growth Revisited. *World Development, 19*, 1153–1165.

Dominguez, L. V., & Sequeira, C. G. (1993). Determinants of LDC Exporters' Performance: A Cross-National Study. *Journal of International Business Studies, 24*(1), 19–40.

DuPont, W., & Noy, I. (2012). What Happened to Kobe? A Reassessment of the Impact of the 1995 Earthquake in Japan. *Economic Development and Cultural Change, 63*(4), 777–812.

English, P., & Wulf, D. L. (2002). Export Development Policies and Institutions. In B. Hoekman, A. Mattoo, & P. English (Eds.), *Development, Trade, and the WTO* (pp. 160–170). Washington, DC: World Bank.

Farole, T. (2010). *Second Best? Investment Climate and Performance in Africa's Special Economic Zones*. World Bank. Available via https://openknowledge.worldbank.org/handle/10986/3930. Accessed 16 Aug 2018.

Fisman, R., & Love, I. (2003). Trade Credit, Financial Intermediary Development, and Industry Growth. *Journal of Finance, 58*(1), 353–374.

Gertler, P. J., Martinez, S., Premand, P., et al. (2011). *Impact Evaluation in Practice*. Washington, DC: World Bank.

Gil, S., Llorca, R., & Serrano, J. A. M. (2008). Measuring the Impact of Regional Export Promotion: The Spanish Case. *Papers in Regional Science, 87*(1), 139–146.

Harrison, A., & Rodríguez-Clare, A. (2010). Trade, Foreign Investment, and Industrial Policy for Developing Countries. In D. Rodrik & R. Rosenzweig (Eds.), *Handbook of Development Economics* (pp. 4039–4214). The Netherlands: North-Holland.

Hausmann, R., Hwang, J., & Rodrik, D. (2007). What You Export Matters. *Journal of Economic Growth, 12*, 1–25.

Heckman, J. J., Hichimura, H., & Todd, P. (1998). Matching as an Econometric Evaluation Estimator. *Review of Economic Studies, 65*, 261–294.

Helleiner, G. K. (2002). *Non-traditional Export Promotion in Africa*. Hampshire and New York: Palgrave Macmillan.

Keesing, B. D., & Singer, A. (1991). Assisting Manufactured Exports Through Services: New Methods and Improve Policies. In P. Hogan, B. D. Keesing, & A. Singer (Eds.), *The Role of Support Services in Expanding Manufactured Exports in Developing Countries*. Washington, DC: World Bank.

Kotabe, M., & Czinkota, M. R. (1992). State Government Promotion of Manufacturing Exports: A Gap Analysis. *Journal of International Business Studies, 23*(4), 637–658.

Lederman, D., Olarreaga, M., & Payton, L. (2010). Export Promotion Agencies: Do They Work? *Journal of Development Economics, 9*(12), 257–265.

Levine, R., Loayza, N., & Beck, T. (1999). Financial Intermediation and Growth: Causality and Causes. *Journal of Monetary Economics, 46*(1), 31–77.

Mah, S. J. (2011). Export Promotion Policies, Export Composition and Economic Development of Korea. *Law and Development Review, 4*, 1–27.

Malouche, M. (2009). *Trade and Trade Finance Developments in 14 Developing Countries Post September 2008: A World Bank Survey*. World Bank. Available via https://openknowledge.worldbank.org/handle/10986/4329.

Marcelin, I., & Mathur, I. (2014). Financial Development, Institutions and Banks. *International Review of Financial Analysis, 31*, 25–33.

Marcelin, I., & Mathur, I. (2015). Privatization, Financial Development, Property Rights and Growth. *Journal of Banking & Finance, 50*, 528–546.

Marcelin, I., & Mathur, I. (2016). Financial Sector Development and Dollarization in Emerging Economies. *International Review of Financial Analysis, 46*, 20–32.

Martincus, V. C., & Carballo, J. (2008). Is Export Promotion Effective in Developing Countries? Firm-level Evidence on the Intensive and the Extensive Margins of Exports. *Journal of International Economics, 76*(1), 89–106.

Martincus, C. V., Carballo, J., & Gallo, A. (2012). The Impact of Export Promotion Institutions on Trade: Is It the Intensive or the Extensive Margin? *Journal of International Trade & Economic Development, 21*(4), 127–132.

Mathur, I., & Marcelin, I. (2014). Unlocking Credit. In Jonathan A. Batten, Niklas F. Wagner (Eds.), *Risk Management Post Financial Crisis: A Period of Monetary Easing (Contemporary Studies in Economic and Financial Analysis).* (Vol. 96, pp. 221–252). Emerald Group Publishing Limited.

Mathur, I., & Marcelin, I. (2015). Institutional Failure or Market Failure? *Journal of Banking & Finance, 52*, 266–280.

Melo, A. (2001). *Industrial Policy in Latin America and the Caribbean at the Turn of the Century.* Inter-American Development Bank. Available via https://papers.ssrn.com/sol3/papers.cfm?abstract_id=181725700230023. Accessed 15 Aug 2018.

Milner, C. (1990). *Export Promotion Strategies—Theory and Evidence from Developing Countries.* Hertfordshire: Harvester Wheatsheaf.

Nannicini, T., & Billmeier, A. (2011). Economies in Transition: How Important Is Trade Openness for Growth? *Oxford Bulletin of Economics and Statistics, 73*(3), 287–314.

Nogués, J. (1990). The Experience of Latin America with Export Subsidies. *Weltwirtschaftliches Archiv, 126*(1), 97–115.

Panagariya, A. (2000). *Evaluating the Case for Export Subsidies.* World Bank. Available via http://documents.worldbank.org/curated/en/8366214687505 45367/Evaluating-the-case-for-export-subsidies. Accessed 16 Aug 2018.

Pangestu, M. (2002). Industrial Policy and Developing Countries. In B. Hoekman, A. Mattoo, & P. English (Eds.), *Development, Trade, and the WTO* (pp. 160–170). Washington, DC: World Bank.

Piñeres, A. G. S., & Ferrantino, J. M. (1997). Export Diversification and Structural Dynamics in the Growth Process: The Case of Chile. *Journal of Development Economics, 52*, 375–391.

Rajan, G. R., & Zingales, L. (1998). Financial Systems, Industrial Structure, and Growth. *Oxford Review of Economic Policy, 17*(4), 467–482.

Rodrik, D. (2004). *Industrial Policy for the Twenty-First Century*. Available via http://www.vedegylet.hu/fejkrit/szvggyujt/rodrik_industrial_policy.pdf.

Somé, Z. M. (2013). *Africa's Wars of Liberation: Impact and Economic Recovery*. Unpublished Working Paper: Department of Economics, University of California, Santa Barbara.

Spence, M. (2008). Commission on Growth and Development. 2008. *The Growth Report: Strategies for Sustained Growth and Inclusive Development*. World Bank. Available via https://openknowledge.worldbank.org/handle/10986/6507. Accessed 16 Aug 2018.

Stein, H. (1992). Deindustrialisation, Adjustment, the World Bank and the IMF in Africa. *World Development, 20*(1), 83–95.

Trindade, V. (2005). The Big Push, Industrialisation and Internationalisation Trade: The Role of Exports. *Journal of Development Economics, 78*, 22–48.

United Nations Economic Commission for Africa. (2011). *Industrial Policies for the Structural Transformation of African Economies: Options and Best Practices*. Economic Commission for Africa. Available via http://repository.uneca.org/handle/123456789/17788.

Wells, H., & Thirlwall, A. P. (2003). Testing Kaldor's Growth Laws Across the Countries of Africa. *African Development Review, 15*(2–3), 89–105.

7

Exploring Multidimensional Fiscal Incentives and Firms' Productivity in a Developing Country

Rapuluchukwu Efobi Uchenna,
Belmondo Tanankem Voufo and Beecroft Ibukun

Introduction

Firms' productivity is determined by firm-specific characteristics and external factors that are peculiar to the environment where the firm operates. The impact of fiscal incentives (which is an important external factor that is peculiar to the environment where the business operates) on firms' productivity, especially in developing countries, has not reached consensus In this paper, we investigate the impact of different forms of fiscal incentives on firms' productivity in Cameroon. Firm level

R. Efobi Uchenna (✉)
College of Business and Social Sciences, Covenant University, Ota, Nigeria
e-mail: uche.efobi@covenantuniversity.edu.ng

B. Tanankem Voufo
Ministry of Economy, Planning and Regional Development, Yaounde, Cameroon

B. Ibukun
Department of Economics, Covenant University, Ota, Nigeria
e-mail: ibukun.beecroft@covenantuniversity.edu.ng

© The Author(s) 2019
A. B. Elhiraika et al. (eds.), *Governance for Structural Transformation in Africa*,
https://doi.org/10.1007/978-3-030-03964-6_7

221

data from the World Bank Enterprise Surveys data were used to achieve our objective. The survey consists of over 300 manufacturing firms and we use information on firms' input and output to compute the productivity of firms. The enterprise survey also contains unique measures of fiscal incentives, such as firms' exemption from import duties, profit tax exemptions, value added tax (VAT) reimbursement, benefits from export financing scheme and benefits from other export/investment incentive scheme. The availability of these measures at the firm level, both as subjective and objective indicators, allows us to exploit the variation in fiscal incentives at the subnational level with a focus on manufacturing firms. Our findings include, among others, that fiscal incentives are beneficial for industrialisation in Cameroon; however, the impact varies across the type of fiscal incentive being observed.

There are immense benefit from industrialisation, including job creation for sustained growth and economic diversification, increased household consumption through improvement in the value of product and price efficiency and the development of other primary sectors through backward linkages that come with the demand for intermediate goods. Despite these identified benefits, most African countries have relied heavily on the trade of low value added primary products as their main export commodity (IMF 2012; UNECA 2013). Some important issues in Africa's industrialisation is the need for appropriate and alternative source of funding (see Gui-Diby and Renard 2015), focus on improving the institutional structure—in terms of corruption (McArthur and Teal 2002), as well as encouraging infrastructural development (Arnold et al. 2008; Escribano et al. 2010). However, government support for the private sector in Africa is slack and has failed to establish an enabling environment for industrialisation (Gui-Diby and Renard 2015).

An important aspect of government involvement is incentives, which can either be fiscal or non-fiscal. We focus on fiscal incentives since they are those fiscal measures used by the government to extend some measurable advantages to specific firms or categories of firms (UNCTAD 2000). They can be in the form of tax holidays, investment allowances and tax credits, reduced corporate income taxes, exemption from indirect taxes and export processing zones.

More so, proponents of fiscal incentive argue that under certain conditions, they improve investment, create jobs and other socio-economic benefits (Bora 2002).[1] Also, fiscal incentives can compensate for possible market failures and can easily be implemented by African government for achieving the industrialisation drive: some African countries are already considering this form of incentive as a viable policy option. For instance, the Nigerian Government has continued over the years to provide some tax incentives to improve investments into various sectors of the economy (Central Bank of Nigeria-CBN 2013). The Ghanaian Government is involved in granting rebates for corporate income tax of manufacturing firms located in some specific regions of the country, carry-forward losses for up to five years, investment guarantees and exemption of import duties (Action Aid 2014). Also, South Africa, Cameroon and a host of others apply specific fiscal incentives. Noting the revamped interest of African government to industrialise and the attention directed at including fiscal incentive as a viable policy option, our study, therefore, examines its impact on productivity by using case studies from Cameroon.

Cameroon is an important case considering that in 2013 the government enacted the investment incentive law No. 2013/004, which establishes the government's commitment towards enhancing fiscal incentives for an improved investment climate. This was the latest legislation by an African government (as at the time of this study) that was directed at using fiscal incentive for improved investment. Hence, it is worth considering an impact evaluation on which new generation of industrialisation policies can be based upon, provided that the political leaders desire to sustain this momentum and move in such direction.

Focusing on fiscal incentive and firm productivity is also important for the following reasons: first, to our knowledge, there is a lack of econometric studies that analyse the impact of government incentives on firms' productivity in Africa. Some studies closest to ours include Cleeve (2008) who used macro data analysis to underscore the

---

[1]While the opponents believe that the cost of fiscal incentives (such as deteriorating governance and corruption) outweighs its benefits (see Cleeve 2008).

importance of fiscal incentive on foreign investment in Africa. Arnold et al. (2008) considers firm-level data, but focused on services inputs. At best, there have been policy documents with country-specific cases that has emphasised on the importance of fiscal incentives on productivity of firms in Africa. They include the CBN (2013) that focused on Nigeria; the OECD (2007) document that focused, in part, on North African countries and the IMF (2012) study that focused on growth sustenance of African countries. Second, our study complements the growing theoretical and policy literature on the importance of developing countries' government involvement with the private sector to provide incentives that will offset the shortcomings of the impending business environment (see UNCTAD 2000, 2004, 2015; Cleeve 2008; IMF 2012). Apart from considering multidimensional measures of incentives, we apply the impact evaluation methodology, which has sparsely been introduced in studies of this nature. This approach is relevant, since it goes beyond showing the linear impact of fiscal incentives on firms' productivity, to understanding the counterfactual effect—what could have been the productivity of firms assuming they did not benefit from the introduction of the incentives.

The remainder of the paper is organised as follows: the next session discusses the review of literature and presents stylised facts. Following immediately is the third section that presents an overview of the data used and addresses econometric and methodological issues, while the fourth and fifth sections are concerned with the descriptive statistics and econometric results. The conclusions of the result are included in the sixth section.

Review of Literature and Stylised Facts

Lee (1996) studied the role of government intervention in enhancing the productivity of manufacturing firms in Korea. The author found that government policies such as tax incentives and subsidised credit were not correlated with total factor productivity of sampled firms. However, they found that government involvement in trade leads to higher productivity. Arnold et al. (2008) linked the productivity of firms to service delivery in Africa and concluded that improved service industries enhance firms' productivity. Closely related to our study—but with a different focus—is Escribano et al. (2010), who observed that African manufacturing firms will require an improved government commitment to infrastructural provision to enhance firm productivity.

The issue of firms' productivity is also of importance from a policy perspective. As noted by UNCTAD (2015), the improvement of firms' productivity is one possible way for developing countries to attain sustainable industrial development. As a result of this, there is an urgent call to relate this phenomenon with government commitment to provide fiscal incentives to firms in order to offset some unfavourable conditions in the business environment (see Gui-Diby and Renard 2015; UNCTAD 2015). Despite the need for enhanced fiscal incentives, some of its adverse consequences are highlighted in the literature. For instance, it is seen as wasteful and propelling corruption due to lack of transparency in its administration (see Cleeve 2008). Notwithstanding the highlighted adverse effect from incentives, it is seen as a viable tool for attracting and sustaining investment. It is suggested that the effectiveness of incentives can be enhanced by focusing it to reward the performance of firm and more development-oriented goals (UNCTAD 2004).

Fiscal incentives in Cameroon are evolving. In 1990, the investment code in Cameroon was established to grant financial concessions to firms (such as free transfer of proceeds from investment capital) in order to encourage and promote investments in Cameroon. This act also granted exemption from export duties and other export-related expenses, and a rebate from the taxable income of firms that are involved in the production of finished or semi-finished products for export. Another important incentive that is granted by the Cameroonian government is the free zone regime, which exempts firms from custom duties and paying of taxes for a period of 10 years of operation. Also, firms in this zone can freely undertake any industrial and commercial activity like installing own power and telecommunication systems, replacing national security scheme with an equal or better valued private scheme, as well as freely negotiate wages of employees. However, a major drawback of this form of incentive is the precarious condition that for firms to benefit from this form of incentive, 80% of their production must be for foreign consumption—i.e. export (Bureau of Economic and Business Affairs 2013).

In 2002, a new investment charter was enacted to replace the 1990 investment code. A major improvement of the 2002 investment code, way beyond the earlier one in 1990, is that it permits 100% foreign equity ownership. This is unlike the 1990 code that had some restrictions on foreign ownership. However, this new charter was not implemented for a long time. In 2013, a new investment incentive law was enacted—law No. 2013/004, which is very applicable to private investors. This law provides two categories of incentives: common incentives and special incentives. The common incentives include those benefits that are directed at firms to promote their productivity and performance. They include tax and custom duty incentives, such as exemption from registration duties, exemption from transfer taxes, exemption from VAT on different categories of provisions, exemption from business licence tax, direct clearing of equipment and materials related to the investment program, among others.

The special incentives are those forms that involve benefits granted to firms that invest in certain government priority sectors like the development of integrated agriculture, real estate development and social housing projects, agro-industry, manufacturing and construction, regional development and decentralisation projects, firms that promote innovation and export, among others. Some of the incentives that these firms benefit from include: exemption from export duty on locally manufactured products, exemption from custom duties for temporary importation of industrial equipment and materials likely to be re-exported, as well as direct customs clearance at investor's request.

To benefit from any of these incentives, however, some criteria are to be met, which includes: the beneficiary firm should be involved in export activities ranging from 10 to 25% of sales, rule of local capacity utilisation, as well as contribute to value addition. Another important aspect of the Cameroonian incentives, just like those of some other developing country, is that it is tied to a period of time. For instance, some of the common incentives are valid for a period of 5 years during the installation stage and 10 years maximum during the operational stage. The government's main intention with these rules is to enhance

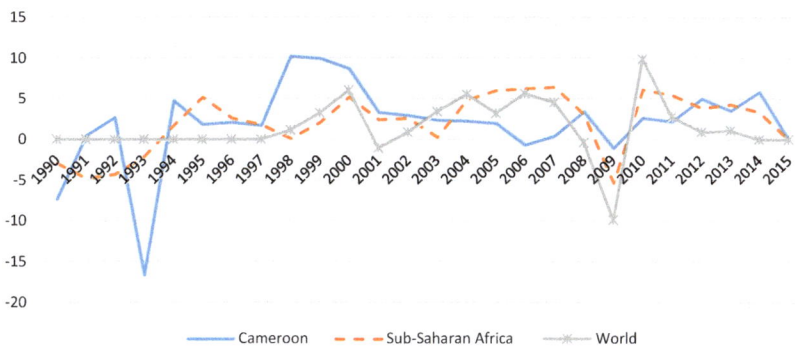

Fig. 7.1 Manufacturing value added as a percentage of GDP (*Source* Authors'
Computation from WDI (2015))

industrialisation and strengthen competitiveness of firms (resident or
non-resident) during these key stages of investment venture's lifecycle
(see Tabi 2005; Biya 2013).

The trend of manufacturing value added as a percentage of GDP
for Cameroon is presented in Fig. 7.1 to understand the productivity
of the manufacturing sector from 1990 to 2015. The aim of this (and
subsequent) stylised facts is to further emphasise the need for government interest (through incentive) in the industrialisation of our sampled
country. Figure 7.1 shows that Cameroon has consistently maintained a
manufacturing value added growth rate of less than 5%. This is except
for few shocks between 1997 and 2000, where the growth rate increased
higher than 5%. Compared to the World average that was along the
boundary of 5% in most of the year,[2] Cameroon has not performed
poorly in this regard. Likewise, the Sub Saharan Africa (SSA) average
was similar to the World average.

The data for the contribution of the manufacturing value added to
the economy of Cameroon as well as the world and SSA average are
presented in Table 7.1. From the Table, we observe that there has been
equivalent contribution of the manufacturing sector to the economy
of Cameroon when compared with the average of the SSA countries as
well as the World average. The manufacturing sector contributed about

---

[2]The trend for the World average began in 1997. There was no data available for earlier years.

Table 7.1 Manufacturing value added as a percentage of GDP

	1991–1995	1996–2000	2001–2005	2006–2010	2011–2015
Cameroon	18.837	20.426	19.946	16.018	14.446
Sub-Saharan Africa	14.410	13.437	12.875	11.304	10.848
World	0.000	19.059	17.484	16.426	15.943

Source Authors' Computation from World Bank (2015)

20.4 and 19.9% for the period 1996–2005. However, in later years, the trend remained on the decrease and this may not be conducive for industrial policy. Although this decrease is not peculiar to Cameroon, however, it suggests that the manufacturing sector is becoming less productive. This trend is also similar to Fig. 7.1.

Data and Empirical Strategy

Data and Variables

Data for the study is from the firm-level panel survey (2007–2009) of the World Bank's *Enterprise Survey* project for Cameroon. The survey data contains different information about the management, ownership and capital structure, performance and other external factors that affects the firm's operation, such as infrastructure facility, government incentives and other institutional bottlenecks like corruption. We focus on manufacturing firms that are involved in some form of cross-border trading. This is because: (i) accounting data is generally collected for only manufactured firms in the Enterprise Survey program; (ii) these firms are involved in the real sector and their productivity is what drives the industrialisation process of countries (Gui-Diby and Renard 2015); (iii) finally, our incentives measures are such that support import and export, as well as profit. Hence, the focus on manufacturing firms that are involved in cross-border trade will be most suitable for our type of analysis. We omit micro-enterprises and informal enterprises and focus on manufacturing firms with over 5 employees. These categories of firms are involved in international trade (i.e. export and import) and their productivity have significant impacts on the economy in terms of job creation and economic diversification (see UNECA 2013).

We identified information on firms' output (using annual sales) and recorded the value of firms' assets (input), which enables us to compute the measure of firms' productivity (i.e. ratio of firms' output to input). The values were converted to US Dollars using the prevailing exchange rate as at the period of the survey. Information regarding fiscal incentives by the government to specific firms is also captured in the survey. There are five categories of these incentives that are identified in the survey. They include: exemptions from duties on imported inputs, profit tax exemption, VAT reimbursement, export financing scheme and export/investment incentive scheme. The impact of each of these incentives is separately examined to underscore the individual effects on productivity and to enhance our policy recommendations. It is important to state that these measures of incentives are popular in Africa, especially for Cameroon.

Some other variables in the econometric analysis include the productive capacity of the firm, the size of the firm, the labour input of the firm and the running cost of the business in generating electricity. The productive capacity of the firm is measured as the current resale value of the machinery and equipment (see Arnold et al. 2008; Clarke 2011). The size of the firm is measured as the value of land owned by the firm. Labour input is measured as the cost of labour (including wages, salaries and bonuses). Firms' overhead cost of generating electricity through yearly expenses on fuel to generate power is another important variable that is included in the econometric estimation (see Ndichu et al. 2015). Table 7.2 presents a summarised overview of the variables in the estimations.

Basic descriptive statistics and kernel density plots were presented to familiarise with the data and briefly evaluate the expected relationships. The quasi-experimental method of propensity score matching was used to evaluate the relationship of interest, such that it estimates the mean effect of benefiting from fiscal incentives on firms' productivity. The main advantage of this form of empirical strategy is its ability to generate a control group that has similar distribution of characteristics as the 'treatment' group. Hence, the actual effect of the program on the

Table 7.2 Main variable description

Variable	Description
Productivity	The ratio of firms' output (sales) to firms' input (total asset available to the firm). This is a ratio measured in the respective year's exchange rate in USD
Fiscal incentives	Three measures are used including: import duty exemption, profit tax exemption and export financing. Firms that benefit from each of the incentives are recorded as "1", and "0" otherwise
Productive capacity	The current resale value of the machinery and equipment. This variable is converted to the respective year's exchange rate in USD
Size	The value of the firm's landed asset. This variable is converted to the respective year's exchange rate in USD
Labour input	The cost of labour (including wages, salaries and bonuses) measured in the respective year's exchange rate in USD
Cost on power	The firms' average yearly expenses on fuel to generate power, measured in the respective year's exchange rate in USD

'treated' groups can be computed by comparing the outcome of similar group that did not benefit from fiscal incentive. The treatment effect is therefore calculated as the difference of the mean outcomes.

Explaining this process in mathematical terms, we assume that there are two groups of firms that are indexed by their fiscal incentives beneficiary status—such that $P = 0/1$ (where 1 (0) indicates that the firm did (did not) benefit from the incentive). Benefiting from the incentives is expected to yield an outcome:

Y_i^1: which is the productivity of the firm conditional on benefiting from the fiscal incentives (i.e. $P = 1$) or

Y_i^0: which is the productivity of the firm if the firm did not benefit from the fiscal incentives (i.e. $P = 0$).

Therefore the Average Treatment on the Treated Effect (ATT) will be:

$$ATT = E(Y_i^1 - Y_i^0 | P_i = 1) \tag{7.1}$$

Further disintegrating this equation, we derive:

$$ATT = E(Y_i^1 | P_i = 1) - E(Y_i^0 | P_i = 1) \tag{7.2}$$

Where $E(.)$ represents the average (or the *expected value*). Equation (7.2) tends to answer the important question: how much would be the productivity of firms that benefited from fiscal incentives compared to what they would have experienced assuming they did not benefit. This is an important policy question that our estimation technique answers.

From our dataset, we are able to access the data on $E(Y_i^1|P_i = 1)$, however we are constrained with accessing the equivalent data for $E(Y_i^0|P_i = 1)$. To derive this data, we will require matching to clearly estimate the average effect of the treatment on the firms that benefited from incentives assuming the specific firms had not benefited. This approach compares the effect of incentives on firms' productivity with those of matched non-participants (those that did not benefit from the incentives) where the matches are chosen on the basis of observed characteristics. The covariates earlier discussed will be included as the observed variables for the matching process as advanced by Rosenbaum and Rubin (1985) and Caliendo and Kopeinig (2005).

A propensity score is then developed based on the observed characteristics, such that the non-beneficiary firms that are similar to the beneficiaries are selected based on the similarity of their propensity scores. The propensity score is computed based on a firm's probability to benefit from fiscal incentives, which is estimated using a logistic regression model.

It is important to state that the underlining assumptions guiding the PSM analysis include: the conditional independence assumption, which states that potential outcomes for non-beneficiary firms are independent of their participation status, given a set of observable covariates "X".

$$i.e.\ Y_i^0 \perp P_i|X$$

Hence, after adjusting for observable differences, the mean of the potential outcome (i.e. productivity of the firm) is the same for both the participating and non-participating group (i.e. $P=1$ and $P=0$). This condition allows for the use of matched non-beneficiary firms to measure outcome of beneficiary firms, had they not benefited from the programme.

Hence,

$$\left(E\left(Y_i^0 | P = 1, X \right) = E\left(Y_i^0 | P = 0, X \right) \right)$$

The second assumption is the common support condition, which is based on the expectation that for each value of "X", there is a positive probability of either being treated or untreated. This assumption supports the overlap condition; such that the proportion of treated and untreated firms must be greater than "0" for every possible value of "X". Hence, it ensures that there is a sufficient overlap in the characteristics of the treated and untreated firms to find adequate matches. Once these two conditions are satisfied, the efficiency of the treatment assignment is certain (Rosenbaum and Rubin 1983; Nkhata et al. 2014).

We apply different matching algorithms for robustness. They include the nearest neighbour matching (NNM), the radius matching (RM), the kernel matching (KM) and the stratification method (SM). The NNM is focused on comparing the outcome of the beneficiary firms with the closest and most similar non-beneficiary firms, based on their propensity scores. The RM is such that the distance between the treated observation and the control observation should fall within a specified radius (r). The KM is such that each treated observation "i" is matched (using the propensity scores) with other control observations that have weights that are inversely proportional to the distance between the two groups (i.e. treated and control observations). While the SM approach is such that matching is based on the intervals or blocks of propensity scores.

Descriptive Statistics

Sample Characteristics

We report (in Table 7.3) the firm characteristics distributed across the fiscal incentive beneficiary status of firms. On average, the firms in the two categories are similar in many respects. There is no significant difference across beneficiary firms and non-beneficiary firms when considering their productivity. Beneficiaries of import duty exemption and

Table 7.3 Basic sample characteristics

	Import duty exemption			Profit tax exemption			Export financing		
	Beneficiary	Non-beneficiary	t-stat	Beneficiary	Non-beneficiary	t-stat	Beneficiary	Non-beneficiary	t-stat
Productivity (Ratio)	4.30	4.29	0.50	1.97	2.78	0.24	4.41	4.29	0.51
	(5.03)	(21.36)		(1.28)	(4.06)		(4.75)	(21.46)	
Productive capacity	0.41	28.70	0.43	0.29	97.40	0.32	0.02	2.90	0.41
	(0.73)	(395.00)		(0.56)	(759.00)		(0.03)	(3.97)	
Firm size	0.01	0.01	0.56	0.01	0.01	0.60	0.01	0.01	0.50
	(0.02)	(0.02)		(0.01)	(0.01)		(0.02)	(0.02)	
Labour cost	3.54	1.23	0.18	8.02	7.18	0.04**	2.58	1.24	0.72
	(8.55)	(6.74)		(25.30)	(30.50)		(7.62)	(6.77)	
Overhead cost	0.05	0.02	0.36	0.04	0.04	0.07***	0.03	0.02	0.57
	(0.09)	(0.07)		(1.09)	(0.04)		(0.07)	(0.07)	

Note The subscript ** and *** imply significance levels at 5 and 10% respectively

Kernel Density Plot: Productivity and Fiscal Incentives

Empirical Strategy (This section benefits from the framework of Pufahl and Weiss (2008))

export financing incentive had a 0.1 and 0.21 higher productivity than non-beneficiary firms. The productivity of the beneficiaries of profit tax exemption incentive was lower by 0.81 compared to the non-beneficiaries. Though some difference exists in the productivity of firms across their beneficiary status, the difference was not significant at 1, 5 or 10% levels of significance. No significant difference was observed for the productive capacity of firms and firm size across their beneficiary status. A significant difference was observed for the labour and overhead cost for only profit tax exemption incentive and across the beneficiary status of firms. However, no significant difference was observed for the import duty and export financing across the firms' beneficiary status.

Since most of the observable characteristics are similar, it is less difficult to identify a comparison firm from our sample. The distance in the mean values of the observable characteristic that differs across the two groups will be reduced in the matching process. Hence, these processes help to satisfy the key concern of the matching estimation technique (i.e. similarity of the two groups). In essence, finding individual firm units in the non-beneficiary group that are similar to those in the beneficiary group.

The productivity of firms (across their fiscal incentive beneficiary status) are considered using the kernel density plots in order to observe their respective biases. The kernel density plot estimates the probability density function of productivity based on the observed sample (see Barron 2014). More so, it allows for a smooth distribution of productivity across the entire and subsamples of the firms based on their beneficiary status.

To understand overall productivity benefit associated with fiscal incentives, it is, therefore, necessary to derive more aggregate fiscal incentive measures, allowing for better comparison of firms that benefited, and those that did not benefit, as well as the overall sampled firms. This measure is such that the firms were attributed 1 if they have benefited from any of the three categories of the incentives (i.e. import duty exemption, profit tax exemption and export financing) and 0 otherwise. The plot is presented in Fig. 7.2 and the three lines in the Figure represent the aggregate sample and the subsamples according to the firms benefiting from any of these forms of incentive.

From the figure, it is observed that firms that benefit from any of these forms of incentives are biased towards the right. Their density

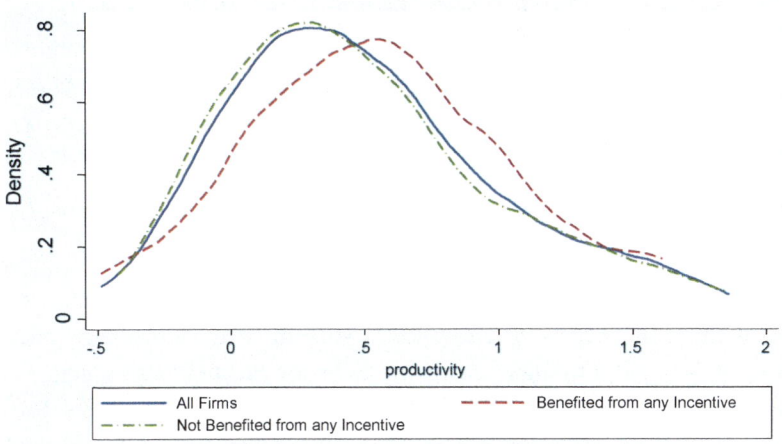

Fig. 7.2 Productivity of firms by their benefiting from any of the incentives (i.e. import duty exemptions, profit tax exemption and export financing)

overlaps with the density of those that did not benefit from any of the incentives, as well as the density of the total firms. This means that firms that enjoy any of these forms of incentives have higher productivity relative to the firms that do not benefit from these incentives. On the other hand, firms that do not benefit from any of these incentives are biased to the left, suggesting that they are less productive than their counterparts. We, therefore, infer that firms that benefit from these forms of incentives have a higher productivity and they tend to be relatively more productive than their non-beneficial counterparts.

Econometric Results[3]

The observed differences in the productivity of firms that have benefited from any of the incentives vis-à-vis those that have not benefited, suggest positive average productivity effects. However, the outcome

---

[3]Please note that henceforth, the word participants and non-participants, as well treated and untreated are used interchangeably.

differences may also be the results of already initial differences in some of the underlining peculiarities of the firms in any of these categories. As a result, we, therefore, apply the econometric methods elaborated in the fourth section. We start by estimating the firms' propensity scores using a probit model; we then use these scores as the basis for the matching procedures.

It is important to note that we are estimating the PSM differently for the three categories of incentives that are of interest to us. The reasons for this is to enable us to have a clearer perspective on the impact of each of these incentives on the productivity of firms across our sample and to enhance the quality of our predictions. As such, using aggregate data to capture the overall incentive may not be relevant henceforth. The firms that benefit from any of these incentives are the participants, while those in the other category are the non-participants.

Variable Selection in the PSM Estimation

There is no consensus on the type of covariates that should be included in the discrete choice model when estimating the propensity scores (see Austin 2011). However, Heckman et al. (1997) suggest that: to eliminate biases due to variable selection, it will be relevant to include all the variables that influence participation and outcome. Therefore, our variables were carefully selected by drawing from the available literature (see preceding section) as well as information available in our database. All the variables had complete data in our main data source.

Determinants of Participation

Table 7.4 shows the estimated probit models used to derive the propensity scores. In the import duty exemption productivity model (see column 1), the firms' overhead expenses such as labour cost and the cost of generating electricity through the purchase of fuel are significantly associated with participation. The positive sign suggests that firms that

Table 7.4 Determinant of participation (excluding the robustness variables)

Variables	Participants benefiting from import duty exemption	Participants benefiting from profit tax exemption	Participants benefiting from export financing
Productive capacity	−0.099	0.042	−0.199**
	(0.298)	(0.676)	(0.034)
Size of the firm	−0.184	−0.164	−0.178
	(0.290)	(0.556)	(0.243)
Labour input	0.594**	1.153**	0.027
	(0.012)	(0.038)	(0.875)
Cost on power	0.220***	0.804**	0.312***
	(0.055)	(0.021)	(0.073)
Constant	−5.167**	−8.221**	−1.306
	(0.029)	(0.014)	(0.349)
Pseudo R2	0.1171	0.189	0.143

Note The subscript *, ** and *** imply significance levels at 1, 5 and 10% respectively

incur more of these overheads have to rely on import duty exemption. Similarly, firms in this category also rely on profit tax exemption since the signs of these variables are positive and significant in the second column of the Table: this column represents the model for participation in the profit tax exemption model. However, moving on to the third column, we observed a slight change: the cost on labour was no longer significant—although it was positive. Nonetheless, the cost of generating electricity through the purchase of fuel remained positive and significant. This suggests that this variable is an important determinant of participation for all the three categories of fiscal incentive that is being observed in this study.

The negative association between firms' productive capacity (in terms of cost of machinery) and the likelihood of participation (see column 3 in Table 7.4) suggests that firms with high productive capacity may be less likely to benefit from the export financing initiative of the government. The non-significance of the size of the firm (measured using value of land owned by the firm) is less straightforward since it was not significant in all the columns. The negative sign suggests that the size of the firm may not be an important determinant of participation. Caution should be applied in interpreting this result considering our measure of firm size.

Overall, our result is consistent with the earlier findings from the descriptive statistics. More so, noting that incentives are supposed to compensate for some deficiencies in the business environment of countries (see UNCTAD 2004), the significance of the firms' overhead variables magnifies this expectation. It can be said that among the main determinants of participation in our analysis, is the fact that the firm incurs huge cost on the purchase of fuel in generating its own electricity and on labour cost. The productive capacity may only be relevant for export financing.

Matching Quality

Before reporting the estimated treatment effects (ATT), we need to ensure that the matching process eliminates any mean differences that may occur after matching between the groups. The existence of mean difference may suggest that some bias exists in the matching process. Therefore to determine the quality of our matching process, we divided the propensity scores into blocks among the groups. This is deemed essential in order to improve the balancing of the covariates.

Table 7.5 presents the propensity scores for the blocks among the treated and untreated groups. The mean propensity scores were not different between import exemption participants and non-participants (i.e. 0.084 and 0.031), between profit tax exemption participants and non-participants (i.e. 0.299 and 0.141) and between participants in export financing and non-participants (i.e. 0.099 and 0.036). More so, the table reveals that, across the models, the scores for both groups are within common range and there is no significant difference existing in the distribution of the scores. These results thereby satisfy the balancing condition suggested by Becker and Ichino (2002).

Table 7.5 Propensity scores of treated and untreated group

Models		Propensity score			
		Min	Max	Mean	Sig
Import duty exemption	Treated	0.023	0.275	0.084	0.999
	Untreated	0.006	0.130	0.031	
Profit tax exemption	Treated	0.146	0.601	0.299	0.994
	Untreated	0.003	0.663	0.141	
Export financing	Treated	0.023	0.293	0.099	0.996
	Untreated	0.001	0.328	0.036	

The common support and overlap assumption of the PSM is another important condition that must be satisfied to ensure that firms with similar covariates have a positive probability of being either participants or non-participants (see Heckman et al. 1999). As earlier stated, the rule of thumb is that the common support must be greater than zero and less than 1. Therefore, we report the common support boundaries for participants from our estimation for each of the estimated models. For the first model that estimates the impact of participating in the import exemption, the common support is within the range of 0.0234 and 0.2748; for the profit tax exemption, the common support is within the range of 0.1462 and 0.6009, while for export financing the common support is within range of 0.0226 and 0.2925. The region of the common support for all the estimated PSM indicates that there was a balance between covariates of participants and non-participants for the groups.

Therefore, having satisfied the two conditions for effectively matching the participants and the non-participants, we go ahead to predict the estimated treatment effect (ATT).

Estimated Treatment Effects

Table 7.6 shows both the bias-adjusted and unadjusted estimates of the ATT from four matching methods to check the consistency of the result. The essence is to evaluate the impact of the different dimensions of fiscal incentives on productivity, using firm productivity data as the

Table 7.6 Average treatment effect for productivity

Treatment	Bias adjustment	Nearest neighbour matching		Kernel matching		Radius matching		Stratified matching	
		ATT	Std. Err.	ATT	Std. Err.	ATT	Std. Err.	ATT	Std. Err.
Import duty exemption	No	0.243	0.216	0.108	0.182	0.017	0.206	0.007	0.206
	Yes	0.243	0.261	0.108	0.182	0.017	0.113	0.007	0.176
Profit tax exemption	No	0.465*	0.059	0.677*	0.056	0.837	0.647	0.273*	0.036
	Yes	0.271*	0.059	0.677*	0.056	0.330*	0.084	0.257*	0.036
Export financing	No	1.054*	0.338	0.401*	0.148	0.638*	0.368	0.661*	0.210
	Yes	0.894*	0.338	0.401*	0.148	0.638*	0.410	0.661*	0.100

Note The subscript *, ** and *** imply significance levels at 1, 5 and 10% respectively. He variables used to determine this statistics are in their log-linear form. This suggests that any coefficient in the table will be interpreted as percentage change outcome variable. Thus, the ATT was estimated using the ATT equation discussed in the third section in the region of common support identified earlier (see preceding section). The common support condition is imposed in our ATT analysis to ensure the groups are within the same range of propensity scores. The treatment effects are derived using four matching estimators, namely, the NNM, the RM, the KM and the SM. The default 0.06 bandwidth is used for the KM and 0.1 caliper for the RM, while five nearest neighbours are used with the NNM and the propensity scores of the closest blocks are used for the SM. Also, from the Table, we observe that the bias adjustment values are consistently lower for all the matching types, which signifies that the PSM is sensitive to the unobserved characteristics. Therefore, for brevity, we report in the text only the results for bias adjustment from nearest neighbour matching.

Considering the participation in the import duty exemption, we find that there was no significant average treatment effect on the productivity of firms in the column that contains the nearest neighbour matching technique. In addition, scanning through the columns for other matching techniques, it was observed that none of the ATT values was significant. This indicates that increase in the productivity of participants in the import duty exemption treatment was not significantly higher above what they could have earned if they did not participate in this treatment. Of course, we cannot conclude in sacrosanct that government involvement in import duty will result in non-significant impact on the productivity of firms. However, we reserve our discussions on this result until we have conducted our sensitivity checks to ensure that our results are not driven by some elements, like the covariates that are included in the computation of the propensity scores for our observations.

For the profit tax treatment, we found that participants in this scheme are able to increase their productivity by about 27.1% above what they could have had assuming they did not benefit from the profit tax exemption. This result is significant at 1% level of significance. For the participants in the export finance scheme, we also observed that the average treatment effect was 89.4%, suggesting that beneficiaries of the export finance scheme had a positive improvement in their productivity by about 89.4% higher of what they could have had assuming they did not benefit from this scheme. This result is also significant at 1%.

Sensitivity Analysis

To be sure that the type of covariates that are included in our PSM model does not drive our results, we decided to try two sensitivity checks. First, we excluded the productive capacity and size variables from the estimation since they were not consistently significant in the PSM logistic regression analysis that was reported in Table 7.4. Then we predicted the ATT estimations again to see whether our results are going to change. The results of this process are presented in Table 7.7 respectively for all the matching techniques.

Before interpreting the results, note that all the preliminary checks have been carried out but not reported in this text for brevity (i.e. they are available from the authors upon request). From Table 7.7, we observe that the participants in the import duty exemption treatment now observed a significant positive improvement in the volume of their productivity (unlike the result in Table 7.4). This result indicates that firms who participate in the import duty exemption treatment are able to increase their productivity by about 85% above the volume they could have produced assuming they did not benefit from this form of incentive. The result for participants in the profit tax exemption treatment as well as those in the export financing treatment remained the same as earlier discussed. They had significant increase as a result of their participation in these two forms of incentives.

The second sensitivity analysis involves the inclusion of other covariates in our analysis to see the possible effect on our results. We prefer the length of years that the firm has been in the particular business and the location of the firm (i.e. whether the firm is located in the capital city and otherwise) because most of the incentives that are granted by the Cameroonian government are tied to specific length of time, which indicates that the likelihood of a firm being a participant in any of the groups will be informed by their length of years of being involved in a particular manufacturing sector. For the location of the firm, we argue

Table 7.7 Sensitivity check 1—average treatment effect for productivity

Treatment	Bias adjustment	Nearest neighbour matching		Kernel matching		Radius matching		Stratified matching	
		ATT	Std. Err.	ATT	Std. Err.	ATT	Std. Err.	ATT	Std. Err.
Import duty exemption	No	0.852*	0.368	0.674*	0.275	0.673**	0.337	0.673**	0.337
	Yes	0.852***	0.484	0.674*	0.275	0.673	0.433	0.673*	0.209
Profit tax exemption	No	0.824 *	0.023	0.435***	0.229	0.579*	0.260	0.474***	0.262
	Yes	0.824*	0.058	0.435***	0.229	0.579***	0.319	0.474***	0.262
Export financing	No	0.592	0.447	0.756*	0.257	0.756*	0.263	0.756 *	0.263
	Yes	0.592**	0.273	0.756*	0.257	0.756*	0.248	0.756 *	0.317

Note The subscript *, ** and *** imply significance levels at 1, 5 and 10% respectively. The variables used to determine these statistics are in their log-linear form. This suggests that any coefficient in the table will be interpreted as percentage change that the chances of firms located in the capital city to be a participant is higher than if they were not located in the capital city. Preliminary checks are also conducted to ascertain the quality of our matching when using these variables (these results are not only reported but are available upon request).

The results of the sensitivity analysis are reported in Table 7.8. The signs and significant value of the ATT estimates for the participants in the import exemption scheme are not significant, but positive in all the columns. This result tends to support the findings from Table 7.6. However, when considering the impact of the other forms of incentive—like the profit tax exemption and the export financing—the results are found to be consistently positive and significant.

Finally, the Rosenbaum checks for sensitivity of our result to unobserved variables was also performed, but not reported, and the result advances the idea that our findings are insensitive to hidden bias.

Discussion

From the analysis, we are cautious in saying that to some extent, the significant improvement in the productivity of our participants in the import exemption treatment is driven by the type of covariates that are included in our analysis. This is because in the first estimation and the second sensitivity test in Tables 7.6 and 7.8, respectively, it was not significant, but later became significant in Table 7.7. These results suggest that the involvement of the government in exempting firms from import duty may not account for a consistent significant increase in their productivity. However, for an increase to occur, there has to be a consideration of some firms' characteristics that may spur such increase. A possible explanation for this is that import duty exemption may drive inefficiency if the recipients are not carefully selected/monitored. Possibly, if firms are allowed to utilise their capital in securing import and all the necessary payment accompanying it, they may likely be optimal in channelling their resources appropriately. Although no consensus is reached on this, it is possible that if firms are granted import duty exemption, there is the likelihood that they may be wasteful in the

Table 7.8 Sensitivity check 2—average treatment effect for productivity

Treatment	Bias adjustment	Nearest neighbour matching		Kernel matching		Radius matching		Stratified matching	
		ATT	Std. Err.	ATT	Std. Err.	ATT	Std. Err.	ATT	Std. Err.
Import duty exemption	No	0.443	0.380	0.341	0.820	0.983	0.730	0.341	0.380
	Yes	0.381	0.330	0.341	0.820	0.983	0.730	0.341	0.290
Profit tax exemption	No	0.409*	0.026	0.367*	0.035	0.203*	0.049	0.212*	0.026
	Yes	0.250*	0.065	0.367*	0.035	0.115*	0.049	0.212*	0.021
Export financing	No	0.821***	0.447	0.873*	0.289	1.002**	0.504	0.868**	0.393
	Yes	0.821*	0.027	0.873*	0.289	1.002**	0.504	0.868*	0.355

Note The subscript *, ** and *** imply significance levels at 1, 5 and 10% respectively. The variables used to determine these statistics are in their log-linear form. This suggests that any coefficient in the table will be interpreted as percentage change

purchase of resources from abroad, knowing that such purchases will not be taxed. OECD (2007) report on tax incentives for investment throws some light on this as they noted that import duty exemption is prone to abuse and easy to divert exempt purchases to unintended recipients.

The consistent positive and significant sign of the profit tax exemption and export financing participants suggest that the forms of incentives that will enhance the productivity of Cameroonian firms should be such that rewards processes. This implies that government incentive should be such that is introduced at later stages of the production process. As seen in our analysis, the import duty exemption incentive was not consistently significant in affecting productivity; however, when considering the other incentives that are introduced at the later stages of the business processes (such as profit tax exemption and export financing) it is seen that there was a significant impact on the productivity of firms. This, of course, suggests that these two forms of incentives can steer up firms' ability to be efficient because; for the firms to benefit from these incentives, they have to be profitable and they should be able to produce outputs that can be consumed beyond the Cameroonian market.

Conclusion

In this study, we contributed to the discussion on the role of incentive in enhancing the productivity of participating in different types of fiscal incentives (i.e. import duty exemption, profit tax exemption and export financing). We applied an econometric analysis using firm data from surveys conducted between 2006 and 2009.

The models suggested that participation in the different forms of incentives are associated with higher productivity, however, the significance differs across the different forms of incentives. The estimations predict that participation in profit tax exemption and export financing is associated with productivity differences of around 27.1 and 89.41%, respectively. While the lack of baseline data and the relatively small sample size require caution in inferring causation, the results may be suggestive of underlying causal impact of participating in fiscal incentive regimes as a manufacturing firm in Cameroon.

It is important to state that this study is not an overall assessment of the impact of fiscal incentives on manufacturing firms' productivity in Cameroon. However, in order to decide on the overall impact, indirect effects within firms have to be taken into consideration. Overall, impact depends on intra-firm decision-making of how to utilise such benefits that are derived from the government to influence its overall productivity. This highlights the need to add further explanatory variables to address this issue particularly as it relates to individual firm basis, which will be advancement to this study.

References

Action Aid. (2014). *Investment Incentives in Ghana: The Cost to Socio-Economic Development*. Action Aid Ghana Report Feb-2014, Accra: Action Aid. Retrieved from http://www.actionaid.org/sites/files/actionaid/investment-tax_incentives_in_ghana_-_an_actionaid_research_report.pdf.

Arnold, J., Mattoo, A., & Narciso, G. (2008). Services Inputs and Firm Productivity in Sub-Saharan Africa: Evidence from Firm-Level Data. *Journal of African Economies, 17*(4), 578–599.

Austin, P. C. (2011). *An Introduction to Propensity Score Methods for Reducing the Effects of Confounding in Observational Studies, Multivariate Behavioural Research*. London: Routledge.

Barron, M. (2014). *Econometric Tools 1: Non-parametric Methods*. Available via https://www.ocf.berkeley.edu/~manuelb/week6/LectureNotes06.pdf. Accessed 1 Oct 2015.

Becker, S. O., & Ichino, A. (2002). Estimation of Average Treatment Effects Based on Propensity Scores. *The State Journal, 2*(4), 358–377.

Biya, P. (2013). *Law N° 2013/004 of 18 April 2013 to Lay Down Private Investment Incentives in the Republic of Cameroon*. Turkish and Cameroonian Business Association. Available via http://turcaba.org/index_htm_files/new-incentive-laws-oninvestment-in-the-republic-of-cameroon.pdf. Accessed 1 Oct 2015.

Bora, B. (2002). *Investment Distortions and the International Policy Architecture*. World Trade Organisation Working Paper, Geneva.

Bureau of Economic and Business Affairs. (2013). *2013 Investment Climate Statement—Cameroon.* Bureau of Economic and Business Affairs. Available via http://www.state.gov/e/eb/rls/othr/ics/2013/204615.htm. Accessed 1 Oct 2015.

Caliendo, M., & Kopeinig, S. (2005). *Some Practical Guidance for the Implementation of Propensity Score Matching.* Institute for the Study of Labour (IZA). Available via ftp.iza.org/dp1588.pdf. Accessed 1 Sep 2015.

Central Bank of Nigeria-CBN. (2013). *Fiscal Incentives in Nigeria: Lessons of Experience.* Abuja: Central Bank of Nigeria.

Cleeve, E. (2008). How Effective Are Fiscal Incentives to Attract FDI to Sub-Saharan Africa? *The Journal of Developing Areas, 42*(1), 135–153.

Escribano, A., Guasch, J. L., & Pena, J. (2010). *Assessing the Impact of Infrastructure Quality on Firm Productivity in Africa: Cross-Country Comparisons Based on Investment Climate Surveys from 1999 to 2005.* World Bank. Available via https://openknowledge.worldbank.org/handle/10986/19901. Accessed 17 Jan 2017.

Gui-Diby, S., & Renard, M. (2015). Foreign Direct Investment Inflows and the Industrialization of African Countries. *World Development, 74,* 43–57.

Heckman, J., Ichimura, H., & Todd, P. E. (1997). Matching as an Econometric Evaluation Estimator: Evidence from Evaluating a Job Training Program. *Review of Economic Studies, 64,* 605–654.

Heckman, J., La Londe, R., & Smith, J. (1999). The Economics and Econometrics of Active Labour Market Programs. In O. Ashenfelter & D. Card (Eds.), *Handbook of Labour Economics, III* (pp. 1865–2097). Amsterdam: Elsevier.

IMF. (2012). *Sub-Saharan Africa-Maintaining Growth in an Uncertain World.* Washington, DC: IMF.

Lee, J. (1996). Government Interventions and Productivity Growth. *Journal of Economic Growth, 1*(3), 391–414.

McArthur, J., & Teal, F. (2002). *Corruption and Firm Performance in Africa.* CSAE working paper, WPS/2002.10, Oxford University.

Ndichu, J., Blohmke, J., Kemp, R., et al. (2015). The Adoption of Energy Efficiency Measures by Firms in AFRICA: Case Studies of Cassava Processing in Nigeria and Maize Milling in Kenya. *Innovation and Development, 5*(2), 189–206.

Nkhata, R., Jumbe, C., & Mwabumba, M. (2014). *Does Irrigation Have an Impact on Food Security and Poverty?* IFPRI. Available via http://ebrary.ifpri.org/cdm/ref/collection/p15738coll2/id/128180. Accessed 17 Jan 2017.

OECD. (2007). *Tax Incentives for Investment—A Global Perspective: Experiences in MENA and Non-MENA Countries*. OECD. Available via www.oecd.org/mena/competitiveness/38758855.pdf. Accessed 17 Jan 2017.

Pufahl, A., & Weiss, C. R. (2008, August 26–19). *Evaluating the Effects of Farm Programs: Results from Propensity Score Matching*. Paper presented at the 12th Congress of the European Association of Agricultural Economists, Ghent, Belgium.

Rosenbaum, P. R., & Rubin, D. B. (1983). The Central Role of Propensity Score in Observational Studies for Causal Effects. *Biometrica, 70,* 41–55.

Rosenbaum, P. R., & Rubin, D. B. (1985). Constructing a Control Group Using Multivariate Matched Sampling Methods that Incorporate the Propensity Score. *The American Statistician, 39*(1), 33–38.

Tabi, A. (2005, February 15–16). *Fiscal Policy and Sectoral Productivity Convergence in Cameroon: Implications for Poverty Reduction*. Paper presented at the Washington Conference, IMF, Washington, DC.

UNCTAD. (2000). *Tax Incentives and Foreign Direct Investment: A Global Survey*. Geneva and New York: UNCTAD.

UNCTAD. (2004). *Incentives: UNCTAD Series on Issues in International Investment Agreements*. Geneva and New York: UNCTAD. Retrieved from https://unctad.org/en/Docs/iteiit20035_en.pdf.

UNCTAD. (2015). *Broadening the Sources of Growth in Africa: The Role of Investment*. Geneva: UNCTAD.

UNECA. (2013). *Making the Most of Africa's Commodities: Industrializing for Growth, Jobs, and Economic Transformation*. Addis Ababa: United Nations Economic Commission for Africa.

World Bank. (2015). *World Development Indicators*. Washington: World Bank.

8

Food and Agriculture Global Value Chains: New Evidence from Sub-Saharan Africa

Jean Balié, Davide Del Prete, Emiliano Magrini, Pierluigi Montalbano and Silvia Nenci

SSA Participation in GVCs and Structural Transformation

Since the last decades of the twentieth century, food and agriculture global value chains (GVCs) keep growing as products cross borders multiple times and the international production networks dominated by modern food processors and retailers become more vertically organised (Reardon et al. 2007; Minten et al. 2009; Balié et al. 2018). As a result, agro-food trade has more than quadrupled in nominal terms during the past three decades, from USD 230 billion in 1980 to almost USD 1100 billion in 2010, and half of this trade can be considered of intermediate

J. Balié
IRRI, Los Baños, Philippines

D. Del Prete (✉) · E. Magrini
FAO, Rome, Italy
e-mail: davide.delprete@fao.org

D. Del Prete
IMT School for Advanced Studies, Lucca, Italy

© The Author(s) 2019
A. B. Elhiraika et al. (eds.), *Governance for Structural Transformation in Africa*,
https://doi.org/10.1007/978-3-030-03964-6_8

usage for global production processes (Maertens and Swinnen 2015; OECD 2016). The common wisdom is that the emergence of GVCs can represent a golden opportunity for supporting the ongoing transformations of Sub-Saharan Africa (SSA), especially in agriculture and food markets, which could move from a subsistence-oriented and farm-centered system to a more commercialised, productive and off-farm centered one (Greenville et al. 2017; Del Prete et al. 2017). GVC participation is indeed supposed to open access to unprecedented flows of knowledge, capital and, in particular, sophisticated inputs (IMF 2015; Montalbano et al. 2016, 2018) which can lead to an accelerated and widespread path of structural transformation and income growth. By generating higher incomes, and because of technology spillovers on food production, participation in the export chains is also supposed to improve income stability and the food security of smallholder households (Cattaneo and Miroudot 2015; Swinnen 2014; Kuijpers and Swinnen 2016; Reardon et al. 2009; Barrett et al. 2012, 2017).

Despite this background, the economic literature has not yet quantitatively assessed the degree of integration of SSA countries in the agriculture and food GVCs, although Balié et al. (2018) is a notable exception. This exercise implies unpacking the different phases of the production process to identify the amount of each country's contribution to trade flows in terms of value-added (i.e. the value that is added by countries/industries in producing goods and services). It requires both the use of multi-region input-output tables (MRIO) to disaggregate the structure of the world economy between countries/sectors and a proper gross exports decomposition methodology. To this end, we apply the methodology developed by Wang et al. (2013) (hereinafter WWZ)—who compute a breakdown of bilateral exports

P. Montalbano
Sapienza University, Rome, Italy

P. Montalbano
University of Sussex, Falmer, UK

S. Nenci
Roma Tre University, Rome, Italy

disaggregated into value-added terms—to the EORA database. This database provides a balanced global MRIO for 186 countries—of which 43 are in SSA—and 25 harmonised ISIC-type sectors in the period 1990–2013 (Lenzen et al. 2012, 2013).[1] Specifically, we focus on agriculture (ISIC codes 1, 2) and food and beverages (ISIC codes 15, 16) sectors.

Our results show that on the one hand, despite low trade shares at the global level, SSA agricultural sector turns out to be deeply involved in GVC participation and the relevance of its international linkages is increasing over time. On the other hand, SSA involvement in GVC is still limited to upstream production stages of the chain and mainly driven by the European market. This suggests a need for a new multi-stakeholder agenda to foster the capacity of SSA to take advantage of GVCs as drivers for their structural transformation, going beyond the simple narrative of upgrading.

The remainder of the chapter is organised as follows: "Measuring GVC Participation: The Methodological Approach" presents the methodology for decomposing trade in value added. "Mapping the Participation of the SSA Countries Along Food and Agriculture GVCs" provides a comprehensive map of food and agriculture GVC participation in SSA and relative trade partners. "Concluding Remarks" concludes and suggests policy implications.

---

[1]The use of EORA database is the only option to look at the issue for a comprehensive set of countries in Sub-Saharan Africa so far. None of the other similar efforts, such as the Asian IO tables (IDE-Jetro), the GTAP project, the OECD-WTO TiVA initiative and the WIOD project has the same extension in terms of country coverage and the same level of detail for end-use categories in Sub-Saharan Africa. Notwithstanding the growing use of the EORA database to carry out GVC studies (see, among others Caliendo et al. 2016; Del Prete et al. 2018), we made additional sensitivity analysis by comparing EORA and WIOD for overlapping sectors and countries. This highlighted consistent trends and a slight upward bias from WIOD (both at the country level and at the world level) likely due to the fact that the latter includes an artificial 'Rest of the World' country whose I–O matrix has been derived through a proportionality assumption based on an 'average' world technology. As pointed by the UNCTAD (2013) this assumption could yield a downward bias in the computed world FVA, as the world average I–O includes by definition large, relatively close, countries, while most excluded countries in the 'Rest of the World' aggregate tend to be small, relatively more open, economies.

Measuring GVC Participation: The Methodological Approach

The increasing international fragmentation of production has challenged the conventional wisdom on how we look at and interpret trade data. As different stages of the same production process are now allocated to different countries, intermediate inputs cross borders multiple times and are then counted each time by gross trade flows. These developments are challenging the way agriculture and food trade data are used and interpreted because conventional statistics have become increasingly misleading as a measure of the value produced by any particular country (Koopman et al. 2014). For instance, using gross trade statistics, the final producer may appear to generate most of the value of goods, while the role of countries providing inputs upstream—such as SSA countries—could be largely underestimated. The relevance of this issue is confirmed by the many initiatives and efforts that try to address the measurement of trade flows in the context of GVCs and try to estimate the so-called trade in value-added.[2] The latter reflects the value that is added by industries in producing goods and services and it is equivalent to the difference between industry output and the sum of its intermediate inputs. Looking at trade from a value added perspective better reveals how upstream domestic industries contribute to exports, as well as how much (and how) participate in GVCs (OECD–WTO 2012).

The recent availability of MRIO data combined with bilateral trade statistics allows us to allocate the value added embedded in trade flows to the countries and sectors of origin and destination. We can then decompose gross exports into their main components (Fig. 8.1), namely: the domestic value added (DVA) (i.e. value added exported in final goods or in intermediates produced at home); the foreign value added (FVA) (i.e. other countries value added in intermediates used in exports) and the "pure double counting" term (DC), that arises when intermediate goods

---

[2]See among others Hummels et al. (2001), Johnson and Noguera (2012), OECD (2012), Timmer et al. (2015), Los et al. (2016).

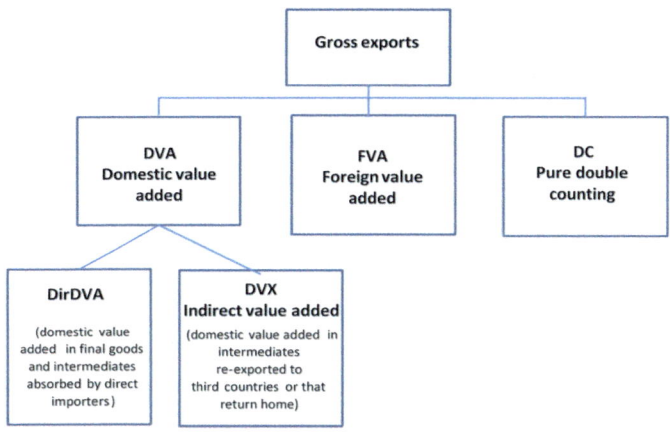

Fig. 8.1 Gross exports decomposition: main buckets (*Source* adapted from WWZ (2013))

cross borders back and forth multiple times. In this work, we calculate these components using the methodology developed by WWZ, as it generalises the gross exports accounting framework proposed by Koopman et al. (2014) from a country-level perspective to one that decomposes gross trade flows at the sector, bilateral or bilateral-sector level.

A simple example borrowed from Balié et al. (2018) concerning cocoa beans' exports of Ivory Coast to France can help to clarify this decomposition. Let us assume that, in order to grow and produce USD 100 cocoa beans eventually exported to France, Ivorian farmers use USD 30 of imported inputs from China (e.g. fertilisers, pesticides, etc.). Conventional trade statistics would show Ivory Coast's exports worth USD 100, although only 70 USD of value added was created there, while USD 30 were imported. Using the jargon of trade in value-added, the value of the cocoa beans exported by Ivory Coast would embed USD 70 of DVA and USD 30 of FVA (which also corresponds to the DVA originating from China) (see Fig. 8.2).

Moreover, let us now assume that USD 20 of the domestic value added of cocoa beans exported from Ivory Coast to France is consumed locally, whereas USD 50 is used as intermediates into the French chocolate production exported abroad, e.g. to the United States.

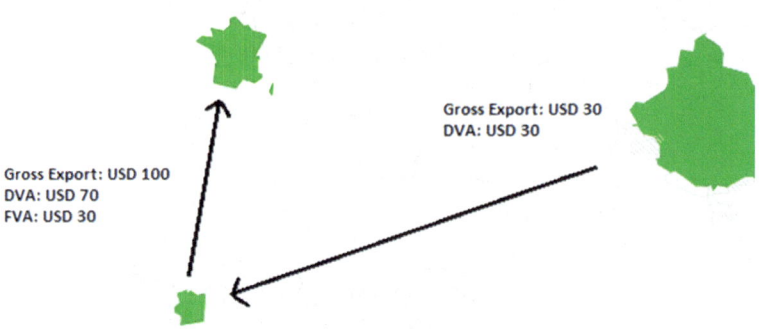

Fig. 8.2 Traditional vs. value-added trade statistics (domestic and foreign value added) (*Source* Balié et al. 2018)

Therefore, the DVA of Ivorian exports should be further decomposed into USD 20 of direct domestic value added (dirDVA), that is the part of cocoa beans' exports directly absorbed—as both final and intermediate goods—by the French market, and USD 50 of indirect domestic value added (DVX), that is, the part of cocoa beans' intermediates further re-exported by France to third countries (e.g. USA), as chocolate primary and confectionary products (see Fig. 8.3). Finally, the chocolate products eventually imported from France include a DC term due to the value of cocoa beans originally exported from Ivory Coast.

Therefore, DVX measures the joint participation of the bilateral trade partners in a GVC since it contains the exporter's value added of a specific sector that passes through the direct importer for a (or some) stage(s) of production before it reaches third countries (or eventually returns home[3]). More specifically, it captures the contribution of the domestic sector to the exports of other countries and indicates the extent of involvement in GVC for relatively upstream industries. This is why it is usually considered as a measure of *forward* GVC participation. On the other hand, since the FVA used in the production of a

---

[3]The DVX component includes also the returned value added (RDV), that is the portion of domestic value added that is initially exported but ultimately returned home by being embedded in the imports from other countries and consumed at home.

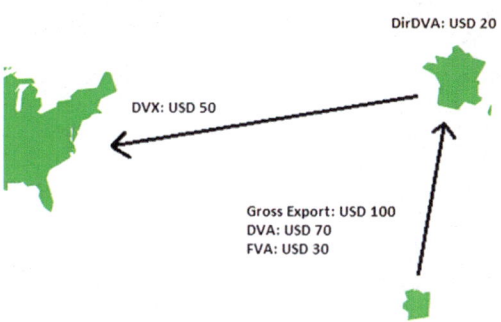

Fig. 8.3   Traditional vs. value-added trade statistics (domestic and indirect value added) (*Source* Balié et al. 2018)

country's exports—which consists of the value added contained in intermediate inputs imported from abroad, exported in the form of final or intermediate goods—captures the extent of involvement in GVC for relatively downstream industries, it is considered a measure of *backward* GVC participation. Eventually, to get a comprehensive picture of trade in value added for a single country across all partners in each sector, we sum up the DVX, the FVA and the PDC components and provide an overall *GVC participation index* (Koopman et al. 2011; Rahman and Zhao 2013). The higher (or lower) the value of the GVC participation index, the larger (or smaller) the participation of a country in global supply chains. The maximum value of GVC index is 1 in the extreme case where all gross exports are entirely determined by GVC related activities.

Mapping the Participation of the SSA Countries Along Food and Agriculture GVCs

An Aggregate View

In this section, we map GVC participation in SSA considering an aggregate estimate of all sectors. Looking at the WWZ decomposition of gross exports, a preliminary remark is that a large part of value

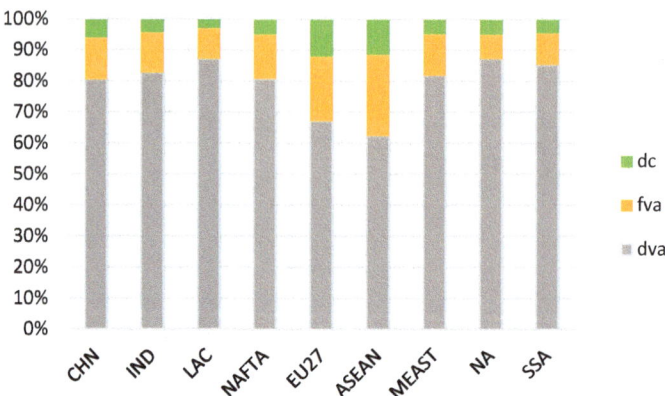

Fig. 8.4 Gross exports decomposition 2013 (*Source* Authors' elaboration on EORA data)

added in SSA is domestic, as the DVA component accounts for more than 80% of gross exports (Fig. 8.4). This is actually in line with what is observed in all the other developing regions, with the relevant exception of ASEAN (which similarly to EU27 produces domestically only about 60% of the value of its exports).[4] It is also consistent with the literature applying different decomposition methods (see, among others, African Development Bank 2015; Foster-McGregor et al. 2015; Del Prete et al. 2018). However, relative to standard methods the WWZ methodology allows to isolate properly the DC component, which appears to be noteworthy (e.g. 0.14 for the EU; 0.04 for SSA). We thus consider that this decomposition provides a more realistic picture of the value added of exports worldwide.

According to our computation, about 10% of SSA exports contains value added actually produced abroad (FVA). This is a similar result compared to the figures in other developing regions (e.g. emerging economies such as China and India register overall 14 and 13% respectively) with the exception of ASEAN. With 26% of foreign value added exports, ASEAN can be considered one of the world "main hubs",

---

[4]Note that the reported measures tend to be inflated by intermediate flows between countries of the same region. This inserts a bias in favor of the EU relative to other large single countries or smaller regional groups (e.g. NAFTA).

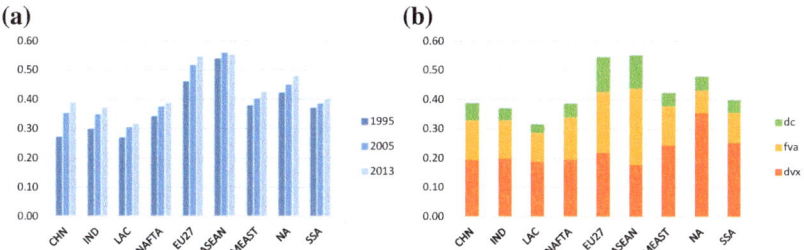

Fig. 8.5 GVC participation index by world areas (all sectors). **a** Total, **b** Composition 2013 (*Source* Authors' elaboration on EORA data)

together with the EU and NAFTA for which the foreign value added content in export is 25 and 16%, respectively.

In terms of GVC participation index, it is worth noting that the involvement of the SSA countries is indeed relevant (40% of SSA gross exports in 2013) and increasing over time (Fig. 8.5a). Again EU27 and ASEAN countries exhibit the highest rates (more than 50% of gross exports), with the EU overtaking ASEAN after the European Monetary Union (EMU), reaching 60%. North Africa shows one of the highest rate of GVC participation in the developing world (48%). Note, however, that this measure does not say anything about the absolute weight of each region in world trade since the value only represents the share of export participating in the GVC with respect to the own region total gross flows.

As expected—due to the limited percentage of FVA embedded in SSA exports—the relative high rate of GVC participation is mainly driven by the domestic value added supplied to other countries' exports (DVX) (Fig. 8.5b). After controlling for double counting, SSA exhibits one of the best performances in terms of DVX (about 25% of the value of gross exports). The best performer in the world is North Africa, where 36% of gross exports embed value added supplied abroad (even higher than the Middle East).

As a matter of fact, the common feature of a very high degree of DVA emphasised in Fig. 8.4 actually hinders different patterns in terms of GVC participation, with Africa (especially North Africa, but also SSA) being the best performer in providing value added to other countries in the world. About 30% of the domestic value added produced in SSA are inputs for other countries' exports (over 40% in the case of

North Africa). For comparison, these figures are close to those of the EU (30%)—that is actually inflated by the high degree of intermediate trade flows within the single market—and higher than those of China, India and NAFTA with figures around 20%.

Therefore, the aggregate view of the GVC participation and position for the 25 sectors included in the EORA database confirms the high degree of involvement of the SSA countries and their relative upstream position that encompasses mainly natural-resource production as well as simple manufacturers. In the next section, we focus on the agriculture and food sectors to provide a more detailed investigation of the agro-food value chain and its involvement in global production networks.

A Focus on the Agriculture and Food Sectors

The left-hand panel of Fig. 8.6 shows that agriculture GVC participation accounts for less than 5% of the total GVC participation worldwide, with the SSA being the most involved area (7%). This suggests that most of the value added in the sector is produced for final demand consumption and does not enter agri-food GVCs. The right-hand panel of Fig. 8.6 also confirms the relatively high share of the DVX component with respect to FVA and DC for agriculture, meaning that its value added is mainly used as input for other countries' exports, likely in the form of unprocessed inputs. It is also worth noting that in the more economically advanced regions, such as NAFTA and EU27, the two main components are more balanced, suggesting an intensive use of foreign agricultural inputs for their exports.

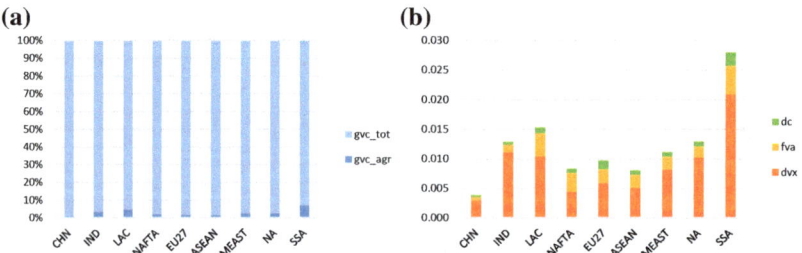

Fig. 8.6 Agriculture GVC participation index by world areas. **a** Total GVC, **b** Composition 2013 (*Source* Authors' elaboration on EORA data)

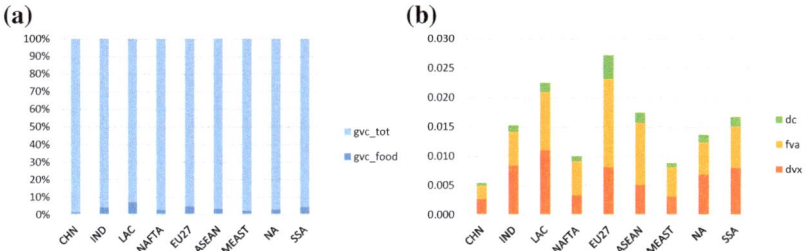

Fig. 8.7   Food GVC participation index by world areas. a Total GVC, b Composition 2013 (*Source* Authors' elaboration on EORA data)

Looking at the food sector, only 4% of the total GVC participation in SSA is due to food activities, while Latin American countries and the EU27 present the highest participation rates (Fig. 8.7a). Unlike the agricultural sector, the position of the food sector lies closer to the final consumers (i.e. downstream position) as shown by the more balanced ratio between the DVX and FVA components (Fig. 8.7b).

However, these overall figures hide a substantial heterogeneity within the region. To shed more light on this, in Table 8.1 we report the same GVC components for the 43 SSA countries present in our data, together with the sectoral contribution of agriculture and food in 2013 (Balié et al. 2018). Some SSA countries, such as DR Congo, Ethiopia, Lesotho and Guinea, register a relatively high involvement into the international fragmentation of production with respect to other countries in the region. This is most likely due to a production structure biased towards the export of natural resources (DR Congo) or the small dimension of their economy (Lesotho). Other countries, such as Benin, Chad and Mali, seem to be more excluded from the global market, likely because of geographical remoteness and/or lack of resources. Note also that in almost all SSA countries, the GVC participation mainly relies on the supply of inputs for other countries' exports (DVX component), whereas only few countries participate mainly as buyers of foreign inputs for their exports (FVA component), among which we can find Botswana, Ethiopia, Lesotho, Namibia, Swaziland and Tanzania. In this latter group, it is interesting to note the peculiar case of Ethiopia, where the GDP has been growing at about 10% over the last ten years. The country is among the most integrated into GVCs and the contribution of the agricultural sector to this process is among the highest in the region (31%). Cote d'Ivoire

Table 8.1 Overall GVC participation by SSA countries in 2013 (*Source* Balié et al. 2018)

Country	DVX	FVA	DC	GVC	*of which:*	
					Agriculture (%)	Food (%)
Angola	0.26	0.04	0.02	**0.32**	0	0
Benin	0.15	0.09	0.02	**0.27**	11	5
Botswana	0.16	0.22	0.07	**0.44**	1	10
Burkina Faso	0.18	0.18	0.06	**0.41**	22	3
Burundi	0.26	0.13	0.05	**0.44**	15	1
Cameroon	0.33	0.05	0.03	**0.41**	15	2
Cape Verde	0.18	0.20	0.06	**0.44**	1	3
Central African Republic	0.36	0.08	0.04	**0.48**	11	1
Chad	0.24	0.04	0.02	**0.30**	28	0
Congo	0.28	0.06	0.03	**0.37**	3	0
Cote d'Ivoire	0.25	0.06	0.02	**0.33**	33	15
DR Congo	0.46	0.06	0.06	**0.58**	4	1
Djibouti	0.21	0.13	0.05	**0.38**	5	3
Eritrea	0.24	0.08	0.03	**0.35**	4	2
Ethiopia	0.15	0.31	0.12	**0.58**	31	5
Gabon	0.27	0.04	0.02	**0.32**	15	0
Gambia	0.22	0.14	0.05	**0.41**	6	9
Ghana	0.31	0.06	0.03	**0.40**	34	14
Guinea	0.44	0.06	0.05	**0.55**	3	1
Kenya	0.19	0.17	0.04	**0.39**	30	15
Lesotho	0.11	0.36	0.10	**0.58**	0	1
Liberia	0.31	0.06	0.03	**0.40**	15	0
Madagascar	0.22	0.10	0.03	**0.35**	38	8
Malawi	0.21	0.10	0.03	**0.34**	39	8
Mali	0.19	0.08	0.02	**0.30**	23	2
Mauritania	0.23	0.13	0.05	**0.41**	1	21
Mauritius	0.13	0.31	0.06	**0.50**	1	15
Mozambique	0.23	0.07	0.03	**0.33**	22	7
Namibia	0.15	0.23	0.05	**0.44**	3	28
Niger	0.24	0.12	0.05	**0.40**	3	1
Nigeria	0.28	0.06	0.02	**0.36**	4	1
Rwanda	0.23	0.20	0.08	**0.51**	9	1
Sao Tome and Principe	0.20	0.21	0.08	**0.50**	7	2
Senegal	0.23	0.09	0.03	**0.34**	11	42
Seychelles	0.21	0.14	0.05	**0.40**	1	36
Sierra Leone	0.20	0.16	0.06	**0.42**	5	5
Somalia	0.21	0.08	0.03	**0.33**	10	4
South Africa	0.25	0.12	0.06	**0.43**	4	2
Swaziland	0.13	0.28	0.08	**0.49**	5	16
Tanzania	0.15	0.24	0.06	**0.45**	15	13
Togo	0.16	0.12	0.03	**0.31**	15	7

(continued)

Table 8.1 (continued)

Country	DVX	FVA	DC	GVC	of which:	
					Agriculture (%)	Food (%)
Uganda	0.19	0.11	0.03	**0.32**	32	11
Zambia	0.23	0.10	0.04	**0.37**	6	2
Total	0.23	0.13	0.05	**0.41**	13	8

(33%), Ghana (34%), Kenya (30%), Madagascar (38%), Malawi (39%) and Uganda (32%) are the other countries in the region where the contribution of the agricultural sector to their total GVC participation is quite remarkable, i.e. above the 30%. Finally, the last column of Table 8.1 clearly shows that the contribution of the food sector to the countries' GVC participation is, on average, much smaller than that of the agricultural sector and it is usually below 10%. The only countries registering noteworthy performances of the food sector are Cote d'Ivoire (15%), Kenya (15%), Mauritania (21%), Namibia (28%), Senegal (42%) and Swaziland (16%).

Bilateral Evidence

As underlined in "Measuring GVC Participation: The Methodological Approach", the WWZ (2013) decomposition method allows us to also disentangle the value added component of the bilateral gross trade flows. Figure 8.8 shows the average percentages of gross exports and value added components (DVX and FVA) that go from SSA countries to groups of partner countries across the main destination regions (Europe, NAFTA, LAC, Africa, South and East Asia). Tables 8.A1–8.A6 reports the same indicators disaggregated by country. Not surprisingly, SSA gross exports in both sectors are mainly absorbed by the European countries that import 51% and 49% of SSA agricultural and food exports, respectively. More interestingly, the percentage of the imports from Africa is similar to figure obtained for other world regions, denoting a low level of regional integration between SSA countries. SSA countries are their main trading partners only for Niger, Uganda and Zambia. For the food sector, the picture looks slightly different. The intra-regional trade accounts for around 20% even if only Angola, Mozambique, Niger, South Africa, Togo, Uganda and Zambia are primarily trading inside the region.

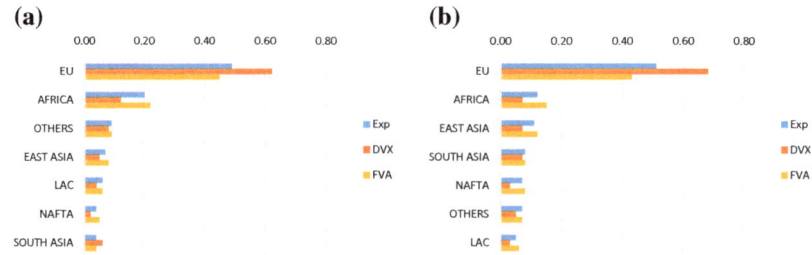

Fig. 8.8 SSA gross export, DVX and FVA, by region of destination (2013). a Agriculture, b Food (*Source* Authors' elaboration on EORA data)

If we focus on the measures of GVC participation, we observe a similar pattern: the European countries are the main importers of FVA and DVX from the SSA countries in both the agricultural and food sectors (Fig. 8.8). However, a significant difference exists. While the percentage of gross export and FVA absorbed by Europe is around or below 50%, the percentage of DVX is 68% for agriculture and 62% for food.[5] In other words, the European countries are mainly importers of intermediates to be processed domestically and re-introduced in the GVC. The same pattern does not apply to the other importing regions (especially Africa) where usually the FVA component is higher than the DVX.

There are two possible explanations for this result. The first one is the so-called "Rotterdam effect"[6] for which some European countries, namely the Netherlands, Germany, France and UK, are traditional gateways to the single market. Indeed, the very high share of the DVX component suggests that the agricultural and food products of SSA are first exported to these hubs and, once processed, further re-exported to third countries. The second reason is related to the fact that the closer the exported products are to the final consumers (the higher is the FVA),

---

[5]In some cases, such as for Uganda, Zambia and Niger, the EU absorbs almost 80% of the DVX despite the main destination for their gross exports is Africa.

[6]It is called "Rotterdam effect" the fact that trade in goods with the Netherlands is artificially inflated by those goods dispatched from or arriving in Rotterdam despite the ultimate destination or country of origin being located elsewhere.

the more difficult for the SSA producers to access the European market because of issues related to preferences as well as public and private safety and quality standards (Lee et al. 2010). The policy implications of our results are not trivial for the SSA economies. If the strategy to increase GVC participation in these two sectors is coupled with the ambition to acquire new downstream stages of production and increase the share of value-added captured by domestic producers, the current trade network needs to be re-oriented towards different regions of the world. In this respect, the simplest choice would be to reinforce the intra-regional agricultural and food networks by removing obstacles to regional trade that are still standing among SSA countries (World Bank 2012).

Concluding Remarks

The above analysis provides an assessment of the SSA participation in food and agriculture global value chains. It shows that (i) despite low trade shares at the global level, SSA countries are deeply involved in GVCs and often more than many other developing regions; (ii) the demand for SSA agricultural production in trade in value added is not regional, but mainly driven by the European and emerging countries and (iii) SSA involvement in GVC is still limited to upstream produc tion stages, i.e. the region is relatively specialised in providing primary inputs to firms in countries further down the value chain. This echoes the difficulties experienced by SSA producers of locally processed inputs or final goods to have direct access to the European market, a restricted access due for the large part to consumer preferences as well as public and private safety and quality standards.

The capacity of SSA to take advantage of GVCs as drivers for the structural transformation of the agricultural sector relies on a complex mix of factors that go beyond the simple narrative of upgrading. These include the characteristics of the comparative advantages of each country but also the availability of ancillary services (including transport and logistics) as well as institutional and socio-economic country features along with human and physical capital. This suggests a need to revisit the development agenda of SSA incorporating the role of GVCs as a part of multi-stakeholder strategies and reinforce the intra-regional agricultural and food networks. Likewise, companies involved in advanced production and trade networks of the agri-food sector can provide unprecedented opportunities to foster the structural transformation of African economies. As such, identifying the sectors involved in GVCs at the bilateral level could help unveil both the extent and conditions of GVC contribution to rural transformation.

Appendix

Table 8.A1 SSA agriculture gross exports (%), by regions of destination (2013)

Exporting country	EU	LAC	NAFTA	Africa	East Asia	South Asia	Others
Angola	0.53	0.07	0.01	0.16	0.04	0.07	0.12
Benin	0.43	0.12	0.02	0.17	0.06	0.18	0.03
Botswana	0.30	0.15	0.02	0.24	0.06	0.09	0.14
Burkina Faso	0.62	0.12	0.01	0.08	0.11	0.05	0.01
Burundi	0.71	0.03	0.07	0.05	0.02	0.04	0.08
Cameroon	0.63	0.00	0.02	0.05	0.26	0.05	0.00
Cape Verde	0.27	0.20	0.04	0.14	0.08	0.10	0.17
Central African Republic	0.73	0.02	0.04	0.05	0.12	0.02	0.03
Chad	0.63	0.01	0.27	0.04	0.01	0.02	0.02
Congo	0.69	0.01	0.02	0.03	0.16	0.07	0.01
Cote d'Ivoire	0.75	0.01	0.10	0.02	0.03	0.09	0.00
DR Congo	0.87	0.01	0.01	0.06	0.02	0.01	0.03
Djibouti	0.40	0.06	0.03	0.10	0.11	0.18	0.11
Eritrea	0.55	0.07	0.03	0.11	0.05	0.07	0.12
Ethiopia	0.30	0.00	0.05	0.01	0.46	0.03	0.15
Gabon	0.14	0.00	0.00	0.01	0.82	0.02	0.00
Gambia	0.57	0.07	0.01	0.12	0.08	0.06	0.09
Ghana	0.72	0.00	0.09	0.01	0.11	0.07	0.01
Guinea	0.76	0.01	0.02	0.12	0.02	0.05	0.02
Kenya	0.70	0.01	0.04	0.05	0.09	0.04	0.07
Lesotho	0.29	0.13	0.05	0.14	0.10	0.11	0.18
Liberia	0.27	0.00	0.66	0.02	0.02	0.02	0.01
Madagascar	0.49	0.00	0.25	0.03	0.16	0.05	0.01
Malawi	0.44	0.01	0.25	0.15	0.07	0.07	0.02

(continued)

Table 8.A1 (continued)

Exporting country	EU	LAC	NAFTA	Africa	East Asia	South Asia	Others
Mali	0.46	0.06	0.03	0.07	0.03	0.34	0.01
Mauritania	0.47	0.10	0.02	0.17	0.04	0.08	0.12
Mauritius	0.50	0.03	0.17	0.08	0.08	0.04	0.10
Mozambique	0.44	0.00	0.01	0.15	0.18	0.21	0.01
Namibia	0.52	0.01	0.01	0.43	0.01	0.01	0.02
Niger	0.36	0.03	0.01	0.52	0.02	0.02	0.04
Nigeria	0.55	0.00	0.02	0.02	0.11	0.29	0.00
Rwanda	0.75	0.04	0.04	0.07	0.02	0.03	0.05
Sao Tome and Principe	0.53	0.10	0.02	0.17	0.03	0.06	0.10
Senegal	0.64	0.01	0.04	0.03	0.27	0.01	0.01
Seychelles	0.36	0.11	0.04	0.15	0.09	0.10	0.15
Sierra Leone	0.58	0.05	0.05	0.10	0.04	0.06	0.11
Somalia	0.22	0.02	0.01	0.03	0.03	0.24	0.44
South Africa	0.53	0.01	0.07	0.18	0.11	0.06	0.05
Swaziland	0.63	0.02	0.00	0.18	0.07	0.03	0.07
Tanzania	0.36	0.01	0.10	0.06	0.33	0.09	0.06
Togo	0.38	0.47	0.02	0.04	0.01	0.07	0.01
Uganda	0.38	0.01	0.06	0.44	0.07	0.01	0.04
Zambia	0.45	0.01	0.02	0.46	0.02	0.02	0.02
Average	0.51	0.05	0.07	0.12	0.11	0.08	0.07

Table 8.A2 SSA agriculture indirect value added DVX (%), by regions of destination (2013) (*Source* Balié et al. 2018)

Exporting country	EU	LAC	NAFTA	Africa	East Asia	South Asia	Others
Angola	0.61	0.06	0.01	0.13	0.04	0.06	0.09
Benin	0.50	0.03	0.01	0.14	0.03	0.27	0.03
Botswana	0.39	0.10	0.02	0.16	0.08	0.11	0.14
Burkina Faso	0.82	0.02	0.01	0.05	0.02	0.07	0.01
Burundi	0.86	0.02	0.01	0.03	0.01	0.03	0.05
Cameroon	0.78	0.00	0.01	0.03	0.15	0.03	0.00
Cape Verde	0.33	0.16	0.03	0.10	0.09	0.12	0.16
Central African Republic	0.85	0.01	0.01	0.03	0.07	0.02	0.02
Chad	0.76	0.01	0.17	0.02	0.01	0.02	0.01
Congo	0.87	0.00	0.01	0.01	0.08	0.02	0.01
Cote d'Ivoire	0.91	0.00	0.03	0.01	0.01	0.03	0.00
DR Congo	0.95	0.01	0.00	0.02	0.01	0.01	0.01
Djibouti	0.58	0.06	0.03	0.08	0.07	0.09	0.10
Eritrea	0.61	0.06	0.01	0.08	0.05	0.08	0.10
Ethiopia	0.63	0.00	0.03	0.01	0.17	0.02	0.14

(continued)

Table 8.A2 (continued)

Exporting country	EU	LAC	NAFTA	Africa	East Asia	South Asia	Others
Gabon	0.23	0.00	0.00	0.02	0.72	0.02	0.00
Gambia	0.65	0.06	0.01	0.08	0.06	0.08	0.08
Ghana	0.90	0.00	0.02	0.00	0.05	0.02	0.01
Guinea	0.84	0.01	0.00	0.10	0.01	0.02	0.01
Kenya	0.90	0.00	0.01	0.02	0.03	0.02	0.03
Lesotho	0.37	0.10	0.03	0.10	0.11	0.13	0.16
Liberia	0.45	0.00	0.48	0.01	0.01	0.04	0.01
Madagascar	0.73	0.00	0.12	0.02	0.07	0.04	0.00
Malawi	0.72	0.01	0.07	0.07	0.04	0.07	0.02
Mali	0.48	0.01	0.01	0.03	0.02	0.44	0.01
Mauritania	0.49	0.09	0.01	0.14	0.04	0.10	0.11
Mauritius	0.57	0.03	0.07	0.08	0.05	0.05	0.14
Mozambique	0.69	0.00	0.00	0.09	0.15	0.06	0.01
Namibia	0.83	0.01	0.00	0.13	0.01	0.01	0.01
Niger	0.47	0.03	0.01	0.39	0.02	0.04	0.05
Nigeria	0.81	0.00	0.01	0.01	0.07	0.10	0.00
Rwanda	0.87	0.02	0.01	0.03	0.02	0.03	0.03
Sao Tome and Principe	0.71	0.05	0.01	0.07	0.03	0.06	0.07
Senegal	0.88	0.00	0.01	0.03	0.07	0.01	0.00
Seychelles	0.43	0.09	0.03	0.11	0.09	0.12	0.13
Sierra Leone	0.74	0.04	0.03	0.05	0.03	0.05	0.06
Somalia	0.45	0.03	0.01	0.04	0.03	0.13	0.31
South Africa	0.78	0.00	0.02	0.10	0.03	0.04	0.03
Swaziland	0.88	0.01	0.00	0.05	0.01	0.02	0.03
Tanzania	0.62	0.01	0.07	0.04	0.14	0.06	0.05
Togo	0.79	0.05	0.01	0.04	0.01	0.08	0.01
Uganda	0.82	0.01	0.01	0.09	0.02	0.01	0.03
Zambia	0.75	0.01	0.01	0.19	0.01	0.02	0.02
Average	0.68	0.03	0.03	0.07	0.07	0.07	0.05

Table 8.A3 SSA foreign value added FVA (%), by regions of destination (2013) (*Source* Balié et al. 2018)

Exporting country	EU	LAC	NAFTA	Africa	East Asia	South Asia	Others
Angola	0.50	0.08	0.01	0.17	0.04	0.07	0.13
Benin	0.41	0.15	0.02	0.18	0.07	0.15	0.03
Botswana	0.28	0.17	0.03	0.26	0.05	0.08	0.14
Burkina Faso	0.56	0.15	0.01	0.09	0.14	0.04	0.01
Burundi	0.61	0.04	0.11	0.07	0.02	0.05	0.10
Cameroon	0.54	0.00	0.03	0.06	0.31	0.05	0.00

(continued)

Table 8.A3 (continued)

Exporting country	EU	LAC	NAFTA	Africa	East Asia	South Asia	Others
Cape Verde	0.24	0.22	0.05	0.15	0.08	0.09	0.18
Central African Republic	0.67	0.02	0.05	0.06	0.15	0.02	0.03
Chad	0.57	0.01	0.32	0.05	0.01	0.02	0.02
Congo	0.56	0.01	0.03	0.04	0.22	0.11	0.02
Cote d'Ivoire	0.66	0.01	0.13	0.02	0.04	0.12	0.01
DR Congo	0.77	0.03	0.01	0.10	0.03	0.02	0.04
Djibouti	0.34	0.06	0.03	0.11	0.12	0.21	0.12
Eritrea	0.53	0.08	0.03	0.12	0.05	0.06	0.13
Ethiopia	0.19	0.00	0.06	0.01	0.56	0.03	0.15
Gabon	0.11	0.00	0.00	0.01	0.85	0.02	0.00
Gambia	0.53	0.07	0.01	0.13	0.09	0.06	0.10
Ghana	0.58	0.00	0.13	0.01	0.15	0.11	0.01
Guinea	0.71	0.02	0.02	0.14	0.02	0.06	0.03
Kenya	0.57	0.01	0.06	0.07	0.14	0.05	0.09
Lesotho	0.26	0.14	0.05	0.16	0.09	0.10	0.18
Liberia	0.21	0.01	0.73	0.02	0.02	0.02	0.01
Madagascar	0.40	0.00	0.30	0.04	0.19	0.06	0.01
Malawi	0.33	0.01	0.32	0.18	0.08	0.06	0.02
Mali	0.45	0.08	0.04	0.08	0.04	0.29	0.02
Mauritania	0.46	0.10	0.02	0.18	0.04	0.07	0.13
Mauritius	0.47	0.03	0.20	0.08	0.09	0.04	0.09
Mozambique	0.35	0.00	0.01	0.17	0.19	0.27	0.01
Namibia	0.38	0.01	0.01	0.57	0.01	0.01	0.02
Niger	0.33	0.03	0.01	0.56	0.02	0.02	0.04
Nigeria	0.46	0.00	0.02	0.02	0.13	0.36	0.01
Rwanda	0.66	0.05	0.06	0.10	0.03	0.04	0.07
Sao Tome and Principe	0.42	0.12	0.02	0.23	0.03	0.06	0.11
Senegal	0.50	0.01	0.05	0.04	0.39	0.01	0.01
Seychelles	0.33	0.12	0.04	0.17	0.09	0.09	0.15
Sierra Leone	0.49	0.07	0.07	0.13	0.04	0.07	0.14
Somalia	0.17	0.02	0.01	0.03	0.03	0.27	0.47
South Africa	0.42	0.01	0.09	0.21	0.14	0.07	0.06
Swaziland	0.43	0.03	0.00	0.29	0.12	0.03	0.09
Tanzania	0.29	0.01	0.10	0.07	0.37	0.09	0.07
Togo	0.28	0.57	0.02	0.04	0.01	0.07	0.01
Uganda	0.25	0.01	0.07	0.54	0.09	0.01	0.04
Zambia	0.33	0.01	0.03	0.57	0.02	0.02	0.02
Average	0.43	0.06	0.08	0.15	0.12	0.08	0.07

Table 8.A4 SSA food gross exports (%), by regions of destination (2013)

Exporting country	EU	LAC	NAFTA	Africa	East Asia	South Asia	Others
Angola	0.27	0.04	0.00	0.20	0.34	0.09	0.06
Benin	0.17	0.02	0.00	0.73	0.01	0.02	0.04
Botswana	0.87	0.01	0.00	0.09	0.01	0.01	0.01
Burkina Faso	0.23	0.50	0.01	0.16	0.02	0.03	0.05
Burundi	0.36	0.13	0.03	0.15	0.06	0.11	0.17
Cameroon	0.51	0.01	0.24	0.24	0.00	0.01	0.01
Cape Verde	0.45	0.10	0.02	0.18	0.05	0.08	0.12
Central African Republic	0.42	0.09	0.03	0.18	0.06	0.08	0.13
Chad	0.29	0.13	0.05	0.17	0.09	0.11	0.17
Congo	0.60	0.06	0.02	0.12	0.06	0.06	0.09
Cote d'Ivoire	0.68	0.00	0.18	0.06	0.05	0.01	0.03
DR Congo	0.69	0.04	0.02	0.08	0.02	0.04	0.11
Djibouti	0.39	0.11	0.03	0.17	0.06	0.10	0.15
Eritrea	0.39	0.11	0.03	0.13	0.07	0.10	0.16
Ethiopia	0.07	0.01	0.22	0.02	0.03	0.01	0.63
Gabon	0.61	0.04	0.01	0.20	0.05	0.04	0.06
Gambia	0.52	0.06	0.01	0.25	0.04	0.05	0.07
Ghana	0.78	0.01	0.11	0.05	0.03	0.01	0.01
Guinea	0.39	0.03	0.01	0.14	0.37	0.03	0.03
Kenya	0.65	0.01	0.06	0.15	0.07	0.01	0.05
Lesotho	0.43	0.10	0.03	0.14	0.06	0.09	0.15
Liberia	0.28	0.13	0.10	0.18	0.05	0.09	0.17
Madagascar	0.75	0.01	0.02	0.09	0.10	0.03	0.01
Malawi	0.65	0.01	0.03	0.28	0.00	0.01	0.02
Mali	0.57	0.05	0.01	0.22	0.02	0.05	0.08
Mauritania	0.64	0.00	0.00	0.09	0.25	0.02	0.01
Mauritius	0.72	0.01	0.03	0.04	0.18	0.02	0.02
Mozambique	0.24	0.01	0.04	0.51	0.18	0.01	0.01
Namibia	0.67	0.01	0.00	0.17	0.08	0.01	0.07
Niger	0.31	0.07	0.04	0.36	0.03	0.09	0.10
Nigeria	0.87	0.00	0.02	0.10	0.00	0.00	0.00
Rwanda	0.30	0.13 ·	0.03	0.18	0.08	0.11	0.18
Sao Tome and Principe	0.47	0.09	0.03	0.11	0.07	0.11	0.13
Senegal	0.89	0.00	0.01	0.05	0.04	0.01	0.00
Seychelles	0.85	0.01	0.00	0.04	0.05	0.04	0.01
Sierra Leone	0.66	0.10	0.12	0.04	0.02	0.03	0.04
Somalia	0.33	0.05	0.01	0.09	0.04	0.05	0.42
South Africa	0.31	0.02	0.07	0.34	0.16	0.04	0.07

(continued)

Table 8.A4   (continued)

Exporting country	EU	LAC	NAFTA	Africa	East Asia	South Asia	Others
Swaziland	0.64	0.01	0.09	0.18	0.04	0.02	0.02
Tanzania	0.49	0.01	0.07	0.20	0.08	0.04	0.11
Togo	0.32	0.02	0.01	0.60	0.01	0.01	0.02
Uganda	0.21	0.05	0.02	0.41	0.16	0.03	0.12
Zambia	0.07	0.02	0.00	0.87	0.01	0.01	0.02
Average	0.49	0.06	0.04	0.20	0.07	0.04	0.09

Table 8.A5   SSA food indirect value added DVX (%), by Regions of destination (2013) (*Source* Balié et al. 2018)

Exporting country	EU	LAC	NAFTA	Africa	East Asia	South Asia	Others
Angola	0.36	0.06	0.01	0.26	0.08	0.15	0.09
Benin	0.35	0.05	0.01	0.42	0.03	0.05	0.08
Botswana	0.89	0.01	0.00	0.04	0.02	0.02	0.02
Burkina Faso	0.46	0.18	0.01	0.12	0.05	0.08	0.10
Burundi	0.43	0.10	0.02	0.11	0.07	0.12	0.15
Cameroon	0.81	0.01	0.08	0.08	0.00	0.01	0.01
Cape Verde	0.49	0.08	0.02	0.16	0.05	0.09	0.11
Central African Republic	0.49	0.07	0.02	0.11	0.07	0.10	0.13
Chad	0.37	0.10	0.03	0.11	0.10	0.13	0.16
Congo	0.63	0.06	0.01	0.08	0.05	0.07	0.10
Cote d'Ivoire	0.85	0.00	0.09	0.02	0.00	0.01	0.02
DR Congo	0.83	0.02	0.01	0.03	0.02	0.03	0.06
Djibouti	0.47	0.09	0.02	0.12	0.06	0.11	0.13
Eritrea	0.50	0.08	0.02	0.09	0.07	0.10	0.14
Ethiopia	0.21	0.03	0.16	0.04	0.02	0.03	0.50
Gabon	0.55	0.06	0.01	0.16	0.05	0.08	0.10
Gambia	0.73	0.04	0.01	0.11	0.03	0.05	0.05
Ghana	0.93	0.00	0.04	0.01	0.00	0.01	0.00
Guinea	0.46	0.04	0.02	0.18	0.17	0.07	0.06
Kenya	0.89	0.00	0.01	0.04	0.02	0.01	0.03
Lesotho	0.52	0.08	0.02	0.09	0.07	0.10	0.13
Liberia	0.38	0.10	0.06	0.12	0.07	0.12	0.16
Madagascar	0.87	0.01	0.01	0.04	0.02	0.05	0.01
Malawi	0.82	0.01	0.01	0.12	0.01	0.01	0.02
Mali	0.62	0.05	0.01	0.13	0.04	0.06	0.09
Mauritania	0.73	0.01	0.00	0.05	0.15	0.05	0.01
Mauritius	0.89	0.01	0.00	0.02	0.04	0.01	0.02
Mozambique	0.30	0.02	0.03	0.52	0.08	0.02	0.03
Namibia	0.89	0.01	0.00	0.07	0.01	0.01	0.01

(continued)

Table 8.A5 (continued)

Exporting country	EU	LAC	NAFTA	Africa	East Asia	South Asia	Others
Niger	0.44	0.07	0.04	0.19	0.05	0.09	0.12
Nigeria	0.96	0.00	0.00	0.02	0.00	0.00	0.00
Rwanda	0.35	0.11	0.02	0.13	0.09	0.13	0.17
Sao Tome and Principe	0.49	0.08	0.02	0.08	0.07	0.11	0.13
Senegal	0.94	0.00	0.00	0.03	0.01	0.01	0.00
Seychelles	0.92	0.00	0.00	0.02	0.01	0.04	0.01
Sierra Leone	0.71	0.04	0.09	0.04	0.02	0.04	0.05
Somalia	0.43	0.07	0.01	0.09	0.06	0.09	0.26
South Africa	0.55	0.01	0.04	0.23	0.08	0.05	0.04
Swaziland	0.83	0.01	0.04	0.07	0.03	0.01	0.01
Tanzania	0.80	0.00	0.00	0.11	0.02	0.03	0.03
Togo	0.66	0.03	0.01	0.20	0.02	0.03	0.04
Uganda	0.62	0.04	0.00	0.17	0.05	0.03	0.08
Zambia	0.31	0.05	0.00	0.47	0.03	0.05	0.07
Average	0.62	0.04	0.02	0.12	0.05	0.06	0.08

Table 8.A6 SSA food foreign value added FVA (%), by Regions of destination (2013) (*Source* Balié et al. 2018)

Exporting country	EU	LAC	NAFTA	Africa	East Asia	South Asia	Others
Angola	0.25	0.03	0.00	0.19	0.39	0.08	0.05
Benin	0.15	0.02	0.00	0.77	0.01	0.02	0.03
Botswana	0.86	0.01	0.00	0.10	0.01	0.01	0.01
Burkina Faso	0.19	0.55	0.01	0.17	0.01	0.02	0.05
Burundi	0.33	0.14	0.03	0.17	0.06	0.10	0.17
Cameroon	0.44	0.00	0.27	0.27	0.00	0.00	0.01
Cape Verde	0.43	0.10	0.02	0.19	0.05	0.08	0.12
Central African Republic	0.39	0.09	0.04	0.20	0.06	0.08	0.14
Chad	0.25	0.14	0.05	0.20	0.08	0.10	0.18
Congo	0.59	0.06	0.02	0.13	0.06	0.06	0.09
Cote d'Ivoire	0.64	0.00	0.20	0.06	0.06	0.01	0.03
DR Congo	0.60	0.05	0.03	0.12	0.02	0.04	0.14
Djibouti	0.36	0.11	0.03	0.19	0.05	0.10	0.15
Eritrea	0.34	0.13	0.04	0.15	0.07	0.09	0.17
Ethiopia	0.06	0.01	0.22	0.02	0.03	0.01	0.64
Gabon	0.62	0.04	0.00	0.21	0.04	0.03	0.05
Gambia	0.42	0.07	0.02	0.32	0.04	0.05	0.08
Ghana	0.74	0.01	0.14	0.06	0.03	0.01	0.01
Guinea	0.38	0.02	0.01	0.14	0.40	0.02	0.03

(continued)

Table 8.A6   (continued)

Exporting country	EU	LAC	NAFTA	Africa	East Asia	South Asia	Others
Kenya	0.57	0.01	0.08	0.19	0.08	0.01	0.06
Lesotho	0.40	0.11	0.03	0.16	0.06	0.09	0.16
Liberia	0.25	0.13	0.11	0.20	0.05	0.08	0.17
Madagascar	0.72	0.00	0.02	0.10	0.12	0.03	0.01
Malawi	0.60	0.01	0.04	0.32	0.00	0.01	0.02
Mali	0.56	0.05	0.01	0.25	0.02	0.05	0.07
Mauritania	0.63	0.00	0.00	0.09	0.26	0.01	0.00
Mauritius	0.66	0.01	0.03	0.05	0.22	0.02	0.02
Mozambique	0.23	0.01	0.04	0.51	0.19	0.01	0.01
Namibia	0.63	0.01	0.00	0.19	0.09	0.01	0.08
Niger	0.27	0.07	0.04	0.42	0.03	0.08	0.10
Nigeria	0.83	0.00	0.03	0.13	0.00	0.00	0.00
Rwanda	0.28	0.14	0.03	0.21	0.07	0.10	0.18
Sao Tome and Principe	0.46	0.09	0.03	0.12	0.06	0.11	0.13
Senegal	0.88	0.00	0.01	0.06	0.04	0.01	0.00
Seychelles	0.82	0.01	0.00	0.05	0.07	0.04	0.01
Sierra Leone	0.64	0.12	0.13	0.04	0.02	0.02	0.04
Somalia	0.31	0.05	0.01	0.09	0.04	0.04	0.46
South Africa	0.26	0.02	0.07	0.36	0.18	0.04	0.07
Swaziland	0.59	0.01	0.11	0.21	0.04	0.02	0.02
Tanzania	0.41	0.01	0.08	0.23	0.09	0.05	0.13
Togo	0.27	0.01	0.01	0.66	0.01	0.01	0.02
Uganda	0.13	0.05	0.03	0.46	0.18	0.03	0.13
Zambia	0.05	0.01	0.00	0.90	0.01	0.01	0.02
Average	0.45	0.06	0.05	0.22	0.08	0.04	0.09

References

African Development Bank, Organisation for Economic Co-operation and Development, United Nations Development Programme. (2015). *African Economic Outlook: Regional Development and Spatial Inclusion*. Tunis, Paris, and New York: African Development Bank, Organisation for Economic Co-operation, and Development, United Nations Development Programme.

Balié, J., Del Prete, D., & Magrini, E., et al. (2018, forthcoming). Does Trade Policy Impact Food and Agriculture Global Value Chain Participation of Sub-Saharan African Countries? *American Journal of Agricultural Economics*.

Barrett, C. B., Bachke, M. E., Bellemare, M. F., et al. (2012). Smallholder Participation in Contract Farming: Comparative Evidence from Five Countries. *World Development, 40*(4), 715–730.

Barrett, C. B., Christiaensen, L., Sheahan, M., & Shimeles, A. (2017, August 1). On the Structural Transformation of Rural Africa. *Journal of African Economies, 26*(suppl_1), i11–i35. https://doi.org/10.1093/jae/ejx009.

Caliendo, L., Feenstra, R. C., Romalis, J., & Taylor, A. M. (2016). *Tariff Reductions, Entry, and Welfare: Theory and Evidence for the Last Two Decades.* National Bureau of Economic Research. Available via https://pdfs.semantic-scholar.org/85e5/57675e3528bee32ca68d3a56e2610f7bca12.pdf. Acessed 1 June 2017.

Cattaneo, O., & Miroudot, S. (2015). From Global Value Chains to Global Development Chains: An Analysis of Recent Changes in Trade Patterns and Development Paradigms. In E. Zedillo & B. Hoekman (Eds.), *21st Century Trade Policy: Back to the Past? Volume in Honor of Professor Patrick Messerlin.* New Haven: Yale University Press.

Del Prete, D., Giovannetti, G., & Marvasi, E. (2017). *Global Value Chains Participation and Productivity Gains for North African Firms.* Review of World Economics. https://doi.org/10.1007/s10290-017-0292-2.

Del Prete, D., Giovannetti, G., & Marvasi, E. (2018). *Global Value Chains: New Evidence for North Africa.* International Economics. https://doi.org/10.1016/j.inteco.2017.03.002.

Foster-McGregor, N., Kaulich, F., & Stehrer, R. (2015). *Global Value Chains in Africa.* United Nations University—Maastricht Economic and Social Research Institute on Innovation and Technology (UNU-MERIT). Available via https://www.merit.unu.edu/publications/working-papers/abstract/?id=5759. Accessed 31 Mar 2016.

Greenville, J., Beaujeu, R., & Kawasaki, K. (2017). *Estimating GVC Participation in the Agriculture and Food Sectors.* OECD Trade and Agriculture Directorate. Available via http://www.oecd.org/officialdocuments/publicdisplaydocumentpdf/?cote=TAD/TC/CA/WP(2016)1/PART1/FINAL&docLanguage=En. Accessed 1 July 2017.

Hummels, D., Ishii, J., & Yi, K.-M. (2001). The Nature and Growth of Vertical Specialization in World Trade. *Journal of International Economics, 54,* 75–96.

International Monetary Fund. (2015). *Regional Economic Outlook.* Sub-Saharan Africa. Washington, DC: International Monetary Fund.

Johnson, R. C., & Noguera, G. (2012). Accounting for Intermediates: Production Sharing and Trade in Value Added. *Journal of International Economics, 86*(2), 224–236.

Koopman, R., Wang, Z., & Wei, S. J. (2011). *Give Credit Where Credit Is Due: Tracing Value Added in Global Production Chains*. National Bureau of Economic Research. Available via http://www.nber.org/papers/w16426.pdf. Accessed 15 July 2015.

Koopman, R., Wang, Z., & Wei, S. J. (2014). Tracing Value-Added and Double Counting in Gross Exports. *American Economic Review, 104*(2), 459–494. https://doi.org/10.1257/aer.104.2.459.

Kuijpers, R., & Swinnen, J. (2016). Value Chains and Technology Transfer to Agriculture in Developing and Emerging Economies. *American Journal of Agricultural Economics, 98*(5), 1403–1418.

Lee, J., Gereffi, G., & Beauvais, J. (2010). Global Value Chains and Agrifood Standards: Challenges and Possibilities for Smallholders in Developing Countries. *PNAS 2012, 109*(31), 12326–12331.

Lenzen, M., Kanemoto, K., Moran, D., & Geschke, A. (2012). Mapping the Structure of the World Economy. *Environmental Science and Technology, 46*(15), 8374–8381.

Lenzen, M., Moran, D., Kanemoto, K., & Geschke, A. (2013). Building Eora: A Global Multi-regional Input-Output Database at High Country and Sector Resolution. *Economic Systems Research, 25*(1), 20–49.

Los, B., Timmer, M. P., & de Vries, G. J. (2016). Tracing Value-Added and Double Counting in Gross Exports: Comment. *American Economic Review, 106*(7), 1958–1966.

Maertens, M., & Swinnen, J. (2015). *Agricultural Trade and Development: A Value Chain Perspective* (No. ERSD-2015-04). World Trade Organization. Available via https://www.wto.org/english/res_e/reser_e/ersd201504_e.pdf. Accessed 23 Mar 2017.

Minten, B., Randrianarison, L., & Swinnen, J. F. (2009). Global Retail Chains and Poor Farmers: Evidence from Madagascar. *World Development, 37*(11), 1728–1741.

Montalbano, P., Nenci, S., & Pietrobelli, C. (2016). International Linkages, Value-Added Trade, and Firm Productivity in Latin America and the Caribbean. *Firm Innovation and Productivity in Latin America and the Caribbean* (pp. 285–316). New York: Palgrave Macmillan.

Montalbano, P., Nenci, S., & Pietrobelli, C. (2018). Opening and Linking Up: Firms, GVCs and Productivity in Latin America. *Small Business Economics, 50*(4), 917–935.

Organisation for Economic Co-Operation and Development, World Trade Organization (OECD). (2012). *Trade in Value-Added: Concepts, Methodologies, and Challenges.* Organisation for Economic Co-operation and Development. Available via https://www.oecd.org/sti/ind/49894138.pdf. Accessed 15 May 2015.

Organisation for Economic Co-operation and Development. (2016). *Evolving Agricultural Policies and Markets: Implications for Multilateral Trade Reform.* Paris: OECD Publishing.

Rahman, J., & Zhao, T. (2013). *Export Performance in Europe: What Do We Know from Supply Links?* International Monetary Fund. Available via https://www.imf.org/~/media/Websites/IMF/imported-full-text-pdf/external/pubs/ft/wp/2013/_wp1362.ashx. Accessed 18 Jan 2016.

Reardon, T., & Timmer, P. (2007). Transformation of Markets for Agricultural Output in Developing Countries Since 1950: How Has Thinking Changed? In R. E. Evenson, P. Pingali, & T. P. Schultz (Eds.), *Handbook of Agricultural Economics* (Vol. 3). Amsterdam: Elsevier.

Reardon, T., Barrett, C. B., Berdegué, J. A., & Swinnen, J. F. M. (2009). Agrifood Industry Transformation and Small Farmers in Developing Countries World Development, *37*(11), 1717–1727.

Swinnen, J. F. (2014). *Global Agricultural Value Chains, Standards, and Development.* http://cadmus.eui.eu/bitstream/handle/1814/31334/RSCAS_2014_30.pdf. Accessed 7 Feb 2017.

Timmer, M. P., Dietzenbacher, E., Los, B., et al. (2015). An Illustrated User Guide to the World Input-Output Database: The Case of Global Automotive Production. *Review of International Economics, 23*(3), 575–605.

United Nations Conference on Trade and Development. (2013). World *Investment Report 2013.* Geneva: United Nations.

Wang, Z., Wei, S.-J., & Zhu, K. (2013). *Quantifying International Production Sharing at the Bilateral and Sector Levels.* National Bureau of Economic Research. Available via http://www.nber.org/papers/w19677.pdf. Accessed 20 Jan 2015.

World Bank. (2012). *Africa Can Help Feed Africa.* Washington, DC: World Bank.

9

The Role of Regional Trade Integration and Governance in Structural Transformation: Evidence from ECOWAS Trade Bloc

Abiodun Surajudeen Bankole and Musibau Adekunle Oladapo

Introduction

Africa's regional economic communities (RECs) are committed to regional integration, as it is considered a necessity for ensuring good socio-economic relationship among the constituent economies which allows for the reaping of the advantage of economies of scale in production and consumption by creating a larger market size. Africa contains small and fragmented economies with low incomes (Karamuriro 2015),

Being a paper presented at the African Economic Conference (AEC) 2017 on the theme **"Governance for Structural Transformation"**, United Nations Conference Centre in Addis Ababa (UNCC-AA), Ethiopia, 4–6 December 2017.

A. S. Bankole · M. A. Oladapo (✉)
Department of Economics, University of Ibadan, Ibadan, Nigeria

A. S. Bankole
e-mail: as.bankole@mail.ui.edu.ng

M. A. Oladapo
Centre for Trade and Development Initiatives (CTDi), Ibadan, Nigeria

© The Author(s) 2019
A. B. Elhiraika et al. (eds.), *Governance for Structural Transformation in Africa*,
https://doi.org/10.1007/978-3-030-03964-6_9

277

and by generating a larger market size, regional integration is one of the factors that can produce structural transformation and economic growth. Atik (2014) defines regional economic integrations as formations serving for the common economic objectives of countries with similar performances. On the other hand, the structural movement of an economy from a primary or rudimentary and subsistence economic activity level to a secondary and tertiary one over a period of time is regarded as economic transformation. In other words, economic transformation constitutes a fundamental change in the structure of the economy and its drivers of growth and development (UNECA 2013).

UNECA (op. cit.) points out that Africa will not be able to achieve wealth creation, tolerable inequalities, poverty reduction, strong productive abilities, improved social environments for its people, and sustainable development without ensuring that its economies are structurally transformed. Economic transformation portends optimal use of the available natural resources in Africa, in addition to bringing about industrial development, enhanced economic growth and ability to withstand commodity price shocks from the international market.

An attainment of regional integration without good governance in each of ECOWAS member states may not produce desired result in terms of economic transformation. As indicated in its Worldwide Governance Indicators (WGI), the World Bank views good governance from six (6) broad dimensions of governance: voice and accountability, political stability and absence of violence, government effectiveness, regulatory quality, rule of law and control of corruption. WGI produces an index that ranges from 1 to 100 in percentile rank, with larger values indicating better governance, and it is expected to have a positive effect on structural transformation in an economy. Therefore, the importance of good governance in transforming an economy cannot be overemphasised.

Trade integration among the member countries of a trade bloc implies the absence of trade restrictions, and in conjunction with good governance, is bound to ensure structurally transformed economies towards industrialisation. It has been argued in the literature that a more open economy tends to be more industrialised (Dodzin and Vamvakidis 1999). By implication, the more restrictive the trade policy of a country, the less industrialised. Liberalisation of an open economy brings about technology transfer, which is facilitated by the market signals. Muuka et al. (2009) assert that removal of the barriers, greater integration and trade openness to the rest of the world will enable companies in a trade bloc to gain from new ideas, technologies and products.

In line with the expectation of the theoretically posited positive link between economic integration and economic growth, the countries in the West African region signed the ECOWAS Treaty in 1975, revised it in 1993 and implemented the ECOWAS Trade Liberalisation Scheme (ETLS) and the common external tariff arrangements with the objective of economic transformation. However, empirical studies on the effect of regional trade integration on the structural transformation of the economies in the trade bloc are not only few but also they do not consider the simultaneous impact of governance. There is a consensus in the literature that regional integration has a potential to structurally transform the economies in a regional bloc and have a positive effect on economic growth. The evidence from the literature shows that there is similarity of the impact of regional integration on economic performance between what is obtained for Europe, America and Asia on one hand and Africa on the other hand. However, COMESA and SADC trading blocs have been the most studied among the recognised RECs in Africa with virtually no empirical studies on some of the remaining RECs. Besides, there is no consensus in the literature regarding the measurement of regional integration. This study fills this gap, by examining the consequences of regional trade integration and governance on structural transformation of economies in ECOWAS trade bloc, thus expecting the latter to be positively affected by the former. To the best of our knowledge, this study is the pioneering work to adopt the methodology for calculating the Africa Regional Integration Index (ARII) developed by African Union Commission (AUC), the African Development Bank (AfDB) and the Economic Commission for Africa (ECA). The ARII will likely form the basis for reaching a consensus for the measurement of regional integration index for future studies on Africa.

The rest of the paper proceeds as follows. "Trends of Sectoral Value-Added in ECOWAS" presents the trends of sectoral value-added shares in ECOWAS while the review of the pertinent literature is provided in "Literature Review". In "Methodology", the paper describes the methodology used to obtain the empirical results in "Empirical Results". "Conclusion and Recommendation" concludes and offers recommendation.

Trends of Sectoral Value-Added in ECOWAS

The 15 countries of the West African region share common economic interest and both cultural and geopolitical bonds. Through the Lagos Treaty, ECOWAS was established on 28 May 1975. The creation of the common market through trade liberalisation among member states is one of the objectives of ECOWAS, which was actualised through the design of the ETLS as the major operational tool. Despite being in existence for over four decades the ECOWAS member economies are still dominated by agriculture, natural resources and/or primary commodities, with little contribution from the manufacturing sector as indicated in Tables 9.1 and 9.2, which present the average percentage sectoral contributions to the value added GDP of all the countries in ECOWAS for the period 2000–2015. Notably, agriculture contributes an average of over 25% to the value added GDP of most of the economies in the bloc. The average contribution is as high as 58.8% in Liberia and only 10.7% in Cape Verde. The average contribution of the industrial sector to the value added GDP of all ECOWAS countries is less than that of Guinea which appears to be the most industrialised in the region while Liberia is the least industrialised. However, the services sector contributed the highest to the value added GDP, recording a regional average of little less than 50% and as high as three-quarters of the economy in Cape Verde (Table 9.1).

Manufacturing is considered as an engine of economic growth (UNCTAD 2016) like trade. Table 9.2 isolates the contribution of the manufacturing subsector of the industrial value added GDP, and this has been very low over the years. The highest manufacturing contribution to the value added GDP of Benin is an average of 19.3%, higher than the regional average during the period 2000–2015.

Table 9.1 ECOWAS countries average sectoral contributions to the value added GDP (%), 2000–2015

Country	Agriculture				Industry				Services, etc.			
	2000–'05	2006–'10	2011–'15	Average	2000–'05	2006–'10	2011–'15	Average	2000–'05	2006–'10	2011–'15	Average
Benin	26.5	27.2	30	27.9	31.9	26.5	28.1	28.8	41.7	46.4	61.9	50.0
Burkina Faso	36.5	36.2	41.1	37.9	19.8	19	27.4	22.1	43.7	44.8	51.5	46.7
Cabo Verde	10.6	9.7	11.9	10.7	19.3	20.1	23.8	21.1	70.1	70.2	84.4	74.9
Cote d'Ivoire	25.5	22.6	28	25.4	21.6	23.7	34.3	26.5	52.8	53.7	57.8	54.8
Gambia, The	26.7	27.2	26.4	26.8	15.1	14.8	17.9	15.9	58.2	58	75.6	63.9
Ghana	40.1	31.3	27.2	32.9	27.8	20.6	33.5	27.3	32.1	48.2	59.4	46.6
Guinea	23.4	24.4	24.7	24.2	33.8	41.4	47.1	40.8	42.7	34.2	48.2	41.7
Guinea-Bissau	42.7	45.5	55.2	47.8	15.7	13.5	16.8	15.3	41.6	41	48	43.5
Liberia	72.4	59	44.9	58.8	5.1	6.5	16.3	9.3	22.4	34.5	58.7	38.5
Mali	35.1	35	48.2	39.4	24.9	26.1	24.6	25.2	40	39	47.2	42.1
Niger	33.7	41.4	46.6	40.6	17	13.9	24.5	18.5	49.4	44.7	48.9	47.7
Nigeria	36.3	31.7	25.5	31.2	41	36.7	29.1	35.6	22.7	31.6	65.4	39.9
Senegal	17.1	15.9	19.4	17.5	24.3	23.5	28.8	25.5	58.5	60.6	71.8	63.6
Sierra Leone	51.8	55.3	67.2	58.1	13.7	8.9	14.4	12.3	34.6	35.8	38.4	36.3
Togo	37.1	35.3	47.4	39.9	17.8	17.5	21.3	18.9	45.1	47.2	51.3	47.9
Regional Average	34.4	33.2	36.2	**34.6**	21.9	20.8	25.9	**22.9**	43.7	46.0	57.9	**49.2**

Source Authors' computation from the WDI, 2015

Table 9.2 ECOWAS countries average manufacturing contributions to the value added GDP (%), 2000–2015

Country	2000–'05	2006–'10	2011–'15	2000–2015 Average
Benin	22.78	17.71	17.39	19.3
Burkina Faso	12.96	9.62	8.03	10.2
Cabo Verde	7.31	5.80*	NA	7.3
Cote d'Ivoire	14.48	13.82	17.08	15.1
Gambia, The	6.63	6.45	6.77	6.6
Ghana	9.85	8.44	6.94	8.4
Guinea	5.2	6.93	8.16	6.8
Guinea-Bissau	NA	NA	NA	NA
Liberia	5.03	5.8	3.96	4.9
Mali	NA	NA	NA	NA
Niger	6.48	5.04	7.54	6.4
Nigeria	3.43	3.31	10.41	5.7
Senegal	15.98	14.16	17.04	15.7
Sierra Leone	3.2	2.48	2.32	2.7
Togo	8.72	8.53	7.34	8.2
Regional average	9.4	8.5	9.4	9.1

Source Authors' computation with data from the World Bank's WDI
Note NA implies Not Available. * Implies data is available for 2006 alone

Thus, manufacturing considered as the engine of economic growth has not shown appreciable performance in the member states of ECOWAS trade bloc.

Figure 9.1 presents the average sectoral shares in the value added GDP for the period 2000–2015. The dominant role of services sector in the ECOWAS trade bloc is manifest suggesting structural transformation. But the agricultural sector's position and the least desirable performance of the manufacturing sector not only reveal the precarious cosmetic and non-qualitative nature of services activities but also it suggests the need for appropriate redefinition and redesign of industrialisation policies and programmes, both at the national and regional level, that will unleash the potential of the manufacturing sector.

Meanwhile, Table 9.3 presents the regional trade integration index (TINT)[1] for all member countries of ECOWAS, together with intra-regional trade intensity index (ITCR) and good governance indicator (GOV).

---

[1]A detailed description of how these figures are derived is presented under Independent Variables.

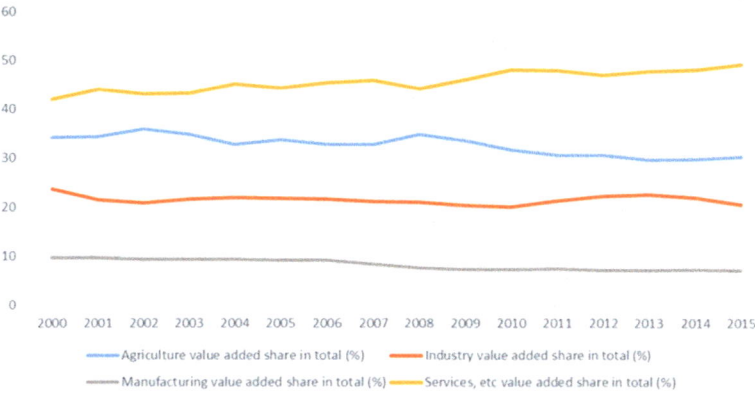

Fig. 9.1   ECOWAS average sectoral share in the value added GDP (%), 2000–2015 (*Source* Drawn by authors from the World Bank's WDI, 2015)

The regional TINT ranges between 0 and 1 and the higher, the more integrated an economy to the ECOWAS trade bloc in terms of trade. Also, ITCR and good governance indicator (GOV) also ranges between 1 and 100 (%) and a higher score indicates a more opened and better governed economy respectively. From Table 9.3, the most regionally integrated economy into the ECOWAS trade bloc is Cote d'Ivoire, while the least integrated is Nigeria[2] over the period 2000–2015. The ITCR show that Cote d'Ivoire and Nigeria are the first and second most opened economies in the bloc while the least opened economy is the Gambia. Table 9.3 also reveals that Cape Verde is the best performer in terms of governance, while the least performing country in terms of governance is Nigeria.

In Fig. 9.2, it is shown that ECOWAS trade bloc's ITCR trend over the period 2000–2015 was falling and indicates that the economies in the bloc as whole imposed trade restrictions despite the trade treaties. The good governance indicator has been stable at an average of slightly above 30%. There was a hollow in the regional TINT trend in 2010 indicating that the

---

[2]This result from our application of the ARII methodology contrast the findings stated in the ARII Reports 2016 where Nigeria is ranked as the highest performer and followed Cote d'Ivoire in the second position.

Table 9.3 Regional trade integration and good governance indicators of ECOWAS countries average regional 2000–2015 (in %)

Country	Regional trade integration index (TINT)				Intra-regional trade intensity index (ITCR)				Good governance indicator (1–100)			
	2000–'05	2006–'10	2011–'15	2000–2015 Average	2000–'05	2006–'10	2011–'15	2000–2015 Average	2000–'05	2006–'10	2011–'15	2000–2015 Average
Benin	0.5	0.4	0.4	0.4	9.4	6.8	5.5	7.2	44.1	42.3	39.7	42.0
Burkina Faso	0.6	0.5	0.5	0.5	15.4	8.8	12.2	12.1	40	42.5	36.4	39.6
Cabo Verde	0.3	0.3	0.3	0.3	0.3	0.2	0.1	0.2	62	66.9	66.3	65.1
Cote d'Ivoire	0.7	0.8	0.6	0.7	81.7	64.8	49.3	65.3	13.1	10.9	22.6	15.5
Gambia, The	0.4	0.2	0.5	0.4	1.1	1	1.8	1.3	40.4	34.8	31.2	35.5
Ghana	0.4	0.3	0.2	0.3	29.3	16.3	23.7	23.1	48.7	54.5	54.5	52.6
Guinea	0.5	0.3	0.3	0.4	6.1	1.6	2.9	3.5	16.8	8.4	13.9	13.0
Guinea-Bissau	0.5	0.5	0.4	0.5	1.1	0.9	0.9	1.0	16.8	16.2	11.8	14.9
Liberia	0.5	0.4	0.6	0.5	2.7	1.8	1.7	2.1	6.1	20.5	23.6	16.7
Mali	0.7	0.6	0.5	0.6	24	18.6	13.4	18.7	43.3	41.3	27	37.2
Niger	0.6	0.4	0.4	0.5	9.5	5.3	5.8	6.9	28.6	28.9	29.2	28.9
Nigeria	0.1	0.3	0.2	0.2	69.1	57	41.2	55.8	12.7	16.1	15.8	14.9
Senegal	0.6	0.6	0.5	0.6	26.3	19.1	15.3	20.2	49.7	40.2	46.2	45.4
Sierra Leone	0.3	0.5	1	0.6	1.3	3.5	9	4.6	16.7	23.8	25.4	22.0

(continued)

Table 9.3 (continued)

Country	Regional trade integration index (TINT)				Intra-regional trade intensity index (ITCR)				Good governance indicator (1–100)			
	2000–'05	2006–'10	2011–'15	2000–2015 Average	2000–'05	2006–'10	2011–'15	2000–2015 Average	2000–'05	2006–'10	2011–'15	2000–2015 Average
Togo	0.7	0.6	0.7	0.7	9.8	6	6.9	7.6	19	18.3	21.3	19.5
Regional average	0.5	0.4	0.5	**0.5**	19.1	14.1	12.6	**15.3**	30.5	31.0	31.0	**30.9**

Source Authors' computation

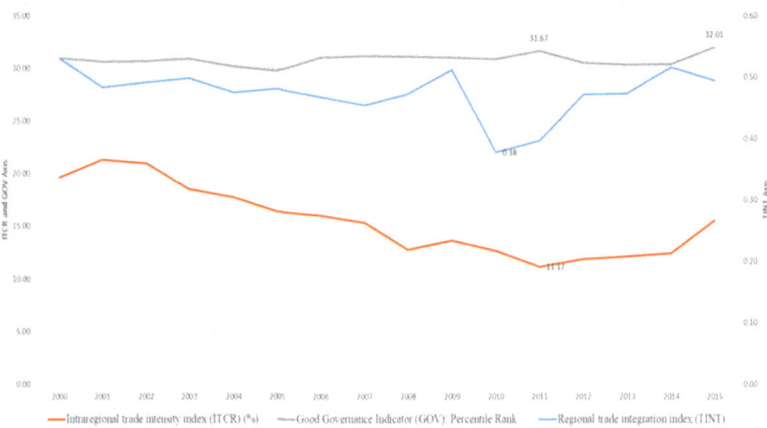

Fig. 9.2 ECOWAS countries average TINT, ITCR and GOV, 2000–2015 (*Source* Drawn by authors from DOT, 2015, WDI, 2015 and WGI, 2015)

economies in the region were less integrated after which there has been an improvement, prompting the need to empirically analyse the relationships among the three variables (TINT, ITCR and GOV) and the structural transformation of the ECOWAS trade bloc.

Literature Review

Different studies have been carried out to analyse the effect of regional integration on the performance of economies in trading blocs under different topics in different regions of the world. These studies cut across Europe, America, Asia and Africa. In respect of Europe, Dreyer and Schmid (2016) examine if the European Union (EU) and Euro Zone (EZ) memberships respectively as forms of economic integration will lead to growth bonuses for their members during the first 15 years of the Euro (1999–2013) by employing augmented Solow growth models using convergence analysis. The results of the study reveal that EU membership has a positive relationship with growth during the period, implying that the growth of the EU countries is higher than non-EU members' growth. The results are in line with Romer's (1990) endogenous growth theory and the work of Baldwin (1992) which maintain that economic integration can result in growth via scale effects. Contrarily, Dreyer and Schmid (2016) observe that how the financial crisis is treated determines the role of EZ membership in economic growth. That is, when the crisis is considered as a consequence of the Euro (an endogenous phenomenon of the EZ) and is not controlled for in the estimations, EZ membership is found to have no impact on growth. But when the crisis is treated as an exogenous variable and its effect is controlled in Euro countries, the results show that EZ membership had a negative effect on economic growth during the period of the crisis compared to EU members that were not in the EZ; while it had no effect on growth in other years.

Kutan and Yigit (2009) examine the effect of globalisation and EU integration efforts on labour productivity growth in 8 Central and Eastern European (CEE) countries that joined the EU in 2004. The authors employ a fixed effects panel estimation for the period 1995–2006 where potential heteroskedasticity in the cross-sectional dimension is corrected for. The results of the study reveal that globalisation and integration factors have direct impact on labour productivity growth through rates of innovation. It is also found that labour productivity level has substantially adjusted towards that of core EU (i.e. EU15), which implies considerable "catching up" and hence real convergence.

Henrekson et al. (1997) examine the implication of European integration in the EC and EFTA for economic growth using base regressions. Their results show that the effect on economic growth of EC and EFTA memberships is positive and significant. The results also reveal that there is no significant difference between EC and EFTA memberships. Their conclusion is that regional integration affects both resource allocation and long-run growth rates. Velde (2011) focuses on the investigation of the impact of regional integration on convergence and growth among developing countries by employing standard growth models covering close to 100 developing countries for the period 1970–2004, and his results show that regional integration does not have robust growth effects. However, the study reveals that there is a positive effect of trade and FDI on growth. The implication is that increased trade and investment can influence regional integration to have positive effect on growth. Besides, the results also show that high levels of regional income disparities make disparities to greatly decrease.

Boltho and Eichengreen (2008) investigate whether or not Europe's economy would have developed the same way without economic integration. In doing this, they employ the methodology applied by Fogel to the railroads and find that today's incomes in Europe would have been 5% lower if there was no EU. Gehringer (2013) examines the effect of financial integration on economic growth and its sources, productivity growth and capital accumulation, in a specific context of the European integration based on an unbalanced panel by applying a dynamic GMM model. The results of the study reveal that there is a strong positive effect of financial openness on economic growth and its sources. Based on an augmented Solow model, the work of Mann (2015) examines the effect of the European integration process of central eastern European countries on their GDP growth. He estimates a convergence equation for a panel of ten countries for the period 1995–2010. The results of the study reveal that there is a small but significant medium-run growth effect of trade integration within the countries of the EU. The study, therefore, concludes that the relatively small yearly growth will become substantial if it is aggregated over a period of several years.

Berthelon (2004) examines the growth effects of regional integration for a group of countries from Africa, Americas, Asia, Europe and Oceania for the period 1960–1999. The study departs from the existing literature which uses simple dummy variables by developing a new measure of regional integration which interacts country membership of a Regional Integration Agreement (RIA) with the partners' share of world GDP. The aim is to capture differentiated effects depending on the size of the partners. To achieve its objective, the study employs cross-country and panel data growth regressions that incorporate the RIA variables constructed in the study. The results reveal that RIAs have had positive effects on growth. Besides, the results also show that there are no significant growth effects of North–North agreements, ambiguous impacts of South–South agreements as the size of the countries joining them dictates and that the impacts of North–South agreements are not clear. The study follows Pritchett (2000) to categorise the OECD countries (excluding Turkey, Mexico, Hungary, Korea and Poland), Malta and Cyprus as North countries, and all other countries as South countries.

There are also some studies on the effect of regional integration on economic performance in America. Gruben (2001) employs a simple regression technique to examine whether or not NAFTA was behind Mexico's high maquiladora growth in the period 1975–1991. The results reveal that NAFTA does not have fast growth effect on maquiladoras; the impact of NAFTA is found to be negative, not positive, albeit statistically insignificant. De Hoyos and Iacovone (2013) investigate whether NAFTA induces Mexican firms to be more productive and if so, they try to determine the channels which it follows using firm-level data from the Annual Industrial Survey (EIA) for the period 1993–2002. They employ a robust microeconometric approach that disentangles the various channels through which integration with the global markets can affect firm-level productivity. The results of the study reveal that Mexican plants productivity is promoted by NAFTA through increase in import competition and positive effect it has on access to imported intermediate inputs. Lopez-Cordova et al. (2003) employ the methodology of Olley and Pakes (1996) to examine the effect of the productivity of a set of manufacturing firms and find that the productivity of the import-competing firms and American owned foreign firms improve with the inclusion of Mexico in NAFTA.

Studies on regional blocs in Asia have also revealed the effect of regional blocs on economic performance in Asia. For instance, Islam et al. (2016) investigate the effect of intra-regional trade creation initiatives through the South Asian free trade agreement (SAFTA) on the efficiency and productivity growth of the countries in the region by applying both stochastic frontier and data envelopment analyses on panel data covering the period 1981–2010. Using labour, capital and output as the major variables for productivity analysis, the results of the study reveal that total factor productivity of most countries in South Asia fall even after when the regional free trade agreement was implemented in 2006. However, the technical inefficiencies and total factor productivity growth are considerably different among the South Asian countries. Therefore, the results suggest that cross-border resource flows could assist lagging countries in improving their productivity.

Considering the implementation of the South Asian Preferential Trade Agreement (SAPTA) in 1995 under the broad framework of the South Asian Association for Regional Cooperation (SAARC), Ansari and Khan (2011) analyse the role of economic integration in increasing FDI inflows and trade in South Asia using percentage computations and graphs. The results of their study reveal that regional integration is yet to increase the SAARC share in world trade, but it has increased FDI inflows and its share is on the increase in Asia and the world respectively.

Wang (2014) examines how regional integration has impacted on the exports of Central Asian countries, and specifically tries to find out whether multiple regional cooperation organisations in the region promote or restrict trade activities by employing panel regression analysis. The results of the study show that exports of Central Asian countries have been boosted by integration agreements. However, the Eurasian Economic Community (EurAsEC), which is considered as the region's most successful integration organisation, has not increased the exports of its member countries. The contradictory results are attributed to the different levels of economic development, defective industrial structures and poor marketisation in EurAsEC member states. The results of the study could also be said to confirm the assertion of Bhagwati et al. (1998) that "spaghetti bowl phenomenon" will arise when a country is in multiple regional trade agreements (RTAs) because their different rules may limit its trading activities.

Africa contains small and fragmented economies with low incomes (Karamuriro 2015), and therefore countries in Africa have considered it necessary to promote economic integration in order to take advantage of economies of scale in both production and consumption (Agbonkhese and Adekola 2014). The African Union only recognises eight RECs[3] (AUC, AfDB and ECA 2016) and there are studies on some of these RECs in Africa as reviews in this study indicate.

---

[3]The eight (8) RECs recognised by the AU are: Community of Sahel–Saharan States (CEN–SAD), Common Market for Eastern and Southern Africa (COMESA), East African Community (EAC), Economic Community of Central African States (ECCAS), Economic Community of West African States (ECOWAS), Intergovernmental Authority on Development (IGAD), Southern African Development Community (SADC) and Arab Maghreb Union (UMA).

Kamau (2010) assess how economic growth is affected by economic integration in Common Market for Eastern and Southern Africa (COMESA), East African Community (EAC) and Southern African Development Community (SADC) trade blocs. To carry out the analysis, an economic integration index based on average Most Favoured Nations (MFN) tariffs and the level of regional cooperation in the three trade blocs is constructed and the system GMM estimation technique is also applied. The results of the study reveal that economic integration is positively related to economic growth. Besides, separately and jointly, economic integration significantly influences economic growth positively.

Negasi (2009) employed augmented gravity model using panel data and random effect estimator methods to examine the effect of regional economic integration in SADC by employing disaggregated data for the period 2000–2007. Their focus is on the analysis of trade creation and diversion effects of SADC. The findings from the study indicate that intra-SADC trade is witnessing a growth in fuel and minerals and heavy manufacturing sectors, but declines in agricultural and light manufacturing sectors. That is, there is a displacement of trade with the rest of the world in both fuel and minerals as well as heavy manufacturing sectors.

Muuka et al. (2009) study the impediments to integration in COMESA which is the Africa's largest regional trading block by investigating the aims of the 22 members of the bloc and types of barriers to integration which are two: World Bank and IMF's structural adjustment programs (SAPs) induced barriers and other factors with limited connection with SAPs. Their conclusion is that the barriers induced by SAP and non-SAP factors have restricted the ability of COMESA to save the economies in the region. However, removal of the barriers, greater integration and trade openness to the rest of the world will enable companies in COMESA to gain from new ideas, technologies and products.

Karamuriro (2015) examines how regional economic integration affects exports in the COMESA region by using the fixed effects regression, random effects regression and instrumental variables GMM regression to estimate an augmented trade gravity model using panel data for the period 1980–2012. The results indicate that intra-regional exports have increased as a result of the establishment of the COMESA trading bloc.

Therefore, there is a need to deepen regional integration in the region in order to promote export flows.

Agbodji (2008) assess the implication of preferential trade agreements and the monetary union for bilateral trade between West African Economic and Monetary Union (Union Économique et Monétaire de l'Afrique de l'Ouest—UEMOA) member countries by employing a dynamic gravity model. The findings of the study show that being a member of a common monetary zone and implementing common economic reforms have significant effect on bilateral trade in the bloc. However, it leads to more imports and exports diversion than creating trade. Trade within a bloc can be negatively affected if there is promotion of informal trans-border trade when economic policy is distorted.

Methodology

Dependent Variables

UNCTAD (2016) submits that the two mostly used measures of structural transformation are: employment shares of sectors in total employment and value-added shares of sectors in total value added. Either the number of workers or the number of hours worked in each sector is usually used to calculate employment shares. Real shares are sometimes used to express the value added shares, but nominal shares are the usual expression for structural transformation. Share of each sector's export as a percentage of GDP is also pointed out by UNCTAD (2016) as another measure of structural transformation. Besides, the real agricultural, service and manufacturing sectors' value added outputs are used by Kumi et al. (2017). This study follows UNCTAD (2016) and measures structural transformation as the nominal value added shares of Agriculture (AGR), Industry (IND) and Services (SER) in total value added as the dependent variables. Manufacturing being an engine of economic growth requires factoring out of industry data for separate and detailed analytical treatment, hence, an additional dependent variable for manufacturing is the nominal value added share of manufacturing (MAN) in total value added.

Independent Variables

The independent variables for this study are lagged or initial values of each sector value added shares of total value added: agriculture (LAGR), industry (LIND) and services (LSER) as well as manufacturing (LMAN). These lagged/initial values of each sector's value added shares of total value added together with capital (CAP) and labour (LAB) are the foundation independent variables of this study. The three independent variables of focus to assess the impacts of regional trade integration and governance on structural transformation are TINT, ITCR and good governance indicator (GOV). Other variables that influence transformation of sectors in an economy considered are fiscal policy (FISP), inflation (INF) and financial development (FIND).

The lagged/initial values of sectors' value added shares in total value added are expressed in nominal term. This follows Kamau (2010) and Kumi et al. (2017) to capture the conditional convergence effects in the model. There is a tendency, according to conditional convergence, for economies to converge towards a steady-state path (Solow 1956). In line with Kumi et al. (2017), this study maintains that the initial value additions have positive effect on each sector contribution to total value addition in ECOWAS member countries. The lagged/initial values of sectors' value added shares in total value added is calculated with data from the World Development Indicators (WDI).

TINT is calculated using the methodology for calculating the ARII jointly developed by AUC, the AfDB and the ECA (2016). Trade integration, regional infrastructure, productive integration, free movement of people and financial integration and macroeconomic convergence are the five major regional integration components on which ARII is based. The five dimensions are further split into 16 indicators. However, this study focuses on the effect of regional trade integration in the ECOWAS bloc on structural transformation. We, therefore, estimate the TINT for each ECOWAS member countries employing the four components of TINT in ARII methodology.

The four components of TINT are: level of customs duties on imports index (CII), share of intra-regional goods exports index (IRGEI), share of intra-regional goods imports index (IRGMI) and share of total intra-regional goods trade (percentage of total intra-REC trade) index. The level of CII is calculated as the simple average of the tariff rate applied to the most-favoured nation (MFN) using the harmonised system 6-digit code based on the imports from the REC. The formula for estimating the level of CII is:

$$CII = 1 - \left(\frac{CR - Min}{Max - Min} \right) \qquad (9.1)$$

where CR is a country's simple average of the tariff rate applied to the MFN, while Min and Max are respectively the minimum and maximum simple average of the tariff rate applied by ECOWAS countries to the MFN for each year.

Share of IRGEI is calculated using each country's share of intra-regional goods exports, which is the value of intra-regional goods exports as a percentage of the country's Gross Domestic Product (GDP). The formula for estimating the IRGEI is:

$$IRGEI = \left(\frac{CRE - MinE}{MaxE - MinE} \right) \qquad (9.2)$$

where CRM is a country's share of intra-regional goods exports, while Min and Max are the minimum and maximum share of intra-regional goods exports in ECOWAS respectively for each year.

Share of IRGMI is calculated a country's share of intra-regional goods imports which is the value of intra-regional goods imports as a percentage of the country's GDP. The formula for estimating the IRGMI is:

$$IRGMI = \left(\frac{CRM - MinM}{MaxM - MinM} \right) \qquad (9.3)$$

where CRM is the country's share of intra-regional goods imports, while Min and Max are the minimum and maximum share of intra-regional goods imports in ECOWAS respectively for each year.

Lastly, each country's intra-regional goods trade index is calculated as an average of the indices obtained from Eqs. (9.1–9.3), and this is used in this study to measure TINT. TINT is estimated using data from the International Monetary Fund (IMF) Direction of Trade (DOT) statistics. The exception is the data for estimating the level of CII, i.e. the tariff rate applied to the MFN, which is obtained from the WDI. The range of the index is between 0 and 1, and closer values to 1 indicate that an economy is highly integrated to its trade bloc. TINT is expected to have a positive effect on total value addition in ECOWAS member countries.

ITCR is calculated as the intra-regional trade share divided by ECOWAS's share of world trade. This follows Kamau (2010) and it is used as a proxy to measure the openness of each economy in ECOWAS not only to the other members in the bloc but also to the rest of the world. ITCR is estimated using data from the IMF DOT statistics and is expected to have a positive effect on total value addition in ECOWAS member countries. Good governance indicator (GOV) is obtained from the World Bank's WGI. It is calculated as the simple average of the addition of the percentile rank of the six (6) broad dimensions of governance. This index ranges from 1 to 100 in percentile rank, with larger values indicating better governance and it is expected to have a positive effect on total value addition of GDP in ECOWAS countries.

The methodology for constructing the WGI has been criticised in the literature in different aspects: it does not allow for comparisons over time and between countries, different sources of data used in obtaining it affect measures to correct past errors, and there is also the claim that the sources lack transparency. Langbeina and Knack (2010) also argue that the WGI does not provide different ideas of the six broad dimensions of governance. A counter-argument of the transparency of WGI has been provided by Kaufmann et al. (2007) who assert that most of the data used are publicly accessible. Despite the criticism, WGI appears is still being used most especially by international organisation and donors. This, therefore, forms the basis for the adoption of the average of the six dimensions of the indicator in this study.

Capital (CAP) data is the gross fixed capital formation as a share of GDP obtained from WDI used as a proxy for the effect of investments on structural transformation. Labour (LAB) is the percentage of economically active population aged 15–64 years and was obtained from

WDI. Physical capital, such as plant and machinery, and the level of infrastructural development in an economy are important for transforming an economy and ensure economic growth. Labour is important to be combined with capital and therefore important in economic transformation. FISP is measured by general government final consumption expenditure as a percentage of GDP with data from the WDI. The Inflation (INF) is used to measure macroeconomic instability and is the annual change in the Consumer Price Index (CPI) with data from the WDI. It is important to consider inflation and FISP because a rising inflation and unpredictable FISP can cause economic uncertainty and instability, and therefore can have negative impact on structural transformation.

Last but not the least, FIND is domestic credit to private sector as a percentage of GDP by other depository banks except central banks with data from the WDI. This variable is considered because the more developed the financial sector of a country, the more access the investors will have access to different sources of finance and the greater will be its effect in structurally transforming its economy. CAP, LAB, FISP and FIND are expected to have positive effects on total value addition while FIND is expected to have a negative effect on total value addition of GDP in ECOWAS countries.

Model Specification

This study adopts a panel regression model to examine the effect of trade integration and governance on structural transformation in ECOWAS trade bloc. In order to correct for heteroscedasticity, robust standard errors are estimated for each coefficient. Considering a model with just one dependent variable which can be stated as:

$$Y_{it} = a + BX_{it} + \varepsilon_{it} \tag{9.4}$$

The implication of the constant 'a' and coefficient 'B' in Eq. (9.4) is that both of them are unchanged for all units and for all years. If we assume a change in constant 'a' which implies some level of heterogeneity in the simple panel model, Eq. (9.4) becomes:

$$Y_{it} = a_i + \delta X_{it} + \varepsilon_{it} \tag{9.5}$$

'a_i' implies that there are some differences in how the economies being studied behave.

For this study, our empirical model stems from the neoclassical augmented Solow model. This model depends on a Cobb-Douglas production function with labour-augmenting technological progress. The model allows for an extension to a panel data formulation. Given the description of the dependent and independent variables in the previous two subsections, the panel model to be estimated to is specified as follows:

$$\begin{aligned} \mathrm{SEC}_{it} =& \alpha_{0it} + \alpha_1 \mathrm{SEC}_{it-1} + \alpha_2 \mathrm{CAP}_{it} \\ &+ \alpha_3 \mathrm{LAB}_{it} + \alpha_4 \mathrm{ITCR}_{it} + \alpha_5 \mathrm{TINT}_{it} \\ &+ \alpha_6 \mathrm{GOV}_{it} + \alpha_7 \mathrm{FISP}_{it} - \alpha_8 \mathrm{INF}_{it} + \alpha_9 \mathrm{FIND}_{it} + \varepsilon_{it} \end{aligned} \tag{9.6}$$

where SEC_{it} and SEC_{it-1} are used to represent current and lag nominal value added shares respectively of each of the sectors: agriculture (AGR and LAGR); industry (IND and LIND), services (SER and LSER) or manufacturing (MAN and LMAN). Equation (9.6) includes the 3 variables of interest: ITCR, TINT and good governance indicator (GOV), and the other variables to assess their impacts on each sector of the economy. In Eq. (9.6), ε_{it} is the error term and the equation implies that structural transformation is positively related to all the independent variables except inflation (INF). Therefore, the priori expectation of each of the parameter of the independent variables in Eq. (9.6) are stated in the following expressions:

$$\alpha_1 > 0, \alpha_2 > 0,\ \alpha_3 > 0, \alpha_4 > 0, \alpha_5 > 0, \alpha_6 > 0, \alpha_7 > 0, \alpha_8 < 0, \alpha_9 > 0 \tag{9.7}$$

That is, the parameters or coefficients of all of the variables in Eq. (9.6) are expected to be positive except for the parameter of INF (inflation) which is expected to be negative.

Data

The data for this study are annual secondary data for the period 2000–2015. The period was chosen because of the paucity of data especially for the import tariffs for each country. Import tariff data is one of the important variable components needed to compute regional TINT for ECOWAS member countries. Data for calculating all the dependent variables, the nominal value added shares of agriculture (AGR); industry (IND), services (SER) and manufacturing (MAN) are obtained from the WDI. Data for the gross fixed capital formation as a share of GDP which measures capital (CAP), labour (LAB) data which is the percentage of economically active population aged 15–64 years, FISP data which is measured by general government final consumption expenditure as a percentage of GDP, macroeconomic instability which is measured by inflation which is the annual change in the CPI and FIND which is measured by domestic credit to private sector as a percentage of GDP by other depository banks except central are also obtained from the World Bank's WDI. TINT and ITCR are estimated with data from the IMFs' DOT statistics. Finally, data for the six (6) broad dimensions of governance to calculate the good governance indicator (GOV) are obtained from the World Bank's WGI.

Determinants of Structural Transformation

ECOWAS comprises of 15 member countries and they form the sample for this study. We adopt descriptive statistics to examine the individual and group statistical features of the series for each country to detect potential outliers using the mean value. Tables 9.4–9.6 presents the descriptive statistics of only the variables that have outliers. Table 9.4 shows that Cabo Verde is an outlier in the capital (CAP) series, Table 9.5 reveals that Cote d'Ivoire and Nigeria are outliers in the Intra-Regional Trade Index (ITCR) index while Cabo Verde is also shown as the only outlier in the FIND series. These countries with outliers are included first and then excluded from both the bivariate and multivariate panel regressions as appropriate to reveal how they affect the results.

Bivariate fixed-effects regression for each sector is estimated to determine which variables have influence on each sector and therefore to be included in the panel regression estimation. Tables 9.7–9.10 presents the bivariate fixed-effects regression results for each sector.

Table 9.4   Descriptive statistics of capital (CAP)

Country	Mean	Min	Max	Std. dev.	No. of obs.	Comment
All ECOWAS countries	20.41	0.29	49.79	10.25	255	–
Benin	23.41	17.81	28.57	2.98	17	–
Burkina Faso	24.36	13.79	32.83	5.72	17	–
Cabo Verde	44.98	31.63	49.79	5.79	17	Outlier
Cote d'Ivoire	12.63	4.70	20.71	4.36	17	–
Gambia, The	20.30	4.56	33.06	9.39	17	–
Ghana	24.66	19.70	31.78	3.58	17	–
Guinea	16.44	10.57	21.62	3.29	17	–
Guinea-Bissau	7.04	3.55	16.80	3.33	17	–
Liberia	19.97	7.50	26.10	3.95	17	–
Mali	20.08	15.75	24.24	2.60	17	–
Niger	25.94	10.22	39.95	11.30	17	–
Nigeria	10.82	5.47	17.29	4.05	17	–
Sierra Leone	14.07	0.29	42.04	10.36	17	–
Togo	17.77	13.34	24.56	3.49	17	–

Source Authors' computation

Table 9.5   Descriptive statistics of Inter-Regional Trade Index (ITCR)

Country	Mean	Min	Max	Std. dev.	No. of obs.	Comment
All ECOWAS countries	15.73	0.06	95.62	20.72	255	–
Benin	7.35	3.93	13.01	2.44	17	–
Burkina Faso	12.51	6.51	25.60	5.94	17	–
Cabo Verde	0.19	0.06	0.60	0.12	17	–
Cote d'Ivoire	66.30	29.22	95.62	16.89	17	Outlier
Gambia, The	1.42	0.53	3.74	0.81	17	–
Ghana	23.93	3.99	51.83	12.94	17	–
Guinea	4.26	0.27	13.43	3.62	17	–
Guinea-Bissau	0.99	0.45	1.50	0.28	17	–
Liberia	2.10	0.89	4.30	0.91	17	–
Mali	19.80	10.74	32.95	6.19	17	–
Niger	7.16	2.81	11.56	2.50	17	–
Nigeria	56.37	29.68	77.81	14.23	17	Outlier
Sierra Leone	4.42	0.62	12.74	3.92	17	–
Togo	7.98	3.27	12.69	2.78	17	–

Source Authors' computation

Table 9.7 shows that the coefficients of CAP, ITCR and TINT are not statistically significant to exert effect on the AGR. When the countries with outliers in CAP, ITCR and FIND series are dropped from the

Table 9.6 Descriptive statistics of financial development (FIND)

Country	Mean	Min	Max	Std. dev.	No. of obs.	Comment
All Countries	16.07	0.41	66.95	12.24	255	–
Benin	16.30	6.81	22.19	5.49	17	–
Burkina Faso	16.66	9.55	26.84	5.53	17	–
Cabo Verde	50.02	29.24	66.95	13.54	17	Outlier
Cote d'Ivoire	15.15	9.68	22.70	3.91	17	–
Gambia, The	12.23	6.51	15.98	2.87	17	–
Ghana	14.78	11.02	19.37	2.41	17	–
Guinea	6.51	3.39	14.14	3.57	17	–
Guinea-Bissau	5.53	0.41	12.10	4.37	17	–
Liberia	11.32	3.06	20.44	6.27	17	–
Mali	15.91	9.88	25.51	4.42	17	–
Niger	9.06	3.96	14.07	3.90	17	–
Nigeria	16.96	11.79	38.35	7.78	17	–
Sierra Leone	4.52	1.54	8.04	2.01	17	–
Togo	22.20	8.63	39.79	10.41	17	–

Source Authors' computation

regression, the coefficient of CAP and ITCR remains statistically insignificant while that FIND still remains statistically significant.

Table 9.8 shows that the coefficients of LIND, ITCR, GOV and FISP are statistically significant and can exert impact on IND. When the countries with outliers in CAP, ITCR and FIND series are dropped from the regression, the coefficients of CAP and FIND are still not statistically significant. However, the coefficient of ITCR changes from being significant to being insignificant.

Table 9.9 shows that only the coefficients of ITCR, GOV and INF are not statistically significant to exert impact on MAN. The coefficient of CAP and FIND are still not statically significant when the countries with outliers in their series are dropped. However, the coefficient of ITCR becomes statistically significant after dropping Nigeria and Cote d'Ivore.

For the services sector, Table 9.10 shows that only the coefficients of LSER, ITCR, GOV and FISP are statistically significant to exert impact on SER. The coefficient of CAP is still not statically significant when Cabo Verde with an outlier in its series is dropped. However, the coefficient of ITCR becomes statistically insignificant after dropping Nigeria and Cote d'Ivore while coefficient of FIND becomes statically significant when Cabo Verde is dropped.

Table 9.7 Agriculture bivariate fixed-effects regressions—dependent variable: AGR

Variable	With outliers			Without outliers			Outliers country
	Coefficient	P value	R-sq.	Coefficient	P value	R-sq.	
LAGR	0.8453 (0.0381)	0.0000*	0.9430	–	–	–	–
CAP	−0.0146 (0.0613)	0.8120	0.1326	0.0234 (0.0707)	0.7410	0.0561	Cabo Verde
LAB	−0.4167 (0.2475)	0.0940**	0.0525	–	–	–	–
ITCR	0.0791 (0.0487)	0.1050	0.0463	0.0766 (0.0827)	0.3550	0.0807	Nigeria and Cote d'Ivore
TINT	0.9096 (2.7039)	0.7370	0.0466	–	–	–	–
GOV	−0.4381 (0.0700)	0.0000*	0.2480	–	–	–	–
FISP	−1.0865 (0.1432)	0.0000*	0.0275	–	–	–	–
INF	0.1660 (0.0690)	0.0170**	0.0022	–	–	–	–
FIND	−0.1135 (0.0568)	0.0470**	0.2839	−0.2564 (0.0796)	0.0020*	0.1575	Cabo Verde

Note * and ** denote 1 and 5% significance levels respectively. Figures in parentheses are standard errors
Source Authors' Estimation

Table 9.8 Industry bivariate fixed-effects regressions—dependent variable: IND

Variable	With outliers			Without outliers			Outliers country
	Coefficient	P value	R-sq.	Coefficient	P value	R-sq.	
LIND	0.7457 (0.0476)	0.0000*	0.8911	–	–	–	–
CAP	0.0049 (0.0435)	0.9100	0.0021	0.0434 (0.0384)	0.2600	0.0288	Cabo Verde
LAB	0.0221 (0.1766)	0.9000	0.0007	–	–	–	–
TINT	–0.5364 (1.9178)	0.7800	0.0547	–	–	–	–
ITCR	0.1065 (0.0340)	0.0020*	0.1841	0.0528 (0.0450)	0.2420	0.1063	Nigeria and Cote d'Ivore
GOV	0.1204 (0.0530)	0.0240**	0.0006	–	–	–	–
FISP	0.2964 (0.1115)	0.0080*	0.0122	–	–	–	–
INF	–0.0608 (0.0493)	0.2190	0.0924	–	–	–	–
FIND	0.0464 (0.0405)	0.2530	0.0049	–0.0072 (0.0446)	0.8720	0.0148	Cabo Verde

Note * and ** denote 1 and 5% significance levels respectively. Figures in parentheses are standard errors
Source Authors' Estimation

Table 9.9 Manufacturing bivariate fixed-effects regressions—dependent variable: MAN

Variable	With outliers			Without outliers			Outliers
	Coefficient	P value	R-sq.	Coefficient	P value	R-sq.	
LMAN	0.9056 (0.0326)	0.0000*	0.9687	–	–	–	–
CAP	−0.0426 (0.0226)	0.0600***	0.0165	−0.0761 (0.0222)	0.0010*	0.0263	Cabo Verde
LAB	−1.6340 (0.1842)	0.0000*	0.0002	–	–	–	–
TINT	1.7081 (0.9758)	0.0820***	0.0375	–	–	–	–
ITCR	0.0035 (0.0177)	0.8430	0.0538	0.0726 (0.0276)	0.0090*	0.1386	Nigeria and Cote d'Ivore
GOV	0.0333 (0.0309)	0.2820	0.1668	–	–	–	–
FISP	−0.2688 (0.0558)	0.0000*	0.0711	–	–	–	–
INF	−0.0067 (0.0255)	0.7930	0.0981	–	–	–	–
FIND	−0.1903 (0.0214)	0.0000*	0.0592	−0.2108 (0.0222)	0.0000*	0.0979	Cabo Verde

Note * and *** denote 1 and 10% significance levels respectively. Figures in parentheses are standard errors
Source Authors' Estimation

Table 9.10 Service bivariate fixed-effects regressions—dependent variable: SER

Variable	With outliers			Without outliers			
	Coefficient	P value	R-sq.	Coefficient	P value	R-sq.	Outliers country
LSER	0.8301 (0.0401)	0.0000*	0.8868	–	–	–	–
CAP	0.0296 (0.0724)	0.2236	0.2236	−0.0668 (0.0680)	0.328	0.0299	Cabo Verde
LAB	0.3751 (0.2932)	0.2020	0.0590	–	–	–	–
TINT	1.3605 (3.1948)	0.6710	0.0017	–	–	–	–
ITCR	−0.2311 (0.0558)	0.0000*	0.0112	−0.1295 (0.0794)	0.105	0.0103	Nigeria and Cote d'Ivore
GOV	0.3493 (0.0863)	0.0000*	0.3295	–	–	–	–
FISP	0.8491 (0.1804)	0.0000*	0.0892	–	–	–	–
INF	−0.1234 (0.0821)	0.1340	0.0857	–	–	–	–
FIND	0.0823 (0.0674)	0.2230	0.3189	0.2635 (0.0765)	0.001*	0.1854	Cabo Verde

Note * denotes 1% significance level. Figures in parentheses are standard errors
Source Authors' Estimation

Empirical Results

Table 9.11 presents the results of the panel regression for agriculture. The results without suppressing the outliers show that the signs of the coefficients of the lagged value of agriculture share in total value added (LAGR), inflation (INF) and FIND are positive, while the signs of the coefficients labour (LAB), good governance indicator (GOV) and FISP are negative. Considering the magnitude of each variable, the results indicate that every 1% increase in LAGR, INF and FIND will lead to 75.59, 8.77, 9.14 and 7.15% increases in the AGR. However, only LAGR is positive and statistically significant, according to a priori expectation, and indicates that it can cause more structural movement towards

Table 9.11 Panel regression results—dependent variable: AGR

Variable	With outliers		Without outliers	
	Coefficient	P value	Coefficient	P value
LAGR	0.7559	0.0000*	0.7378	0.0000*
	(0.0900)		(0.1017)	
LAB	−0.1855	0.2970	−0.3001	0.3900
	(0.1711)		(0.3351)	
GOV	−0.1054	0.0280**	−0.1332	0.0270**
	(0.0429)		(0.0524)	
FISP	−0.3219	0.0080*	−0.3060	0.0350**
	(0.1038)		(0.1271)	
INF	0.0877	0.1640	0.0857	0.2030
	(0.0597)		(0.0634)	
FIND	0.0715	0.2420	0.0213	0.7670
	(0.0586)		(0.0701)	
Constant	23.4684	0.0560**	32.2908	0.1640
	(11.2409)		(21.6718)	
Overall R-sq	0.9076		0.8942	
F-Statistics	62.1400		84.2400	
F-Statistics (Prob.)	0.0000*		0.0000*	
Hausman test (Chi^2)	36.6400		30.1500	
Hausman test (Prob.)	0.0000*		0.0000*	

Note * and ** denote 1 and 5% significance levels respectively. Figures in parentheses are Robust Standard Errors
Source Authors' Estimation

agricultural sector in the member countries of the ECOWAS regional trading bloc. Contrarily, the results in Table 9.11 indicate that every 1% increase in LAB, GOV and FISP cause AGR to fall by 18.55, 10.54 and 32.19% respectively. Since only good governance indicator (GOV) and FISP are negatively significant, they can lead to a movement away from the agricultural sector in ECOWAS trading bloc, and perhaps to other sectors of the economies. That is, there is a negative impact of governance on agricultural value added contribution to total value added in ECOWAS trading bloc. This implies that when poor governance prevails in the economies, structural transformation of the economy becomes unattainable. The results in Table 9.11 also reveal that there is no difference in our results when the outliers are suppressed. The only major exception is that FISP is now statistically significant at 5% as against 1% obtained when the outliers are not suppressed.

Table 9.12 Panel regression results—dependent variable: IND

Variable	With outliers		Without outliers	
	Coefficient	P value	Coefficient	P value
LIND	0.7158	0.0000*	0.6392	0.0000*
	(0.0894)		(0.1222)	
ITCR	0.0488	0.2900	0.0656	0.0320**
	(0.0444)		(0.0267)	
GOV	0.0364	0.4850	−0.0005	0.9940
	(0.0508)		(0.0665)	
FISP	0.0705	0.5120	0.1279	0.3100
	(0.1049)		(0.1201)	
Constant	3.2114	0.1480	4.9778	0.1230
	(2.0983)		(2.9767)	
Overall R-sq	0.8771		0.8869	
F-Statistics	33.1700		14.8900	
F-Statistics (Prob.)	0.0000*		0.0002*	
Hausman test (Chi²)	24.2800		35.3500	
Hausman test (P value)	0.0001*		0.0000*	

Note * and ** denote 1 and 5% significance levels respectively. Figures in parentheses are Robust Standard Errors
Source Authors' Estimation

Table 9.12 presents the estimation results for the industrial sector. When the outliers are not suppressed, the results indicate that the coefficients of all the relevant independent variables are positive. That is, the coefficients of the lagged value of industry shares in total value added (LIND), ITCR, good governance indicator (GOV) and FISP are positive. As regards the magnitude of each variable, it is revealed in the results in Table 9.12 that when there is a 1% increase in any of LIND, ITCR, GOV and FISP, there will also be an increase of 71.58, 4.88, 3.64 and 7.05% in IND as well. However, only LIND is statistically significant and the implication is that this brings about a structural transformation of the economy towards the industrial sector of the economy.

There is a significant difference in the results in Table 9.12 when the outliers are suppressed. As it can be seen, the coefficients of the lagged value of industry shares in total value added (LIND), ITCR and FISP are still positive; while the coefficient of good governance indicator (GOV) is now negative. Looking at the magnitude of each variable, it can be observed that as each of LIND, ITCR and FISP increases by 1%, IND increases by 63.92, 6.56 and 12.79%; but IND falls by

0.00% as GOV increase by 1%. In terms of statistical significance, LIND is still statistically significant and ITCR is now also statistically significant and positive. This implies that LIND and ITCR bring about a structural transformation of the economy towards the industrial sector of the economy. The positive and significant impact of the ITCR, which is one of the variable of focus of this study, imply that the more opened the economies in ECOWAS trading bloc not only to members but also to the rest of the world, the more the economies are structurally transformed from the other sector towards the industrial sector. Besides, concerning the coefficient of independent variables which are statistically significant, the coefficients of LIND and ITCR follow our a priori expectations as given by the expressions in Eq. (9.4)

Table 9.13 presents the panel estimation results for manufacturing and shows that without suppressing outliers, the coefficients of lagged value of manufacturing shares in total value added (LMAN), capital (CAP) and regional TINT are positive; while FISP and FIND are negative. By implication, a 1% rise in each of LMAN, CAP and TINT results in 84.48, 1.66 and 42.17% rises in the manufacturing shares in total value added (MAN) respectively. As it can be seen in Table 9.13, only the coefficients of LMAN is positive and statistically significant, and play important role in transforming the economies in the ECOWAS trade bloc towards the manufacturing sector. On the other hand, only the coefficient of FIND is negative and statistically significant, and play negative role in transforming the economies in the ECOWAS trade bloc away from the manufacturing sector. The conclusion from the results in Table 9.13 is essentially the same when the outliers are suppressed.

The estimation results of the panel model for services is presented in Table 9.14, and it reveals that when the outliers are not suppressed the coefficients of the initial value of service sector value added shares of total value added (LSER), good governance indicator (GOV) and FISP are positive, while the coefficients of ITCR is negative. With respect to the magnitude of the independent variables, increases in LSER, GOV and FISP by 1% result in an increase in the service sector value added shares of total value added (SER) by 77.81, 7.27 and 22.30% respectively. However, only LSER and FISP are statistically significant, and

Table 9.13 Panel regression results—dependent variable: MAN

Variable	With outliers		Without outliers	
	Coefficient	P value	Coefficient	P value
LMAN	0.8448	0.0000*	0.8381	0.0000*
	(0.0264)		(0.0263)	
CAP	0.0166	0.1820	0.0077	0.4570
	(0.0116)		(0.0100)	
TINT	0.4217	0.5250	0.2956	0.6570
	(0.6416)		(0.6438)	
FISP	−0.0302	0.2430	−0.0371	0.1370
	(0.0245)		(0.0228)	
FIND	−0.0387	0.0000*	−0.0412	0.0020*
	(0.0072)		(0.0092)	
Constant	1.6575	0.0190**	1.9825	0.0010*
	(0.6019)		(0.4292)	
Overall R-sq	0.9655		0.9698	
F-Statistics	248.9300		373.4800	
F-Statistics (Prob.)	0.0000*		0.0000*	
Hausman test (Chi^2)	17.3000		14.3100	
Hausman test (P value)	0.0040*		0.0138**	

Note * and ** denote 1 and 5% significance levels respectively. Figures in parentheses are Robust Standard Errors
Source Authors' Estimation

imply that the initial value of service sector value added shares of total value added (LSER) and FISP are important for structural transformation of the economies in the ECOWAS trade bloc to the service sector. In contrast, as shown in Table 9.14, an increase in ITCR by 1% will bring about a decrease in the service sector value added shares of total value added (SER) by 6.05%. However, the coefficient of ITCR is not statistically significant. The results also reveal that there is no appreciable difference in the results when the outliers are suppressed.

Conclusion and Recommendation

This study examines the effect of regional trade integration and governance on the structural transformation in the ECOWAS trade bloc covering the period 2000–2015. The structural transformation which is the dependent variables is measured as the value added shares of each

Table 9.14 Panel regression results—dependent variable: SER

Variable	With outliers		Without outliers	
	Coefficient	P value	Coefficient	P value
LSER	0.7781	0.0000*	0.6376	0.0000*
	(0.1011)		(0.1261)	
ITCR	−0.0605	0.3260	−0.0482	0.2560
	(0.0594)		(0.0402)	
GOV	0.0727	0.4160	0.1637	0.1770
	(0.0868)		(0.1136)	
FISP	0.2230	0.0970***	0.3262	0.0400**
	(0.1254)		(0.1399)	
Constant	6.2236	0.0460**	7.3090	0.0850***
	(2.8353)		(3.8598)	
Overall R-sq	0.8601		0.7739	
F-Statistics	60.6800		30.4200	
F-Statistics (Prob.)	0.0000*		0.0000*	
Hausman test (Chi^2)	16.1300		24.6300	
Hausman test (P value)	0.0028*		0.0001*	

Note *, ** and *** denote 1, 5 and 10% significance levels respectively. Figures in parentheses are Robust Standard Errors
Source Authors' Estimation

of sector in the total value added; agriculture (AGR), industry (IND), services (SER) and manufacturing (MAN). The independent variables of the study are lagged/initial values of each sector value added shares of total value added: agriculture (LAGR), industry (LIND) and services (LSER) as well as manufacturing (LMAN). These lagged/initial values of each sector value added shares of total value added together with capital (CAP) and labour (LAB) are the foundation independent variables of this study. The three independent variables of focus for this study to assess the impacts of regional trade integration and governance on structural transformation are TINT, ITCR and good governance indicator (GOV). Other variables that influence transformation of sectors in an economy considered in this study are FISP, inflation (INF) and FIND.

In carrying out the empirical analysis, panel regression method was used in the estimation and the results in respect to the variable of interest of this study reveal that: First, there is a negative impact of governance on agricultural value added contribution to total value added in

ECOWAS trading bloc. That is, when bad governance prevails in the economies, structural transformation of the economy becomes unattainable. Second, the ITCR, which is one of the variable of focus of this study, imply that the more opened the economies in ECOWAS trading bloc not only to members but also to the rest of the world, the more the economies are structurally transformed from the other sector towards the industrial sector. Third, with 77.81% positive and significant coefficient of regional TINT, this emphasises the high importance of the positive role that regional trade integration can play in structurally transforming the economies in the ECOWAS trading bloc. That is, when there is deeper trade integration in the ECOWAS trading bloc, the economies in the bloc will be more and highly structurally transformed towards the manufacturing sector which is considered as the engine of economic growth. Fourth, however, regional TINT plays no role in the transformation of the economies in the ECOWAS trade bloc towards manufacturing sector when each of the economy is closed not only to the ECOWAS members but also to the rest of world. Fifth and lastly, the initial value of each sector's shares in the total value addition is consistent for all the sectors and suggest that the sectoral output will not converge to a stable equilibrium.

Based on the results obtained, it is therefore recommended that each economy in the ECOWAS trade bloc should improve on good governance to structurally transformed their economies. Specifically, the implication is that if all of the economies in the trade bloc desire to achieve structural transformation towards agriculture, they need to improve on all the six (6) broad dimensions of governance: voice and accountability, political stability and absence of violence, government effectiveness, regulatory quality, rule of law and control of corruption as stipulated by the World Bank's WGI. As the aim of every developing economy is to be industrialised, economies in the ECOWAS regional trading bloc have to trade not only with the ECOWAS member countries alone but also with the rest of the world in order to structurally transformed from the other sector towards the industrial sector. This in line with what holds in the literature that increase in openness of a country will lead industrialisation of its economy (Dodzin and Vamvakidis 1999). The trade integration efforts of the ECOWAS so far need to be sustained and improved upon. The achievement of deeper trade integration in the ECOWAS trade bloc will make the economies in the bloc to be more and highly structurally transformed towards the manufacturing sector which is considered as the engine of economic growth. However, in the process of achieving this, the economies in the trading bloc should not restrict their trading with the rest of the world.

References

African Union Commission, African Development Bank, Economic Commission for Africa. (2016). *Africa Regional Integration Index (ARII) Report 2016*. Economic Commission for Africa, Addis Ababa.

Agbodji, A. E. (2008). *The Impact of Subregional Integration on Bilateral Trade: The Case of UEMOA*. African Economic Research Consortium. Available via https://www.africaportal.org/documents/6554/RP186.pdf. Accessed 28 July 2017.

Agbonkhese, A. O., & Adekola, A. G. (2014). Regional Economic Integration in Developing Countries: A Case Study of Nigeria; A Member of ECOWAS. *European Scientific Journal, 10*(19), 1857–7881.

Ansari, N., & Khan, T. (2011). *FDI and Regional Economic Integration in SAARC Region: Problems and Prospects*. Available via https://mpra.ub.uni-muenchen.de/32365/6/FDI and Regional Economic_Integration_in_SAARC_Region_pdf. Accessed 30 July 2017.

Atik, S. (2014). Regional Economic Integrations in the Post-Soviet Eurasia: An Analysis on Causes of Inefficiency. *Procedia—Social and Behavioural Sciences, 109*(2014), 1326–1335.

Baldwin, R. (1992). Measurable Dynamic Gains from Trade. *Journal of Political Economy, 100*(1), 162–174.

Berthelon, M. (2004). *Growth Effects of Regional Integration Agreements*. Central Bank of Chile. Available via https://dialnet.unirioja.es/descarga/articulo/1064705.pdf. Accessed 28 July 2017.

Bhagwati, J., Greenaway, D., & Panagariya, A. (1998). Trading Preferentially: Theory and Policy. *Economic Journal, 108*(449), 1128–1148.

Boltho, A., & Eichengreen, B. (2008). *The Economic Impact of European Integration*. Centre for Economic Policy Research. https://eml.berkeley.edu/~eichengr/econ_impact_euro_integ.pdf. Accessed 2 Aug 2017.

De Hoyos, R., & Iacovone, L. (2013). Economic Performance Under NAFTA: A Firm-Level Analysis of the Trade-Productivity Linkages. *World Development, 44,* 180–193.

Dodzin, S., & Vamvakidis, A. (1999). *Trade and Industrialisation in Developing Agricultural Economies.* International Monetary Fund. Available via https://www.imf.org/external/pubs/ft/wp/1999/wp99145.pdf. Accessed 30 July 2018.

Dreyer, J. K., & Schmid, P. A. (2016). Growth Effects of EU and EZ Memberships: Empirical Findings from the First 15 Years of the Euro. *Economic Modelling.* http://dx.doi.org/10.1016/j.econmod.2016.09.007.

Gehringer, A. (2013). Growth, Productivity and Capital Accumulation: The Effects of Financial Liberalization in the Case of European Integration. *International Review of Economics and Finance, 25*(2013), 291–309.

Gruben, W. C. (2001). Was NAFTA Behind Mexico's High Maquiladora Growth? *Economic and Financial Review Third Quarter, 3*(2001), 11–21.

Henrekson, M., Torstensson, J., & Torstensson, R. (1997). Growth Effects of European Integration. *European Economic Review, 41*(1997), 1537–1557.

Islam, A., Salim, R., & Bloch, H. (2016). Does Regional Integration Affect Efficiency and Productivity Growth? Empirical Evidence from South Asia. *Review of Urban and Regional Development Studies (RURDS).* https://doi.org/10.1111/rurd.12048.

Kamau, N. L. (2010). The Impact of Regional Integration on Economic Growth: Empirical Evidence from COMESA, EAC and SADC Trade Blocs. *American Journal of Social and Management Sciences, 1*(2), 150–163.

Karamuriro, H. T. (2015). Regional Economic Integration and Exports Performance in the COMESA Region (1980–2012). *International Journal of Business and Economics Research, 4*(1), 11–20.

Kaufmann, D., Kraay, A., & Mastruzzi, M. (2007). *The Worldwide Governance Indicators Project: Answering the Critics.* The World Bank. http://documents.worldbank.org/curated/en/979231468178138073/pdf/wps4149.pdf. Accessed 2 Aug 2017.

Kumi, E., Ibrahim, M., & Yeboah, T. (2017). *Aid Volatility and Structural Economic Transformation in Sub-Saharan Africa: Does Finance Matter?* Economic Research Southern Africa. Available via https://researchportal.bath.ac.uk/en/publications/aid-volatility-and-structural-economic-transformation-in-sub-saha. Accessed 28 July 2017.

Kutan, A. M., & Yigit, T. M. (2009). European Integration, Productivity Growth and Real Convergence: Evidence from the New Member States. *Economic Systems, 33*(2009), 127–137. https://doi.org/10.1016/j.ecosys.2009.03.002.

Langbein, L., & Knack, S. (2010). The Worldwide Governance Indicators: Six, One, or None? *The Journal of Development Studies, 46*(2), 350–370.

Lopez-Cordova, E., Hernandez, G. E., & Monge-Naranjo, A. (2003). NAFTA and Manufacturing Productivity in Mexico. *Economia, 4*(1), 55–98.

Mann, K. (2015). *The EU, a Growth Engine? The Impact of European Integration on Economic Growth in Central Eastern Europe.* FIW. Available via https://ideas.repec.org/p/wsr/wpaper/y2015i136.html. Accessed 30 July 2017.

Muuka, G. N., Harrison, D. E., & McCoy, J. P. (2009). Impediments to Economic Integration in Africa: The Case of COMESA. *Journal of Business in Developing Nations, 2*(1998) Article 3, 1–19

Negasi, M. Y. (2009). *Trade Effects of Regional Economic Integration in Africa: The Case of SADC (Evidence from Gravity Modelling Using Disaggregated Data).* Trade and Industrial Policy Strategies. Available via http://www.tips.org.za/files/13.Trade_effects_of_Regional_Economic_Integration_-_SSD.pdf. Accessed 30 July 2017.

Olley, G. S., & Pakes, A. (1996). The Dynamics of Productivity in the Telecommunications Equipment Industry. *Econometrica, 64*(6), 1263–1297.

Pritchett, L. (2000). Understanding Patterns of Economic Growth: Searching for Hills among Plateaus, Mountains, and Plains. *The World Bank Economic Review, 14,* 221–250.

Romer, P. M. (1990). Endogenous Technological Change. *Journal of Political Economics, 98*(5), 71–102.

Solow, R. M. (1956). A Contribution to the Theory of Economic Growth. *The Quarterly Journal of Economics, 70*(1), 65–94.

te Velde, D. W. (2011). Regional Integration, Growth and Convergence. *Journal of Economic Integration, 26*(1), 1–28.

United Nation Conference on Trade and Development. (2016). *Virtual Institute Teaching Material on Structural Transformation and Industrial Policy.* United Nations Conference on Trade and Development, New York and Geneva.

United Nations Economic Commission for Africa. (2013). *Economic Transformation for Africa's Development.* United Nations Economic Commission for Africa. Available via https://www.uneca.org/sites/default/files/uploaded-documents/Macroeconomy/africaeconomictransformation_en.pdf. Accessed 30 July 2017.

Wang, W. (2014). The Effects of Regional Integration in Central Asia. *Emerging Markets Finance and Trade, 50*(sup2), 219–232.

Index